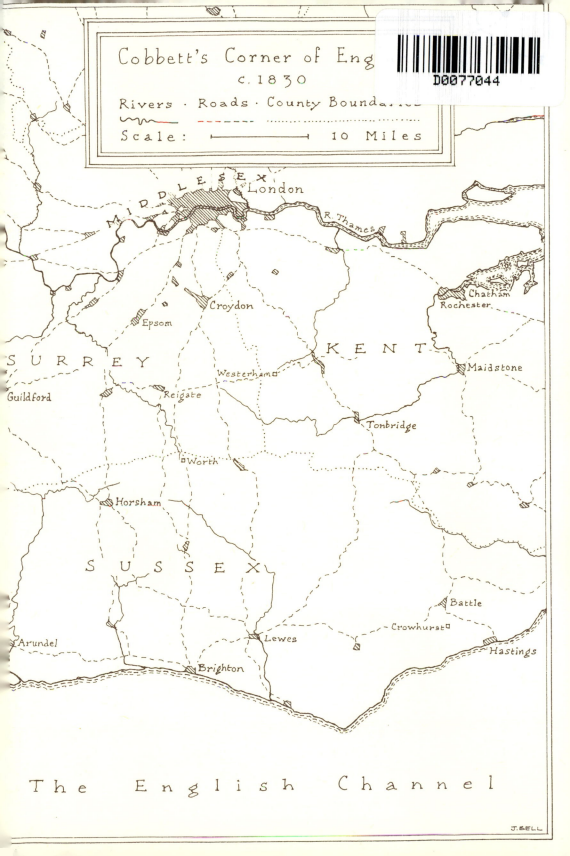

Cobbett's Corner of Eng...

c. 1830

Rivers · Roads · County Boundar...

Scale: |———————| 10 Miles

MIDDLESEX

London

R. Thames

Chatham

Rochester

Croydon

Epsom

SURREY

KENT

Maidstone

Westerham

Guildford

Reigate

Tonbridge

Worth

Horsham

Battle

SUSSEX

Crowhurst

Arundel

Lewes

Hastings

Brighton

The English Channel

J. BELL

William Cobbett

The Poor Man's Friend

Volume 1

Cobbett in 1800. This portrait by John Raphael Smith has previously been known to the public only through a frequently reproduced engraving by Bartolozzi

WILLIAM COBBETT

The Poor Man's Friend

GEORGE SPATER

Volume 1

CAMBRIDGE UNIVERSITY PRESS

Cambridge

London   New York   New Rochelle

Melbourne   Sydney

Published by the Press Syndicate of the University of Cambridge
The Pitt Building, Trumpington Street, Cambridge CB2 1RP
32 East 57th Street, New York, NY 10022, USA
296 Beaconsfield Parade, Middle Park, Melbourne 3206, Australia

First published 1982

Printed in the United States of America

Library of Congress catalogue card number: 81-3859

British Library cataloguing in publication data
Spater, George
William Cobbett
vol. I
1. Cobbett, William – Biography
I. Title
828'.6'08   PR4461.C324
ISBN 0 521 22216 8 vol. 1
ISBN 0 521 24077 8 vol. 2

To HOPE

From one who "on honey-dew hath fed,
And drunk the milk of Paradise"

Contents

VOLUME 1

CONTENTS

VOLUME 2

Illustrations

ix

ILLUSTRATIONS

ILLUSTRATIONS

Preface

The Life of William Cobbett by G. D. H. Cole has been the standard source of information about Cobbett for more than fifty years. Originally published in 1924, it went through three regular editions and has recently been reprinted. The writings on Cobbett since Cole have been either broad-brush sketches derived from Cole or specialized studies concentrating on a limited aspect of Cobbett's life or work. There has been, up to now, no attempt to produce a full-scale life paralleling Cole's admirable undertaking of a half century ago.

Yet a large quantity of new material has appeared since 1924. Much of it was collected by Cole himself, including three finds of major importance: the letters of Cobbett to Edward Thornton from 1797 to 1800, which Cole edited and published in a separate volume in 1937; twenty bundles of papers and some account books from the files of Cobbett's solicitor; and more than a hundred letters written by Cobbett and his sons to one of Cobbett's close friends, S. Sapsford, a master baker of London. Cobbett's last manuscript diary, "running right to the eve of his death," also came into Cole's possession. These finds are now a part of the great Cobbett archive held by Nuffield College library in Oxford, which includes Cole's own large collection of Cobbett papers and several hundred letters and manuscripts deposited there by the Cobbett family.

Despite the mass of new material, Cole did not rewrite his life of Cobbett. He explained this in 1952 when he wrote that there "remain certain obscure points in Cobbett's private life, which cannot be cleared up until more of the letters are found or recovered." One of the major areas of obscurity was mentioned in Cole's preface to the third edition of his life of Cobbett published in 1947:

I had hoped at one time to be able to add to my own *Life* fresh material relating to Cobbett's last years, derived from a considerable collection of his letters now in my possession. From these it appears that in the last year of his life there was in progress an acrimonious family dispute, in which Cobbett and his wife were the principal parties, and the four sons seem to have been ranged, two and two, on opposite sides. Unhappily, the letters I have been able to see give so incomplete an account of the quarrel that I am entirely unable to discover what it was all about.

The information which Cole sought, and much more besides, reposed quietly in American libraries. Materials at Columbia, Cornell, Illinois, Rutgers, and Yale Universities, when added to the previously known correspondence, provide the story of the last years of Cobbett's life that eluded Cole, as well as casting new light on his earlier years. But that is not all. Adelphi University holds Cobbett's letters to Henry Hunt – the flamboyant "Orator" Hunt – written from 1809 to 1829. Yale has some interesting material relating to Cobbett's early life as a soldier, in addition to important letters from a later period. The library at Haverford College is the repository of manuscripts and letters dealing with Cobbett's petitions to the Pennsylvania legislature in 1818–19 and several other subjects. Other missing pieces at various points throughout Cobbett's life are supplied by the university libraries at Buffalo, Duke, Iowa, Kansas, Pennsylvania State, Princeton, Scripps, Stanford, and Swarthmore; by the Morgan library in New York; and by the American Philosophical Society in Philadelphia. Correspondence during Cobbett's first stay in America (1792–1800), together with material relating to later periods, is found at the Boston Public Library, Harvard University, the Historical Society of Pennsylvania, the Massachusetts Historical Society, the New York Public Library, and the New York Historical Society, much of which is reflected in a fine work of American scholarship, *Peter Porcupine in America* by Mary Elizabeth Clark, published in 1939, too late to be used in Cole's biography, but generously acknowledged by him in the preface to his third edition. A more recent work has augmented still further our knowledge of Cobbett's activities in America: *William Cobbett and the United States 1792–1835: A Bibliography with Notes and Extracts* by Pierce W. Gaines, published in 1971.

Two lucky finds in England in the past several years conclude the list of major new materials relating to Cobbett that have become available since 1924. One of these is a Cobbett manuscript pertaining to the court-martial initiated by Cobbett against his superior officers in 1792, which adds a bit more to what was previously known of that incident. The other, and the more important, is a notebook of over a hundred pages containing valuable information gathered by James Paul Cobbett in preparation for writing a life of his father – a project which he barely started. The first of these documents is now in the Nuffield library in Oxford; the second is in the possession of the heirs of the late General Sir Gerald Lathbury, great-great-grandson of William Cobbett.

The present biography attempts to incorporate what we now know about Cobbett with the improved knowledge we have gained in the past fifty years of many of Cobbett's contemporaries and of the economic, social, and political movements of the period. I am indebted in this effort not only to the prior workers in the Cobbett vineyard who are referred to in the bibliography, but also to the unnamed librarians and archivists of the fifty or so institutions on both sides of the Atlantic who provided Cobbett letters and other materials; to members of the Cobbett family, particularly General Lathbury and Mrs. Sybil Cobbett, both of whom took a keen interest in this work but did not live to see its completion; to J. W. Stone, senior partner of Messrs. Cobbett, solicitors of Manchester, England, for his non-legal services of a varied and valued nature; to D. C. L. Holland for his generosity in making the Perceval papers available; and to those who read the text before it was sent to the publisher. These include Paul Showers of Palo Alto, California; Professor J. F. C. Harrison, Professor Norman MacKenzie and Jeanne MacKenzie of Sussex, England; M. L. Pearl of London, England, who read a draft of the preface, the final chapter, and the epilogue; and Professor Marcus Cunliffe, currently of Washington, D.C., who read Chapters 3 through 6, dealing with Cobbett's life in America. Finally, I owe an immeasurable debt to Jane Van Tassel, subeditor, who from "mony a blunder" freed me.

I have taken a few liberties in quoting from Cobbett's letters and from his printed works as well, especially in regard to his compulsive underlining of words and phrases. These (and italics in printed works) I have deleted where, in my opinion, they detract from the readability of the text. I have also made occasional changes in capitalization, spelling, and grammar, in most cases to correct what seem to have been errors in the original. However, I have left untouched a number of examples of Cobbett's idiosyncratic orthography, as for example "gulph," "skaiting," "graff," "ideot."

Money is expressed in the currency of Cobbett's day, and no attempt has been made to translate it into modern values.

The great uses of history are, to enable us to profit from experience of the past, to implant in the minds of the present and future generations, a just opinion of those who have acted in past events. How are either of these to be accomplished by writing so long after the events as to make the facts so many points in dispute?

Cobbett

... a biography is considered complete if it merely accounts for six or seven selves, whereas a person may well have as many thousand.

V. Woolf

Provided a man is not mad, he can be cured of every folly, but vanity.

Rousseau

Introduction

WILLIAM COBBETT, self-educated son of a tavern-keeper, who rose from ploughboy to soldier, from soldier to journalist, and from journalist to member of parliament, occupied a unique position of power in England and America for nearly forty years – from the last decade of the eighteenth century to his death in 1835. This was an extraordinary period embracing the formative years of the new American republic, the French revolution, the Napoleonic wars, the British–American war of 1812, and the adolescence of the industrial revolution. No other private person before or since has had such a dominating influence in public affairs on both sides of the Atlantic.

Born and bred in England, Cobbett acquired a first-hand knowledge of America equalled by few of his countrymen. He served for seven years (1785–91) as a British soldier on the American–Canadian border in the midst of large numbers of loyalists who had fled from the colonies as a result of the war of independence. He lived in America for another eight years (1792–1800), mostly in the national capital at Philadelphia, rising quickly to prominence as a vigorous supporter of George Washington's administration and a truculent defender of Britain in America. Later, he spent two and a half years (1817–19) on Long Island, New York. On his return to England in 1800 he had been embraced by the rulers of the country as a stalwart conservative, but a view of the government at close quarters shortly converted him into a fiercely independent radical reformer, a position he occupied for the last thirty years of his life.

Cobbett's power was derived from his pen. It was both a brilliant and a savage pen, combining common sense, humor, and blistering invective. The English scientist and theologian Joseph Priestley, writing from America, where he had migrated at the end of the eighteenth century, declared that Cobbett was "by far the most popular writer in this country." The *Edinburgh Review* wrote in 1807 that Cobbett had more influence in England than all the other journalists put together. To the historian Spencer Walpole, Cobbett was "the comet of the literary hemisphere, dazzling the world with his brilliancy, per-

1

plexing it with his eccentricity, alarming it with his apparent inflammability." Daniel O'Connell, the Irish Liberator, called Cobbett "one of the greatest benefactors of literature, liberty and religion."[1]

When Cobbett died in 1835, *The Times,* after noting that Cobbett was "in some respects a more extraordinary Englishman than any other of his time," added that he had been "by far the most voluminous writer that has lived for centuries," and it is doubtful whether anyone since has produced a larger body of published work.[2] His first writings in America are represented by twelve substantial volumes. His writings in England consist of eighty-eight large volumes of a weekly journal published by him from 1802 to 1835, *Cobbett's Weekly Political Register,* and another twenty or so volumes of books on such diverse subjects as the poor laws, grammar, politics, agriculture, the protestant reformation, the life of the American president Andrew Jackson, and the raising of children. Cobbett's *Rural Rides,* first published in book form in 1830 and never out of print for long in the past century and a half, the book for which Cobbett is best known today, is a minute fraction – less than a hundredth part – of his writings, roughly estimated at something in excess of twenty million words. Immured within this vast edifice of words is some of the finest writing our language has produced. Lord Holland called Cobbett "unrivalled and matchless" in perspicuity of statement, and the critic William Hazlitt, after describing Cobbett as the most powerful political writer of the day, added that he was "one of the best writers of the language."[3] The appeal of Cobbett's writing lies in a combination of circumstances: he wrote about subjects in which he was intensely interested (including himself); he was inventive, seeing similarities in outwardly dissimilar subjects; he had a rare sense of humor; and he had a wonderfully lucid style. Writing, to be really good, he said, "must be plain to plain men." Most of Cobbett's writing is the spoken word which has happened to find its way into print. A large part was dictated – "dictated and not read" – for he rarely looked over what he had written either when he put it down himself or when it was taken down by others.[4] This, to Montaigne, was the ideal style: "simple and natural speech, the same on paper as on the lips." And Cobbett's writing had the other characteristics that Montaigne admired. It was "vehement and brisk . . . free from affectation, loose, irregular and bold; every piece to form a body in itself; not in the manner of the professor, the preaching friar or the pleading advocate, but rather soldier-like." A sample will illustrate:

In every thing where *horses* are the chief instruments (and horses are second only to men) the English so far surpass all the rest of the world, that there is no room for comparison. The man who has a mind to *know* something of

England in this respect, should walk from the Tower of London to Charing Cross a little after day-light in the morning, while the streets are clear of people. He would then see the teams of immense horses, drawing up from the bank of the Thames, coals, timber, stone, and other heavy materials. One morning last summer I counted, in various places, more than a hundred of these teams, worth *each of them*, harness, waggon, load and all, little less than a thousand pounds. The horses, upon an average, weigh more than a *ton*. But, next after a *fox-hunt*, the finest sight in England is a stage coach just ready to start. A great sheep or cattle fair is a beautiful sight; but, in the stage coach you see more of what man is capable of performing. The vehicle itself, the harness, all so complete and so neatly arranged; so strong and clean and good. The beautiful horses impatient to be off. The inside full and the outside covered, in every part, with men, women, children, boxes, bags, bundles. The coachman, taking his reins in one hand and his whip in the other, gives a signal with his foot, and away go, at the rate of seven miles an hour, the population and property of a hamlet. One of these coaches coming in, after a long journey is a sight not less interesting. The horses are now all sweat and foam, the reek from their bodies ascending like a cloud. The whole equipage is covered, perhaps, with dust or dirt. But still, on it comes as steady as the hand of the clock. As proof of the perfection, to which this mode of travelling has been brought, there is one coach, which goes between Exeter and London, the proprietors of which agree to forfeit *eight-pence* for every *minute* that the coach is behind its time at any of its stages; and this coach, I believe, travels eight miles an hour, and that, too, upon a very hilly, and, at some seasons, very deep road.[5]

Coupled with the freshness and vigor of oral writing are some negative aspects: good talkers talking over a long period tend to repeat themselves, to be discursive, to resort to exaggeration, to be inconsistent; and Cobbett was guilty of all of these on occasion. He was repeatedly taken to task by his many enemies for his exaggeration and inconsistency, but there is no reason why these failings need spoil a reader's enjoyment of the rich fare Cobbett has to offer. It is only necessary to remember that when Cobbett wrote that Richard Brinsley Sheridan, after taking public office, abandoned "every great principle that he ever before professed" and "every pledge he ever gave," this is simply his hyperbolic way of saying that Sheridan made little effort to fulfill all the fine promises he had made earlier.[6] Cobbett's unfriendly contemporaries were quick to call such exaggeration "lies," but in most instances the fault Cobbett was trying to criticize was there; he was holding it under a magnifying glass; he was, in a word, a caricaturist. Pitt, as portrayed by Gillray, had a longer nose than Pitt in real life; as portrayed by Cobbett he was more vicious than the real Pitt. And while Cobbett more often than not provided a one-sided picture of the individuals and events about whom and which he wrote, it is a side that cannot be ignored in any serious analysis of the political, economic, or social life of the time.

In the case, too, of Cobbett's frequent boastful remarks about himself, there was nearly always some solid basis for what he claimed. In 1819 he wrote: "It is very certain that I have been the great enlightener of the people of England." Five years later this claim was picked up by the *Westminster Review* in its first issue. It began by extolling Cobbett's "shrewd and manly intellect," his "inexhaustible store of facts on all subjects of political economy," his "clear, unaffected vigorous style of English," and then quoted Cobbett's boastful remark about his role as enlightener of the English people. "It was impossible to avoid laughing at him," the *Westminster Review* continued, "and yet at the same time feeling, in our hearts, that the impudent fellow had some ground for his boast."[7]

Cobbett's statement that his employees on his farm liked him "personally better than they like any other man in the world" meant no more than that he was generally well liked by those who worked for him on the farm.[8] Like most good talkers, Cobbett regarded the exact fact as unimportant; it was the impression that he wished to create. In a discussion about the disappearance of small farms in England, he once said that "three farms had been turned into one within fifty years." At a later date he claimed that five or six farms had been made into one. In another six months he wrote that "nothing is more common" than a man occupying land that had once been "twenty farms."[9] The successive figures were not intended to be statistics; they were intended to convey the thought that small farms were rapidly decreasing.

The single most often repeated accusation against Cobbett was his inconsistency. He had once praised Pitt, now he condemned him. He had once been a tory, now he was a radical. Pamphlet after pamphlet was published comparing his views at one time with those of a later date. Cobbett made some trenchant comments on the subject:

The doctrine of *consistency*, as now in vogue, is the most absurd that ever was broached. It teaches, that, if you once think well of any person or thing, you must always think well of that person or thing, whatever changes may take place either in them, or in the state of your information respecting them. For instance, if you praise a man to-day, and, to-morrow, receive proof of his having long been a thief, you must still continue to praise him. Where is the man, who has not changed his opinions of men as well as of things? Those who write every day, or every week, must express what they think at the time; but, if new sources of information open to them, they must express what they *then* think, and not with any regard to what they have given as their opinion before. – But, how would this doctrine suit my opponents, if I were to attempt to hold them to [it]. If I am to say, to some of the friends of corruption, "you used to praise me, and why do you not praise me now?" They would, doubtless, answer: "Oh! but, you *then* wrote to please us; and *now* you do not: Owing to your ignorance of us and our views, we *then* were objects of your applause, and *now* we are objects of your censure". To be sure, nothing could be more reasonable than this. There is nothing at all *inconsistent* in it; but, then, the argument is just as good for me as it is for them. – The truth is, that, as to opinions, no man is to be blamed for a change, except there be strong reason to conclude that the change has proceeded from *a bad motive*; or, rather, that it is not real, but a pretended change, for the purpose of something selfish or wicked.[10]

Addressing William Huskisson years later, Cobbett wrote: "I do not blame you for changing your opinions: I blame you for changing from good to bad . . . And, I have a full right to blame you, because your opinion, or, rather, your professed opinion, has changed in accordance with your interest."[11]

Personal advantage – in the form of profit or advancement or popularity – was never discernible in Cobbett's changed views. Despite the repeated attacks on him for inconsistency, it seems probable that he changed his mind no more often than anyone else in public life who expressed himself over an extended period. Indeed, if objectives are to be used as the measure, a good case should be made for the position that Cobbett was a model of consistency compared with his contemporaries, and particularly as compared with the "great men" of the period or the leading newspapers. In the article which first brought Cobbett to public attention in 1794 he wrote: "Happiness being the end of all good government, that which produces the most is consequently the best." In 1830 he wrote: "Happiness ought to be your great object."[12] Throughout the whole of Cobbett's public life he had wielded his power for the benefit of the poor and the weak. During the yellow fever epidemic in Philadelphia in 1797 he strongly condemned the failure of the civic authorities to make provision for the removal of the poor from the city: "If the treasury be full, as it is said to be, let it be emptied instantly, that the poor may have the same chance of living as the rich."[13] In 1801 he supported the fairness of the existing English poor laws, and on his deathbed in 1835 he wrote an article attacking harsh amendments to those laws which parliament had passed, over Cobbett's protests, the year before. In 1808 James Mill wrote of Cobbett: "He has assumed the patronage of the poor, at a time when they are depressed . . . and when the current of our policy runs to depress them still farther."[14] It was a patronage, Mill might have added, that offered no opportunity of material reward. For a lifetime of service in this unrewarding cause Cobbett earned what he prized more than money: the title of the Poor Man's Friend.

Another of the cliches about Cobbett is that he looked to the past rather than to the future. This is true only in a most limited sense: he saw various features of the past that he liked, and wished to see them preserved. In other cases his opponents sought to scotch reform proposals by denouncing them as "innovations" – the accepted label for rash and impractical Jacobin experiments. Hence, Cobbett was often driven to the device of defending his proposals by demonstrating that they were not new, but had been applied in the past. But here the past was used as a defense for reforms, rather than the reason for them.

The charge of looking to the past was, in any event, a more effective condemnation in the late nineteenth century when "Progress" was the shibboleth and newer was always better. A citizen of the late twentieth century would hardly think ridiculous Cobbett's charge that the large city, with its smoke, noise, dirt, and overcrowding, was a "wen." We cannot be too hard on Cobbett for preferring country life to city life, the rose-covered cottage to the sleazy city flat, homemade bread to baker's bread, cottage industry to factory industry. Today it cannot be to Cobbett's discredit that he consistently stood in opposition to the establishment. He was for wider suffrage and the ballot; for the selection of civil servants on the basis of merit rather than rank or family; for the correction of such church abuses as nonresidency and plural livings; for the elimination of sinecures and the public workhouse; for the abolition of the Bank of England as a privately owned establishment profiting from its dealings with the government; for stricter child labor laws; for the termination of the unfair game laws; for the cessation of flogging in the army; for the freedom of Ireland from protestant domination. Was it he, or the rulers of England, who looked to the past rather than to the future?

We must, therefore, approach the life of Cobbett with an open mind, without too much regard to the calumnious charges of his enemies which have been thoughtlessly repeated so many times as almost to become gospel. This is not to claim that he was a saint. Far from it. He was often wrong; he was a supreme egotist; he was harder on both his friends and his enemies than he should have been; he lied on occasion, possibly as much as the "great men" of his day; his attainment frequently fell short of his goals. Yet there were elements of greatness in the man. He reminds one at times of Rousseau, of Tolstoy, of Jonathan Swift, of King Lear, of old Harlov in Turgenev's *A Lear of the Steppes,* or of an Old Testament prophet.

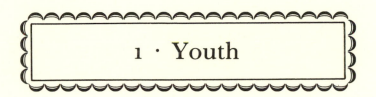

1 · Youth

An extraordinary *man,* indeed, Sir James; but, as far as my observation and experience have gone, a ten thousand times more extraordinary *boy.*

"I WAS BRED AT the plough-tail," wrote William Cobbett, "and in the Hop-Gardens of Farnham in Surrey, my native place, and which spot, as it so happened, is the neatest in England, and, I believe, in the whole world. All there is a garden."[1] Farnham, where Cobbett was born in 1763, lies in the valley of the Wey, forty miles west of London.[2] Arthur Young called the vale between Farnham and Alton the finest ten miles in England. And in Defoe's day, Farnham, next to London, was "the greatest corn-market in England." A gentleman told Defoe that one day he counted "eleven hundred teams of horse, all drawing waggons or carts, loaden with wheat at this market."[3] The garden-like quality of the area was produced by the manicured grounds of its great residences, the well-tended fields of the prosperous farmers, and the pretty cottages of those who tilled the fields. Towering over the village on the rising ground to the north was the huge castle occupied by the bishops of Winchester, notable for its fine lawns and gardens and gravelled terrace "rolled over and over and over again, till it had little white specks on it."[4] Not much more than a mile to the east of Farnham lay Waverly Abbey, reputedly the inspiration for Walter Scott's first novel and, during Cobbett's boyhood, the residence of Sir Robert Rich. Not far from Waverly Abbey was Moor Park, once the home of Sir William Temple and his bride Dorothy Osborne, a place distinguished by the presence of Jonathan Swift and his beloved Stella.

William Cobbett's grandfather was a day laborer, a road-wagoner, who worked for one farmer from the day of his marriage to that of his death, upwards of forty years.[5] Cobbett's father, who owned the Jolly Farmer, a public house in Farnham where Cobbett and his three brothers were born, was a man of considerable talents. As a boy he had driven a plough for twopence a day, and used his small earnings to attend an evening school. He learned some mathematics there, and

7

on occasion was employed as a land surveyor. He even acquired some knowledge of writing in shorthand. To one of his sceptical neighbors who disbelieved in the usefulness of the strange symbols employed in such writing, he gave a note to be carried to a mutual friend, a Mr. Jarratt, chief gardener at the castle, a fellow practitioner of the art. Cobbett said to the sceptic, "he'll tell you something that he dont know now, but you do." When Jarratt received the message, he said to the bearer, "Ah, I see; you've got a spade, and hav'nt paid for it."[6]

William Cobbett was the third of the four sons, the eldest of whom

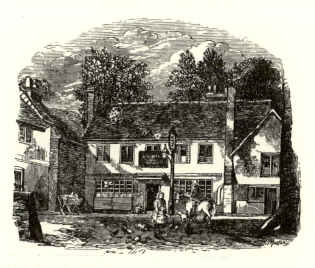

Cobbett's birthplace, the Jolly Farmer tavern in Farnham. This woodcut was made around 1860 at the request of Cobbett's son James, who intended to use it in a life of his father

was less than four years older than the youngest. He began to work on the farm as a little boy, driving the small birds from the turnip seed, and the rooks from the peas. He learned to tie hop shoots around the bottoms of the poles with rushes which had first been made pliant by trampling them with bare feet.

I do not remember the time when I did not earn my living . . . When I first trudged a-field, with my wooden bottle and my satchel swung over my shoulders, I was hardly able to climb the gates and stiles, and, at the close of the day, to reach home was a task of infinite difficulty. My next employment was weeding wheat, and leading a single horse at harrowing barley. Hoeing peas followed, and hence I arrived at the honour of joining the reapers in harvest, driving the team and holding plough. We were all of us strong and laborious, and my father used to boast, that he had four boys, the eldest of whom was but fifteen years old, who did as much work as any three men in the parish of Farnham. Honest pride, and happy days![7]

When Cobbett learned to plough he was so small that he had to "get up upon a gate to put the bit-halter upon a cart-horse's head." When he was fifty-five years old he wrote: "The two first fingers of my right hand are still somewhat bent, from having been, more than forty years ago, so often in close embrace with the eye of the spade and the handle of the hoe."[8]

One suspects as he reads Cobbett's account of his own life that he tended to overemphasize the innocence of his youth, but it is probably true that he had little formal schooling. He claimed "some faint recollection of going to school to an old woman who, I believe, did not succeed in teaching me my letters." His father taught him to read and write, including some shorthand, and gave him "a pretty tolerable knowledge of arithmetic." Cobbett also asserted that the family neither knew nor thought anything about politics, that he did not remember ever seeing a newspaper in the house. His brother Tom, however, claimed that their father frequently read aloud from the papers and that Bill was intensely interested (the only one of the four boys who was) in the political news they contained: "for Bill to be taken up with it, he too who was always foremost in all frolic and daring, was very odd, Uncle Tom said." The American war was the one political topic that was of general interest in the family.

My father was a partizan of the Americans: he used frequently to dispute on the subject with the gardener of a nobleman who lived near us. This was generally done with good humour, over a pot of our best ale; yet the disputants sometimes grew warm, and gave way to language that could not fail to attract our attention. My father was worsted without doubt, as he had for antagonist, a shrewd and sensible old Scotchman, far his superior in political knowledge; but he pleaded before a partial audience: we thought there was but one wise man in the world, and that one was our father.[9]

Cobbett had the same respectful and loving recollection of his mother, although he recognized that the four small boys were often a trial that tested her patience: "when I and my brothers were little children, and used to run about the house, tearing at our mother's gown or apron in order to worry her into giving us apples or something or other, she used, when we had tired out her most exemplary patience, to exclaim, 'Be quiet, you plagues of Egypt, do!' "[10]

Life for small boys in rural Surrey was not all work on the farm. Every year one of the four Cobbett sons accompanied their father to the great hop fair at Weyhill as a reward for the labors of the summer. There were also regular visits to the house of grandmother Cobbett.

It was a little thatched cottage with a garden before the door. It had but two windows; a damson tree shaded one, and a clump of filberts the other. Here I and my brothers went every Christmas and Whitsuntide, to spend a week or two, and torment the poor old woman with our noise and dilapidations. She used to give us milk and bread for breakfast, an apple pudding for our dinner, and a piece of bread and cheese for supper.

At their grandmother's house the fire was made of turf cut from the neighboring heath. Cobbett and his brothers were lighted to bed with rushes that had been dipped in grease and were kept in a long piece of oak bark.[11]

The giant sandhill that extended from the heath down to a rivulet that emptied into the Wey near Moor Park was the scene of another source of entertainment.

As a due mixture of pleasure with toil, I, with two brothers, used occasionally to *desport* ourselves, as the lawyers call it, at this sand-hill. Our diversion was this: we used to go to the top of the hill, which was steeper than the roof of a house; one used to draw his arms out of the sleeves of his smock-frock, and lay himself down with his arms by his sides; and then the others, one at head and the other at feet, sent him rolling down the hill like a barrel or a log of wood. By the time he got to the bottom, his hair, eyes, ears, nose, and mouth, were all full of this loose sand; then the others took their turn, and at every roll, there was a monstrous spell of laughter . . . This was the spot where I was receiving my *education;* and this was the sort of education; and I am perfectly satisfied that if I had not received such an education, or something very much like it; that, if I had been brought up a milksop, with a nursery-maid everlastingly at my heels; I should have been at this day as great a fool, as inefficient a mortal, as any of those frivolous idiots that are turned out from Winchester or Westminster School, or from any of those dens of dunces called Colleges and Universities.[12]

From his earliest youth Cobbett was an admirer of field sports, and in after years remembered that he had "scores of times" dropped the hoe to follow the hounds – not always, though, for the joy of the kill.

a huntsman, named George Bradley, who was huntsman to Mr Smither of Hale, very wantonly gave me a cut with his whip, because I jumped in amongst the dogs, pulled a hare from them, and got her scut, upon a little common, called Seal common, near Waverly Abbey. I was only about eight years old; but my mind was so imbued with the principles of natural justice, that I did not rest satisfied with the mere calling of names, of which, however, I gave Mr. George Bradley a plenty. I sought to inflict a just punishment upon him; and as I had not the means of proceeding *by force,* I proceeded by cunning . . .

Hounds (hare-hounds at least) will follow the trail of a red-herring as eagerly as that of a hare, and rather more so, the scent being stronger and more unbroken. I waited till Bradley and his pack were trailing for a hare in the neighbourhood of that same Seal common. They were pretty sure to find in the space of half-an-hour, and the hare was pretty sure to go up the common and over the hill to the south. I placed myself ready with a red-herring at the end of a string, in a dry field, and near a hard path, along which, or near to which, I was pretty sure the hare would go. I waited a long while; the sun was getting high, the scent bad; but by-and-by, I heard the view-halloo and full cry. I squatted down in the fern, and my heart bounded with the prospect of inflicting justice, when I saw my lady come skipping by, going off towards Pepper-harrow; that is to say, to the south. In a moment, I clapped down my herring, went off at a right angle towards the west, climbed up a steep bank very soon, where the horsemen, such as they were, could not follow; then on I went over the roughest part of the common that I could find, till I got to the pales of Moor Park, over which I went, there being holes at the bottom for the letting in of the hares. That part of the park was covered with short heath; and I gave some twirls about to amuse Mr. Bradley for half-an-hour. Then off I went, and down a hanger at last, to the bottom of which no horseman could get without riding round a quarter of a mile. At the bottom of the hanger was an alder-moor, in a swamp. There my herring ceased to perform its service. The river is pretty rapid; I tossed it in that it might go back to the sea, and relate to its brethren the exploits of the land. I washed my hands in the water of the moor; and took a turn, and stood at the top of the hanger to witness the winding-up of the day's sport, which terminated a little before dusk in one of the dark days of November. After overrunning the scent a hundred times; after an hour's puzzling in the dry-field, after all the doubles and all the turns that the sea-born hare had given them, down came the whole *posse* to the swamp; the huntsman went round a mill-head not far off, and tried the other side of the river: "No! d—n her, where can she be?" And thus, amidst conjectures, disputations, mutual blamings, and swearings a plenty, they concluded, some of them half-leg deep in dirt, and going soaking home at the end of a drizzling day.[13]

Alongside Cobbett's picture of the idyllic life in Farnham – the neatest, the most fertile, the most beautiful in the world, where the most hard-working boys lived with the most loving parents – one must place the fact that from an early age Cobbett was so often found away from Farnham for one reason or another.[14] When he was "about ten or eleven years of age" (Cobbett thought he was born in 1766 rather than in 1763; hence the ages he gives may be similarly distorted) he was sent down with a horse to Steeple Langford, a small village in Wiltshire, near Salisbury, where he stayed "from the month of June till the fall of the year."[15] In the following year he was off again:

At *eleven* years of age my employment was clipping of box-edgings and weeding beds of flowers in the garden of the Bishop of Winchester . . . I had always been fond of beautiful gardens; and a gardener, who had just come from the King's gardens at Kew, gave me such a description of them as made me instantly resolve to work in these gardens. The next morning, without saying a word to any one, off I set, with no clothes, except those on my back, and with thirteen half-pence in my pocket. I found that I must go to Richmond, and I, accordingly, went on, from place to place, inquiring my way thither. A long day (it was in June) brought me to Richmond in the afternoon. Two-penny worth of bread and cheese and a pennyworth of small beer, which I had on the road, and one half-penny that I had lost somehow or other, left three pence in my pocket. With this for my whole fortune, I was trudging through Richmond, in my blue smock-frock and my red garters tied under my knees, when, staring about me, my eye fell upon a little book, in a book-seller's window, on the outside of which was written: "TALE OF A TUB; PRICE 3d". The title was so odd, that my curiosity was excited. I had the 3d. but, then, I could have *no supper*. In I went, and got the little book, which I was so impatient to read, that I got over into a field, at the upper corner of Kew Gardens, where there stood a *hay-stack*. On the shady side of this, I sat down to read. The book was so different from any thing that I had ever read before: it was something so *new* to my mind, that, though I could not at all understand some of it, it delighted me beyond description; and it produced what I have always considered a sort of birth of intellect. I read on till it was dark, without any thought about supper or bed. When I could see no longer, I put my little book in my pocket, and tumbled down by the side of the stack, where I slept till the birds in Kew Gardens awaked me in the morning; when off I started to Kew, reading my little book. The singularity of my dress, the simplicity of my manner, my confident and lively air, and, doubtless, his own compassion besides, induced the gardener, who was a Scotsman, I remember, to give me victuals, find me lodging, and set me to work. And, it was during the period that I was at Kew, that the present king and two of his brothers laughed at the oddness of my dress, while I was sweeping the grass plat round the foot of the Pagoda. The gardener, seeing me fond of books, lent me some gardening books to read; but, these I could not relish after my *Tale of a Tub*, which I carried about with me wherever I went, and when I . . . lost it in a box that fell overboard in the Bay of Fundy in North America, the loss gave me greater pain than I have ever felt at losing thousands of pounds.[16]

After the Kew Gardens experience Cobbett seems to have spent two years (1779–81) in Guildford working for a William Parson for £10 10s. a year the first year and £14 the next. At some point Cobbett worked in Guildford for the Reverend James Barclay, author of *A Complete and Universal English Dictionary* (1774). Barclay had a good library and allowed Cobbett to have the use of his books. "It was prob-ably here that he [Cobbett] first showed his inclination to compose something of his own, for here he made a small manuscript book, containing a history in Epitome of all the Kings & Queens of England" – anticipating by a few years the mock history of the mon-archs written by his younger contemporary Jane Austen.[17]

In 1781 Cobbett apparently was in London, for he tells of hearing John Wesley (whom Cobbett irreverently calls "Jack") preach there:

Old Jack had talent. He could pick the pockets of his audience without their perceiving it. I never saw Jack but once. I was quite a boy; but I have always remembered his familiar slang. He gave out a hymn, to be sung to the tune of Nancy Dawson, observing, that he was resolved, that the Devil should not have *all the pretty tunes to himself* any longer, but that *God should have some* of them too. That was at Wapping in the year 1781.

From the same talk, presumably, he remembered hearing Wesley tell his audience: "You do not *like* to be damned: you *like* to be wicked . . . but you do not *like* to be burnt."[18] Was it on this stay in London that Cobbett "lodged with a widow and her two daughters at a cottage at Ham Common"? He told his children, that "he sometimes read their newspaper to them of an evening, and afterwards would go out on the Common and practise speech making. He said he had a feeling within him *then,* that he should one day be in Parliament, making speeches."[19]

In 1782 we find Cobbett staying with an uncle near Portsmouth, where he remained "some little time," assisting at a school run by the uncle or one of his cousins.

From the top of Portsdown, I for the first time beheld the sea, and no sooner did I behold it than I wished to be a sailor. I could never account for this sudden impulse, nor can I now. Almost all English boys feel the same inclination: it would seem that, like young ducks, instinct leads them to rush on the bosom of the water. But it was not the sea alone that I saw: the grand fleet was riding at anchor at Spithead. I had heard of the wooden walls of Old England: I had formed my ideas of a ship and of a fleet; but what I now beheld so far surpassed what I had been able to form a conception of, that I stood lost between astonishment and admiration . . . My heart was inflated with national pride. The sailors were my countrymen, the fleet belonged to my country, and surely I had my part in it, and in all its honours; yet, these honours I had not earned; I took to myself a sort of reproach for possessing what I had no right to, and resolved to have a just claim by sharing in the hardships and the dangers . . . For a sixpence given to an invalid I got permission to go upon the battlements; here I had a closer view of the fleet, and at every look my impatience to be on board increased. In short, I went from the castle to Portsmouth, got into a boat, and was in a few minutes on board the Pegasus man of war, commanded by the Right Honourable George Berkley, brother to the Earl of Berkley.

The captain had more compassion than is generally met with in men of his profession; he represented to me the toils I must undergo, and the punishment that the least disobedience or neglect would subject me to. He persuaded me to return home, and I remember he concluded his advice with telling me, that it was better to be led to church in a halter, to be tied to a girl I did not like, than to be tied to the gang-way, or, as the sailors call it, married to *Miss Roper*. From the conclusion of this wholesome counsel, I perceived that the captain thought I had eloped on account of a bastard. I blushed, and that confirmed him in his opinion . . . I in vain attempted to convince Captain Berkley, that choice alone had led me to the sea; he sent me on shore, and I at last quitted Portsmouth; but not before I had applied to the Port-Admiral, Evans, to get my name enrolled among those who were destined for the service. I was, in some sort, obliged to acquaint the Admiral with what had passed on board the Pegasus, in consequence of which my request was refused, and I happily escaped, sorely against my will, from the most toilsome and perilous profession in the world.[20]

Cobbett's stay in the neighborhood of Portsmouth was followed by a short return to Farnham, but by the next year he had left home forever.

It was on the sixth of May 1783, that I, like Don Quixote, sallied forth to seek adventure. I was dressed in my holiday clothes, in order to accompany two or three lasses to the Guildford fair. They were to assemble at a house about three miles from my home, where I was to attend them; but, unfortunately for me, I had to cross the London turnpike road. The stage-coach had just turned the summit of a hill and was rattling down towards me at a merry rate. The notion of going to London never entered my mind until this very moment, yet the step was completely determined on, before the coach came to the spot where I stood. Up I got, and was in London about nine o'clock in the evening.

It was by mere accident that I had money enough to defray the expenses of this day. Being rigged out for the fair, I had three or four crown and half-crown pieces (which most certainly I did not intend to spend) besides a few shillings and half-pence. This my little all, which I had been years in amassing, melted away like snow before the sun, when touched by the fingers of the inn-keepers and their waiters. In short, when I arrived at Ludgate-Hill, and had paid my fare, I had but about half a crown in my pocket. By a commencement of that good luck, which has hitherto attended me through all the situations in which fortune has placed me, I was preserved from ruin. A gentleman, who was one of the passengers in the stage, fell into conversation with me at dinner, and he soon learnt that I was going I knew not whither nor for what. This gentleman was a hop-merchant in the borough of Southwark, and upon closer inquiry, it appeared that he had often dealt with my father at Weyhill. He knew the danger I was in; he was himself a father, and he felt for my parents. His house, became my home, he wrote to my father, and endeavoured to prevail on me to obey his orders, which were to return immediately home. I am ashamed to say that I was disobedient. It was the first time I had even been so, and I have repented of it from that moment to this. Willingly would I have returned, but pride would not suffer me to do it. I feared the scoffs of my acquaintances more than the real evils that threatened me.

My generous preserver, finding my obstinacy not to be overcome, began to look out for an employment for me. He was preparing an advertisement for the news-paper, when an acquaintance of his, an attorney, called in to see him. He related my adventure to this gentleman, whose name was Holland, and who, happening to want an understrapping quill-driver, did me the honour to take me into his service, and the next day saw me perched on a great high stool, in an obscure chamber in Gray's Inn, endeavouring to decypher the crabbed drafts of my employer.

I could write a good plain hand, but I could not read the pot-hooks and hangers of Mr. Holland. He was a month in learning me to copy without almost continual assistance, and even then I was of but little use to him; for, besides that I wrote a snail's pace, my want of knowledge in orthography gave him infinite trouble; so that for the first two months I was a dead weight upon his hands. Time, however, rendered me useful, and Mr. Holland was pleased to tell me that he was very well satisfied with me, just at the very moment when I began to grow extremely dissatisfied with him.[21]

Cobbett later claimed that the eight or nine months he spent in Mr. Holland's dungeon was the only part of his life totally unattended with pleasure. "When I think of the *saids* and *soforths,* and the counts of tautology that I scribbled over," he wrote; "when I think of those sheets of seventy-two words, and those lines two inches apart, my brain turns." His working hours were from five in the morning to eight or nine at night, and sometimes all night long. The office was so dark that candles had to be lighted on cloudy days.[22]

I never quitted this gloomy recess except on Sundays when I usually took a walk to St. James's Park, to feast my eyes with the sight of the trees, the grass, and the water. In one of these walks I happened to cast my eye on an advertisement, inviting all loyal young men, who had a mind to gain riches and glory, to repair to a certain rendezvous, where they might enter into His Majesty's marine service, and have the peculiar happiness and honour of being enrolled in the Chatham Division. I was not ignorant enough to be the dupe of this morsel of military bombast; but a change was what I wanted; besides I knew that marines went to sea, and my desire to be on that element had rather increased than diminished by my being penned up in London. In short I resolved to join this glorious corps; and, to avoid all possibility of being discovered by my friends, I went down to Chatham, and enlisted in the marines as I thought, but the next morning I found myself before a captain of a marching regiment. There was no retreating: I had taken a shilling to drink his Majesty's health, and his further bounty was ready for my reception. When I told the captain (who was an Irishman, and who has since then been an excellent friend to me), that I thought myself engaged in the marines: "By Jasus! my lad," said he, "and you have had a narrow escape."[23]

2 · The soldier's friend

I have a quarrel with abuses of all sorts; I have a quarrel with peculation and plunder, under whatever specious names they may be disguised.

THE MARCHING regiment into which Cobbett had enlisted was His Majesty's 54th (or West Norfolk) Regiment of Foot. It had rendered service in North America during the American war of independence, which had ended in 1783, and, when Cobbett joined on February 4, 1784, the main body of men were in Nova Scotia – a terrestrial paradise, according to the Irish captain who had complimented Cobbett on his escape from the marines.[1]

Since the country was at peace, the military services were particular about those it accepted; "they used to make us swear before they would accept of our voluntary offers, that we were not, and never had been, chimney-sweeps, colliers, or miners; that we were not papists, that we were not Irishmen, and that we were not troubled with fits, including love fits, for ought I know to the contrary." They also insisted on having "straight and tall fellows, and used to stare into our eyes to see if we squinted." Cobbett presumably took the oath; plainly he met the standards. He was about six feet tall with flaxen hair and an extremely florid complexion. He had, according to his own account, "a plump and red and smiling face." His eyes were gray, rather small, but straight enough. So he had signed on and been given his shilling.[2]

After enlistment, Cobbett spent thirteen months at Chatham, learning military exercises and taking his tour in the duty of the garrison.

My leisure time, which was a very considerable portion of the twenty-four hours, was spent, not in the dissipations common to such a way of life, but in reading and study. In the course of this year I learnt more than I had ever done before. I subscribed to a circulating library at Brompton, the greatest part of the books in which I read more than once over. The library was not very considerable, it is true, nor in my reading was I directed by any degree of taste or choice. Novels, plays, history, poetry, all were read, and nearly with equal avidity.[3]

What Cobbett read may be guessed by a look at his later writings. He was, of course, already familiar with the Bible in the detailed way that was characteristic of men in the eighteenth century. It is too much to say that he knew it by heart, but he always seemed capable of producing the relevant quotation. We know that he had read *A Tale of a Tub* as a small boy, and by the time he became a journalist he had read a great deal more of Swift. He seemed as familiar with Shakespeare as with the Bible, and quoted him more often than any other author. By the peak of his career he had read the poetry of Dryden, Pope, and Goldsmith, who were his favorites, and he also read Milton, Marvell, Butler, Cowley, Churchill, Thomson, and Cowper.[4] He knew all 400-odd lines of Goldsmith's poem "The Traveller." He had read some Byron, and mentions Wordsworth and Southey, but not Keats or Coleridge. The novels Cobbett read included those by Fielding, Sterne, Le Sage, and Cervantes. In addition to the plays of Shakespeare, he was familiar with those of Wycherley, Congreve, Beaumont and Fletcher, Otway, and Foote, as well as those of his contemporary Sheridan. He read some of Molière, Voltaire, La Fontaine, and Rousseau. He occasionally mentioned Virgil and Horace. He had carefully studied Blackstone's *Commentaries*, Watts's *Logic*, and Blair's *Lectures on Rhetoric*. He had read some of Fortescue, Bacon, Evelyn, Gibbon, Addison, Paley, Samuel Johnson, and William Temple.

Cobbett's reading in the army was mainly recreational; but it was accompanied by a large amount of hard studying, particularly in the field of grammar. His father "made us get the rules by heart but we learnt nothing of the principles." He soon had occasion to remedy the deficiency. Because he was able to write a fair hand, he was made copyist to Colonel (later General) Hugh Debbieg, commandant of the garrison at Chatham, who, seeing Cobbett's shortcomings, "strongly recommended study," which he enforced "with a sort of injunction, and with a promise of reward in case of success." Cobbett bought a Lowth's *Grammar*. He wrote out the entire text of the 190-page book two or three times and repeated it to himself every morning and every evening until he had it by heart. When on guard, he said it all over once each time he was posted sentinel. "I learned grammar," he wrote, "when I was a private soldier on the pay of sixpence a day":

The edge of my berth, or that of the guard-bed, was my seat to study in; my knapsack was my bookcase; a bit of board, lying on my lap, was my writing-table; and the task did not demand any thing like a year of my life. I had no money to purchase candle or oil; in winter time it was rarely that I could get any evening light but that of the fire, and only my turn even of that. And, if I, under such circumstances, and without parent or friend to advise or encourage me, accomplished this undertaking, what excuse can there be for

Cobbett as soldier. "I was at the time, much more intent upon the beauty of my cap and feathers than upon any thing else." This silhouette of Cobbett with traditional bearskin and pigtail was drawn in 1784 or 1785 by his friend Benjamin Garlike, later British minister in Copenhagen, D.C.L. (Hon.) Oxon. 1810 any youth, however poor, however pressed with business, or however circumstanced as to room or other conveniences? To buy a pen or a sheet of paper I was compelled to forego some portion of food, though in a state of half-starvation: I had no moment of time that I could call my own; and I had to read and to write amidst the talking, laughing, singing, whistling, and brawling of at least half a score of the most thoughtless of men, and that, too, in the hours of their freedom from all control. Think not lightly of the farthing that I had to give, now and then, for ink, pen, or paper! That farthing was, alas! a great sum to me! I was as tall as I am now; I had great health and great exercise. The whole of the money, not expended for us at market, was two-pence a week for each man. I remember, and well I may! that, upon one occasion I, after all absolutely necessary expenses, had, on a Friday, made shift to have a half-penny in reserve, which I had destined for the purchase of a red-herring in the morning; but, when I pulled off my clothes at night, so hungry then as to be hardly able to endure life, I found that I had lost my half-penny! I buried my head under the miserable sheet and rug, and cried like a child![5]

It is quite possible that Cobbett learned more than grammar while working for Debbieg, who, as the great British authority on fortification, may have been the stimulus to Cobbett's interest in that subject, and as one of the most outspoken, obstinate, and hot-tempered officers in the British army, may have developed Cobbett's tendencies in that direction as well. One of Cobbett's tasks for Debbieg was transcribing "the famous correspondence between him and the duke of Richmond," which would have included that intemperate letter which Debbieg in 1784 wrote to the duke, his superior officer, leading to Debbieg's trial before a court-martial for insubordination. The nettlesome nature of Cobbett's mentor was conclusively proved in 1789 when Debbieg again assailed the powerful duke and was subjected to a second court-martial in which he was sentenced to be deprived of his rank and pay for six months.[6]

Cobbett was soon promoted to corporal, "a rank, which, however contemptible it may appear in some people's eyes, brought me in a clear twopence *per diem,* and put a very clever worsted knot upon my shoulder too." As corporal, he was sent off from Chatham to join his regiment in Halifax, Nova Scotia in March 1785. The barrenness of the country that met his eye was far from the terrestrial paradise he had been led to expect. And the country was populated, when he landed, by thousands of refugees: the loyalists from the thirteen colonies who fled from the United States following the treaty of Paris in 1783, and many of the British military personnel who had been in the theater of war.

Nova Scotia had no other charm for me than that of novelty. Every thing I saw was new; bogs, rocks and stumps, musquitoes and bull-frogs. Thousands of Captains and Colonels without soldiers, and of 'Squires without stockings or shoes. In England, I had never thought of approaching a 'Squire without a most respectful bow; but, in this new world, though I was but a Corporal, I often ordered a 'Squire to bring me a glass of grog, and even to take care of my knapsack.[7]

The 54th regiment remained in Halifax for only a few weeks. It was then ordered to New Brunswick, 150 miles to the west, where Cobbett spent the next six years peacefully engaged in guarding the trouble-free border between Canada and the United States. The regiment was first assigned to the village of St. John on the bay of Fundy, but after about two years was sent nearly a hundred miles up the St. John river to Fort Howe at Fredericton, the new capital of New Brunswick, a community consisting predominantly of loyalist immigrants from the United States. The principal geographic features of Fredericton were (and are) the great St. John river, nearly a mile wide at this point, and the long and extremely cold winters. The men going on guard duty "were wrapped up in great cloth coats lined with flannel, their heads covered with caps of the same sort, leaving only an opening for the eyes and the nose." The St. John river and all the creeks running into it were completely frozen over early in November.

"In about ten days the snow came; until storm after storm, coming at intervals of a week or fortnight, made the mass upon an average, ten feet deep; and there we were, nine days out of ten, with a bright sun over our heads, and with snow, dry as hair-powder, screeching under our feet." The snow did not begin to melt until the end of April; a month later the St. John river became a huge mass of ice moving "downwards with accelerating rapidity towards the sea." This was followed by about five months of summer.[8]

Cobbett learned the full value of his knowledge of grammar after he had joined his regiment. He was first made clerk of the regiment, then the whole business of the regiment fell into his hands. At the end of about a year, "neither adjutant, paymaster, or quarter-master could move an inch without my assistance." He drew up the returns, reports, and other official papers.

Then I became the Serjeant Major to the Regiment, which brought me in close contact at every hour, with the whole of the Epaulet gentry, whose profound and surprizing ignorance I discovered in a twinkling. But, I had a very delicate part to act with these gentry; for, while I despised them for their gross ignorance and their vanity, and hated them for their drunkenness and rapacity, I was fully sensible of their power, and I knew also the envy, which my sudden rise over the heads of so many old serjeants had created. My path was full of rocks and pit-falls; and, as I never disguised my dislikes or restrained my tongue, I should have been broken and flogged for fifty different offences, given to my supreme jack-asses, had they not been kept in awe by my inflexible sobriety, impartiality, and integrity. . .

My custom was this: to get up, in summer, at day-light, and in winter at four o'clock; shave, dress, even to the putting of my sword-belt over my shoulder, and having my sword lying on the table before me, ready to hang by my side. Then I ate a bit of cheese, or pork, and bread. Then I prepared my report, which was filled up as fast as the companies brought me in the materials. After this I had an hour or two to read, before the time came for any duty out of doors, unless when the regiment or part of it went out to exercise in the morning. When this was the case, and the matter was left to me, I always had it on the ground in such time as that the bayonets glistened in the rising sun, a sight which gave me delight, of which I often think, but which I should in vain endeavour to describe. If the *officers* were to go out, eight or ten o'clock was the hour, sweating the men in the heat of the day, breaking in upon the time for cooking their dinner, putting all thing out of order and all men out of humour. When I was commander, the men had a long day of leisure before them: they could ramble into the town or into the woods; go to get raspberries, to catch birds, to catch fish, or to pursue any other recreation, and such of them as chose, and were qualified, to work at their trades. So that here, arising solely from the early habits of one very young man, were pleasant and happy days given to hundreds.[9]

Perhaps it was this delight in the image of marching men with bayonets glistening in the rising sun that caused Cobbett to write twenty years later: "I did many things, which I would not now do, if possessed of similar power . . . I made no allowances for the weaknesses, or lukewarmness of others."[10]

In 1788 when new rules were issued relating to military exercises, most of the officers did not bother to learn them. So when the time came for the annual review, Cobbett "had to give lectures of instruction to the officers themselves, the colonel not excepted." For several of them, Cobbett drew the successive positions of the regiment on large cards, with the words of command the officers were to give at each point during the maneuvers.[11]

Cobbett continued to apply himself to his own improvement. He taught himself French. He read Vauban on fortifications. He refused, however, to study astronomy: "I will confine my studies to things which pass upon the earth." He studied geometry and made "for the teaching of young corporals and serjeants, a little book on arithmetic; and it is truly surprising in how short a time they learned all that was necessary for them to know of that necessary department of learning . . . I have, in my tossings about the world, lost the manuscript; but I recollect the substance very well; and, as it will cost me little time, I think I shall put it in print some of these days." He did not do that, but the lost manuscript has recently turned up. It is eloquent evidence of the thoroughness of Cobbett's studies.[12]

He found time for much else besides:

I built a barrack for four hundred men, without the aid of either draughtsman, carpenter, or bricklayer; the soldiers under me cut down the timber and

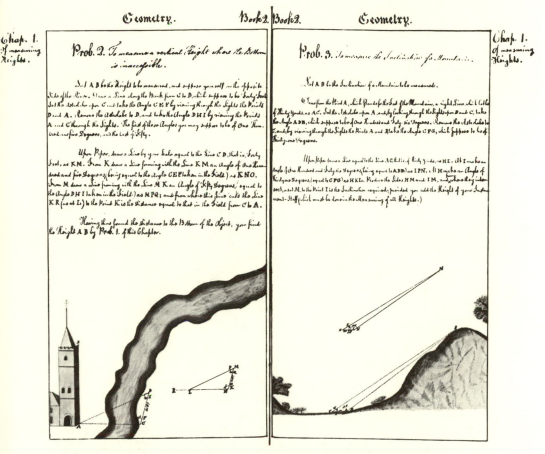

Cobbett's "Little Book of Arithmetic." Two pages from the exercise book written by Cobbett in 1789 for teaching mathematics to young corporals and sergeants

dug the stones, and I was the architect; I went through a tract of woods, of above a hundred miles where no man had ever ventured before to go alone; and this I did for the purpose of putting a stop to desertion, by showing the regiment that I myself was able to follow the fugitives, and, accordingly, after that we had no more desertion to the United States. With all these occupations (of which I mention only a few particulars that occur to me at the moment) I found time for skaiting, fishing, shooting, and all the other sports of the country, of which, when I left it, I had seen, and knew, more than any other man.[13]

Much of the work performed by Cobbett beyond that required in the strict line of duty was exacted of him by his superiors. Some of this was paid for by them, but more was not. Cobbett took particular

_ The Life of WILLIAM-COBBETT . ...written by himself.

London. Publish'd Sep.t 29 1809 by H. Humphrey. 27 St James's

2.ᵈ Plate .

_ as I shot up into a hobble-dehoy, I took to driving the Plow for the benefit of mankind, which was always my prime object ; _ hearing that the Church Wardens were after me, I determined to become a Hero. and secretly quitting my agricultural pursuits. and Sukey Stubbs, _ Volunteered as a Private-Soldier. into the 51.ˢᵗ Regiment. commanded by that tried Patriot and Martyre Lord Edw.d Fitzgerald, _ and embarked for the Plantations. _

Cobbett's enlistment as seen by Gillray. In 1809, when the tory government was being harassed by Cobbett, the artist James Gillray, a minion of the administration, did a series of eight cartoons in which Cobbett's own account of his life was rudely parodied. This and the next four illustrations deal with Cobbett as a soldier

The Life of **WILLIAM-COBBETT**, _ written by himself.

London P.dsd.1.? Sept.25.1809 by H.Humphrey 27 St James's Street

3.ᵈ Plate . _

    arrived in safety (according to the proverb), being a Scholard, (for all the world knows that I can Read and Write,) I was promoted to the rank of a Corporal, and soon after appointed to teach the Officers their duty _ found them all so damnably stupid, that 'though I took the pains to draw up my instructions on Cards, I could not with all my Caning and Kicking, drive one manual movement into their thick heads! _

    _ NB: These Cards were so much admired by Genᶜ Dundas, that he made them the foundation of his New Military Systemn.

Cobbett's dominion over his officers as seen by Gillray

25

delight in sparring with the adjutant, a lieutenant to whom the sergeant major was a sort of deputy. Cobbett claimed that "he was a keen fellow, but wholly illiterate." He could read and write, but had no literary skills beyond that. Since both sergeant major and adjutant entered the orders of the day in the same book, the contrast between the entries was inescapable. The adjutant looked with amazement on Cobbett's writings, which had punctuation and paragraphing, and while attempting to conceal his own obvious ignorance, tried to find out the meaning of these esoteric signs and divisions. Embarrassed by his shortcomings, the adjutant decided to "dictate" to Cobbett. When that failed, he "used to tell me *his story*, and leave me to put it upon paper; and thus we continued to the end of our connection."

When a commission sent out from England to report on the state of affairs in Novia Scotia and New Brunswick ended their work at Fredericton, the adjutant had offered to draw up their report for them, presumably believing that he could somehow induce Cobbett to do the work for him. But his subtle approaches to Cobbett on the subject met with little success, as the project was not part of Cobbett's regular duties. Finally, an opportunity to effect his purpose offered itself:

At this time I had long been wanting to go and see an old farmer and his family and to shoot wild pigeons in his woods; and, as the distance was great, and a companion on the journey necessary, I wanted a serjeant to go with me. The leave to do this had been put off for a good while, and the Adjutant knew that I had the thing at heart. What does he do now, but come to me and after talking about the Report again, affect to lament, that he should be so much engaged with it, that here was no hope of my being permitted to go on my frolic, 'till he had finished the Report. I, who knew very well what this meant, began to be very anxious for this finishing, to effect which I knew that there was but one way. Tacked on to the pigeon-shooting the Report became an object of importance, and I said "perhaps I could do something, Sir, in putting the papers in order for you." That was enough. Away he went, brought me the whole mass, and, tossing them down upon the table: "There," said he, "do what you like with them; for d—n the rubbish, I have no patience with it." . . . I d——d the papers as heartily as he did, and with better reason; but, they were to bring me my week's frolic, and, as I entered into every thing with ardour, this pigeon-shooting frolic, at the age of about 23, was more than a compensation for all the toil of this Report and its appendix. To work I went, and with the assistance of my shooting-companion serjeant, who called over the figures to me, I had the Appendix completed in rough draft in two days and one night. Having the detail before me the Report was short work, and the whole was soon completed. But, before a *neat copy* was made out, the thing had to be shown to the Commissioners. It would not do to shew it them in my handwriting. The Adjutant got over this difficulty by copying the Report; and having shown it, and had it highly applauded, "well, then," said he, "here, Serjeant Major, go and make a fair copy."

Cobbett eventually managed to get full credit for the work he had performed on the report. When he stopped in Halifax in 1800, he learned that the Duke of Kent, then commander-in-chief of the provinces, "had a copy of it made to be kept in the office, and carried the original with him to England as a curiosity, and of this fact informed me himself. The Duke, from some source or other, had heard that it was I who had been the penman upon this occasion, though I never mentioned it to any body."[14]

While the regiment was still in St. John, Cobbett met Anne Reid – Nancy Reid – the girl he was ultimately to marry. She was the daughter of a sergeant of artillery, and at the time Cobbett first saw her she was thirteen years old. He was then twenty-four, although, because of the error in his birth year, he thought he was three years younger. She was small: five feet two inches high or thereabouts, plump, dark, and exceptionally beautiful.[15]

I sat in the same room with her, for about an hour, in company with others, and made up my mind that she was the very girl for me. That I thought her beautiful is certain, for that I have always said should be an indispensable qualification; but I saw in her what I deemed marks of that sobriety of conduct of which I have said so much, which has been by far the greatest blessing of my life. It was now dead of winter, and, of course, the snow several feet deep on the ground, and the weather piercing cold. It was my habit, when I had done my morning's writing, to go out at break of day to take a walk on a hill at the foot of which our barracks lay. In about three mornings after I had first seen her, I had, by an invitation to breakfast with me, got up two young men to join me in my walk; and our road lay by the house of her father and mother. It was hardly light, but she was out on the snow, scrubbing out a washing-tub. "That's the girl for me," said I, when we had got out of her hearing . . .

From the day that I first spoke to her, I never had a thought of her ever being the wife of any other man, more than I had thought of her being transformed into a chest of drawers; and I formed my resolution at once, to marry her as soon as we could get permission, and to get out of the army as soon as I could. So that this matter was, at once, settled as firmly as if written in the book of fate. At the end of about six months, my regiment, and I along with it, were removed to Frederickton, a distance of a hundred miles up the river of St. John; and, which was worse, the artillery were expected to go off to England a year or two before our regiment! The artillery went, and she along with them; and now it was that I acted a part becoming a real and sensible lover. I was aware that when she got to that gay place Woolwich, the home of her father and mother, necessarily visited by numerous persons not the most select, might become unpleasant to her, and I did not like, besides, that she should continue to work hard. I had saved a hundred and fifty guineas, the earnings of my early hours, in writing for the paymaster, the quartermaster, and others, in addition to the savings of my own pay. I sent her all my money before she sailed; and wrote to her, to beg of her, if she found her home uncomfortable, to hire a lodging with respectable people: and, at any rate, not to spare the money, by any means, but to buy herself good clothes, and to live without hard work, until I arrived in England; and I, in order to induce her to lay out the money, told her that I should get plenty more before I came home.[16]

The hundred and fifty guineas had been hard won: "for four years together I never tasted a morsel of fresh meat, never drank any thing stronger than spruce beer."[17]

The discovery of Nancy Reid in 1787 was not the only event of that year that brought about a change in Cobbett's life. He discovered blatant dishonesty among the officers of his regiment, and made a resolution to expose it.

The project was conceived so early as the year 1787, when an affair happened, that first gave me a full insight into regimental justice. It was shortly this: that the Quarter Master, who had the issuing of the men's provisions to them, kept a fourth part to himself. This, the old serjeants told me, had been the case for many years; and, they were quite astonished and terrified at the idea of my complaining of it. This I did, however, but the reception I met with convinced me, that I must never make another complaint 'till I got safe to England, and safe out of the reach of that most curious of courts, a Court Martial. – From this time forward, I began to collect materials for an exposure, upon my return to England. I had ample opportunities for this, being the keeper of all the books, of every sort, in the regiment, and knowing the whole of its affairs better than any other man. But, the winter previous to our return to England, I thought it necessary to make extracts from books, lest the books themselves should be destroyed. And . . . in order to *prove* that these extracts were correct, it was necessary that I should have a witness as to their being true copies. This was a very ticklish point. One foolish step here, would have sent me down to the ranks with a pair of bloody shoulders. Yet, it was necessary to have the witness. I hesitated many months. At one time, I had given the whole thing up. I dreamt twenty times, I dare say, of my papers being discovered, and of my being tried and flogged half to death. At last, however, some fresh act of injustice towards us made me set all danger at defiance. I opened my project to a corporal, whose name was William Bestland, who wrote in the office under me, who was a very honest fellow, who was very much bound to me, for my goodness to him, and who was, with the sole exception of myself, the only sober man in the whole regiment. – To work we went, and during a long winter, while the rest were boozing and snoring, we gutted no small part of the regimental books, rolls, and other documents. Our way was this: to take a copy, sign it with our names, and clap the regimental seal to it, so that we might be able to swear to it, when produced in court. – All these papers were put into a little box, which I myself had made for the purpose.[18]

In September 1791 the 54th regiment was relieved and sent home to England. As the soldiers prepared to leave, the governor of New Brunswick issued a public order expressing his thanks for the work that Cobbett had performed there; no other man, from the commanding officer down, was so honored.[19] Cobbett arrived in Ports-

The Life of WILLIAM-COBBETT, — written by himself.

London. Published Sept 1 1809 by H. Humphrey 27 St James's Street

4th. Plate.

— I was now made Sarjeant-Major, and Clerk, to the Regiment, and there
being only One Man in it, besides myself, who could read, or keep him-
-self sober (viz — poor little Corporal-Bestland). I constituted him my
Deputy ; — being intrusted with the care of the Regimental-Books, the
Corporal and myself (tho' both of us blastedly afraid of a pair of
Bloody Shoulders.) — purloined, and Copied by night such Documents
as promised to be serviceable in the great National Object which I had
in view; — namely, to Disorganize the Army preparatory to the
Revolutionizing it all. . . . . .

Cobbett's copying of regimental records as seen by Gillray

29

mouth on November 3 with his box of papers.[20] He had formed a warm attachment to his major, the handsome and intrepid Lord Edward Fitzgerald, and through him managed to secure his discharge from the lifetime service to which he had engaged himself.[21] The discharge was no perfunctory one. It was granted "in consideration of his good Behaviour and the Services he has rendered the Regt.," while the orders, issued in the garrison of Portsmouth on the day of Cobbett's discharge, December 19, 1791, stated: "General Frederick has ordered Major Lord Edward Fitzgerald to return the Sergeant Major thanks for his behaviour and conduct during the time of his being in the regiment, and Major Lord Edward adds his most hearty thanks to those of the General."[22]

Cobbett found Nancy – they had been separated for nearly three years – working as a servant at five pounds a year, in the home of a Captain Brisac, "and without hardly saying a word about the matter, she put into my hands the whole of my hundred and fifty guineas unbroken!" Nancy and her Billy were married at Woolwich on February 5, 1792. He was almost twenty-nine; she was nearly eighteen. Nancy signed the marriage register with her mark – she could not read or write, and never acquired these skills in later life.[23]

In the meanwhile Cobbett had set on foot the other project he had begun in New Brunswick. On January 17 he had delivered to the office of Sir George Yonge, secretary at war, a petition addressed to the king accusing four officers in Cobbett's regiment of various acts of misconduct. In general, these were of two types: overstatements of expenditure, principally "the making of false musters of non-commissioned officers and soldiers," thereby defrauding the government; and withholding benefits from the noncommissioned officers and soldiers, such as selling their allowances of bread and firewood for the personal advantage of the officers, thereby defrauding the men.[24] The petition was followed by a letter from Cobbett to Yonge dated January 22 asking that the books of the regiment for the period from "1 Sept. 1781 to 1 Oct. 1791 be secure in order to give me the opportunity of making good my accusations."[25] Cobbett was summoned to Yonge's office on January 25. At this meeting Cobbett was assured that orders had been given to secure the regimental books as requested. He also was told that one of the four accused, Colonel Bruce, had recently died, leaving three defendants: Captain Richard Powell, Lieutenant Christopher Seton, and Lieutenant John Hall. Cobbett was asked to redraw his charges omitting Bruce and making the charges "more particular" in respect of the three others. The charges as thus redrawn were delivered to Yonge on the day immediately following the meeting. "Sir George Yonge told me, I should hear from him in a day or two."[26]

Up to this point, all seemed to be going well, but from there on Cobbett was given one cause after another to suspect that there was no genuine interest at headquarters in exposing the corruption which he had so rudely brought to their attention. He did not hear from Yonge "in a day or two." Two weeks went by, and he found it necessary to write again to Yonge, explaining that he had no business in London other than that which he had put before Yonge, and he wanted to know when his attendance would be necessary. The regimental books, Cobbett learned, had still not been secured, and he pointed this out to Yonge.[27]

A royal warrant authorizing the convening of the court-martial was signed on February 18. Sir Charles Gould, judge advocate general, notified Cobbett that it was proposed that the hearings would be "holden at Portsmouth or Hilsea Barracks." This was especially alarming, as Cobbett pointed out in his reply: "There the regiment is quartered, there the accused must have formed connexions, and there all the witnesses who I may call upon will be totally in their power." Cobbett's suggestion that the court-martial be held in London was vigorously resisted by Powell, and so concerned was Cobbett over the issue that he addressed a letter to William Pitt, the prime minister, which he personally delivered to his house in Downing Street, declaring that "if the court-martial is not held in London there may as well be no court martial at all."[28]

Two days later, on March 9, Cobbett was notified that he had won: the court-martial would be held in London, and shortly thereafter he learned that it would be convened on Saturday, March 24. Cobbett then found himself involved in a new wrangle with Gould over whether one of the essential witnesses, a Joseph Margas, no longer an active soldier but one who had retired on a pension, would or would not be legally subject to an official summons which would require his presence at the hearing. A penultimate bombshell was Cobbett's discovery, on examining more carefully the papers Gould had sent him several weeks before, that Gould had rewritten the accusations against the three officers to eliminate some of the charges made by Cobbett and to exclude all matters that had occurred more than three years antecedent to the warrant. Cobbett nevertheless agreed to accept "for the present" the reduced scope of the inquiry, "being as much unwilling as any one can be to delay the assembling of the court." Cobbett had previously advised Gould that he had "good reason to believe that every method had been taken to represent my accusations as

The Life of WILLIAM-COBBETT._ written by himself.

5ᵗ Plate _

— my next step was to procure a Discharge from my ever lamented associate the Lord Edwᵈ. Fitzgerald; with this I returned to England and directly set about writing "the Soldier's Friend" which I nightly dropt about the Horse Guards; and drank "Damnation to the House of Brunswick!" more over, I wrote 27 Letters to my Royal Master, to Mr. Pitt and the Judge Advocate, against my Officers 23 of which Letters were stolen by the public Robbers, and never came to hand, so that I had no means of obtaining Credit for my Charges, & procuring a Court Martial but by solemnly Pledging my precious Soul to the Devil in the presence of Judge Gould for the Truth of my alegations, and my ability to support them by evidence !!! _____

Cobbett's court-martial charges as seen by Gillray

32

malicious and groundless." He assured Gould that this was not the case: "If my accusation is without foundation, the authors of cruelty have not yet devised the tortures I ought to endure. Hell itself, as painted by the most fiery bigot, would be too mild a punishment for me!"[29]

On Monday, March 19, five days before hearings were to commence, Cobbett wrote to Gould giving him a list of the witnesses he wanted to call, and stating that "a private concern obliges me to go into the country" – he would return on Friday, March 23, the day before the court-martial was to be convened. The witnesses on the list included only one officer: Cobbett's friend Lord Edward Fitzgerald ("the only sober and the only honest officer I had ever known in the army," Cobbett later told Pitt), and Corporal William Bestland, the man who had assisted Cobbett in copying out the incriminating records. Since fifty other noncommissioned officers and soldiers were included on Cobbett's witness list, the mere inclusion of Bestland's name could not create any special suspicion directed at him.[30]

On the appointed day, Saturday, March 24, at ten o'clock in the morning, the court-martial, a board of seventeen officers headed by three major generals, convened at the Horse Guards. The three defendants were there, the witnesses were there, the requested books were there, but there was no prosecutor. After waiting more than an hour, a messenger was dispatched to 3 Felix Street, southward of Westminster bridge, where Cobbett had been staying. On his return the messenger reported "that the said William Cobbett was not to be found, and that the answer obtained at the house where he had lodged was, that he had removed from those lodgings on Wednesday evening last, since which he had not been seen or heard of, nor was it known where he now resided."

The hearings were adjourned to the following Tuesday, March 27. Cobbett's landlady was summoned as a witness. She confirmed that she had no knowledge of Cobbett's current whereabouts. The only additional information she could give to what was already known was that a Captain Lane of the 54th regiment had called on Cobbett on Monday, March 19. Captain Lane said that he could add nothing to what was known. The three defendants were then "put on their trial." They each denied the charges; no person came forward to support the charges. The court thereupon declared that the charges were unfounded, and the defendants were acquitted.[31]

Within a few days Gould submitted to the attorney general and the solicitor general a memorandum setting out the facts of the case, declaring that "There is every reason to suppose that the accusation was destitute of foundation, and wilfully and maliciously set on foot for the purpose of calumniating the characters of the three officers in question," and asking whether Cobbett could be criminally prosecuted for his conduct. On May 25, the chief law officers of the government reported that Cobbett could not be criminally prosecuted "unless he could be proved to have conspired with others wilfully and maliciously to prefer these charges," but that the "parties injured by his conduct, which is certainly most highly blameable," might maintain a civil action against him.[32]

Cobbett had left England with his bride and was in France, where no civil action could be brought against him. There was very little public interest in the conduct of an obscure William Cobbett, former sergeant major of His Majesty's army, and he made no effort to explain his conduct for seventeen years. By then, that is by 1809, Cobbett had become a prominent thorn in the side of the government, and a great public stir was created when a pamphlet containing an account of the incident was widely circulated in order to discredit him.[33]

The story from Cobbett's side seems to be this: When Captain Lane called on Cobbett at his lodgings on March 19, he apparently either told Cobbett that something damaging to Cobbett's case was going on in Portsmouth, or said enough to cause the already suspicious Cobbett to investigate the situation himself.[34] Cobbett went down to Portsmouth on March 20. From the start, he had been concerned about the regimental books. Now he found that they had not been secured until March 15.[35] If they had been tampered with in the two months that had passed since he had filed his charges, he would have to call Bestland as a witness, but if Bestland testified, the officers would find some fancied infringement of army rules to justify flogging him near to death. Hence, writing from Fratton, a village near Portsmouth, Cobbett dispatched a letter to Gould demanding the discharge of a man whom Cobbett would hereafter name, as the only condition on which Cobbett would attend the court-martial. "I requested him to send me an answer by the next day . . . and told him that unless such an answer was received, he and those to whom my repeated applications have been made might do what they pleased with their Court-Martial; for, that I confidentially trusted, that a few days would place me beyond the scope of their power. No answer came."[36]

There was another development which Cobbett added as the final entry in his copy of the correspondence relating to the court-martial. "March 20. I went by coach to Portsmouth in order to reconnoitre, and to my astonishment met Lahif, Body, Phillpot, Holmes, the Music Master, a man from their band and several others who were marching from Portsmouth to London to give evidence against me for having

The Life of WILLIAM·COBBETT. *written by himself.*

London Publish'd Sept.r 19. 1809 by H Humphrey 2.r S.t James's Street

Plate .6.th —

— the Court-Martial was assembled at Chelsea as I requested, and Capt.n Powell and the other accused Persons were placed at the Bar; — — when — blast-my-Eyes ! — I saw the whole of that damn'd 51.st Regiment Drummers, Fifers and all, marching boldly into the Hall to bear Testi-mony against Me !! — on this, I instantly ran to a boat which I had Providentially secured, and crossed the Thames — —
— damn'd infernal-Ideots ! — did the Judge-Advocate and his Gang of Publick Robbers think that I would stay to witness my own Exposure and condemnation?

The court-martial as seen by Gillray

35

damned and drunk to the destruction of the house of Brunswick! At Portsmouth I found this confirmed, and the whole set of scoundrels I was going to serve leagued against me; even Phillpot would not speak to me on the road. I gave them all to the devil together, returned to London, went the next day to Dover, and so to France."[37]

Cobbett left behind him a token of his feelings toward his former superiors. Sometime between the middle of February and June 1792 an anonymous pamphlet, twenty-two pages long, entitled *The Soldier's Friend*, appeared in London. It was sold at 6d. In 1793 there was another edition sold at 2d. or 10s. 6d. per hundred. It appeared again at the time of the Nore mutiny in 1797. The pamphlet quoted from a statement made in parliament by the secretary at war in February 1792, that the private soldier, although legally entitled to receive three shillings a week for his subsistence, was actually receiving only half or, at best, two-thirds of that amount. The minister approached the subject delicately. He did not explain the reason for the discrepancy: "perhaps he could not," wrote the author of *The Soldier's Friend*, "for the secrets of the Army are something like those of Free Masonry; it is absolutely necessary to become a brother of the blade before you can become at all acquainted with the *arcana* of the profession." The "'secret," of course, as the pamphlet explained, was that the officers followed the regular practice of buying things for the men and charging more than they paid for them. The secretary at war, instead of proposing that the officers be compelled to cease this dishonest practice, suggested that the pay of the private soldier be augmented, which (*The Soldier's Friend* stated) "points out in the clearest light the close connection that exists between the *ruling Faction* in this Country and the military Officers."[38]

The anonymous pamphlet, as the law was then being interpreted, was almost certainly seditious. In 1803 Cobbett denied writing it. He made a similar disclaimer in 1805.[39] But in 1832 and again in the following year he confessed to the authorship.[40] This is confirmed by the style, and there are other clues too. The motto on the title page was a line from a poem that Cobbett knew by heart and frequently quoted, Goldsmith's "The Traveller": "Laws grind the poor, and rich men rule the law."[41] The title of the pamphlet may itself be revealing. For when Captain Lane left Cobbett at his lodgings on March 19, the last words Cobbett said to him were that "he was and ever would be a soldier's friend."[42]

Billy and Nancy Cobbett spent their honeymoon at the village of Tilque, near St. Omer, about twenty-five miles south of Calais. The stay in France, Cobbett wrote many years later, was "the six happiest months of my life." The timing of their departure from England had not been planned, but their destination may have been. Cobbett seems to have been thinking about opening a school in Farnham, and wanted to improve his French before undertaking the venture. In addition to working on his French, Cobbett was able to advance his interest in continental fortifications of the types he had read about in Vauban.[43]

In August the honeymooners set off for Paris. They had gone only sixty miles when, on arriving at Abbeville on August 11, they learned of the massacre of the royal Swiss Guard at the Tuileries and of the arrest of Louis XVI and Marie-Antoinette. Instead of continuing south to the capital, they turned west and headed for Le Havre, about a hundred miles away. This journey took four or five days. They were frequently interrupted by soldiers looking for fleeing aristocrats. Nancy was suspect, since she had no passport. They reached Le Havre on August 15 or 16. After a fortnight they found passage on a small American ship bound for New York, the sloop *Mary* of ninety-ton burden or thereabouts, under the command of Captain Grinnell. The Cobbetts and one other passenger, a young Frenchman, made up the total passenger list on a voyage that lasted forty-five or forty-six days, during much of which they were "tossed about upon the ocean like a cork."[44]

3 · Joseph Priestley

... as an Englishmen, as a calf of John Bull, I shall hope to be permitted, in short, I will be permitted, to bellow out the truth without disguise.

THE COBBETTS arrived in America in October 1792, three years after a new government, operating under an untried constitution, had been established in that country. The constitution represented a series of compromises between those who wanted a strong central government and those who wanted a weak central government. The leaders of the country had some doubt whether such a structure could survive. The president, George Washington, saw an "ocean of difficulties" facing the experiment and questioned whether he had "the competancy ... to manage the helm."[1] The vice-president, John Adams, wrote that "Our new government is an attempt to divide a sovereignty ... It cannot, therefore, be expected to be very stable or very firm."[2] But even this watered-down solution had gone too far for many Americans; the constitution had been ratified only by the combined efforts of individuals of all shades of opinion who called themselves "federalists," against the opposition of a large body of "anti-federalists" who would have been quite satisfied with the most loosely knit confederation of states, such as had existed during the war of liberation.

The constitution made no provision for political parties, and Washington had never thought of himself as belonging to any party. The idol of the American people was elected the first president without contest. In the same way, John Adams was elected vice-president. Washington's cabinet appointments were also made on a nonpartisan basis. The position of secretary of the treasury was given to the brilliant, hard-driving, and practical Alexander Hamilton, the leader of the "federalists" and an advocate of a strong central government. The position of secretary of state was given to the brilliant, easy-going, and philosophical Thomas Jefferson, the drafter of the Declaration of Independence, who had been in France as American minister during the writing and ratification of the constitution but who was known to favor a relatively weak central government. These appointments had been made in 1789 at the outset of Washington's first term. It did not take long to establish the essential incompatibility between the conservative Hamilton and the liberal Jefferson. To Hamilton the first order of business was to put the new republic on a sound financial footing. Two weeks after congress met in 1789, Hamilton recommended the funding at par and assumption by the federal government of the debt which the states had incurred during the revolution. This was distasteful to Jefferson, but he accepted it in return for an agreement that the national capital should be moved south, on the Virginia border. In the following year Hamilton urged the establishment of a national bank. Jefferson thought this proposal put too much power in the central government and was too friendly to creditors and businessmen. He argued that the creation of a national bank was beyond the constitutional authority of the national government. Washington, however, backed Hamilton, and congressional approval was secured for the measure.

The differences in temperament and philosophy that separated Hamilton and Jefferson were further widened by events concurrently taking place in France. The fall of the Bastille occurred in July 1789, three months after Washington's inauguration. This opening move toward greater freedom in France was widely acclaimed in America. There were other issues on which the country was divided, but "in its first stage," wrote John Marshall, future chief justice of the United States supreme court, "but one sentiment respecting it prevailed."[3] It was not long, however, before the excesses in France raised doubts among more conservative leaders outside that country. Edmund Burke, who had been a passionate supporter of the American cause during the 1770s, saw little to commend on the French scene. "Their humanity is savage and brutal," he wrote in 1790; "it seems as if it were the prevalent opinion in Paris, that an unfeeling heart, and an undoubting confidence, are the sole qualifications for a perfect legislator."[4] Doubts of this order existed in the minds of Washington, Adams, and Hamilton. But Jefferson, who was more optimistic about the perfectibility of mankind, maintained his enthusiasm for the events in France, believing that there was more good than bad in what was happening there, and that in the end all would become orderly and humane.

Not surprisingly, Jefferson became increasingly dissatisfied with the direction being taken by the administration, and particularly with what he perceived as the pernicious influence of Hamilton. In the summer of 1791 he attempted to develop an antidote. Jefferson and his fellow Virginian James Madison, leader of the House of Representatives, made what they called a "botanizing" tour of New York and New England for the purpose of forming an alliance with the old anti-federalist interests.[5] The resulting group became the "democrats" or, by Jefferson's preference, the "republicans,"[6] an emotionally charged name judiciously preempted by Jefferson to reflect his opinion that the opposition – the "federalists", the party of Hamilton and Adams – were not true believers in a republican form of government, but at heart favored return to a monarchy. At about the same time Jefferson hired Philip Freneau, propagandist, poet, and satirist, as "translation clerk" in the state department, in order to induce Freneau to establish a newspaper, the *National Gazette,* as a counterirritant to the pro-Hamilton *Gazette of the United States,* edited by John Fenno.[7] In 1792, the new *National Gazette* launched a savage attack on Hamilton's economic policies. Hamilton replied with a number of anonymous articles in which he asserted that Jefferson was opposed to the constitution and to Washington's administration.[8] Thus what had started as a cabinet with two key members holding somewhat different views on matters of principle rapidly developed into a cabinet with its two key members in a state of not too well concealed warfare. Try as he did, Washington was unable to effect a reconciliation between his principal ministers. In the autumn of 1792 Jefferson advised Washington that he would leave the government the following year, at the end of Washington's first term.

It was into this city of brotherly love – Philadelphia, second in population only to London in the English-speaking world – the temporary capital of the United States of America, the center of intrigue and character assassination, that the Cobbetts, William Cobbett, aged twenty-nine, and Nancy Reid Cobbett, aged eighteen, about to give birth to her first child, stepped late in 1792.[9]

It is doubtful whether Cobbett at this juncture knew much about the American political scene. But he had brought with him a letter of introduction to Jefferson from William Short, U.S. minister at The Hague, a young Virginian who had served under Jefferson when Jefferson had been minister to France. Short's letter of introduction, dated August 6, 1792, stated that Cobbett was a "man of worth & merit" who had "been formerly in the English possessions to the Northwards & intends now to go & settle in the United States." Short plainly did not know Cobbett personally. He wrote, his letter explains, at the instance of "a Gentleman in the family of the English Ambassador here."[10] This was Lord Auckland, His Majesty's ambassador extraordinary and plenipotentiary at The Hague during the French revolution. How Cobbett, an English runaway living in a tiny village in France, a former noncommissioned officer without family connections, managed to get such a letter of introduction has never been explained, and was a puzzle to his heirs. Was it, as one of his sons suggested, through Cobbett's old friend of London days, the rather obscure Benjamin Garlike, who had served in the British embassy at Copenhagen in 1791?[11] Or was it, as a romantic biographer might hope, through Cobbett's major "in the English possessions to the Northwards," the handsome and adventuresome Lord Edward Fitzgerald, who was to lose his life in the Irish rising of 1798? Cobbett was strongly attached to Fitzgerald; he had been, "when abroad, frequently honoured with his conversation"; and had even seriously considered following Fitzgerald after leaving military service.[12] Fitzgerald, son of the Duke of Leinster and brother of Lord Robert Fitzgerald, ambassador to France in 1789, was quite capable of securing such an introduction for Cobbett.[13] The answer to this question might provide further insight into the remarkable ability of this self-educated farmer boy to create friendships among persons of distinction.

Although Cobbett spent a week in Philadelphia after landing in New York, he did not deliver Short's letter while he was in the city. He waited until he and his wife had moved thirty miles downriver to Wilmington, Delaware. From there he wrote to the secretary of state on November 2, 1792:

Sir,

My friend, whom Mr. Short has mentioned in the enclosed letter, procured it for me thinking you might have it in your power to serve me upon my landing in this country; but, conscious that I can have no other pretension to your notice at present than merely that founded on a recommendation, and wishing to avoid the importunate part too often acted by men in my situation, I have chosen this as the least troublesome way of paying my respects to you.

Ambitious to become the citizen of a free State, I have left my native country, England, for America: I bring with me youth, a small family, a few useful literary talents and that is all.

Should you have an opportunity of serving me, my conduct shall not shew me ungrateful, or falsify the recommendation I now send you. Should that not be the case, I shall feel but little disappointment from it, not doubting but my industry and care will make me a happy and useful member in my adopted country.

> I am, with great respect,
> Sir,
> Your most obedient servant
> Wm Cobbett

Thomas Jefferson
Secretary of State
Philadelphia

P.S. Sir, I am but a few days landed in America, and am settled here for the winter, if no employment offers itself during that time.[14]

Three days later Jefferson, in a politely worded reply, explained that he wished it were in his power to assist Cobbett, but "public offices in our government are so few, and of so little value, as to offer no resource to talents."[15] This was not simply a gracious excuse: the total employment of the American state department in 1792 was seven persons including the secretary himself.[16]

There is nothing to suggest that Cobbett felt any serious disappointment at his failure to secure government employment. Both Wilmington and Philadelphia offered a ready-made outlet for his talents. French-speaking people, by the thousands, had come there in waves beginning in 1789, first from France itself and then in 1791 from the French West Indies, where there had been Negro uprisings. The total has been estimated at from 10,000 to 25,000.[17] Since many spoke no English, Cobbett became a teacher of his native tongue to the French. He took a few boarders into the house he had rented at Wilmington, and gave lessons to others in their lodgings.

The newcomers were very welcome in America. In the thirty years that had passed since the cry of "no taxation without representation" had first been raised, a generation had grown up which from the cradle had learned to hate Britain and admire everything French. Louis XVI had supplied money and men when the Americans needed them, and the Americans were grateful, even though they were generally aware that to a great extent the French may have been motivated more by the desire to hurt the British than to help the Americans. Under the treaty of 1778 with the Americans, the French had been given the commercial rights of a most favored nation. Portraits of Louis XVI and his queen hung on the wall of the United States Senate chamber; however, the American admiration for the French was not particularly discriminating, since it was broad enough to encompass, at the same time, both the French royal family and the revolution that deposed them.[18] When a choice had to be made between the two, it was plain where the American loyalties lay – they loved the revolution better than the monarchs and, in fact, better than the French people. The Americans were not only grateful; they also thought of liberty as good, and wanted others to gain some of this good. But there was far more involved; the Americans were themselves revolutionists and, like many who overthrow political doctrine, were fired by a religious fanaticism to proselytize. It was flattering to the young, primitive Americans to view themselves as the authors of a creed that had been adopted by one of the cultured powers of the old world. It was comforting to find their own disrespectful attitude toward authority, about which there may have been some lingering feelings of guilt, justified by even more disrespectful conduct toward authority on the part of the French. Some unconscious stirrings of this order are needed to account for the explosive force, the passion, the frenzy, that were released in America by the French revolution – a force, passion, and frenzy that have enchanted and dismayed historians from that time to this.

To the great mass of Americans, as distinguished from their conservative leaders, each event that occurred in France in the years immediately following 1789 was greeted with a rising enthusiasm that finally neared hysteria. Since 1783, Philadelphia had boasted a triumphal arch with a bust of Louis XVI inscribed "Merendo memores facit": His merit makes us remember him.[19] The French king had been publicly toasted on July 4, 1792, American Independence Day. But a few months later the news that their old ally had been deposed and was on trial for his life set off wild celebrations throughout the cities of America, large and small. The civic feast held in Boston on January 24, 1793 to celebrate French victories over the Prussians and Austrians after Louis XVI had been deposed was "an event long famous in the annals of that town." It commenced with an early morning salute of cannon. A great procession began at eleven o'clock, in this order: two citizens on horseback carrying flags; the parade marshal Citizen Waters; a band; masses of marchers on foot eight deep; twelve citizens in white frocks with cleavers and knives; a roast ox decorated with ribbons, its gilded horns ornamented with a French and an American flag; more massed citizens eight deep; a horse-drawn cart with eight hundred loaves of bread; another with a hogshead of punch; a cart with more bread and more punch. The procession, having saluted the houses of the governor of the state and the French consul, drew up in State Street where a sixty-foot liberty pole had been erected, and where, on tables stretching from the Old State House to near Kilby Street, the bread and punch were served. Children were given cakes decorated with the words "Liberty and Equality."

At two o'clock another procession moved from the State House to Faneuil Hall, where a great banquet was held, Citizen Samuel Adams presiding. The Hall was elaborately decorated. At the west end, over the head of the president, rose an obelisk, having in front the figure of Liberty, her left hand supporting her insignia and her right displaying "The Rights of Man". Under her feet lay broken in a hundred pieces the badges of Civil and Ecclesiastical Despotism – a crown, sceptre, mitre and chains. Over her head a descending cherub presented in its right hand a wreath as the Reward of Virtue, and in its left the Palm of Peace. Over the whole there was an eye supposed to be the benign eye of Providence, which appeared to view with approbation the scene below. The French and American flags were everywhere, and many were the mottoes and inscriptions to Liberty and Equality, to Justice and to Peace. So fervid was the feeling aroused by the incidents of the day that "amidst other displays of urbanity" a purse was raised for the release of the prisoners in the town jail; "the doors of the prison houses were thrown open, and those who had long been immured therein were invited to join their festive brethren and again breathe the air of Liberty."[20]

The exultation of the good people of Boston on January 24, 1793 over the French victories in the field was not perceptibly dampened by what had occurred in France immediately before those victories: those notorious September massacres of 1792 when the Princesse de Lamballe, intimate friend of Marie-Antoinette, was killed, her body subjected to abuse and her head fixed on a pike paraded by a howling mob beneath the queen's window; when 43 boys at the Bicêtre reformatory, aged twelve to fourteen, were put to death; when a total of 1,600 helpless persons were senselessly and savagely slaughtered.[21]

Only the more reflective Americans seemed upset when the September massacres were followed up, within four months, by the execution of Louis XVI and his queen in January 1793. At a dinner in Philadelphia, we are told, "the head of a pig was severed from its body, and being recognised as an emblem of the murdered King of France, was carried round to the guests. Each one placing the cap of liberty upon his head, pronounced the word 'tyrant!', and proceeded to mangle with his knife the head of the luckless creature."[22] For three shillings (children half price) the people of Philadelphia were able to witness, from nine o'clock in the morning until nine at night, an "Exhibition of figures in Composition at full Length" portraying the execution of Louis XVI: "the executioner drops the knife, and severs the head from the body in one second; the head falls in a basket, and the lips which are first red, turn blue; the whole is performed to the life by an invisible machine, without any perceivable assistance."[23] Referring to the democratic press in Philadelphia, Cobbett wrote: "I have seen a bundle of Gazettes published all by the same man, wherein Mirabeau, Fayette, Brissot, Danton, Robespierre, and Barras, are all panegyricised and execrated in due succession."[24] This period, for reasons that must be apparent, is known to historians of the American scene as the "French frenzy." Cobbett described it as "that enthusiastic season, when the sun of liberty bore with such violence on our skulls, as made us dance the whirligig, like ducks under the tropics."[25]

In February 1793 the French declared war on England, and three months later Edmond Charles Edouard Genêt, the first minister to the United States appointed by the new French republic, arrived in Charleston, South Carolina on a French man-of-war. Welcomed by the governor of that state and enthusiastically received by its citizens, he promptly began to enlist troops and fit out ships to fight against England. As he travelled northward by land he was hailed everywhere as a hero. Farmers along the way pledged themselves to provide France with 600,000 barrels of flour at less than market prices.[26] The reception was so tumultuous that President Washington, to dispel any misconception among the American people, issued a neutrality proclamation (without using the word "neutrality") on April 22. This did little to diminish public enthusiasm. When Genêt arrived in Philadelphia in May, a town meeting was called to congratulate him. Seven leading citizens delivered an address of welcome declaring that the cause of France was "dear to all the human race."[27] The Fourth of July, American Independence Day, was celebrated in Philadelphia "more as a French than an American holiday." At the festivities on the fourteenth of July, attended by Genêt and the governor of Pennsylvania, eighty-five rounds were fired in honor of the eighty-five departments of the French republic.[28] The French minister was greeted with the same enthusiasm in New York. Liberty caps and the tricolor were worn, bells were rung, cannon were fired – men called themselves citizen this and citizen that. "What hugging and tugging," exclaimed Alexander Graydon, "what addressing and caressing! What mountebanking and chanting! with liberty caps and the other wretched trumpery of *sans culotte* foolery. 'Give me an ounce of civet, good apothecary, to sweeten my imagination.'"[29]

Such displays convinced Genêt that he had the support of the American public. He became increasingly arrogant, and in July 1793 refused to hold up the departure from Philadelphia of a French ship, *The Little Democrat,* which had been armed there in violation of American neutrality. Claiming that he had been ill-treated by the American government, Genêt threatened to appeal directly to the American people over the head of President Washington. Years later, John Adams wrote of "the terrorism excited by Genêt in 1793 when ten thousand people in the streets of Philadelphia day after day *threatened to drag* Washington out of his house and effect a revolution in the government or compel it to declare war in favor of the French Revolution and against England."[30] But Genêt had gone too far; even Jefferson was disgusted with him. Washington's cabinet unanimously agreed to ask the French government for Genêt's recall.

Genêt's performance, astounding as it was, did little more than create further doubts about the French among those who already doubted. The bulk of the active public continued their worship of everything French. The youthful Stephen Decatur, future hero of the naval war against the Barbary pirates, was assailed by a crowd for wearing the American colors instead of the French cockade.[31] In New York, Queen Street became Pearl, and Crown Street was changed to Liberty.[32] Thus Cobbett's first year in America – the year highlighted by Genêt's rise and fall – was what a distinguished American historian called "a year utterly without parallel, so far as I am aware, in the history of this country."[33] Cobbett himself, a few years later, spoke of Genêt's rapturous reception as "a variety of such nonsensical, stupid, unmeaning, childish entertainments as were never thought or heard of till Frenchmen took it into their heads to gabble about liberty."[34]

Throughout this year Cobbett had continued to live in Wilmington, taking care, with his young wife, of their first child, a boy born there on January 3, 1793; teaching English to French who had settled in Wilmington; writing a book on English grammar for French-speaking people; gardening; occasionally hunting; borrowing money against future prospects; offering advice to his friends.[35] In Wilmington, Cobbett not only saw the French frenzy at first hand – "they caballed, and harangued, and remonstrated with more industry and virulence than even the virtuous town meetings of Boston and Philadelphia" – but heard, at first hand, Frenchmen of all persuasions (aristocratic émigrés from mainland France and the heterogeneous white French population forced to flee the Negro uprisings in Santo Domingo) debate the changes taking place in France. "Every time the newspapers arrive," Cobbett wrote in July 1793, "the aristocrats and democrats have a decent quarrel to the admiration of all the little boys in the town."[36]

Cobbett's single public utterance during this period, published in February 1793, was a translation from the French of materials relating to the impeachment of Lafayette by the National Assembly.[37] Lafayette was a figure of enormous popularity in the United States, having voluntarily joined the American forces at an early stage in the revolution, before France became an ally. A youth at the time, he became a close friend of Washington. Many in America were stunned by the news that Lafayette, a lifelong believer in the sovereignty of the people, had been declared a traitor by the French government. The episode on which the charges were based had occurred while Cobbett was living in France. After France declared war against Austria in April 1792, Lafayette was made commander of one of the three French armies. He soon perceived that the greatest threat to his country was not her external enemies but the trend toward intolerance and lawlessness that the revolution was taking at home. In June 1792, he courageously spoke out against the rise of the Jacobins and warned of the impending danger of this faction to the National Assembly and the king. The leaders of the radical factions promptly inaugurated proceedings to impeach Lafayette on a variety of vague charges; he had, for example, "endeavoured to debase the National Assembly in supposing it governed by a faction."[38] The eighty-page pamphlet translated by Cobbett included copies of the charges against Lafayette, the papers on which the accusations were based, and two of the speeches to the Assembly – one for and one against impeachment. Cobbett, as his introduction stated, "observed the most scrupulous impartiality" in his translation and notes.[39] It was not necessary to do otherwise. The charges against Lafayette were so hollow and the sophistry of his principal accuser, Jacques-Pierre Brissot, so nauseous, that there could hardly be two views on the merits of the case. The National Assembly itself, though riddled with extremists, voted against the impeachment by 406 to 224.[40] But this was an expiring gasp of French justice; and with the minor exception noted below, it was where the pamphlet ended. As every reader of the pamphlet knew, on August 10, two days after Lafayette's acquittal, the Paris mob took over: The Swiss Guard was massacred; the king was suspended from his functions; he and the queen were held hostage.[41] Lafayette, after making one last attempt to protect the sovereign he, and the other officers of state, had sworn to serve, was declared a traitor by a rump National Assembly which, to quote Cobbett's notes in the pamphlet, "under the absolute authority of the mob" revoked Lafayette's acquittal in the impeachment proceedings.[42] Lafayette fled the country and did not return until 1799. His warnings against a rising faction proved uncomfortably accurate in short order. The year 1793 witnessed the execution not only of the French monarch but also of the antimonarchist Brissot, Lafayette's chief accuser in the impeachment proceedings. It was against Cobbett's nature to play the role of bystander: *Impeachment of Mr. Lafayette* made it plain that he was not able to accept the popular view among Americans that anything done in the magic name of Liberty and Equality was justifiable. And he soon found other opportunities for making these views known in more dramatic form.

In December 1793, after thirteen months in Wilmington, Cobbett began to think about moving to Philadelphia. Nancy Cobbett did not like Wilmington, and the far larger French population in Philadelphia offered greater teaching opportunities for her husband.[43] A small house at 81 Callowhill Street was found through a friend, and on February 3, 1794 Cobbett loaded the family possessions into a wagon, and put himself, wife, and small child on a stagecoach bound for Philadelphia.[44] There Cobbett found plenty of work, but the ill-luck which had plagued him since the London court-martial quickly struck twice more: in mid March, Nancy was delivered of her second child, but it was dead on delivery; and less than three months later, on June 3, "Toney," their first child, died. "All I ever felt before," wrote Cobbett, "was nothing – nothing at all to this . . . a settled sadness seems to have taken possession of my mind; nor do I wish to be diverted from it. For my poor Nancy, I cannot paint to you her distress – for several days she would take no nourishment. We were even afraid for her – never was a child so adored."[45]

The bitterness in Cobbett's soul from these personal misfortunes and the smoldering resentment engendered by the French frenzy, with the concomitant animosity toward the country of his birth which he had borne quietly for the past year, were vented on the world in the form of Cobbett's first polemic: a stinging attack on Joseph Priestley, distinguished English theologian and scientist, and a warm supporter of the French revolution, who had arrived in New York on June 4.[46] The Democratic Society of New York, one of the many pro-French groups created by Genêt's proselytizing, greeted Priestley as a martyr to British "tyranny," welcoming him to a land where, in contrast to England, "reason has successfully triumphed."[47] This was followed a week later by a similar address of the Republican Natives of Great Britain and Ireland resident in the city of New York, which declared that "a republican representative Government was not merely best adapted to promote human happiness, but that it is the only rational system worthy of the wisdom of man to project."[48] Priestley's reply acknowledged the martyr's role: "I rejoice," he said, "in finding an asylum from persecution." In *this* country, he continued, he no doubt would find "that protection from violence which . . . I have not found in my own."[49]

These fine words from an admirer of the revolution in France, where violence was rampant, and delivered in America, where reason seemed to have been abandoned by the pro-French public, were more than Cobbett could bear. Priestley, he asserted, had been a troublemaker for most of his life, and had brought down on his head whatever ill-treatment he had suffered in England. As one of those "who entertained hopes of bringing about a revolution in England upon the French plan," he had delivered a series of sermons attacking the English constitution from the pulpit of the same unitarian meeting house in Birmingham from which he had long been assailing the church of England.[50] On July 14, 1791, a rowdy crowd, crying "Church and King," broke up a dinner being held in Birmingham to celebrate the French revolution, and then went on to destroy Priestley's meeting house and his personal dwelling place with all its contents. The rioting lasted several days during which other houses ware destroyed. Order was not restored until a detachment of dragoons arrived in Birmingham. Fortunately, not a person was injured except among the rioters themselves.[51]

Eleven of the ringleaders were indicted; seven were freed, four found guilty, and two hanged. Priestley brought an action for damages against the town of Birmingham for £4,122 and obtained a verdict for £2,502.[52] Cobbett contrasted this result with what had been going on in France, where men, women, and children were being killed by the hundreds, where there was no attempt to maintain order, where there was no redress for damage done:

A man who had for many years been the avowed and open enemy of the government and constitution, had his property destroyed by a mob, who declared themselves the friends of both, and who rose up against him because he was not. This mob were pursued by the Government whose cause they thought they were defending; some of them suffered death, and the inhabitants of the place where they had assembled were obliged to indemnify the man whose property they had destroyed. It would be curious to know what sort of protection this reverend Doctor, this "friend of humanity", wanted. Would nothing satisfy him but the blood of the whole mob? Did he wish to see the town of Birmingham, like that of Lyons, razed, and all its industrious and loyal inhabitants butchered . . . ?[53]

Cobbett, even at this early date, had a good nose for the weakness of his opponents, and he struck hard at what appears to be an almost universal defect in the radical position: their tendency to condone violence and injustices when applied to serve their ends, but to condemn similar means when applied to serve conservative ends. While attacking the government of England, Priestley had preached that "When the majesty of the people is insulted" or they feel themselves "oppressed by any set of men, they have the power to redress the grievance." Yet Priestley complained when the Birmingham mob rose to redress what they conceived as their grievance against *him*. "And therefore," wrote Cobbett, "he says to the people of Birmingham 'You have been misled'. But had they suffered themselves to be misled by himself into an insurrection against the Government; had they burnt the churches, cut the throats of the clergy, and hung the magistrates, military officers, and nobility to the lamp-posts, would he not have said that they exercised a sacred right?"[54]

Publishing a pamphlet attacking a prominent French sympathizer was no simple thing in democratic Philadelphia. Cobbett had felt maltreated by the publisher of his first venture – "I'll be damned if I dont take care how they cheat me again"[55] – so he sought a new connection, a process that became a familiar one throughout his life. His first choice, Mathew Carey, prominent democrat, turned him down.[56]

Thomas Bradford, the second choice, after some expressions of doubt, finally agreed to publish on Cobbett's agreement to delete from the title the opening words: "The Tartuffe Detected," but he left his name off the pamphlet.[57] The author's name, as was common in those days, was also omitted. "Poor little innocents!" – wrote Cobbett about this and his succeeding pamphlet, which similarly appeared without the name of either author or publisher – "They were thrown on the parish like foundlings; no soul would own them, till it was found that they possessed the gift of bringing in the pence." And that they did. When published in August 1794, the doubly anonymous *Observations on the Emigration of Dr. Joseph Priestley* proved an immediate success. There were five Philadelphia editions of the pamphlet. It was reprinted in New York, in Birmingham, and in London.[58] The publishers were quite glad, after the first edition, to be identified with the publication, and Cobbett too had reason to be pleased, for he had hit upon a career that was to keep him at the center of controversy for the next forty years.

4 · George Washington

I have endeavoured to make America laugh instead of weep.

COBBETT'S PAMPHLET on Priestley had, by chance, arrived at a critical time for the governments of Britain and the United States. The year 1794 was characterized on both sides of the Atlantic by a general atmosphere of lawlessness. In England, there were bad harvests and widespread unrest. The French example simultaneously produced hope for change among the lower classes and fear of change among the governing classes. In the United States, an excise tax on distilleries met with organized resistance in western Pennsylvania which was put down in the autumn of 1794 with militia provided by four states, an incident that became known as the Western Insurrection or, more commonly, the Whiskey Rebellion, although it was a rebellion on a most modest scale.[1] However, the incident had frightening implications beyond the numbers involved: The governmental structure was in its infancy – five years old – and no one knew how fragile or durable it might prove in a crisis. The federal government had an army of approximately 2,000 men committed to keeping the Indians in check on the western frontiers and no way of enforcing its decrees except through state cooperation. Hence, Cobbett's pamphlet against Priestley, with its condemnation of violence and respect for lawfully constituted authority, was heralded by moderates everywhere. But there was another feature of the tract that had special significance to the American audience: Cobbett's attack on Priestley was also an attack on the societies, and particularly the Democratic Societies, that had so warmly welcomed him to America. These Democratic Societies had sprung up all over the country shortly after Genêt had arrived in 1793, and immediately after they were formed they began to agitate for the French cause and against the neutral course being pursued by President Washington. In the very issue of the semiofficial *Gazette of the United States* announcing the address to Priestley by the Democratic Society of New York, there also appeared an article beginning with these words: *"Says a Correspondent,* The

53

Democratic Society resolve one thing, the President of the United States resolves another – A House divided against itself cannot stand – One cannot serve God and Mammon."[2] Washington, who had been unanimously reelected for a second term a few months before and had the complete confidence of the American public, had no intention of allowing these organizations to set the policy of the United States. He was thoroughly sceptical of their goals. In 1790 Burke had warned of French societies created "to cabal and correspond at home and abroad for the propagation of their tenets,"[3] while Cobbett's translation of the Lafayette impeachment published in 1793 contained Lafayette's accusation that a *faction* had been the cause of the disorders in France.[4] Washington suspected that the Democratic Societies, besides the general trouble they had been making, were behind the Whiskey Rebellion, and when he reported on that event to congress on November 19, 1794, he specifically denounced "certain self-created societies" that sought to defeat government decisions by "formal concert."[5] This criticism was all that was needed. Although Washington was bitterly attacked for his accusations, his prestige was sufficient to put an end to serious difficulty from this source. The societies did not immediately disappear, but their following dwindled and they never again assumed a position of such importance.

From the federalist point of view, Cobbett's opening attack on French sympathizers had arrived at the right moment. Most of the American periodicals were pro-French and constantly pressing for entering the war against the British. Washington was determined to remain neutral, but the republican argument for war had been given further impetus by the British themselves through orders in council issued in June and November 1793 for the purpose of stopping neutral trade with France and its possessions in the West Indies. As a result, American ships were captured and condemned with their cargoes. Sailors on American ships were pressed into service by the British. And there were many other complaints. But Washington, instead of yielding to the popular demand for war with Britain, took the unpopular course of sending a special envoy to England – John Jay, chief justice of the United States supreme court – to attempt to resolve the outstanding issues between the two countries.[6]

On November 19, 1794, the day Washington was condemning "certain self-created societies" in his report to congress, Jay signed a treaty with Lord Grenville, British foreign secretary. The treaty from one point of view decided nothing, since it left untouched the prevailing law of nations relating to the rights of neutrals on the high seas and referred to commissions a pending dispute relating to the Canadian–U.S. boundary line as well as the American claim for maritime confis-

cations and the counterclaims for American debts to the British arising before the revolutionary war. But from another point of view it
decided everything, because the improved relations between the two
nations avoided a war that otherwise was almost unavoidable. The
Americans also gained certain rights to trade with British India and
the British West Indies.

The terms of the Jay treaty did not reach the American capital until
March 1795, and they were withheld from the public until June, while
the agreement was being debated in the Senate. But the terms were a
secondary consideration; to the democrats *any* treaty with Britain was
anathema. And unfortunately, the details of Jay's treaty were peculiarly vulnerable to fault-seeking opponents. While in practice (possibly because of British forbearance) the treaty worked out tolerably
well for the Americans, on paper it looked, or was made to look, like
an extremely bad bargain.[7] The public outcry led one historian to
claim that it was the most unpopular treaty in American history.[8]
Plainly, feeling ran strongly against ratification.

Cobbett threw himself into the battle. For more than a year nearly
all of his writings were directed at the issues underlying the treaty.
The first of these, published in January 1795, was an anonymous
pamphlet with the delightful title *A Bone to Gnaw, for the Democrats:* "I
throw it in amongst them, as amongst a kennel of hounds: let them
snarl and growl over it." The ostensible reason for Cobbett's essay was
the publication in Philadelphia of *The Political Progress of Britain,* the
work of James Callender, an earnest democrat who had recently fled
to America from England; but, as Cobbett confessed, Callender's
work "has acted only the part of an usher": It served to introduce a
theme on which Cobbett was able to improvise with great ingenuity.[9]
Callender's thesis was that Britain was finished as a major power, and
the country was ripe for revolution. In all, not an attractive partner
for a commercial treaty. Cobbett's pamphlet was more than an answer
to Callender's charges; it was also a calm exposition of the relationships of Britain, France, and the United States, and the importance
of ties between Britain and the United States. Its calmness and geni-
ality, in contrast to the vituperation in the Priestley pamphlet, and the
sureness of the author's hand, demonstrate Cobbett's virtuosity. The
tone is set by the opening passage: "If you have a Shop to mind, or
any other business to do, I advise you to go and do it, and let this
book alone; for I can assure you, it contains nothing of half so much
importance to you, as the sale of a skein of thread or a yard of tape."[10]

Callender's work had catalogued his troubles with the English
authorities that led to a prison sentence. According to Callender,
Thomas Jefferson, having read the book, had declared that "it con-

tained the most astonishing concentration of abuses, that he had ever heard of." Cobbett insisted that Jefferson had been slightly misquoted, that the word "abuses" should read "abuse," and that, correctly rephrased, Callender's book contained the "most astonishing concentration of *abuse*, that he had ever heard of."[11]

Callender was not the only democrat who predicted an English revolution. James Madison did too, and stated that when the British peerage came thronging to the United States he would treat them with "all that hospitality, respect and tenderness to which misfortune is entitled." Cobbett was amused by Citizen Madison's sympathy for the British nobility:

'Tis a pity the poor devils are not apprized of all this. It would certainly be an act of humanity in our good Citizen to let them know what blessings he has in *store* for them: they seem attached to their Coronets and Coach-and-sixes at present; but were they informed that they can have as much homony and fat pork as they can gobble down (once every day of their lives), liberty to chew tobacco, and smoke all the week, and to ride out on the meeting-going mare on Sundays, it might tempt them to quit their baubles and their poor bit of an Island without a struggle, and fly to the free State of Virginia.[12]

And so, for sixty pages, quoting Shakespeare, Goldsmith, Pope, Molière, La Fontaine, and Arbuthnot – flicking his whip to one side and then the other – first on the barbarities and fickleness of the French and then on the pretensions and inconsistencies of the American democrats, with such digressions as suited his purpose, Cobbett took his course.[13] He pleaded, in the meanwhile, the British cause: that there was no sign of Britain's dissolution ("is she not the undisputed Mistress of the Ocean?");[14] that if there were a revolution in Britain it would, according to democratic philosophy, make her stronger rather than weaker; that Britain and the United States had common enemies; that the British had no animosity toward the Americans; that because a state of war once existed between the two countries, that was no reason why they should hate each other.[15] Underlying these homilies were very material trade relationships – Britain was the principal source of American imports as well as the largest customer for American exports. In keeping with the morality of political writing in the eighteenth century, Britain's case was presented as though the anonymous author were an American who had been attending Christ Church in Philadelphia for the past thirty years: "the English are no favorites of mine; I care very little if their Island were swallowed up by an Earthquake."[16]

A Bone to Gnaw enjoyed enormous popularity. "It was read in all companies, by the young and by the old."[17] Three editions of the pamphlet were published in less than three months.[18] According to

Cobbett, William Bradford, attorney general of the United States, was delighted with it and "said he should have loved me for ever, if I had not been so severe upon the French." He had also been rather severe on some of the high gods and lesser gods among the American democrats, which provided a base for Cobbett's troubles in later years.

A month after *A Bone to Gnaw* was published, it drew the attention of the *American Monthly Review,* a new periodical edited by Samuel Harrison Smith. The reviewer, presumably the editor himself, was no fool. He referred to Cobbett's "magical pen" – probably the first critic to do so – and went on to explain that with it, Cobbett "throws every object into a ludicrous light, and determined to make the most of the ridiculous, he laughs almost without cessation from the beginning of his book to the end of it."[19] One would hardly think that such a review would offend the author of a publication intended to be humorous, but Mr. Smith had committed two sins: First, his publication consisted principally of articles reprinted from the *London Review,* "because its authors have ever been among the foremost in opposing the tyranny of the British government,"[20] and second, Mr. Smith had the temerity to criticize Cobbett's grammar! A prompt reply by Cobbett, entitled *A Kick for a Bite,* devoted nine pages to a detailed analysis of Mr. Smith's grammatical errors and several more pages to a denunciation of the materials taken from the London publication, ending with what appears to be a wholly unrelated subject: a lengthy dissertation on the literary demerits of Mrs. Susanna Haswell Rowson, actress and playwright who was currently entertaining the people of Philadelphia. The only known connection between Mrs. Rowson and Mr. Smith or Mr. Smith's periodical was that Smith had clearly implied his opposition to the "tyranny of the British government," while Mrs. Rowson, although British-born, had been guilty of "a sudden conversion to republicanism," and like Smith was addicted to syntactical howlers.[21] Perhaps Cobbett intended *A Kick for a Bite* to continue the amiability that characterized his prior publication. If so, it did not come off. There are, it is true, some genial aspects of the pamphlet: the title page identified the author as "Peter Porcupine," the first time Cobbett had used this pseudonym, and the text explains that "if you should see a person with one ear hanging down upon his cheek, like the ear of an old sow, that is PETER PORCUPINE, at your service."[22] But if *A Kick for a Bite* provided laughter to some, its major impact was to add to the list of enemies Cobbett was rapidly accumulating in Pennsylvania. While pillorying Mrs. Rowson, Cobbett found the opportunity to attack the wife of Frederick Muhlenberg, Speaker of the House of Representatives.[23] Throughout his life Cobbett was rarely able to resist publicly flailing anyone who thought differently from him or poking fun at anyone he regarded as funny. This was a luxury of a generally simple-living man that was to prove expensive as time went on.

As Cobbett may have expected, and possibly hoped, Mrs. Rowson found her supporters. Peter Porcupine was roundly, but not very effectively, assailed by an anonymous pamphlet bearing a long title: *A Rub from Snub; or A Cursory Analytical Epistle: Addressed to Peter Porcupine, Author of the Bone to Gnaw, Kick for a Bite &c. &c. Containing, Glad Tidings for the Democrats, and a Word of Comfort to Mrs. S. Rowson, Wherein the Said Porcupine's Moral, Political, Critical and Literary Character Is Fully Illustrated.* "Citizen Snub," the author of this attack, was easily identifiable as John Swanwick, member of the House of Representatives from Philadelphia. Beginning with a relatively small role in *A Bone to Gnaw,* he soon became one of Cobbett's favorite comic characters. He was small; he was a would-be poet; he was a fussy bachelor who liked to talk with little girls at boarding school; he had decorated his bedchamber "with lascivious pictures, *Leda and her Swan,* and such-like stimuluses"; and he was a democrat – a combination Cobbett found irresistible.[24] Renamed "Scrub" by Peter Porcupine, he was frequently recalled to the stage by Cobbett to receive a fresh quota of raps on the skull. "Was I Johnny Swanwick, which by the bye, I thank God I am not," begins a letter from Henry Van Schaack of Pittsfield, Massachusetts, a better federalist than a grammarian, "the seat of Congress should be instantly renounced and remove to where P. Porcupine could not probably get access."[25]

Minor characters like John Swanwick and Mrs. Rowson had a distinct purpose in Cobbett's tactics; they were used to illustrate the silliness of those attracted by libertarian doctrine. But Cobbett never took his eye off the main game: the ratification of the Jay treaty by the United States Senate. Resisting the temptation to reply to "Scrub," Cobbett produced a new pamphlet, Part II of *A Bone to Gnaw.* This did not deal with the substantive terms of the treaty, but struck at the underlying objection to the agreement: the love-France and hate-Britain emotionalism. A popular verse of the time put it neatly:

> Englishman no bon for me,
> Frenchmen fight for liberty.[26]

Cobbett recognized that a large part of the problem was due to the failure to distinguish between what the French were saying and what they were doing. Benjamin Franklin Bache, editor of the *Aurora,* chief democratic paper in America, had blandly assured his readers that it was "an easy matter to apologise for all the murders committed in France."[27] He said nothing about the extent of the slaughter, the savagery, and the cruelty displayed, the senseless destruction of innocent women and children for reasons that had nothing to do with liberty or equality. Cobbett's newest pamphlet told this story, using as an example the terrible massacres that had occurred in Lyons, France's second city, where half of the population had been wiped out since France "called itself a Republic."[28] The Jay treaty itself was not mentioned until the last few pages of the pamphlet. There, in a few words, Cobbett summarized the factual arguments that justified the treaty: that Britain was both the chief customer of the United States and the chief supplier of American needs. Then Cobbett returned to the true issue:

Think not, reader, whatever advantages we are about to derive from the treaty with Great Britain, that I wish to see such a marked partiality shown for that nation, as has hitherto appeared for the French . . . No; let us forget that it is owing to Great Britain that this country is not now an uninhabited desert; that the land we possess was purchased from the aborigines with the money of an Englishman; that his hands traced the streets on which we walk. Let us forget from whom we are descended, and persuade our children that we are the sons of the gods, or the accidental offspring of the elements; let us forget the scalping knives of the French, to which we were thirty years exposed; but let us never forget that we are not Frenchmen.[29]

Part II of *A Bone to Gnaw* appeared approximately a week before the treaty was sent to the Senate for its consideration, on June 8. When the Senate voted on June 24, the two-thirds majority required by the constitution was barely secured; there was not a single vote to spare.[30] When the result became known, French sympathizers mounted a nationwide campaign of unparalleled intensity to prevent Washington from signing the treaty. Town meetings were called in major cities, "Everywhere Jay was burned in effigy," and remonstrances endorsed by the meetings poured in on the president.[31] In Richmond, Virginia – largest city in Washington's home state – a town meeting, calling Jay a "d—n'd Arch Traitor," declared that if the treaty were signed, the state legislature would be petitioned to "recede" from the union. At Portsmouth, New Hampshire, the people were told that the treaty *"will be the death warrant of your Trade,* and entail beggary on us, and our posterity for ever!!!" In New York, opponents of the treaty marched behind the French flag to the Battery at the foot of Manhattan, where a copy of the treaty was burned.[32] "The cry against the Treaty," wrote Washington from his home in Mount Vernon, "is like that against a mad-dog."[33]

Those making most of the noise probably had little idea of what the treaty contained, and the newspapers, being largely pro-French, did little to enlighten them. Cobbett sought to remedy this in *A Little Plain*

English, a pamphlet describing the twenty-eight articles of the treaty and discussing the objections that had been raised under three main titles: I – that a commercial treaty with Great Britain was unnecessary and dangerous, II – that the terms of the treaty were disadvantageous to the United States, and III – that President Washington had been guilty of misconduct in appointing Jay and in other aspects of the negotiation. It had even been contended by some that Washington should be impeached. Cobbett's defense of the treaty and of the conduct of the principal parties was rushed to completion, appearing sometime in August 1795, probably, but not certainly, after Washington had precipitately signed the treaty on August 14.[34] A curious event had intervened. Secret French dispatches captured by the British and turned over by them to Washington suggested that Edmund Randolph (who had succeeded Jefferson as secretary of state) had been guilty of indiscreet conversations with the French minister, Fauchet; there even were implications of possible bribery. This had occurred the year before, during the Western Insurrection, but it confirmed the allegations by Cobbett and others that the French were continually meddling in the internal affairs of the United States.[35] The captured dispatches were shown to Randolph on August 19, and he huffily resigned that day without admitting the truth of the charges.

But the execution of the treaty by Washington did not finally settle the issue. The Senate approval had been conditional on the elimination of an objectionable clause from the treaty relating to trade with the West Indies, so final British approval was needed.[36] And on the American side of the Atlantic the enforcement of the treaty required funds, and funds could be voted only by a bill initiated in the House of Representatives, which was far more pro-French than the Senate. Still another campaign was launched against the treaty, this time directed to the House of Representatives. Cobbett's *A Little Plain English* was still pertinent, but no longer complete. Randolph's resignation had presented a new complication. He himself, after waiting four months, had published *A Vindication of Mr. Randolph's Resignation,* consisting of an extremely indecisive defense of his innocence and an extremely bitter attack on the president. He claimed, to use Cobbett's words, that Washington had signed the Jay treaty "not from a persuasion that it was a good one, not from the obligations of his constitutional oath . . . but from motives of resentment against France and her faction, which resentment had been excited by the intercepted dispatches."[37]

Randolph's *Vindication* was published on December 18, 1795.[38] Hot on its trail, on January 9, 1796, came Peter Porcupine's response: *A*

*New-Year's Gift to the Democrats; or, Observations on a Pamphlet Entitled
"A Vindication of Mr. Randolph's Resignation".*[39] Randolph was made to
appear an utter scoundrel, not simply through an analysis of his dealings with Fauchet, but by his subsequent conduct, including the manner in which the *Vindication* was prepared and published. Cobbett
rarely missed an opening. He pointed to the title of the publication
itself: Randolph was trying to vindicate his *resignation,* and what the
public wanted to know was how he could vindicate his relations with
the French minister. There was also the four months it took Randolph, a trained lawyer, to prepare his answer, "and we now find it to
contain no more original matter than any man, accustomed to writing, would have prepared for the press in the space of six or seven
days at most." Further, Randolph had seemingly attempted to black-
mail Washington by asking his consent to the publication of correspondence at the risk of having "the whole of this affair, howsoever
confidential and delicate, being exhibited to the world." Washington
was not be be caught in this trap. Without hesitating, he replied that
Randolph was "at full liberty to publish, without reserve, any and
every private and confidential letter I ever wrote you; nay more, every
word I ever uttered to or in your presence, from whence you can
derive any advantage in your justification." Then Cobbett pointed to
the unusual manner of putting the *Vindication* before the public:
instead of giving it the widest possible circulation by sending it to a
gazette, "requesting at the same time all the other printers of gazettes,
in the United States, to republish it," it was being offered for sale at
2s. 9¾d., and its republication was expressly forbidden. To Randolph's description of his *Vindication* as "an appeal to the people,"
Cobbett remarked: "Civilians have long been divided as to the precise
import of the word *people;* this question is now resolved by the rules
of arithmetic, and that to a fraction, as far at least as relates to the
United States: the people, are all those who are able and willing to
give Mr. Randolph, or his printer, two shillings and nine pence three
farthings good and lawful money of Pennsylvania! *O Respublica! O
Mores!"*

   Randolph, according to Cobbett, did not vindicate himself; his
paper was nothing more than an attempt "to balance the crime laid to
his charge, against another supposed crime, which he imputes to the
President, concerning the ratification of the treaty" – a matter in no
way related to Randolph's dealings with Fauchet. Finally, Randolph
asserted that when he had given his advice in favor of ratification of
the treaty he had in mind that "if the people were averse to the
Treaty, it was the constitutional right of the House of Representatives
to refuse, upon original grounds, unfettered by the Senate and the

President, to pass the laws necessary for its execution." Randolph thus made it quite clear that he had gone over to the opposition, and that he looked to the House of Representatives to stop the treaty.

Cobbett began his summing up with these words:

Thus has the Vindicator failed in all his attempts. On the article of corruption, of which we before doubted, we now doubt no longer; and as to his indirect accusation against the President, it only serves to show that one who, with unblushing front, can ask a bribe, will never be ashamed to publish his ingratitude and apostacy.[40]

Madison wrote to Jefferson ten days after *A New Year's Gift* was published: "Randolph's 'Vindication' has just undergone the lash of the author of the 'Bone to Gnaw'. It is handled with much satirical scurrility, not without strictures of sufficient plausibility to aid in the plan of running him down."[41] Another republican called it a "witty billingsgate performance, very droll."[42] William Plumer, a federalist, thought that the "wit and satire must wound the feelings of Randolph and friends, if feelings they have."[43] It seems likely that both sides may have missed the point; that is, that the purpose of Cobbett's attack on Randolph was to support the Jay treaty, and only incidentally to castigate the former secretary of state.

A New Year's Gift was followed, in February 1796, by a Peter Porcupine pamphlet entitled *A Prospect from the Congress-Gallery*, which reported on congressional action during the session beginning in December 1795. It had opened with a speech by the president on the state of the nation. The Jay treaty was mentioned briefly: The Senate had approved subject to a condition; the president had signed; the result on the part of His Brittanic Majesty was unknown. "When received, the subject will, without delay, be placed before Congress."

Extended debate occurred in both houses on how the president's speech should be answered, and more specifically, what should be said in response to Washington's express hope that "the causes of external discord, which have heretofore menaced our tranquillity" had been extinguished.[44] This invited a reopening of the Jay treaty debate. In the Senate the question was speedily resolved, but in the House of Representatives the proposed address voicing "undiminished confidence" in the president was watered down by the dominating pro-French faction, who replaced these words with the phrase "affectionate attachment." The revered George Washington, twice unanimously elected to the presidency, was thus presented with "the cup of humiliation, filled to the brim."[45]

In March 1796, Peter Porcupine had still another pamphlet on sale, the third since the beginning of the year. It was a piece in Cobbett's continuing campaign. Randolph had stated, in his *Vindication*, that the

House of Representatives, when acting on the request for funds to implement the Jay treaty, should defer to the opinion of the *people*. Cobbett made this direct appeal to the people, in the strongest terms he knew, in his pamphlet *The Bloody Buoy*, or, to give its complete title; *The Bloody Buoy, Thrown Out as a Warning to the Political Pilots of America; or A Faithful Relation of a Multitude of Acts of Horrid Barbarity, Such as the Eye Never Witnessed, the Tongue Never Expressed or the Imagination Conceived, until the Commencement of The French Revolution, to Which Is Added An Instructive Essay, Tracing These Dreadful Effects to Their Real Causes*. Previous political publications of Cobbett ran, at most, to around 100 pages. *The Bloody Buoy* was 240 pages. The first half of the volume was devoted to a detailed description of the barbarous acts committed in the name of Liberty during the French revolution – acts which the greatest part of American newspapers "have most industriously concealed, or glossed over . . . on the false, but specious pretence, that they were conducive to the establishment of a free government."[46] The facts marshalled by Cobbett from French publications for the period 1792 to 1795 show that the sufferers were not simply nobility or their successors in office, or even their sympathizers, but were from all classes of society; that men, women, and children were tortured and murdered with unparalleled lewdness and savagery. People were reduced to the level of beasts, churches were defiled, priests were massacred, the rights of private property were extinguished. Any American reader who believed in the substance of civil rights, as distinguished from the words, or in human dignity or religion or private property could see, without being told, what could happen if French principles were to be transported across the Atlantic. But Peter Porcupine did not take any chances that this point would be missed:

Shall we say that these things never can take place among us? Because we have hitherto preserved the character of a pacific and humane people, shall we set danger at defiance? Though we are not Frenchmen, we are men as well as they, and consequently are liable to be misled.

Nor are men of the same stamp wanting among the native Americans. There is not a single action of the French revolutionists, but has been justified and applauded in our public papers, and many of them in our public assemblies.

The attacks on the character and conduct of the irreproachable Washington, have been as bold, if not bolder, than those that led to the downfall of the unfortunate French Monarch. His impudent and unprincipled enemies have represented him as cankered with every vice that marks a worthless tyrant; they have called him the betrayer of the liberties of his country, and have even drawn up and published *articles of accusation* against him!

. . . sure I am, that had the friends of virtue and order shown only a hundredth part of the zeal in the cause of their own country, as the enemies of both have done in the cause of France, we should not now have to lament the existence of a hardened and impious faction, whose destructive principles, if not timely and firmly opposed, may one day render the annals of America as disgraceful as those of the French Revolution.[47]

These were sobering words, and they fell on an audience made up largely of property-owning, law-abiding, church-going Americans. The problem created by loving everything French and hating everything British, being an emotional one, gradually succumbed to an argument that was both emotional and practical: Think of yourselves.[48] *The Bloody Buoy* went through a great number of editions in America and England. In America it was even printed in German (for the German population of Pennsylvania) and was republished in the state as late as 1823, long after the bloody French revolution was over.[49]

The House of Representatives began debating the treaty in April 1796, the month after *The Bloody Buoy* made its appearance. There was a noticeably more balanced view than the year before. A "decided majority" of the citizens of Richmond, Virginia, at a meeting held there on April 25, 1796,[50] approved a resolution favoring the treaty, whereas at a similar meeting in July 1795 only four or five individuals had been for it.[51] The leading democratic papers in Boston and Philadelphia protested against the changing opinion in their communities, claiming that it was due to personal influence, intrigue, and fear tactics.[52] A Maryland representative in the House, Gabriel Christie, who thought the treaty was the "worst of all hard bargains" decided to vote for it because he was satisfied that "a large majority of his constituents wished it to be carried into effect."[53] Fisher Ames, staunch federalist from Massachusetts, in a stirring speech to the House on April 28, 1796, declared that public opinion was no longer opposed to the treaty as perhaps it had been the year before, when "The alarm spread faster than the publication of the treaty. There were more critics than readers." Now passions had cooled and a majority supported it. The next day the issue was put to the House sitting as a committee of the whole. "The tally revealed a tie, and all eyes turned to Frederick Muhlenberg, who sat in the chair." Muhlenberg, Pennsylvania congressman, had formerly been an outspoken critic of the treaty. "Visibly tense . . . Muhlenberg hesitated, mumbled an explanation, then voted 'aye', and the victory was won. The next day in a roll call vote which was really an anticlimax, the bill passed by a vote of fifty-one to forty-eight." Those voting against the treaty were nearly all from agricultural states south and west of the Potomac.[54]

The outcome of the debate over the Jay treaty was a personal triumph for Cobbett: "It was, in a great measure, owing to me , that the Congress finally ratified the treaty," he wrote forty years later.[55] He, or rather "Peter Porcupine," since Cobbett had still not yet revealed himself as the author of these writings, had become the outstanding journalist supporting the Washington administration. He was read everywhere. The seven pamphlets from *Observations on Priestley* in August 1794 to *A Prospect from the Congress-Gallery* early in 1796 were published in a total of more than twenty editions in the brief period 1794–6, and most of them continued to be reprinted in both America and Britain for years to follow.[56] Oliver Wolcott, who had succeeded Hamilton as secretary of the treasury, was reported as having said that some of the officers of the government had intended to write an answer to Randolph's *Vindication* but that Cobbett's *New Year's Gift* had done its business so completely that nothing further was necessary.[57]

Cobbett received personal gratification also from his meeting with Talleyrand. This famous statesman, who had fled France after the fall of the monarchy, asked to be introduced to Cobbett, and this was arranged by a friend sometime in 1796 before Talleyrand's return to France in June of that year:

At last this modern Judas and I got seated by the same fire-side. I expected that he wanted to expostulate with me on the severe treatment he had met with at my hands: I had called him an apostate, a hypocrite, and every other name of which he was deserving; I therefore leave the reader to imagine my astonishment, when I heard him begin with complimenting me on my *wit* and *learning*. He praised several of my pamphlets, the New Year's Gift in particular, and still spoke of them as mine. I did not acknowledge myself the author, of course; but yet he would insist that I was; or, at any rate, they reflected, he said, *infinite honour* on the author, let him be who he might. Having carried this species of flattery as far as he judged it safe, he asked me, with a vast deal of apparent seriousness, whether I had received my education at *Oxford,* or at *Cambridge!* Hitherto I had kept my countenance pretty well; but this abominable stretch of hypocrisy, and the placid mien and silver accent with which it was pronounced, would have forced a laugh from a Quaker in the midst of meeting. I don't recollect what reply I made him; but this I recollect well, I gave him to understand that I was no trout, and consequently was not to be caught by tickling.[58]

Was Talleyrand, as Cobbett suggests, trying to buy Cobbett by this talk and through his subsequent proposal to take English lessons at $20 a month (Cobbett usually charged $6),[59] or was he, as Duff Cooper concluded, merely curious "to meet a remarkable man"?[60] In either case, the visit was enormously flattering, and further recognition of Cobbett's extraordinary skill as a writer.

While this recognition was fuel to Cobbett's heroic-sized ego, most of the financial reward from his efforts was going to his Philadelphia printer and publisher, Thomas Bradford. For the seven widely acclaimed pamphlets, Cobbett received a total of $403.21.[61] Fortunately, this was not his sole source of income. During the same period Cobbett published a 340-page French text on English grammar. This was reprinted in France, where (although almost certainly without payment of royalties to Cobbett) it went through some forty editions.[62] He also translated from French into English a treatise on international law, Martens's *Law of Nations.*[63] Without legal training, except for the months he spent copying documents in Mr. Holland's office in Gray's Inn, he performed this translation "for a quarter of a dollar (thirteenpence halfpenny) a page; and . . . I made it a rule to earn a dollar while my wife was getting breakfast in the morning, and another dollar after I came home at night, be the hour what it might; and I have earned many a dollar in this way, sitting writing in the same room where my wife and only child were in bed and asleep."[64] But the principal earnings of this enormously energetic man came from tutoring. "I taught English to the most respectable Frenchmen in the city," he wrote; this produced the surprisingly large income of $140 a month.[65]

In 1796 Cobbett angrily broke with his publisher, Bradford. Two of Cobbett's works that were immediately available for the press were farmed out to a rival Philadelphia printer, Benjamin Davies. Meanwhile, Cobbett leased a large house in the center of Philadelphia at 25 North Second Street, opposite Christ Church, where he had decided to establish himself as publisher, printer, and bookseller, a combination of occupations typical of this period. Presumably this would have left little time for tutoring, but since it had become generally known with the leasing of the house that the French tutor William Cobbett and the French scourge Peter Porcupine were the same person, it is likely that there would have been fewer "respectable Frenchmen" available for instruction.

The shop at the front of the house on Second Street, painted a bright blue, was opened with a flourish on July 11, 1796, three days before Philadelphia's annual celebration to commemorate the fall of the Bastille. Cobbett had let it be known in advance among his close acquaintances that the pro-British sentiments expressed in his writings would be evident in the stock carried in his shop.

As the time approached for opening my shop, my friends grew more anxious for my safety. It was recommended to me, to be cautious how I exposed, at my window, any thing that might provoke the people; and, above all, not to put up any *aristocratical portraits*, which would certainly cause the windows to be demolished.

Christ Church, Second Street, Philadelphia. Cobbett's shop was across the street from Christ Church, the largest religious edifice in America when it was built (1727–54). James Abercrombie, vicar of the church, was a close friend of Cobbett. The woodcut was commissioned by James Cobbett in about 1860

I saw the danger, but I also saw, that I must, at once, set all danger at defiance, or live in everlasting subjection to the prejudices and caprice of the democratical mob. I resolved on the former; and, as my shop was to open on a Monday morning, I employed myself all day on Sunday, in preparing an exhibition, that I thought would put the courage and the power of my enemies to the test. I put up in my windows, which were very large, all the portraits that I had in my possession of *kings, queens, princes,* and *nobles.* I had all the English Ministry, several of the Bishops and Judges; the most famous Admirals; and, in short, every picture that I thought likely to excite rage in the enemies of Great Britain.

Early on the Monday morning, I took down my shutters. Such a sight had not been seen in Philadelphia for twenty years. Never since the beginning of the rebellion, had anyone dared to hoist at his window the portrait of George the Third.[66]

Among the pictures thought likely to enrage British enemies was an engraving four feet long by two wide and a smaller print of the same subject portraying Lord Howe's victory over the French fleet on June 1, 1794, when the British captured seven French men-of-war.[67] This seems to have been satisfactorily provocative. Although no windows were broken, Cobbett's landlord received a semi-illiterate, anonymous letter complaining of "certain prints indicative of the prowess of our enemies the British and the disgrace of the French" and threatening damage to the property unless the landlord would compel Cobbett to vacate the premises or "oblige him to cease exposing his abominable productions or any of his courtley prints at his window for sale."[68]

The letter had no effect on the landlord, a calm quaker merchant who had received a year's rent in advance, and a wholly predictable effect on the tenant, who used it as a text for a new pamphlet assailing local French sympathizers. In this pamphlet, *The Scare-Crow,* the first in which Cobbett's name appears, he facilely treats the threat from the single anonymous letter writer as though it were a manifesto from the Jacobins as a group:

Had they studied for years, they could not have found out any thing that would have pleased me so well. It will for ever silence their clamours about the liberty of the press; it will prove to the people, most fully, the truth of what I have always told them; that is, that these "pretended patriots", these advocates for liberty and equality, would, if they had become masters, have been a divan of cruel and savage tyrants. That they know nothing of liberty but the name, and that they make use of that name merely to have the power of abolishing the thing.[69]

The disclosure that Cobbett was the author of the Peter Porcupine pamphlets, the opening of his bookshop retailing federalist and loyalist propaganda, and the publication of *The Scare-Crow,* all coming at about the same time, kept the Philadelphia presses busy with unfriendly retorts. These served only to stimulate further the irrepressible Cobbett, whose "Remarks on the pamphlets lately published against Peter Porcupine" began:

"Dear Father, when you used to set me off to work in the morning, dressed in my blue smock-frock and woollen spatter dashes, with my bag of bread and cheese and bottle of small beer swung over my shoulder on the little crook that my old god-father Boxall gave me, little did you imagine that I should one day become so great a man as to have my picture stuck in the windows, and have four whole books published about me in the course of one week." – Thus begins a letter which I wrote to my father yesterday morning, and which, if it reaches him, will make the old man drink an extraordinary pot of ale to my health. Heaven bless him! I think I see him now, by his old-fashioned fire-side, reading the letter to his neighbours. "Ay, Ay," says he, *Will* will stand his ground wherever he goes." – And so I will, father, in spite of all the hell of democracy.[70]

The "picture" Cobbett referred to showed a porcupine sowing the "seeds of discord" at the urging of the devil with a bag of gold and a British lion with a jay on his back holding a copy of the treaty.[71] The attacks in the four "books" published in a week (and others published about the same time) were founded on two principal charges: that Cobbett was an adventurer with a disreputable career before coming to America and, as the picture implied, was in the pay of the British government, an allegation Cobbett was to hear many times during his stay in America.[72] To the last charge Cobbett pointed out that the only business he ever had with the British agent in Philadelphia (he did not know the two British ministers there) was "as the interpreter

Peter Porcupine "sowing the seeds of discord." A 1796 cartoon occasioned by Cobbett's support of the British–American treaty negotiated by John Jay. A jay, with the treaty in its beak, sits on the back of the British lion, which declares: "Go on dear Peter, my friend & I will reward you." The "friend," the devil, offers Peter a bag of gold. Peter writes: "I hate this country, & will sow the seeds of discord in it." At the left Liberty weeps on a monument to Benjamin Franklin

69

of Frenchmen, who wanted certificates from him, in order to secure their property in the conquered colonies . . . I have every reason to believe that the British Consul was far from approving of some, at least, of my publications. I happened to be in a bookseller's shop, unseen by him, when he had the goodness to say, that I was a *'wild fellow'*. On which I shall only observe, that when the King bestows on me about five hundred pounds sterling a-year, perhaps, I may become a *tame fellow,* and hear my master, my countrymen, my friends and my parents, belied and execrated, without saying a single word in their defence."[73]

In response to the allegations and innuendoes about a shady past, Cobbett wrote a delightful *Life and Adventures of Peter Porcupine*—a tale of 50-odd pages of his family background, youth, army service, honorable discharge, visit to France, journey to America armed with a letter of introduction to Jefferson, and finally his activities in America since arrival.[74] Written in his most forthright and amiable style, it is a story that can still be read for sheer enjoyment; it has several times been reprinted, and is the basis for much of Chapters 1 and 2. Indeed, from what we know of Cobbett's life, this account is *almost* complete in all essential details; not quite, because it made no reference of any sort to the court-martial proceedings in 1792 nor, more strangely, to Cobbett's marriage.[75] If its amiability was broken here and there (as it was) by an occasional rude remark about Benjamin Franklin, perhaps this might be forgiven when we recall that one of the most scurrilous attacks on Cobbett's past life originated in the *Aurora,* a paper edited by Benjamin Franklin Bache, grandson of "Old Lightning Rod."[76] Just as human, and just as typical of Cobbett, was his decision to include in the *Life and Adventures of Peter Porcupine* a detailed statement of his dealings with the printer Thomas Bradford. Cobbett was seriously offended by certain rumors: "I have been well informed, that it is currently reported, that Mr. Thomas Bradford, the bookseller, 'put a coat upon my back,' and that when I was first favoured with his patronage, I had not a 'second shirt to my back.' "[77] Never, at any time during his long career, could Cobbett tolerate the suggestion that his accomplishments were due to anything but his own personal efforts, and here this "hatter-turned-printer, this sooty-fisted son of ink and urine, whose heart is as black and as foul as the liquid in which he dabbles," was taking credit for Cobbett's success![78]

The story told by Cobbett was that he had gone to Bradford with his *Observations on Priestley* after it had been turned down by another printer. Bradford hesitated, "wanted to know if I could not make it a little *more popular,* adding that unless I could, he feared that the publishing of it would endanger *his windows."* This, Cobbett said, opened his eyes to the boasted liberty of the press in America:

I had not the least idea, that a man's windows were in danger of being broken, if he published any thing that was *not popular*. I did, indeed, see the words *liberty* and *equality*; the *rights of man,* the *crimes of kings,* and such like in most of the booksellers' windows; but I did not know that they were placed there to save the glass.

Cobbett refused to alter the text but, as we have seen, did accommodate Bradford to the extent of changing the title of the pamphlet; yet Bradford was still so concerned about the pamphlet's popularity that he omitted his name from the title page.

The agreement for publishing the *Observations,* this pamphlet that had gone into so many editions, provided that Cobbett and Bradford should share the profits equally after deducting Bradford's expenses, a system called "publishing together." Cobbett's share under this arrangement came to 1s. 7½d. in Pennsylvania currency, not enough to "cover the back of a Lilliputian." There was no more "publishing together" with Bradford after that; Cobbett sold his pamphlets outright, receiving an average of around $65 for each of the next six. When Cobbett went into business for himself, he offered to buy back the copyrights at what he had sold them for, leaving Bradford with a clear profit for all editions previously published, but Bradford refused.

The straw that proved too much for Cobbett's back related to the last pamphlet he sold to Bradford: *A Prospect from the Congress-Gallery.* This publication sold well, and Bradford decided that he would like to have it continued. His son offered Cobbett $100 a number as contrasted with the $18 he was paid for the first.

I should have accepted his offer, had it not been for a word that escaped him during the conversation. He observed, that their customers would be much disappointed; for that, his *father had promised* a continuation, and *that it should be made very interesting.* This slip of the tongue, opened my eyes at once. What! a bookseller undertake to promise what I should write, and that I should write to please his customers too! No; if all his *customers,* if all the Congress, with the President at their head, had come and solicited me; nay, had my life depended on a compliance, I would not have written another line.[79]

Overly dramatic perhaps, and certainly reflecting an overly touchy personality, but when Cobbett made this statement and the parallel remark in the same publication "I never was of an accommodating disposition in my life," he was accurately describing an essential element of his character that explains much of his career. He was not in the habit of working *with* others, much less of working *for* others. In later years he frequently signed his letters "your most humble and most obedient servant," but from the time he left the army until his death more than forty years later he was never one or the other.

The foregoing account of Cobbett's relations with Bradford appeared in *The Life and Adventures of Peter Porcupine*, published on August 8, 1796. Within three weeks the Bradfords had retaliated with *The Impostor Detected, or A Review of Some of the Writings of "Peter Porcupine"*, providing Cobbett with a platform for a renewed assault on the printer and his family. This time the Bradfords accused Cobbett of writing stuff of poor quality – "dirty water," they called it; and Cobbett was able to show not only that they wanted more of it, but that both they and many of their distinguished customers had highly praised the work. Cobbett modestly added that since the Peter Porcupine pamphlets were ascribed "to almost every gentleman of distinguished talents among the friends of the Federal Government, it would be mere grimace for me to pretend, that they have no merit at all."[80]

The Bradfords also published a letter signed "A Correspondent" which Cobbett had written to the *Aurora* (it was not printed by that paper), denouncing Part II of *A Bone to Gnaw*. This, Cobbett explained, was a "puff indirect," a piece written by an author attacking his own performance, "thereby to excite opposition" and to "awaken the attention of the public," resorted to by authors such as Addison and Pope. The puff had been proposed by the Bradfords, said Cobbett; they did all the "dirty work" and they were the only ones who could profit by the device, as Cobbett had sold the copyright to them outright.[81]

Cobbett ended his reply with a series of amusing and gossipy morsels that would tend to discredit his former publisher. The dedication of Martens's *Law of Nations* to George Washington, for example, had been written by Cobbett, although Bradford took the credit by signing his name to it; when Cobbett was engaged in drafting the dedication, Bradford had urged him to "give the old boy a little more oil."[82]

Cobbett had hardly concluded the first round of these personal feuds of 1796 before he was again in the forefront of a second major political war. The Jay treaty was safe, but a presidential election was due at the end of 1796 under the old electoral system, which existed until 1804. Washington had served two terms and was determined to serve no more. "I desire to be buffeted no longer in the public prints by a set of infamous scribblers," he wrote. His decision was announced on September 17, 1796 in the form of a farewell address in which he urged internal unity and external detachment: "cultivate peace and harmony with all . . . The Nation which indulges towards another an habitual hatred or an habitual fondness is in some degree a slave." And then the phrase which has been so often misquoted: " 'Tis our true policy to steer clear of permanent alliances, with any portion of the foreign world."[83]

The obvious candidate to succeed Washington was his federalist vice-president, John Adams, but Adams was sure to be opposed by Thomas Jefferson, leader of the pro-French democratic party. The unanimity that had put Washington into the presidency and kept him there for eight years would never occur again. There could be no question where Cobbett stood in the election, and his willingness to assist in the cause was made easier by a strange step taken by Pierre Adet, the French minister – a step that almost paralleled the master blunder committed by Genêt in 1793. Adet, by letter to the American secretary of state, Timothy Pickering, dated October 27, 1796, announced that thereafter the French would treat neutral vessels in the same manner as they were treated by the English.[84] Since the Jay treaty acknowledged the right of the English to confiscate French goods carried in American vessels, the French would confiscate English goods carried in American vessels. This was an angry but natural reaction of the French to the Jay treaty. The Franco-American compact of 1778 provided that "free ships should make free goods." Hence the enforcement of the French decree constituted a *de facto* renunciation of that compact, but this was something that the Americans must have foreseen when the Jay treaty was negotiated. Presumably the controlling element was a pragmatic one: The British navy dominated the high seas, whereas that of the French could be only an incidental scourge.

Two weeks after his first letter Adet again wrote to Pickering, stating that the French ministry in the United States was being suspended as a "mark of just discontent, which is to last until the government of the United States returns to sentiments and to measures more conformable to the interests of the alliance and the sworn friendship between the two nations."[85] Both of Adet's letters were given by him to Bache's *Aurora* for publication. No one could doubt that Adet meant: Turn out the federalists, and we shall take you back in our good graces.

So blatant was the appeal that Cobbett's first retort was simply to reprint Adet's letters under a title that spoke for itself: *The Gros Mousqueton Diplomatique; or Diplomatic Blunderbuss.* In a short preface Cobbett coyly denied that he had used the word "blunderbuss" to mean "an unprincipled, shameless bully" who "acts in such a bungling, stupid manner, as to excite ridicule and contempt in place of fear" – no, the word was used to refer to "a species of fire arms that exceeds all others . . . in the noise of its discharge."[86]

This tract was quickly followed by Porcupine's *Political Censor* for

November 1796, in which Cobbett took up, and answered in typical Cobbett fashion, Adet's allegation that seven "crimes" had been committed by the Washington administration against the French government.[87] The fifth of Adet's claims, for example, was that the United States government had "allowed" the French colonies in the West Indies to be blockaded by the British navy. "Had he complained that they *allowed* it to rain," Cobbett asserted, "his complaint would have not been more absurd."[88] To Adet's claim of France's traditional generosity and friendship toward the Americans, Cobbett reviewed their actions in the past forty years: They had been charged by Benjamin Franklin with "perfidy," "cruelty," and "treachery" during the French and Indian war; their participation in the American revolution had been for the purpose of weakening Great Britain and not to gain freedom for the Americans (besides, the French soldiers "were never engaged. They only seemed to come to look on a bit, and go home and brag about *giving liberty to America*"); they sent Genêt to America to raise an insurrection; they replaced him with Fauchet, whom "we find dabbling in the Western rebellion"; and finally they sent over Adet, who was trying to interfere in the election of a chief magistrate.[89] While Adet purported to offer his complaints in the capacity of a friend, he described his government as "terrible to its enemies, but generous to its allies."[90] To this Cobbett replied: " 'A *friend*,' says Citizen Adet, 'injured by a *friend* may safely complain, without fear of giving offence.' – Yes, but he must complain *like a friend*, and not like a bully. He must not talk of his horsewhip or his cane."[91] Cobbett had nothing good to say about Jefferson, the French candidate for the presidency. Unnamed, he is described by Cobbett as

... a man as much fit to be a President as I am to be an Archbishop! A man who is a deist by profession, a philosopher by trade, and a Frenchman in politics and morality . . . a man, in short, who is at the head of the prostituted party by whose intrigues he has been brought forward and is supported. If this man is elected President, the country is sold to the French; and as plantations are generally sold with the live stock on them, I shall remove my carcass; for I am resolved never to become their property. I do not wish my family vault to be in the guts of cannibals.[92]

Cobbett's *Political Censor* for November 1796 was on sale by December 20 – too late to have any effect on the voting of the electors, although it was not until December 30 that Adams was confident that he had won.[93] When the ballots were officially counted on February 8, 1797, Adams had seventy-one votes – one more than the necessary majority. Jefferson had sixty-eight votes and therefore was elected vice-president. According to Adams's son, John Quincy Adams, Adet had cost Jefferson thirteen or more votes in the electoral college.[94]

Cobbett had obviously enjoyed the contest, and was even more obviously pleased by the result. We have a taciturn testimonial, from a well-qualified source, to the general effectiveness of Cobbett's pamphlet on Adet. In a letter dated January 8, 1797 George Washington wrote: "Enclosed also, you will receive a production of *Peter Porcupine,* alias Wm. Cobbet. Making allowances for the asperity of an Englishman; for some of his strong and coarse expressions; and a want of official information of many facts; it is not a bad thing."[95]

5 · John Adams

Professions of impartiality, I shall make none.

JOHN ADAMS, second president of the United States, took the oath of office on March 4, 1797. Cobbett's skills as the leading federalist writer during Washington's administration were to prove more of a burden than a blessing to Adams during the four stormy years of his tenure.

It is difficult to visualize two people more different than Adams and the man he succeeded. Washington and Adams shared the virtues of integrity, patriotism, and courage, but not much more. Washington was tall, taller even than Cobbett, while Adams was a mere five feet seven or eight inches.[1] Washington was a self-educated surveyor, soldier, and farmer; Adams was a graduate of Harvard and a practicing lawyer. Washington spent his lifetime in North America; Adams had lived in Europe for nearly a quarter of his adult life, serving as American minister in France, Holland, and Britain. Washington was a quiet man, a good listener, a natural leader, a moderator between individuals of differing views; Adams was contentious, impetuous, vain, stubborn, and opinionated. Adams revealed more of himself than he intended when he told Gilbert Stuart, the portrait painter, that "Washington got the reputation of being a great man because he kept his mouth shut."[2]

In Adams's inaugural address his remarks about Washington followed a more traditional pattern. Washington's "prudence, justice, temperance, and fortitude," said Adams, "merited the gratitude of his fellow-citizens, commanded the highest praises of foreign nations, and secured immortal glory with posterity."[3] Unfortunately, Washington had not reaped such encomiums from all quarters. That perpetual troublemaker, Benjamin Franklin Bache of the *Aurora*, asserted that "If ever a nation was debauched by a man, the American nation has been debauched by Washington"; he rejoiced that Washington, "who is the source of all the misfortunes of our country, is this day reduced to a level with his fellow citizens, and is no longer possessed of power to multiply evils upon the United States." Bache was not alone in his attacks. The democratic majority in the House of Representatives had refused to pass a resolution declaring that Washington's life had been "strongly marked by wisdom, in the cabinet, by valour, in the field, and by the purest patriotism in both."[4]

And then there was the terrible attack on Washington by the resurrected Tom Paine.[5] For some time it had been generally believed that the champion propagandist of the American revolution had died following his release from a French prison in November 1794. Cobbett had published an epitaph that appeared in the *Political Censor* for May 1796:

> Tom Paine for the Devil is surely a match;
> In hanging Old England he cheated Jack-Catch,
> In France (the first time such a thing had been seen)
> He cheated the watchful and sharp Guillotine,
> And at last, to the sorrow of all the beholders,
> He march'd out of life with his head on his shoulders.[6]

But Paine was still very much alive in France (he did not die until 1809) and still capable of producing one more polemic. Although Paine owed his release from prison to the intervention of James Monroe, American minister to France, he felt that Washington had been indifferent to his fate.[7] Paine's return to life was trumpeted by a letter to Washington published in Bache's *Aurora* in November 1796. The two-year wait before Paine aired his complaint, its timing to appear on the eve of the American election, its publication by the pro-French Bache, and the inclusion within the complaint of an attack on features of the constitution which were resented by the pro-French faction in America, all strongly suggested that Paine's letter was still another effort by the French to influence American opinion against the federalists.

Cobbett, who disliked Paine for many reasons (Paine was not only anti-religion and anti-British but was, allegedly, a wife-beater, a bigamist, and a drunk) and who had inherited from his father a strong attachment to Washington, wrote a forceful tract in Washington's defense. In two sets of parallel columns Cobbett compared the harsh words Paine now used with the eulogies Paine had applied to the same subjects four years before in the *Rights of Man*. Paine now contended that the vices of the constitution were "naturally to be expected," since it was "a copy, not quite so base as the original, of the form of the British government." In 1792, Cobbett pointed out, Paine had called the American government the "only real Republic . . . that now exists" and "the admiration and model" of the present world. Paine now charged that Washington had been a poor general ("Old Mrs.

Thompson, the house-keeper of headquarters . . . could have done it as well") and that as president he had become the "patron of the fraud," "treacherous in private friendship," and "a hypocrite in public life." In the *Rights of Man,* Paine had praised Washington's "benevolence" and his "exemplary virtue."[8]

No matter what Cobbett or anyone else might have said in Washington's defense, the president was deeply wounded by these attacks on the service he had rendered to his country and on his character as a man. He was, therefore, quite ready to turn over the cares of office to John Adams. The day after the inauguration Adams wrote to his wife, Abigail, that during the formal ceremonies he had noticed that Washington's "countenance was as serene and unclouded as the day. He seemed to me to enjoy a triumph over me. Methought I heard him say, 'Ay! I am fairly out and you fairly in! See which of us will be happiest!' "[9]

Adams's inaugural address, in addition to giving "the old boy a little more oil," was directed at the issue that had created so much trouble for Washington: the perennial question of dealing with the changing leadership of the French revolution. Adams held out the olive branch, speaking of his "personal esteem for the French nation, formed in a residence of seven years chiefly among them, and a sincere desire to preserve the friendship which has been so much for the honor and interest of both nations." He also promised "an earnest endeavor to . . . remove every colorable pretence of complaint."[10] Bache's *Aurora* was ecstatic: "although the task will be an arduous one, [it] cannot fail of giving the highest satisfaction to his constituents. It is a course of conduct which they have long been earnestly looking for in the Executive of the Union."[11]

The *Aurora*'s ecstacy was not long-lasting. Between the date of the inaugural address and the opening of congress two months later, Adams received exceedingly upsetting news: The French Directory had refused to receive Charles Pinckney, who had been appointed by Washington as minister to France, and had notified the outgoing minister, James Monroe, that they would receive none "until after a reparation of the grievances demanded of the American Government, and which the French Republic has a right to expect." Pinckney was ordered to leave France, and Monroe departed after a high-handed lecture from the president of the Directory, described by Adams, when he reported to congress on May 16, as "studiously marked with indignities towards the Government of the United States."[12]

Unfortunately, the indignities were not limited to talk. Up to the time of the ratification of the Jay treaty in 1796 the French had intermittently honored the 1778 Treaty of Amity and Commerce with the United States, but now all semblance of compliance was abandoned. The French did not declare war against the Americans. Instead, they issued letters of marque by the hundreds to shipowners, operating from the islands they held in the West Indies – principally Santo Domingo, Guadaloupe, and Martinique – and these descended like aroused hornets on the hundreds of American vessels, mostly small ships, engaged in the West Indian trade. Apparently letters of marque were even issued to American shipowners willing to participate in the profitable trade of capturing ships operated by their fellow countrymen.[13] Insurance premiums for American merchant vessels in the Caribbean trade, which had been 6 percent of the combined value of hull and cargo per voyage, rose to 15 percent and then to 25 percent

Masthead of *Porcupine's Gazette*. The origin of the name "Peter Porcupine" is not known, but Cobbett made the most of it. His daily newspaper *Porcupine's Gazette*, published 1797–9, attained the largest circulation of any contemporary newspaper in America

in 1797.[14] Events were moving so rapidly that Cobbett decided that they could no longer be adequately reported in the *Political Censor* issued at monthly intervals. He therefore replaced it by a daily paper called *Porcupine's Gazette*.[15] The first issue appeared on March 4, 1797, the day of Adams's inauguration. In it Cobbett declared that he felt "the strongest partiality for the cause of order and good government, such as we live under, and against everything that is opposed to it."[16] Thereafter *Porcupine's Gazette* regularly and conscientiously recorded the plundering of the American merchant marine by its erstwhile friends. In its first week of publication, an article satirically headed "French Fraternity" reported that French privateers and gunboats had captured and carried into Santo Domingo fifty-four vessels in the course of about one month, of which forty-two had been condemned, three had been abandoned, and seven were awaiting trial, with only two having been cleared. Throughout the month of March 1797 individual episodes were featured: Captain Benjamin Henderson of Salem, Massachusetts, captured by a French privateer, was beaten until he was black and blue, and robbed of cash and goods to the amount of £350. Captain Thomas Calvert was starved in prison after his boat and cargo were condemned. Captain Henry Holden was robbed of his watch, a barrel of flour, "all his cabin stores, firewood ... and everything they could see." Captain Town of Philadelphia had $16,000 stolen from him.[17] American sailors captured by the French raiders were traded like prisoners of war for French prisoners captured by the British. Meanwhile, the American government forbade the arming of its merchant ships on the ground that arming "raises a presumption that it is done with hostile intentions against some one of the belligerent nations."[18] Cobbett had provocatively written: "I have heard, or read, of a fellow that was so accustomed to be kicked, that he could distinguish by the feel, the sort of leather that assailed his posteriors. Are our buttocks arrived at this perfection of sensibility?"[19]

A declaration of war by the Americans would, at best, have been little more than a gesture. The American army of some 2,000 men was barely adequate to restrain the Indians on the western frontiers.[20] There was no navy of any kind. The construction of six frigates had been authorized by congress in 1794, but work on them had ceased in the following year and had not been resumed until 1796, and then only on three.[21] Even this tiny fleet would not be in the water until 1798. Adams followed the only practical course available. He sent a peace mission to Paris, as he had virtually promised to do in his inaugural address. The mission, appointed in July 1797, contained elements that implied both willingness to compromise and the clear suggestion that the compromise could not go too far, for it consisted of Elbridge Gerry, a known friend of France; federalist lawyer John Marshall, close associate of George Washington; and the previously rejected Charles Pinckney. The mission arrived in Paris in October 1797, requested an interview with Talleyrand, the French foreign minister, and promptly found itself party to a sequence of events more appropriate to a comic opera than a diplomatic negotiation. Instead of securing an official audience with Talleyrand, the mission was waited on by three gentlemen without official status. These three, designated X, Y, and Z in the subsequent reports of the American mission, claimed to speak for Talleyrand. They sometimes came singly, and sometimes two of them came together, but they came with a common message: The Americans must pay money, "a great deal of money" (finally fixed at £50,000), as a *douceur* to the Directory; they must arrange a loan to France of thirty-two million Dutch florins; President Adams must retract his comments about the French in his May 16 address to congress.[22]

If France had declared war on the United States, the impact would hardly have been as startling as the release of the XYZ story to the American congress in April 1798. "The Jacobins in Senate & House were struck dumb, and opend not their mouths," reported Abigail Adams.[23] The federalists, at no loss for words, promptly introduced bills for improved coastal defenses, an expanded navy, the arming of merchant ships, and the establishment of a provisional army. All such measures to arm the nation against the French had hitherto been successfully resisted by the democrats in congress. Whether they would succeed once again was the issue of the hour. Cobbett's first contribution to this issue was a complete failure. Seeing the funny side of the XYZ episode, he quickly produced a 26-page poem in Hudibrastic couplets describing the negotiations. In *French Arrogance; or, "The Cat Let Out of the Bag"*, published in May 1798, the French were properly boastful:

> . . . Buonaparte the Gallic god,
> Who has *ten millions* at his nod,
> . . . cou'd if he was firmly bent
> Turn upside down your continent.

The American commissioners were properly manly:

> We will not Adams e'er disgrace,
> Nor from his speech a word erase;
> He spoke what every heart shou'd feel;
> And prov'd his patriotic zeal.

But Cobbett could not resist adding a few Rabelaisian touches in describing the approach that had been made to the three dignified American commissioners (after X, Y, and Z had failed to budge them) by the charming Madame de Villette, another of Talleyrand's agents:

> I love all handsome Plenipos,
> Such *satisfaction* with them goes;
> They have most noble gen'rous hearts,
> And then of course they're men of *parts*,
> Of *sense* I mean, and penetration,
> And schollars at negociation.[24]

Not many Americans were prepared to laugh at the humorous side of French corruption, for Cobbett's account book indicates that only ninety copies of *French Arrogance* were sold to other booksellers.[25] (We have no record of the number sold at the Cobbett shop on Second Street.) However, Cobbett's second response to the XYZ episode was one of his greatest successes. He had recently received a pamphlet translated from the German describing French cruelties during their invasion of Bavaria. This he abridged and reprinted with appropriate comments of his own, under the title *The Cannibals' Progress*. In the portion of the text written by him, Cobbett reminded his readers of the earlier sanguinary French conquests of Holland, Genoa, Venice, and Switzerland:

Thus, *Americans,* have *all the republics of Europe,* for their endeavouring to *conciliate* with France; for their tame submission to *injury* and *insult;* for their whining, cringing, and crawling for *peace,* been finally rewarded by the subversion of their governments, by the loss of their property, by the massacre of their people, by being reduced to the last degree of national wretchedness and disgrace, and by being rendered the scorn and contempt of the universe.

Independence, with all its attendant blessings, is yet within your power; but as it was obtained by arms, so it must be maintained; and you have not a month, nay, not a day left you to consider, whether you shall assume those arms, or basely bend your necks to the galling yoke of the insolent, blood-thirsty tyrants of France.[26]

The Cannibals' Progress was published in June 1798. According to Cobbett, over 100,000 copies were sold. "The little boys and the poor people buy it, and it is read in every family."[27] It fanned the flame of patriotism and anti-French sentiment that had spread across the country. The critical bills in congress moved forward rapidly under the slogan "Millions for defense, but not a cent for tribute." By the end of July 1798, twenty laws for arming the country had been enacted by congress, a navy department had been created, and George Washington had been recalled from retirement to become commanding general of the newly authorized provisional army. Alexander Hamilton was appointed second-in-command.[28]

But the external defenses were not the only concern of the Adams administration. Cobbett had constantly stressed the internal threats to the nation's safety from disaffected persons within the country: the French sympathizers, including the many recent immigrants, particularly those from Ireland, who had been rebels in their homelands. In May 1798 Cobbett had published a short pamphlet entitled *Detection of a Conspiracy, Formed by the United Irishmen, with the Evident Intention of Aiding the Tyrants of France in Subverting the Government of the United States of America.* The pamphlet contained a copy of the declaration and constitution of the American Society of United Irishmen dated August 8, 1797 with comments by Cobbett designed to show that the real purpose of the society was to upset the United States government. The pamphlet, by itself, would hardly convince a twentieth-century reader, but those of 1798 were almost certainly influenced by several contemporary elements: The Irish pouring into the United States at the end of the eighteenth century in such large numbers were an especially unruly lot. "Of all the people I have met here," wrote the Irish patriot Wolfe Tone while visiting America, "the Irish are incontestably the most offensive. If you meet a confirmed blackguard you may be sure he is Irish."[29] The intention of the Irish to unite with the French against the British was an established fact, and the French had boasted more than once of their powerful friends in America. The American mission to France was told that "we have a very considerable party in America who are strongly in our interest."[30] The *Moniteur,* organ of official information under Napoleon, announced that "the *friends of liberty* in the United States, supported by a great part of the House of Representatives, will probably not wait for the next elections, but in the mean time will destroy the fatal influence of the President and Senate *by a Revolution.*"[31] Irishman John Burk, living in New York, was alleged to have declared that "he believed the French would come here, and he wished to God they would, when every scoundrel in favour of this Government would be put to the guillotine."[32] Cobbett probably expressed the view of a great number of conservatives when he stated: "I should not wonder if there were, and I really believe there are, thousands of desperate villains already *enrolled in the service of France,* and ready to declare in her favour, the moment an opportunity arrives."[33] There were approximately 700,000 blacks in the United States; might there be a Negro uprising such as had occurred in French Santo Domingo?

Out of a welter of such considerations rose the new Naturalization Act and the alien and sedition laws passed by congress in June and July of 1798 closely following the external defense measures. Under these latest acts the residence requirement for would-be citizens was increased from five to fourteen years; aliens could be deported by presidential order without trial; combinations opposing the execution of national laws were made illegal, as were malicious and scandalous writing against the president and other government officials. The fear of internal disorder led to even more stringent acts in Britain during the last decade of the eighteenth century: the suspension of habeas corpus in 1794, the Seditious Meetings and Assembly Act in 1795, and the Combination Acts in 1799 and 1800.

Cobbett was a warm advocate of such legislation: "Surely we need a sedition law to keep our own rogues from cutting our throats, and an alien law to prevent the invasion by a host of foreign rogues to assist them."[34] In the belief that the new laws would be enforced to put many of the Jacobin journalists out of business, Cobbett compiled a list of the worst of them. The *Baltimore Intelligencer* was described as "a sink of abuse, scurrility and democracy" whose editor "was an imp of democracy, as wicked & depraved as his master the Devil."[35]

At this point Cobbett had reached the peak of his popularity in America. *Porcupine's Gazette* was the most widely read paper in the country. As early as August 1797, five months after the first issue,

daily sales had climbed to more than 2,500, which was comparable to
that of the successful London papers of the period.[36] Peter Porcupine
no longer limited his scope to top-level governmental decisions, but
became the arbiter of both public and private virtue. As such, he
periodically pointed out American shortcomings, including the "great
depravity and corruption" of their morals, the low level of their liter-
acy, and the poor quality of their officials.[37] He ridiculed the Pennsylvania legislature's description of a new highway as an "artificial
road," declaring that more sensible people would have called it a
"turnpike."[38] He criticized the composition of the Philadelphia board
of health on the ground that doctors composed "nearly half of its
members."[39] He scorned the wax figures displayed in the museum
opened in Philadelphia by the painter Charles Willson Peale: "if you
mean to have my company, get me half a dozen Democrats stuffed
with straw."[40] He thought that the ladies of Middletown, Connecticut
behaved "too much in the bacchanalian style" when they celebrated
Independence Day by meeting in a grove where, after a cold collation
and six patriotic toasts, they were *joined by a number of gentlemen!*[41]
These gratuitous observations on his neighbors were used as amusing
fillers to flesh out Cobbett's daily criticism of the president, his cabinet, and various members of congress. John Quincy Adams, son of
the president and later himself president (1825–9), quietly pointed
out in a family letter:

If an American should go to London and set up a daily newspaper, and fill it
from one week's end to another with abuse however ingenious and witty upon
the English king, Parliament, judges and people, upon their friends and
allies, upon every man and measure which should cross his own ideas of right,
or his national partialities as an American, Lord Kenyon would very shortly
send him to muse upon the liberty of the press in the king's bench prison, or
a cockney mob would spare the courts of justice all trouble about him, by
breaking his head and pulling down his print shop about his ears.[42]

Despite this criticism, John Quincy Adams was a genuine admirer of
Cobbett: "I am convinced that his publications have done much good
in our country, and I heartily wish that many of our well meaning
printers, instead of engaging themselves in silly and unequal contests
with him, would catch a little of his wit and humor."[43]

Cobbett himself, as an individual, was an object of enormous interest. "I have a great curiosity to see the Creature," wrote Abigail
Adams. "There is a strange mixture in him. He can write very hand-
somely, and he can descend & be as low, and vulgar as a fish
woman."[44] Cobbett became one of the tourist attractions of Philadelphia and the subject of numerous stories: "As to Porcupine I was this
day told of a very witty bon mot of his. Whether it be genuine or not,

I cannot tell, I think it may be. – A Gentleman – a strong democrat, went to his shop and entered into political dispute with him. After some time he was going away, but turning round, he asked for a bundle of quills. Cobbet gave him them: 'These', said the Gentleman, 'are, I suppose, Porcupine's quills.' 'They *were*', said Cobbet, 'but they are now *Goose quills*.' "[45]

Cobbett had also acquired a substantial reputation in England, where most of his writings had been reprinted, and was thus assured of an outlet for his talents in his homeland when the moment came to return. "Pray tell me something of Peter Porcupine," wrote a Sussex vicar to his brother in the United States in April 1796. "I am one of his admirers, of whom there are many in England. I think America ought to be vain of him."[46] While the collected works of most authors appear at the end of their lives, or even more often posthumously, editions of Cobbett's collected works were being published in 1796, when he was thirty-two years old and only two years after he had initially come to public notice. The first volume of these collected works went through four printings in twelve months.[47]

Cobbett could take credit (he probably took a little too much credit) for dramatic changes that had occurred in American attitudes since that time:

It is astonishing, but not less astonishing than true, that it was I, and I alone, that re-exalted the character of Great Britain in America . . . Not a man, 'till I took up my pen, dared mention the British Government with respect. The very best of the newspapers were obliged to satirize it occasionally in order to keep well with their readers. My God! how things are changed! The same presses, and under the very same editors, that used to call the king a monster, now sing forth his praises incessantly. I have *beat* the rascals into reason.[48]

The French reaction to Cobbett's writings is a fair measure of their influence. In 1798 Talleyrand complained to the United States government that the British were paying for pamphlets published in America "containing insults and calumnies against the French Republick & her agents." Robert Liston, British minister in the United States, explained to Lord Grenville, foreign secretary, that Talleyrand was referring to the publications of William Cobbett, "a man of uncommon ability & strength of mind," who had "attacked the French revolution and its partisans with equal spirit and success." Liston assured Grenville that Cobbett had not been paid for his articles.[49]

Cobbett had reason to be vain. He had put down Joseph Priestley, one of the great controversialists of the period: "The Goliath of Literature has fled from the sling of the shepherd's boy."[50] He had been on the winning side in the Jay treaty controversy, and in the election of 1796. He had not only been in the forefront of the battle against the Jacobin faction, but now he had them nicely on the run. His remaining ambition was to get the United States to join forces with Britain in its war against France, an aim he shared with Alexander Hamilton, Theodore Sedgwick, and others of the more conservative federalists. Things seemed to be moving satisfactorily in that direction after the XYZ episode. "The Marseillaise," which had almost become a national anthem in America, was loudly hissed when played at a public gathering in Baltimore. Eleven hundred young men of Philadelphia marched in the streets to demonstrate their readiness to take up arms in defense of their country. A similar demonstration took place in New York.[51] The American cockade, a rose of black ribbon with a white fastening, which had been worn on the hats of soldiers in the revolution, became the symbol of support for the government. "The black cockade is now universally worn in town and country," an observer reported. (In derision, a Jacobin of Roxbury, Massachusetts appeared on July 4, 1798, American Independence Day, wearing a cockade made of dried cow dung.)[52] The cities of New York and Philadelphia, following the example set by the town of Newburyport, Massachusetts, voted to build armed ships to be loaned to the federal navy.[53] John Adams transmitted a four-sentence message to congress in June 1798 saying: "I will never send another minister to France without assurances that he will be received, respected, and honoured as the representative of a great, free, powerful, and independent nation." Many of the high federalists "considered this sentence the equivalent of a declaration of war, or at least of an intention to make war."[54] The new United States navy, taking to sea in the summer of 1798, captured two armed French vessels in August and September, and by year-end had established bases in the Caribbean for the protection of American merchant ships.[55] The attorney general gave an opinion that "a maritime war existed between France and the United States, authorized by both nations."[56]

The American successes in the war continued into 1799. In the first nine days of February, three more armed French vessels, including the frigate *Insurgente,* were captured.[57] Cobbett, with one eye on the British struggle against the traditional enemy, could not have hoped for more. Then came the shock.

A democratic paper, the *True American,* announced that President Adams proposed to reopen peace negotiations with France, and to entrust such negotiations to William Vans Murray, minister at The Hague. Cobbett angrily denounced the report, stating that he had not made any inquiry into the matter, nor did he think it worth while to do so:

I have such respect for the President, too much confidence in his wisdom, to suppose the thing possible . . .
And shall we believe, that a negotiation, which was thought of such impor-

tance, as to require the united wisdom of three of the most profound and experienced politicians in America, can now be entrusted to one man, and he of very slender political abilities?[58]

Although it was like a bad dream to Cobbett, there was no relief in the awakening. The report was true. Adams had received indirect assurances from more than one source that the French were now prepared to deal honorably with an American envoy. The proposal for new negotiations and the designation of Murray, "one of the most stunning surprises in the history of American foreign policy,"[59] was submitted to the Senate on February 18, 1799. After discussions with other leading federalists, Adams agreed to expand the mission to three members, a change for which Cobbett claimed credit.[60] If credit was due, it was his last service to the Adams administration, although he remained in America for another year. As events were to prove, the crisis with France had passed. The issue of Franco-American relations, which had helped split Washington's cabinet into federalists and democrats in 1793–6, assisted in splitting the federalists into two groups in 1797–9: the "high federalists" led by Alexander Hamilton, who favored the hard line with France (to which Cobbett was naturally attached), and the "small federalists," or moderates, led by Adams. This alignment had been steadily growing more apparent. "Poor sinking Cobbett" read an article in the *Philadelphia Gazette* at the peak of the anti-French sentiment in America, "having no more Frenchmen in this country to devour, begins to cram his insatiable maw of defamation with federalists."[61] The moment it was rumored that Adams had made new overtures to France, Cobbett predicted that this step would be "instantaneously followed by the loss of every friend worth his preserving."[62] It probably lost Adams the chance of a second term as president. Adams knew the price. He later wrote: "I desire no other inscription over my gravestone than 'Here lies John Adams, who took upon himself the responsibility of the peace with France in the year 1800.' "[63] Adams credited Cobbett with much of the blame for his failure to gain reelection, claiming that "Porcupine's Gazette and Fenno's Gazette from the moment of the mission to France, aided, countenanced, and encouraged by *soi-disant* Federalists in Boston, New York and Philadelphia, have done more to shuffle the cards into the hands of Jacobin leaders than all the acts of administration and all policy of opposition from the commencement of the government."[64]

After the events of February 1799, Cobbett's influence in America declined even more rapidly than that of Adams, for while Adams was still the leader of the larger part of the federalists, Cobbett's following was now limited to the extreme right wing of that disjointed party. It was rumored that Cobbett had been ordered by the president to leave the United States, but this Cobbett stoutly denied: "I *know* that he never thought of ordering me away." This strongly suggests that Cobbett had consulted Timothy Pickering, secretary of state, with whom he seems to have been on especially cordial terms.[65] As might be expected, Cobbett's paper suffered a severe decline in circulation. It continued to be published as a daily for only six months after the new mission to France had been announced. Then, with the outbreak of another yellow fever epidemic in Philadelphia, the paper dwindled to a weekly, finally expiring altogether at the end of 1799.

Despite the gloomy predictions of Cobbett and others among the high federalists, the United States survived a treaty signed with France in 1800, just as it had survived the Jay treaty signed with Britain in 1796. The erroneous predictions stemmed from a commonly held belief that America, as an extension of Europe, must be either for Britain and against France or for France and against Britain. One exceptional French official of the time saw it more clearly:

Our agents wished to see only two political parties in the United States, the French party and the English party; but there is a middle party, much larger, composed of the most estimable men of the other two parties. This party, whose existence we have not even suspected, is the American party which loves its country above all and for whom preferences either for France or England are only accessory and often passing affections.[66]

6 · Some personal feuds

I have not yet brought myself to adopt the Quaker maxim, that it is the *second* blow which is most sinful.

COBBETT'S NATIVE BELLIGERENCE, sharpened by his training under General Hugh Debbeig, found a natural outlet in American journalism of the 1790s. Abusive language directed at Britain had become a habit in America during the eighteen-year period between parliament's enactment of the Stamp Act in 1765 and the withdrawal of British troops in 1783. The end of the war was followed by a huge influx of immigrants (the population more than doubled from 1783 to 1800). Many were rough and turbulent, often rebels in their homelands, to whom angry words came naturally. Not surprisingly, angry language appeared in the American press, and it was particularly pronounced in the democratic, anti-British newspapers where leadership was assumed by the youthful Benjamin Franklin Bache: He was only twenty-one years old when he established his *Aurora* in 1790 (and only twenty-nine when he died of yellow fever in 1798); his entire life prior to entering journalism had been colored by the violence and direction of revolutionary propaganda.[1] Cobbett accepted the practices as he found them, adopting the principle that "as much zeal might be shown in defending the general government and administration, as in accusing and traducing them; and that as great warmth would be admissible in the cause of virtue, order, and religion, as had long been tolerated in the wicked cause of villainy, insurrection, and blasphemy."[2]

Many of Cobbett's readers, even those friendly to the federalist cause, thought he went too far. Abigail Adams wrote that he "frequently injures the cause he means to advocate for want of prudence and discretion." Robert Liston, British minister to the United States, unsuccessfully tried to persuade Cobbett to omit from his writings "that gross personal abuse which has frequently marred their complete effect." In contrast, at least one contemporary thought his

91

"blunt vulgar language" suited and had great effect among "the middle and town classes."[3] Years later Cobbett offered this justification:

My opponents contended that *nothing* was good that belonged to England. I contended that nothing was good that *did not* belong to her. I was quite sincere; and I solemnly declare, that I believed, that even the poultry and apples were not half so good as those in England.

You may call this folly, enthusiasm, fanaticism; but you cannot call it baseness. The principle by which I was actuated was good. It was love *for my country* . . . and . . . I was in too high a state of irritation, to enter into a fair discussion of the merits of her cause. Besides, my antagonists were equally violent, and had, in most cases, been the aggressors.[4]

Responding to Cobbett's zeal and warmth, personal antagonisms developed almost as a matter of course. The simplest of these exceedingly complicated contests was Cobbett's feud with Noah Webster, the great American lexicographer to whom we owe the record of and sanctions for some of the most characteristic differences between English and American pronunciation and spelling.[5] Webster had migrated from Connecticut to New York to become the editor of the federalist paper the *Minerva*. He had not yet written the first of his several dictionaries, and was known principally for his elementary spelling book, "the Blue-Backed Speller," which ultimately became a standard school textbook throughout the United States – year after year selling a million or more copies. Obviously intelligent, he also was a vain man; he was opinionated; and he was, at times, inconsistent; and these were three traits which Cobbett – finding full measure in himself – detested in others. And while Webster was a federalist, it developed that he was not high enough to suit Cobbett; even worse, he was one of those "most estimable men" who tended to place England on the same footing as France in its relations with the United States. Early in 1797 it had appeared likely that the *Minerva* and the newly established *Porcupine's Gazette* would join hands as "friends of order" in supporting the federalist administration against the attacks of the Jacobin–democrat–republicans, but hardly a month had passed before verbal brickbats were flying back and forth between New York and Philadelphia over the issue of whether it was proper to link the American and British flags in joint display "against an ambitious enemy."[6] Two other men might have been able to debate this issue with a fair amount of goodwill, but not Cobbett, and surely not Cobbett with an antagonist as pugnacious as Webster. As those who fought with Cobbett were sure to learn, his tactics were not limited to a formal series of statements and responses, rebuttals and surrebuttals. Instead he kept up an incessant gunfire of hectoring and, as John Quincy Adams soberly put it, was not always "sufficiently careful to confine his censure within the limits of justice."[7] The shortcomings of Webster as seen through the eyes of Cobbett became a regular feature of *Porcupine's Gazette*. At the outset, Cobbett called Webster such names as "wretch," with the mollifying admission that he was "in the common concerns of life, a man of good sound understanding."[8] But a year later Webster had become a "spiteful viper" and a "tool in service of sans-culottism."[9] Webster's opinions, to which Cobbett took such violent exception, seems to have been nothing more than the quite widely held view that the Americans did not want to get too closely allied with *either* Britain or France.

One of the stories about Webster which Cobbett originated or popularized related to Webster's appearance in Philadelphia to take up his appointment as teacher in the Episcopal Academy. Dr. Rush (another of Cobbett's major antagonists) met him and exclaimed: " 'How do you do, my dear friend. I congratulate you on your arrival in Philadelphia.' Webster replied, 'You may if you please, Sir, congratulate Philadelphia on the occasion.' "[10]

In Cobbett's mock "Will and Testament" published in April 1797, he bequeathed to Webster "six Spanish milled dollars, to be expended on a new plate of his portrait at the head of his spelling-book, that which graces it at present being so ugly that it scares the children from their lessons."[11]

The sight of these two conservative champions expending their efforts on a public free-for-all must have been distressing to other members of the party; early in the battle we find Webster writing to fellow federalist Jedidiah Morse, the distinguished geographer:

Porcupine is evidently attempting to create or rally an English party in our country as violent and devoted to foreign government as the French party. I judged it prudent to apprize my countrymen of these intentions. But if he is not attempting this, his prejudices, his birth, and his violent principles will do great injury to the true American interests. Besides he is a mere bully.[12]

Bully? In a sense, yes. Cobbett was a bully just as were the Old Testament prophets. Like them, he believed in the holiness of his cause, placing it above any personal advantage. Yet Cobbett nearly always directed his blasts at someone well above his level in social standing, education, and public position. Can a ploughboy be said to "bully" a prime minister?

Cobbett's quarrels with Webster were slight – one might almost say nonexistent – compared with his campaigns against the democrats. His fundamental disagreement with the democrats stemmed from his belief based on his observation of the French scene, that atheism (or deism) and an egalitarian society, including a broader franchise, led directly to lawlessness. As his stay in America lengthened, every rash

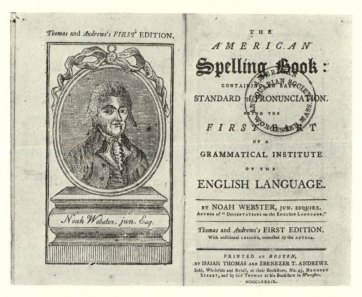

Noah Webster. This woodcut, a feature of Webster's *American Spelling Book*, used by every schoolchild in America, caused Cobbett, in his mock will, to leave Webster six Spanish milled dollars for a replacement portrait, "the present being so ugly that it scares the children from their lessons"

act, miscarriage of justice, or evidence of corruption was ascribed by him to the corroding influence of republicanism. "Health," he wrote in 1820, "you will hardly fail to secure by early-rising, exercise, sobriety, and abstemiousness as to food."[13] "Freedom and order," he might have written in 1796, "you will hardly fail to secure by an established Christian church, parliamentary government, and a class-ordered society headed by a hereditary monarch." Cobbett was for a system that produced a society in which the average man could live happily. Looking around, he decided that the French system did not produce such a society, but the British did. This was the foundation of his earliest political philosophy.

Cobbett's initial attacks on French principles were directed mainly against the action of groups of American democrats: the groups that had welcomed Priestley and the French minister Adet and those that fought the Jay treaty. Gradually, certain names began to appear in Cobbett's writing with greater frequency – the Virginia political philosophers Jefferson, Madison, and Monroe, and the Pennsylvania activists John Swanwick and Albert Gallatin, members of the federal

94

House of Representatives; Mathew Carey, the Philadelphia publisher and his brother James; Benjamin Franklin Bache, editor of the *Aurora;* Alexander Dallas, secretary of state of Pennsylvania; and Thomas McKean, chief justice of the state supreme court. "There are no gallows in Pennsylvania" was one of Cobbett's frequent comments on his numerous Pennsylvania enemies. Some of Cobbett's targets (including the three distinguished Virginians) endured him in silence. Swanwick, as we have seen, essayed a brief and highly unsuccessful response to Cobbett's gibes. Mathew Carey, stung by Cobbett's reference to him as "O'Carey" and the charge that he was associated with the United Irishmen, sought revenge in a pamphlet in which he abused Cobbett as roundly as Cobbett had abused him, and followed this up with a series of bitter denunciations in verse.[14] The newspaper *Aurora,* under the editorship of Bache and his successor, William Duane, along with the lesser democratic papers, kept up a continuous barrage of charges and countercharges, but they probably caused Cobbett more amusement than anguish.[15] Only the jurist, Judge Thomas McKean, was able to draw blood.

McKean, sixty-two years old in 1796, had served as chief justice of the highest court in Pennsylvania for nearly twenty years. Earlier, he had developed a successful law practice, had been a warm advocate of cutting ties between the American colonies and the mother country, and had signed the Declaration of Independence. McKean's portrait, painted by Rembrandt Peale, confirms a description of him: "Boldly energetic, courageously independent, never flinching before an opposition however great; always driving straight to his point . . . and withal, proud, vain, and domineering in his ways; manifesting pronounced predilections for his friends and inveterate scorn for his enemies, his personality readily aroused antagonisms." These are the words of a McKean biographer.[16] Those of one of his enemies – "vain conceited rusty old weathercock" – round out the picture.[17]

It took very little, at any time, to arouse Cobbett's animosity, and he found much in McKean that was distasteful. In addition to being a democrat and "a little, upstart tyrant," he seems to have been henpecked (Cobbett often referred to him as "Mrs. McKean's husband") and to have occasionally enjoyed a "morning's dram."[18] Cobbett accused McKean of "boozing and bawling with . . . the rabble" when he attended a public banquet on February 9, 1797 (called by Cobbett a "festival of fools") to celebrate the anniversary of the 1778 alliance between the United States and France.[19] When McKean solicited an office for his son (having refused to do so for a friend), Cobbett described this as "an instance of dirty meanness, hardly to be equalled

95

in the annals of democracy . . . A *Chief Justice!* Good Heaven, preserve me from his clutches. I would almost as soon, God forgive me, fall under those of *his wife!*"[20]

These last pleasantries were published in July 1797, only a few weeks before Cobbett began to realize what Judge McKean's clutches might entail. The first round between McKean and Cobbett involved McKean's prospective son-in-law, Don Carlos Martinez de Yrujo, Spanish minister to the United States. Chevalier de Yrujo had arrived in America early in 1796, in the midst of the controversy over the Jay treaty. A few months later Spain allied itself with France by declaring war against Great Britain. The Jay treaty had been signed and ratified, but Yrujo began a newspaper war with Timothy Pickering, American secretary of state, over the effect of the treaty on Spain and over Yrujo's assertion, which he had imparted to Pickering, that the British were preparing to attack Spanish Louisiana from a base in Canada, thus violating American territory.[21] Cobbett joined this contest with his usual enthusiasm, and in the course of his discussion on the merits of the case, he frequently referred to Yrujo and his employer in terms that were not highly respectful. Among other things, the Spanish minister was called "Don Sans-culotta de Carmagnola Minor" and "the little Don"; his communication to Pickering was called "stupid, vain, insolent"; and the king of Spain was called a "degenerate Prince" whose acts were "directed by the crooked politics of France."[22] These and other assaults were part of a repetitious campaign appearing day after day in *Porcupine's Gazette* during the first three weeks of July 1797. On July 21 Yrujo complained to Timothy Pickering, the secretary of state, and three days later his letter of complaint was transmitted to the attorney general to determine whether the papers would support a charge against Cobbett.[23] No sooner had Yrujo filed his complaint than a new idea struck him (or, more likely, was suggested to him by a third party): that his case would stand a better chance in the state courts of Pennsylvania, where McKean, whose daughter Yrujo was courting, presided as chief justice. By letter dated July 31, Yrujo asked Pickering to transfer the case to the state court, and when Pickering refused to accede to the request, Yrujo sent him a second letter making still another plea for the transfer.[24] By this time a federal action had already been initiated against Cobbett, and on August 8 (eighteen days after Yrujo's first letter of complaint) Cobbett had appeared before federal judge Peters and given bond to answer the charges against him at the next term of the court.

Ten days later, on August 18, Judge McKean issued a warrant for Cobbett's arrest returnable in the Pennsylvania state court, charging

Thomas McKean, signer of the Declaration of Independence, chief justice of the supreme court of Pennsylvania, governor of the state, called by one of his enemies "a vain conceited rusty old weathercock." The portrait is attributed to Rembrandt Peale

Cobbett with publishing libelous matter against the king of Spain and his minister. Cobbett was immediately arrested and ninety minutes later was brought before Judge McKean at the judge's home. He was not accompanied by counsel. McKean declared that Cobbett had the choice of going to jail immediately or giving security "to be of good behaviour towards the Commonwealth and all her liege people until the next court of Oyer and Terminer." In accordance with the terms laid down by McKean, Cobbett entered into a recognizance in the sum of $2,000, and two of Cobbett's friends, Benjamin Davies, a bookseller, and Richard North, a stonecutter, executed additional recognizances in the amount of $1,000 each.[25] McKean's imposition was of doubtful legality, as the only specific requirement in any Pennsylvania statute for the giving of such security was in the case of a threat of physical violence to a person or his property.

In August 1797 Philadelphia was in the grip of another epidemic of yellow fever, and the court did not meet until November. The bill of indictment presented to the grand jury on November 27, 1797, describing Cobbett as "a person of wicked and turbulent disposition," claimed that libels appeared in three articles published in *Porcupine's Gazette* which were not included in the federal complaint. As it happened, none of the three articles had been written by Cobbett: two of them were letters from *Gazette* readers, and the third was a reprint of an article that had appeared in the federalist *Gazette of the United States* edited by John Fenno.[26]

The "Hon. Thomas McKean Esq." was one of the witnesses before the grand jury; he also acted as judge, delivering himself of a long and ringing charge. To the portion of the charge relating to the law of libel, largely lifted from Blackstone, McKean added some comments of his own:

Every one who has in him the sentiments of either a Christian or gentleman, cannot but be highly offended at the envenomed scurrility that had raged in pamphlets and newspapers printed in Philadelphia for several years past, insomuch that libelling has become a kind of national crime . . . This evil, so scandalous to our Government, and detestable in the eyes of all good men, calls aloud for redress.

After commenting that defamatory language in such pamphlets directed towards the French and their allies had "a tendency to . . . provoke a war between sister republics," McKean declared:

Impressed with the duties of my station, I have used some endeavours for checking these evils, by binding over the editor and printer of one of them, licentious and virulent beyond all former example, to his good behaviour, but he still perseveres in his nefarious publications; he has ransacked our language for terms of reproach and insult . . . It is now with you, Gentlemen of the Grand Jury, to animadvert on his conduct; without your aid it cannot be corrected.[27]

The grand jury, made up of nineteen citizens of Philadelphia, was split almost down the middle, nine voting for indictment and ten voting against. In the quaint language of the clerk of court, "the said Bill was returned Ignoramus [we ignore] by the said Grand Jury." The split in the grand jury was on party lines, the democrats voting for the indictment and the federalists voting against it.[28] A few months later a federal grand jury voted down the second indictment.[29]

Cobbett had won. But McKean made it plain that if Cobbett had won, he had only won the first skirmish and not the war. The attorney general of the state commenced another action against Cobbett and his two sureties, Davies and North, claiming that the three recognizances, in total amount of $4,000, had been forfeited by Cobbett's failure to maintain "good behaviour," as required by their terms. This action, returnable December 1797, was based on the allegation that between the date of the recognizances on August 18, 1797 and the date the court had convened in November 1797, Cobbett had published a number of libels on "the general government of the Union, the principles of republican government," and various individuals including Jefferson, Monroe, the king of Spain, the French and Spanish nations and their ministers, former Governor Mifflin, the deceased Benjamin Franklin, and David Rittenhouse.[30] Cobbett's attempt to remove this newest action to a federal court was also denied by McKean, but at the time no effort was made by the state attorney general to bring the suit to trial.[31]

In the midst of these cases originating from Yrujo's complaint, Cobbett found himself a defendant in another libel action for articles that had appeared in *Porcupine's Gazette,* although that paper had been in existence for only seven months. The new action was brought by the Philadelphia physician Dr. Benjamin Rush. Rush came under Cobbett's attack at almost the same time as Yrujo; first, for being a democrat, and second for being a democrat who believed that the yellow fever could be cured by massive purges and copious bleeding.[32] Rush's action against Cobbett was commenced in October 1797 while Philadelphia's second great yellow fever epidemic was still raging. During the 1793 epidemic Rush had tried every remedy known to him before developing his theory of "depletion," which he contended was appropriate for all ailments.[33] Specifically, yellow fever patients should be given "mercurial" purges three times daily, of ten grains of calomel and fifteen grains of jalap (five more grains of jalap than the strongest purges given to soldiers in the U.S. army), and should have as much as four quarts of blood drawn from the body.[34] If the patient

was brought to him early enough, yellow fever was no more dangerous, Rush declared, than "the measles or the influenza." At another
point he stated that it was about as offensive as "the common cold."[35]

Not all Philadelphia's doctors accepted Rush's drastic treatment.
This did not diminish the tenacity of Rush's belief in the cure. His
self-deception went so far that the refusal of other physicians to
administer his cure was attributed by him to envy and hatred: "They
blush at their mistakes, they feel for their murders."[36] Dr. Rush was
not a stupid person, but his character was blemished by an excessive
dose of vanity without any leavening sense of humor; and his judgment in this instance was further impaired by an error of fact: He
thought that the human body contained twelve quarts of blood, or
about twice the actual quantity.[37] This combination of vanity and factual error enabled him to conclude that each patient who recovered
did so because of, rather than despite, his treatment.

In a broader view, Rush was a man of exceptional ability. He had
been a friend of Franklin (no commendation to Cobbett) and of the
colonial leaders who became the first four presidents of the United
States: Washington, Adams, Jefferson, and Madison.[38] At the invitation of Sir Joshua Reynolds, he had dined with the Literary Club at
the Turk's Head, sitting between Sir Joshua and Oliver Goldsmith.
He was one of the fifty-six American demigods who signed the Declaration of Independence and had married the daughter of one of
the other fifty-five. He was a member of the American Philosophical
Society, and is regarded by twentieth-century American psychiatrists
as the founder of their profession. He also was "the most powerful
physician our nation has ever known. Sir William Osler's influence on
his colleagues did not compare with the influence of Rush, whose
medical theories were accepted by succeeding generations of practi-
tioners as direct from God."[39] For fifty years after Rush's death "half,
if not more, of all college-trained physicians in the United States
propagated views and prescribed cures absorbed from Rush's lectures
at the College of Philadelphia." Presumably most of his theories were
better founded than his cure for yellow fever.

Vanity was not the only trait shared by Rush and Cobbett. Rush,
like Cobbett, was a pugnacious and domineering man who made
many enemies. He was notoriously indiscreet; he thought prudence
was "a rascally virtue." He was a vehement reformer who disliked
mild reformers, particularly clergymen who were "too good to do
good." He was sustained by a high sense of his own rectitude: "Our
cause is the cause of virtue and heaven." He exultingly proclaimed:
"Expect to be persecuted for doing good, and learn to rejoice in persecution." All of these quotations from Rush could have come from

the pen of Cobbett.[40] These similarities in traits may explain similarities in conduct. Both Rush and Cobbett, as soldiers, had initiated or attempted to initiate court-martial proceedings against superior officers for corruption. Both, after reaching forty, were converted from arch-conservatives to radicals. But in 1796, when they first bumped heads, Cobbett was in his thirties and still a tory, while Rush, nearly twenty years older, had already turned his back on conservatism.

In March 1797 Peter Porcupine declared that he thought Dr. Rush was "a very fine man," but that he thought less of the republican principles expressed in Rush's eulogium of David Rittenhouse, deceased president of the American Philosophical Society.[41] Rush's medical quirks were noted only in passing. But with the reappearance of the yellow fever epidemic in the summer of 1797, both *Porcupine's Gazette* and the *Gazette of the United States,* edited by John Fenno, turned their attention to the pestilence that was raging in the city. And beginning in mid September 1797, the two papers attacked the cure identified with Rush. He was called a quack and Dr. Sangrado after the bloodletting doctor in *Gil Blas:*

> The times are ominous indeed
> When quack to quack cries, *Purge* and *bleed.*

Rush's "mercurial" purges (calomel is mercurous chloride) were included in the attacks:

Dr Rush, in that emphatical style which is peculiar to himself, calls *mercury* "the *Samson* of medicine." In his hands and in those of his partisans, it may, indeed, be justly compared to *Samson*; for I verily believe they have slain more Americans with it, than ever Samson slew of the Philistines. The Israelite slew his thousands, but the Rushites have slain their tens of thousands.

Additionally, Rush was accused of puffing his cure by writing anonymous letters to publications and producing self-serving correspondence with his fellow bleeders.[42]

In October 1797, after two weeks of such assaults, Rush sued Cobbett and Fenno for libel. Rush's trial counsel, who from the outset had doubted the advisability of the actions, managed to persuade his client that the suit against Fenno, at least, should be dropped.[43] Clearly Cobbett was the easier target: an alien with a reputation slightly soiled by the charges of libel which had been brought against him in the two Yrujo cases initiated earlier in 1797 and still pending when Rush commenced his action in October. Rush's case was noticed for December trial, and Cobbett's petition to remove the case to federal court was denied by McKean.[44] Rush's counsel chose to defer the trial from term to term, so that the matter did not finally come to hearing until December 1799.[45]

It seems possible, at this distance, that the Rush case might never have been brought to trial and that the Yrujo cases (including the action on the recognizances) might have been forgotten if Cobbett had not insisted that it be otherwise. The government and the public were fully preoccupied at this period with issues of transcending importance: the impending conflict between France and the United States, the startling XYZ episode revealed in April 1798, the ensuing excitement over preparations for war, and the passage of the controversial Alien and Sedition Acts in the summer of 1798. Cobbett, however, was not satisfied with his victory over McKean in the Yrujo case; he was determined to expose the judge's perfidy. The result was a pamphlet of over a hundred pages entitled *The Democratic Judge* issued in March 1798. A substantial portion of this pamphlet was devoted to a demonstration that the words Cobbett had published about the Spanish king and his minister, for which he had been so virulently assailed by McKean, were milder ("what the glare of a taper is to a city in flames") than the repeated vilification that had been heaped by the democratic press of America on George Washington, president of the United States, and on John Jay, its chief justice, or on the heads of various foreign states, including the king of England – yet there had been no prosecution for these statements.[46] The injustice of the action against Cobbett was magnified by the scandalous manner in which McKean had taken jurisdiction over a matter already pending in the federal courts, his dual role as witness and judge, the malice apparent in his charge to the grand jury, and his participation as judge in a case involving his daughter's fiancé. Plainly, McKean's judicial conduct was inexcusable. It is not possible to say, at this distance, whether McKean was a thoroughgoing scoundrel, or whether the angels would have excused his misuse of judicial process when weighed against Cobbett's nagging abuse of the McKean family. If so, they would have had much more to forgive before the rivalry ended. Cobbett, on his part, conscious of his own industry, intelligence, sobriety, and honesty, felt fully justified in saying whatever came into his head about others whose industry, intelligence, sobriety, or honesty seemed to him less perfect. So now Cobbett was not content with showing that the judge was wrong, but must needs keep the judge's wounds fresh by applying the lash of scurrility. This he did in a revised version of the pamphlet, renamed *The Republican Judge,* which was published in England in April 1798 for the purpose of showing that the people of England, under their monarch, were "happier and more free than the people of America" under a republican form of government.[47] In the revision (which was almost certain to be circulated in America) he added a two-page account of Judge McKean:

His private character is infamous. He beats his wife, and she beats him . . . He is a notorious drunkard. The whole bar, one lawyer excepted, signed a memorial, stating, that so great a drunkard was he, that, *after dinner, person and property were not safe in Pennsylvania*. He has been horsewhipped in the City Tavern, and kicked in the street for his insolence to particular persons; and yet this degraded wretch is *Chief Justice of the State*.[48]

No one, not even a chief justice, liked to be reminded of such homely truths. But Cobbett did not stop there. When McKean, early in 1799, announced that he was a candidate for governor of Pennsylvania, Cobbett declared that it was his duty to oppose McKean and that he would leave the state if McKean were elected:

I will never live six months under his sovereign sway. As soon as he is in his saddle, I shall begin to look out for a horse. Nor will a migration of this sort give me a moment's uneasiness. It would be a durable source of satisfaction to me, that I had scorned to live amongst a set of beings, who could voluntarily and deliberately choose such a man to reign over them.[49]

At the election held in September 1799, it developed that approximately 54 percent of those voting in Pennsylvania were beings of this sort.[50] McKean, the new governor, was to take office on December 18. When the jury panel was announced for the December term of the Pennsylvania supreme court, Cobbett sensed that the Rush case, which had been deferred two years, was finally going to be tried: "The moment I saw the *jury list*, 'Ah!' said I, to a friend that happened to be with me, 'the action of Rush is to be tried this time.' "[51] There does not seem to have been much confidence in Pennsylvania juries of the period. Theodore Sedgwick, federalist senator from Massachusetts, thought the situation was self-explanatory: "Juries are returned by sheriffs & sheriffs are chosen by the people," he wrote to a friend.[52]

Cobbett left Philadelphia for New York on December 9, and the Rush case opened on December 13 before a three-judge court, Justice Edward Shippen presiding.[53] The three judges had been McKean's colleagues on the bench for many years.[54] The appointment of a chief justice to replace McKean was in the discretion of the newly elected governor. Shippen's son-in-law, Burd, was prothonotary of the supreme court, in charge of jury lists, an office held at the pleasure of the governor.[55]

Rush's lead counsel was the twenty-nine-year-old Joseph Hopkinson, who, in addition to being the author of the patriotic hymn "Hail Columbia," had excellent political connections. He was clerk of both the mayor's court of the city of Philadelphia and the orphans' court of Philadelphia county. He was nephew of McKean, son of a federal judge, and son-in-law of outgoing Governor Thomas Mifflin, who had appointed Shippen and the other two judges to the bench.[56]

Another of McKean's counsel was Jared Ingersoll, former attorney general of the state (now in private practice), who had drawn the Yrujo indictment against Cobbett. Cobbett had retained two experienced lawyers to defend him, but at the last minute added Robert G. Harper, federalist member of the House of Repesentatives from South Carolina, who took a leading role in Cobbett's defense. Harper had been admitted to the South Carolina bar in 1786 and the Pennsylvania bar in 1797 but had been principally occupied in land speculation, with little actual legal experience and virtually no courtroom practice. Cobbett had frequently helped Harper with his congressional speeches.[57]

The hearings were concluded on the second day of the trial. Judge Shippen then delivered a spirited charge to the jury, in some respects reminiscent of McKean's charge in the Yrujo case:

Every one must know that offenses of this kind have for some time past too much abounded in our city; it seems high time to restrain them – that task is with you, Gentlemen. To suppress so great an evil, it will not only be proper to give compensatory, but exemplary damages; thus stopping the growing progress of this daring crime – at the same time the damages should not be so enormous as to absolutely ruin the offender.[58]

After two hours of deliberation, the jury brought in a verdict for Rush in the amount of $5,000. That was on December 14, 1799. Four days later Edward Shippen was appointed chief justice by Governor McKean.[59] Mahlon Dickerson of New Jersey, a lawyer who had a distinguished public career as governor of the state, United States senator, and secretary of the navy – a staunch democrat – wrote in his diary: "Trial of Rush and Cobbett finished, Verdict Plff [plaintiff] $5,000 – a ruinous verdict, and therefore a rascally one."[60] Several years later, Cobbett, in a philosophical mood induced by the passage of time, declared that Rush "gave me a dose almost as injurious as he would have sent me from his own shop."[61]

December 14, 1799 was distinguished by another event. On that day George Washington died at his home in Mount Vernon. The report of the attending physicians stated that Washington, suffering from "an inflammatory affection of the upper part of the wind-pipe," was, in the space of twenty hours, bled four times and took three doses of the mercurial purges of the type recommended by Rush. According to Cobbett's computations, the blood drawn from Washington amounted to about nine pints. He wrote:

Thus, on the fatal 14th of December, on the same day, in the same evening, nay, in the very same hour, that a Philadelphia court and jury were laying on me a ruinous fine for having reprobated the practice of Rush, GENERAL

Washington *was expiring while under the operation of that practice!* On that day the victory of RUSH and of DEATH was complete.[62]

The Rush suit had been completely mishandled, and the blame must be equally distributed among Cobbett, his counsel, and McKean's friend Judge Shippen. Cobbett's presence was essential to the defense: to be seen by the jury, to testify to the truth of his assertions as well as to his motives in making them, to contradict testimony of witnesses appearing on behalf of Rush, and to provide his counsel with material for cross-examination. Harper performed miserably. One of Cobbett's friends said that he "should have done well to have given him (H.) a hundred guineas to stay away," and Rush, leaning over the rail to speak to his counsel, was overheard to say, "Why, *I* did not *fee* Harper!"[63] Harper not only went out of his way to praise Rush at every opportunity and to condemn his client's articles as "indecent," "improper," "ill-tempered" and "impertinent," but managed to top this by declaring that Cobbett's statements about Rush's system were "very untrue."[64] Presumably Harper believed that purges and bleeding did cure yellow fever, and no contrary testimony was produced in Cobbett's defense, although many competent doctors in the Philadelphia area agreed with the substance of Cobbett's allegations. Finally, Shippen's charge to the jury was not only biased, but contained at least one important misstatement of fact.[65] The historian Henry Adams, great-grandson of John Adams, waggishly commented that "Cobbett found to his cost that the Philadelphians were glad to be bled, or at least to seize the opportunity for silencing the libeler."[66]

The December 14 issue of the federalist *Gazette of the United States*, although containing no account of the trial, carried this advertisement:

WILLIAM COBBETT

Having (in order to avoid the disgrace of living under the Government of M'Kean) removed from Philadelphia to the City of New-York, requests any one in Pennsylvania, who may have a demand against him, to deliver an account thereof to Mr. JOHN MORGAN, No. 3 South Front Street, Philadelphia, or to forward it by post to New York.

Immediately following was a notice of an auction to be held "on Thursday next" of certain of Cobbett's household furniture, including "an excellent roasting jack" and "a complete printing press." Rush's counsel promptly attached the property and caused an edition of Cobbett's works, then in process of being printed, to be sold as wastepaper.[67]

The bulk of Cobbett's furniture and the entire stock of his bookshop had been packed up and sent off to New York by sea the month before the trial took place.[68] *Porcupine's Gazette,* following the resumption of yellow fever in the summer of 1799, had been gradually closed down, appearing only once a week during September and October.[69] A final number, published in New York in January 1800, explained that the *Gazette,* which had never yielded Cobbett "a farthing of clear profit," had now lost its utility, since its principal object was to assist the administration of John Adams in combating French principles, but "he suddenly tacked about, and I could follow him no longer."[70]

The final issue of the *Gazette* was not Cobbett's final word on the events that were still so fresh in his mind. He now published in New York, in the period February to May 1800, five issues of a publication called the *Rush-Light,* the first four of which dealt almost wholly with the Rush case.[71] In these pamphlets he chastised Harper and Shippen for the parts they had played in the case, demolished Rush's claims for the virtue of purges and bleeding, and, in the process of stating the facts, demonstrated how severely the cause had suffered through his own failure to attend. He showed by a statistical analysis that "from the day on which Rush declared that his discovery had reduced the Fever to a level with a common cold" the daily death rate began to increase – doubling, tripling, and finally quadrupling – "though the lancet was continually unsheathed; though Rush and his subalterns were ready at every call." But that was not all, for the doctor who claimed that yellow fever was no more dangerous than a common cold had lost his own sister and three of his five apprentices to yellow fever while they were under his personal care.[72]

Cobbett also demonstrated that many experienced doctors violently opposed Rush's cure, one stating that "the mode of treatment advised by Dr. Rush cannot, in the Yellow Fever, fail of being certain death." Additionally, Cobbett showed that Rush was not the saintlike figure pictured by his counsel, but abusive to doctors who did not accept his cure, calling them "assassins"; accusing them of "murders"; asserting that they had "slain more than the sword."[73] When it was suggested by nonbelievers that the heavy doses of mercury could loosen one's teeth, Rush, whom a supporter had called the "American Hippocrates," replied that he had "met with but two cases in which there was a loss of teeth from this medicine." To which Cobbett remarked: "But, my dear 'Hippocrates', there is some little difference between *loosening* and *losing* one's teeth. You think it's nothing, I suppose, unless your patient's teeth drop into his porridge?"[74] Cobbett had an adequate answer to every question raised in the hearings as well as factual material which would have created serious problems for Rush's witnesses: "their evidence," wrote Cobbett, "would have appeared very different from what it did appear, if I had had the cross-examining of them."[75] Why then, was he not in attendance where he could feed his lawyers with the questions to be asked? We know that he was in New York during the hearings. He claimed in no. IV of the *Rush-Light* that his counsel had written to him there on December 11 stating that the case was again to be put off to another term, "but the *very next day*, it was all at once resolved to bring it to trial immediately." This may be true, but what Cobbett failed to state is that when he left Philadelphia on December 9, he fully expected that both the Rush case and the Yrujo recognizance case would be tried in his absence, and in a letter to his counsel he outlined the procedures to be followed "In case of a decision against me, in both or either of the cases."[76] Since Cobbett does not blame his counsel for his absence, it almost certainly was a decision he made himself. We can do no more than guess the reason for the decision. Possibly he thought that any recovery in the Rush case would be nominal. No one could have imagined a verdict for anything like $5,000, which was larger, according to Cobbett, than the aggregate of all damages assessed against all defendants in all libel cases in the states "from their first settlement to the present day."[77]

Cobbett's ability to meet an award of this size was extremely doubtful. His assets consisted principally of his stock of books (now installed in a shop he had opened in New York at 141 Water Street) and uncollected accounts due from customers of the Philadelphia shop and subscribers to *Porcupine's Gazette*. Cobbett, from the start, refused to take any steps to avoid payment. Declaring "I will fight as I retreat to the very water's edge," he spurned the suggestion that he "flee the persecution." He also vetoed a proposal that an attempt be made to reduce the award by "*softening* Rush."[78]

Rush's counsel did not give Cobbett much time. As soon as the Pennsylvania decree was handed down, they instituted an action in New York to enforce the judgment.[79] However, the pressure this placed on Cobbett was almost immediately relieved by "the noble disposition which my friends have discovered" – a plan, presumably, by which Cobbett's admirers were to lend him the money to pay off the judgment, but which eventually developed into an outright gift. The names of the donors have never been revealed; it is not clear whether Cobbett knew who they were.[80] The only solid information we have is that Edward Thornton, secretary to the British legation, and a Mr. John Ashley, about whom we know very little, took an active part in finding the money, and that the amount finally paid to Rush in a negotiated settlement was $4,250.[81] Rumors that Cobbett's Pennsylvania enemies might attempt further legal harassment caused him to consult Alexander Hamilton, who by now had resumed his law practice in New York. Hamilton declared that he would be honored to defend Cobbett, without fee, if any attempt should be made to initiate other legal proceedings in New York; in that state, he asserted, Cobbett "had nothing to fear from injustice."[82]

Secure on the legal front, Cobbett was also enabled to liquidate a large part of his investment in the New York bookshop, and thereby to complete arrangements for a return to England, where he saw "another and better world opening to receive me." The shop and its contents were to be sold to young John Ward Fenno, editor and owner of the *Gazette of the United States,* the other Philadelphia newspaper devoted to the high federalist cause. Fenno, after disposing of his paper, would pay Cobbett $5,000 to $7,000 down, the balance over a period of time. This meant, according to Cobbett, that he would "be able to carry off 10,000 dollars, which will give me a pretty tolerable start in London."[83]

Thus, on June 1, 1800, Cobbett and his small family – his wife, their daughter Anne, nearly five years old, and their son William, not yet two, set sail for England on the *Lady Arabella.* He had arranged for a farewell message to be inserted in the newspapers the day before. It ended with these words:

When people care not two straws for each other, ceremony at parting is mere grimace; and as I have long felt the most perfect indifference with regard to the vast majority of those whom I now address, I shall spare myself the trouble of a ceremonious farewell. Let me not, however, depart from you with indiscriminating contempt. If no man ever had so many and such malignant foes, no one has ever had more friends, and those more kind, more sincere, and more faithful. If I have been unjustly vilified by some, others have extolled me far beyond my merits; if the savages of the city have scared my children in the cradle, those children have, for their father's sake, been soothed and caressed by the affectionate, the gentle, the generous inhabitants of the country, under whose hospitable roofs I have spent some of the happiest hours of my life.

Thus and *thus,* Americans, will I ever speak of you. In a very little time, I shall be beyond the reach of your friendship, or your malice; beyond the hearing of your commendations or your curses; but being out of your power will alter neither my sentiments nor my words. As I have never spoken any thing but truth to you, so I will never speak any thing but truth of you: the heart of a Briton revolts at an emulation in baseness; and though you have, as a nation treated me most ungratefully and unjustly, I scorn to repay you with ingratitude and injustice.

Taking another breath, Cobbett concluded:

To my friends, who are also the real friends of America, I wish that peace and happiness which virtue ought to ensure, but which, I greatly fear, they will not find; and as to my enemies, I can wish them no severer scourge than that which they are preparing for themselves and their country. With this I depart for my native land, where neither the moth of *Democracy,* nor the rust of *Federalism* doth corrupt, and where thieves do not, with impunity, break through and steal five thousand dollars at a time.[84]

7 · The end of Jacobinism

Life is not life, with me, unless I am master, sole master, of my thoughts *and* my actions.

COBBETT'S RECEPTION by his countrymen began before he and his family could set foot in England. Five days out of New York the *Lady Arabella* put into Halifax, Nova Scotia, where the Cobbetts received a warm welcome from the governor, Sir John Wentworth, and from the representative of the royal family, the Duke of Kent, commanding general of British forces in North America. Cobbett wrote Edward Thornton several days later as the *Lady Arabella* made ready to sail from Halifax:

I have dined out every day, and am bespoke for a week, if we remain so long – I have been visited by all the civil officers, the clergymen, and most of the officers of high rank in the army and navy . . . On Sunday the Duke sent me one of his aides de camp to request me to wait on him. I went, and was extremely well received. We talked about everything which he could suppose me to understand much about, and before I took my leave, he gave me a paper, commanding all officers of the Garrison, forts, posts &c. to suffer me to go wherever I pleased, and to attend me and give me all the information I might want. This regiment was reviewed on Monday, and after the review, he rode up to me on the Grand parade, asked me my opinion on his corps, and conversed with me for some time . . . Nor has Mrs Cobbett been neglected. Several of the first ladies in the place have waited on her; she and her children were carried to the Review by some of the very few persons who keep carriages here.[1]

The contrast between this reception and the status of husband and wife only a few years before was peculiarly gratifying to Cobbett: "When I was last in Halifax I helped, as a soldier in fatigue, to drag the baggage from the wharf to the Barracks; and when my wife was here last, she was employed in assisting her poor mother to wash soldier's shirts!"[2]

The presence in Nova Scotia of a royal duke with the responsibility for repelling any attempt by the French to regain their lost North

111

American colonies tells us something about the situation of Britain in the year 1800. The country had been at war with France since 1793 and, except on the seas, where Nelson and his colleagues had established the ascendancy of the British navy, had not been doing well. France had conquered most of Europe despite the millions in British gold spent on two successive military coalitions of France's continental enemies. The various threats emanating from republican France which had so exercised Cobbett while in Philadelphia – invasion by armed forces, internal uprisings, and the destruction of established religion and orderly government – were far more real to the British than they had ever been to the Americans.

The French controlled all the mainland channel ports; a French 'Army of England' under the command of General Bonaparte, allegedly 275,000 strong, had been in being since 1797; and hundreds of landing craft were readied for use along the coast from Boulogne to Ostend. Irish patriots flowed to and from France with invasion plans designed to overthrow the British government in Ireland. An attempt in the winter of 1796–7 had been frustrated, not by any British military forces, but by one of those sudden storms that had so providentially saved the country once before. Then in 1798 there had been the Irish rising, which was put down only after a good deal of blood had been shed. The union of Great Britain and Ireland had been voted, to become effective January 1, 1801, in the vain hope that this would lead to improved relations.

England itself seemed ripe for an internal explosion. Bad harvests were experienced in four of the first eight years of the war. The price of wheat in 1800 had risen to 113s. a quarter, more than twice the average for the preceding ten years. There were food riots throughout England in 1795 and again in 1800. In the former year, while 200,000 Londoners swarmed through the streets, the king was hissed on his way to parliament and his coach pelted with stones. In 1800 troops had to be withdrawn from Portugal to keep order at home. Poor living conditions on British men-of-war and inadequate pay produced a mutiny at Spithead in April 1797 and then at the Nore a month later, immobilizing a large part of the British navy. In the same year, the Bank of England suspended payments in specie, and British government bonds, the consols, fell to 48. Many British intellectuals (Priestley was only one of many) had been captivated by the high-sounding French principles. Charles James Fox, leader of the liberal whigs in parliament and cousin of Lord Edward Fitzgerald, Cobbett's ex-major, had publicly toasted the "sovereign people" and been immediately removed from the privy council.

A series of repressive acts demonstrated the extent to which fear dominated the British scene at the end of the eighteenth century. The writ of habeas corpus was suspended; it was made a treasonable offense to incite hatred or contempt of the king, constitution, or government; no meeting of over fifty persons could be held without advance notice to a magistrate; Tom Paine's *Rights of Man* was banned. To many of its citizens – probably the vast majority even including the lower classes – the repressive laws passed by parliament were believed necessary to preserve the British way of life and the security of the country. To others – and surely this category included more poor than rich – the period was "the English Reign of Terror."[3]

The passengers on board the packet *Lady Arabella* during her three-week crossing from Halifax to Falmouth were not allowed to forget the beleaguered state of Britain. The ship, hungrily pursued by a fast-sailing French privateer, was enabled to escape only by throwing overboard her armament, cannon and shot, to lighten the load. Apart from this adventure, it had not been a pleasant trip for the Cobbetts. The captain proved to be a "blackguard," the fellow passengers were "vulgar" and sang bawdy songs, and the board and lodgings on the packet were "worse than in a common merchant ship." However, once they were on shore in Falmouth, the family was made comfortable by the collector of customs there, Samuel Pellew, brother of two famous British sailors – all three great admirers of Peter Porcupine. The Falmouth brother, after making one of those vague offers "to oblige ... in any way," proved that he had meant what he said by entertaining the family throughout their six-day stay at Falmouth; placing a horse at Cobbett's disposal the whole time he was there; introducing the family to local gentlefolk of importance in the area; and advancing Cobbett £20 so that he would have sufficient money to cover expenses on the final leg of the trip.[4]

Cobbett arrived in London with his family on July 15, 1800. He was thirty-seven years old and, except for the five months he had been in England during 1791–2, he had been out of the country for the past fifteen years – virtually all of his adult life. He knew no one there of importance, but he had been in correspondence with three Londoners, all fervid anti-Jacobins: John Wright, Piccadilly bookseller and publisher; William Gifford, editor and co-founder with George Canning of the short-lived *Anti-Jacobin or Weekly Examiner* (1797–8); and John Gifford, the assumed name of John Richards Green, editor and founder of the *Anti-Jacobin Review and Magazine* (1798–1821). These three had done much to enhance Cobbett's reputation in England – Wright by publishing Cobbett's writings since 1797 and the two Giffords by the notoriety and acclaim they had accorded to Cobbett in their separate reviews over the same period.[5] Of more immediate importance, Cobbett was armed with letters of introduction from Robert Liston, British minister in the United States, and from Edward Thornton, secretary of the British legation there. These letters included one to George Hammond, undersecretary for foreign affairs. Cobbett called on Hammond directly after his arrival and was invited to dine at his house. There he met, among others, William Windham, secretary at war. And at a succeeding dinner given a few weeks later by Windham, Cobbett met the prime minister, William Pitt – an invariably cold and remote figure – whom Cobbett recalled as being "very polite to me, and whose manners I very much admired."[6] Pitt was almost certainly aware of Cobbett's services in America. One of Cobbett's letters to William Gifford, written in 1799 – a sixteen-page description of affairs in America with a not overly modest account of Cobbett's part in those affairs, ending with the words "You may possibly have an opportunity to show this letter to some one to whom its information may be useful" – still reposes among the papers of William Pitt. The letter also acknowledged a present sent by Gifford for Cobbett's four-year-old daughter – a gold locket containing a strand of Pitt's hair and a "W.P." in letters of gold filigree.[7]

The Cobbett family, after lodging one or two nights at the Bath Hotel, had joined John Wright in the living quarters connected with Wright's bookshop in Piccadilly. Years later Mrs. Cobbett recalled that "many great people" visited them there, but as Wright's quarters were not "fine enough for appearance" – even Queen Charlotte had asked how Peter Porcupine was housed – Cobbett transferred the family into lodgings in St. James's Street, where "everybody of consequence came."[8] Windham must be numbered among the foremost of these. He was a member of an old Norfolk family; he was rich; he had been a friend of Edmund Burke and Samuel Johnson. The latter, writing from Ashbourne, where Windham had visited him, said: "Such conversation I shall not have again till I come back to the regions of literature; and there Windham is *inter stellas Luna minores*."[9] Between Windham and Cobbett a warm relationship soon developed.

Cobbett's professional life was similarly affected by his new acquaintances. He had come to London with two projects: to open a bookshop and to publish his American writings. Hammond "urged, in addition, the undertaking of a daily paper."[10] Pitt's government, constantly under attack by those holding more liberal views, needed that rarest of journalistic phenomena, an effective defender of conservative principles, and for this purpose there was no one on either side of the Atlantic the equal of

Porcupine Peter
The democrat eater.[11]

As a result, Cobbett was offered the proprietorship of the *True Briton,*
one of the government newspapers. Cobbett's answer, to those who
knew him, was obvious and immediately forthcoming. He declined
the government assistance, politely explaining that he desired to render the greatest possible service to his country and that "by keeping
myself wholly free . . . I shall be able to give the government much
more efficient support than if any species of dependence could be
traced to me."[12] His scrupulosity was such that he turned down the
proposal of the treasury to refund the customs duties charged on his
library brought from America.[13] When Cobbett made these brave
decisions he did not have the $10,000 in his pockets he once thought
would be available to start business in London. The sale of his New
York shop did not work out as well as he had originally expected, so
he had arrived in London with some £600 or £700, about one-third
of his first estimate.[14] This was no deterrent to the ebullient Cobbett.
He decided to proceed with the three projects simultaneously: he
would open a bookshop; he would produce a collected edition of his
writings on America, an undertaking that involved editing and printing about 5,000 pages in twelve bound volumes; and he would produce a daily paper.

Everything was done in grand style. Cobbett took a house at 18 Pall
Mall for £308 a year, where the bookshop was to be established with
John Morgan, a Philadelphia friend, as partner.[15] Cobbett and Morgan, at the sign of "The Crown and Mitre," would publish and sell
books supporting the king and the church. The family moved to this
address in October 1800, and the bookshop was opened shortly afterwards with an impressive billhead:

Cobbett & Morgan
Booksellers & Stationers
To Their Royal Highnesses
The Prince of Wales,
The Dukes of Clarence, Kent & Cumberland
& Prince Augustus[16]

In September 1800 Cobbett sent to the printers the proof of the
first part of the edition of his works on the United States – a project
that was completed and published in May of the following year. This
was not simply a reprint of what he had written in America: Two volumes of the twelve were mainly materials which Cobbett had not previously used. The preface to the first volume, dated May 29, 1801,
stated that the disaffection in the British dominions, and particularly

in Ireland, "was chiefly to be ascribed to the deception with respect to America" and that the purpose of the writings now being offered to the public was to contradict the falsehoods on which such deception was founded. The American rebellion had been "against the mildest, the most just, and most virtuous of Sovereigns." Cobbett said that while he was in America, he had "never met with a man in whatever rank or situation of life, who did not regret the separation of the United States from the mother-country" and "did not acknowledge that the country was much happier before the rebellion than it ever had been since."[17]

As a matter of history this is a bit difficult to swallow, but Cobbett was not writing as a historian. He was trying to mold public opinion; to dampen revolutionary ardor in Ireland and at home at a time when, in the midst of widespread economic distress, it was believed that "an Insurrection was in contemplation among the lower orders."[18] To such grounds also must be ascribed Cobbett's extensive emendations to his original text, by which (for example) George Washington, once one of Cobbett's heroes and then referred to as "irreproachable Washington" and a "great and good man," was now converted into "aged Washington," full of "pride" and "cunning," – who "never did one generous action in his life" – as would be expected of the leader of a rebellion against his gracious majesty George III, who now, after forty years on the throne, was facing still another rebellion.[19]

The twelve-volume collection was dedicated to John Reeves, founder of the Loyal Association against Republicans and Levellers, who had been appointed king's printer in 1800. The dedication, like the preface, was dated May 29, the anniversary of the restoration of Charles II: "that happy day, which drove rebellion, republicanism and tyranny from England."[20] Appropriately, the list of subscribers for the collected works, consisting of more than 600 individuals in the United Kingdom, the United States, Jamaica, and Canada, was headed by the Prince of Wales and four royal dukes, and included the archbishop of Canterbury as well as three future prime ministers of England.

Cobbett's third project, the daily newspaper to be called the *Porcupine,* was announced in an eight-page prospectus dated "Pall Mall 29 Sep. 1800." Cobbett had rented separate offices for the paper on Southampton Street at £106 per annum, and was joined in the endeavor by John Gifford.[21] The first issue appeared on October 30, 1800, bearing the legend "Fear God. Honour the King." The *Porcupine,* in the interest of religion, morality, and order, would demonstrate "the injurious and degrading consequences of discontent, disloyalty, and innovation." It was to be independent, having been started "without the aid, without the advice, and even without the knowledge of any person, either directly or indirectly, connected with the Ministry"; it hoped to yield some trifling support to that ministry because "this country owes its preservation to the wisdom and integrity of Mr Pitt and his colleagues"; but it was not to be the "trumpet of indiscriminate applause."

"Mr Pitt and his colleagues" meant those busily engaged in prosecuting the war against Jacobin France, as contrasted with those followers of Pitt who were rather lukewarm about it, as well as the whig followers of Charles James Fox who opposed it. Some of the more conservative whigs who supported the war had joined forces with Pitt and were serving in his cabinet. These included William Windham, Lord Grenville, and Earl Spencer – all intellectual descendants of Edmund Burke, who had died in 1797. Windham, the only one with whom Cobbett was more than casually acquainted, espoused Burke's view that the French principles were an evil that must be exterminated.[22] It was this position that Cobbett, always an admirer of Burke ("this great man . . . the profoundest of statesmen; the ornament of his country"), was prepared to support in the *Porcupine*.[23]

The daily newspapers of London in 1800 had a remarkable uniformity of outward appearance: They all had four pages with four columns a page; they all had advertising on the first page (and as much on other pages as they could manage to capture); they all cost 6d. (of which 3½d. was tax); and they all contained reports of activities in parliament and of law decisions, the king and his family, theatrical performances, and the foreign news – at this point principally pertaining to France as reported in the Hamburg mails. The high tax was designed to restrict government criticism rather than to raise revenues, and was extremely effective. The daily circulation of the leading papers at the beginning of the nineteenth century was tiny: from 1,000 (or even less) to 2,500 or 3,000.[24] Individuals, unless they were actively engaged in politics, rarely subscribed to newspapers; most of them were sold to coffee shops or other reading rooms where a variety of publications was made available to customers, frequently on a subscription basis.[25] An estimate made in 1829 was that each paper was read by an average of thirty persons.[26]

All the papers were politically oriented and they all received, as a matter of course, some sort of financial assistance from the government or political parties or persons.[27] This took the form of periodic grants; fees for insertions, contradictions, or suppressions; the assignment of government advertising; or other government favors. "There were Gatton and Old Sarum newspapers as well as Gatton and Old

Sarum boroughs."[28] The *Sun* and the *True Briton,* both edited by John Heriot, were out-and-out government papers. At the other end of the spectrum were the papers representing the whig opposition, the followers of Fox. In this group were the *Morning Chronicle,* the *Morning Post,* and the *Courier.* The *Morning Chronicle,* edited by James Perry, although not the largest in terms of circulation, was the "most influential journal for thirty years" until overtaken by *The Times* after Perry's death in 1821.[29] *The Times* received financial support from the Pitt and Addington administrations up to 1803 at least, and possibly later.[30] The popular *Morning Post,* edited by Daniel Stuart, had a reputation (inherited from Stuart's predecessor) for "fashionable intelligence" – a euphemism for racy gossip appealing to a below-the-stairs audience – which Stuart successfully combined with a unique stable of competent writers. Coleridge, Southey, Lamb, Wordsworth, and Stuart's brother-in-law, James Mackintosh, author of *Vindiciae Gallicae,* all wrote for the *Morning Post* early in the nineteenth century. Stuart sold the *Post* in 1803 and devoted all his attention to the *Courier,* which he had acquired in 1796. He built that paper into an extremely successful tory publication, using the literary figures who had earlier written for the *Post* but who had since turned more conservative.[31]

The heavy tax and undercover financial arrangements were not the only deterrents to a free press. There was the problem of delivery by the post office, a service to which the publisher was theoretically entitled on payment of the 3½d. tax. Newspapers unpopular with the government often disappeared or were replaced by publications that were politically more acceptable. Likewise, the prompt receipt of news from abroad was dependent on the good graces of the post office; one of the informal perquisites of the staff was the right to levy such charges as they might see fit on incoming reports and on English papers sent abroad. And finally, there were the criminal libel laws which, although erratically invoked, were administered in a manner which left small chance of acquittal once proceedings were initiated by the government. These had sent the editor of *The Times* to prison twice in the latter part of the eighteenth century and carried off two of his colleagues to prison during the same period.

Cobbett's intentions were extreme in two respects. He proposed to run a paper without outside financial assistance, and to support in his columns the small group that viewed the French war as a crusade against evil. The ability of Cobbett to sustain this position was seriously threatened even before he was able to get out the first issue of his new publication. The Austrians, Britain's last important military ally in Europe, had been decisively defeated by Bonaparte at

Marengo in June 1800, and in September of that year peace negotiations began between France and Britain. These continued for several months while Pitt's ministers quarrelled among themselves over the desirability of any settlement with the current rulers of France, and then negotiations broke down. Meanwhile, the Austrians had been able to raise new forces. But the respite was brief. The Austrians were once more defeated in December 1800; Pitt's second coalition against the French had failed. After seventeen years in office, Pitt resigned as prime minister in March 1801, followed by his close friend Henry Dundas and the three members of the cabinet who were violently opposed to the peace: Lord Grenville, William Windham, and Earl Spencer. "Mr Pitt and his colleagues," five months after Cobbett had pledged them his support, were replaced by the dull mediocrity Henry Addington and his mostly undistinguished friends. Lord Hawkesbury succeeded Grenville as foreign secretary, and on October 1, 1801, Hawkesbury signed a preliminary treaty of peace with France. Lady Bessborough wrote: "Ld. Hawkesbury look'd very proud and happy when he came to the House as Minister, and to declare Peace. H [James Hare] said: 'He look'd as he always looks – as if he had been on the rack three times, and saw the wheel preparing for a fourth.' "[32]

The truce was an immediate success with the man in the street, to whom the end of the war meant, or so he thought, the end of food shortages and high prices. "The ratification of the preliminaries is not yet arrived," wrote Cobbett to Windham on October 7, "but is hourly expected, and I am informed that a grand illumination is preparing at all the Public Offices. Two thousand lamps, I am told, are prepared for the War Office and the Horse Guards. The swinish multitude, having nothing better to do, have, all this day long, been assembled to the amount of three or four thousands, in St. James's Park, waiting for the arrival of the ratification, and for the consequent firing of the guns."[33]

Cobbett was determined not to light up, and since he had made his opposition to the truce widely known, he took the precaution of applying to the Bow Street magistrates, who assured him of all practicable protection from the mob at both his house and printing office. The guns were finally fired three days later, on Saturday, October 10 – the date the representatives of the French republic delivered the formal ratification to the British foreign office in London. On the morning of that day, when General Lauriston, Bonaparte's special envoy, emerged from his lodgings on Bond Street with Louis Otto, French agent in Britain, he found an admiring crowd surrounding his carriage. After the two Frenchmen seated themselves, the crowd excitedly took off the horses and placed themselves in the traces, and off they started down Bond Street, like a communally powered rickshaw, a form of transportation traditionally reserved for British heroes. The triumphal carriage, with its huge crowd in attendance, was drawn first to the front of the king's palace, where they stopped and cheered, then to the Prince of Wales's palace, to Downing Street and to the admiralty, finally returning to Bond Street on a route through the Mall "exclusively appropriated to carriages of the Royal family." According to Cobbett's somewhat embroidered account, when Lauriston reached his lodgings:

Those who came within reach of him, *kissed* his hands, his jacket, his pantaloons, and his boots; those who were not able to get at any part of his precious person, went on their knees and kissed the stones he had walked upon; while others were obliged to content themselves with slobbering the coach and the poor unfortunate horses, who, when they passed my door seemed ashamed to accompany the beasts that had usurped their office.[34]

The mob had not concluded their "tumult of exultation and delirium of joy." That evening when the lights came on all over London, crowds appeared outside Cobbett's house on Pall Mall at about eight o'clock. Shouting "Peace and Plenty" and "France for ever," they broke all the windows and were preparing to force their way into the shop when Cobbett ordered lights, "fearing that the cannibals might murder myself and my children." This move stopped further destruction, but the howling and taunts continued until past one in the morning. The Bow Street magistrates, despite their assurances, provided no protection of any sort. Cobbett's offices on Southampton Street were similarly assaulted and damaged.[35] Not all of Cobbett's public were sympathetic with him at this turn of events. "I observe Porcupine has had his windows broke," wrote a citizen of Philadelphia to his brother in England, "pity but that it had been his head."[36]

The *Porcupine* appeared on the following Monday, October 12, but was not published the two succeeding days. The next issue, that of October 15, carried the first of a series of nine letters to Lord Hawkesbury on the terms of the peace that had just been negotiated with the French.[37] The letters were surprisingly restrained, and except for an occasional reference to Hawkesbury as a "suckling statesman" (he was thirty-one, six years younger than Cobbett) were remarkably civil. But they utterly demolished the ministry's contention that the treaty was a good one for Britain, for it required the surrender by the British of two points of vital strategic importance: the Cape of Good Hope and the island of Malta, and it left both Belgium and Holland under French control, contrary to traditional British policy. Underlying Cobbett's objections was his conclusion, quickly proved correct, that further war with France was inevitable and that all the treaty had done was to strengthen France for the next round: "it multiplies her means of attack, and diminishes our means of defence. It leaves our enemy armed and prepared; it compels us to remain also under arms. This Peace, then, my Lord, is a real state of War."[38] George III had similar qualms. Writing to his old friend Richard Hurd, bishop of Worcester, he said: "it is certainly doubtful what reliance can be placed on the Assurances of those who set every Religious, Moral and Social Principle at nought."[39] But the British people were tired of war and, as to the treaty, Robert Southey wrote: "The nation . . . is very well persuaded that no better was to be had, very thankful for a respite from alarm, and a relief of taxation, and very well convinced by its own disposition to maintain the peace that it is in no danger of being broken."[40]

The letters to Hawkesbury were the last gasp of the *Porcupine.* By the end of November 1801, a little more than a year after the first issue, both Cobbett and Gifford had sold their interest in the paper, and on January 1, 1802 it was combined with the government publication the *True Briton.*[41] Cobbett reported that his loss was £450; Gifford's, £300.[42]

But Cobbett was not through with journalism. The *Porcupine* had been a failure, but not enough of a failure to discourage Cobbett. Despite difficulties with the post office, the daily circulation had risen from an initial 700 in October 1800 to upwards of 1,500 by December of that year, exceeding the sale of some of the established papers, although not the racy *Morning Post.*[43] "I could not throw out hints against a man's or woman's reputation in order to bring the party forward to pay me for silence," wrote Cobbett years later.[44] And circulation of all papers suffered a decline at the end of 1801 on the cessation of hostilities against France. The principal problem of these low circulation rates was the narrow margin: a government-prescribed sale price of 6d. and a government stamp tax of 3½d., left only 2½d. for production costs. Cobbett saw a way around this: A weekly publication of sixteen pages, octavo size, with two columns per page, would require half the amount of paper and half the typesetting as a daily newspaper of four standard pages, and it could be sold for 10d.[45] The tax was still 3½d., leaving 6½d. for production costs. At this figure, Cobbett could forgo advertising, which, by the looks of the insertions in the *Porcupine,* would have produced little added revenue in any event. A weekly publication of this type was urged on Cobbett by William Windham and another enthusiastic follower of Burke, Dr. French Laurence, member of parliament and Regius Professor of History at Oxford; they undertook to arrange the necessary capital – about £600 – since by the end of 1801 Cobbett had little left of what he had brought with him from America. According to Cobbett, the money was provided

upon the *express* and *written* conditions, that I should never be under the influence of any body. The money was to be looked upon as sunk in the risk; and *I was never to be looked upon as under any sort of obligation to any of the parties.* It was long before I would consent to the thing at all; but, when I did, it was upon these express and *written* conditions. And never did any of the persons who advanced the money, attempt, in the slightest degree, to influence my opinions, which were frequently opposed to their own.[46]

The new publication was called *Cobbett's Weekly Political Register.*[47] The first issue covered the period January 1–16, 1802; the second was for the fortnight ending January 30; thereafter, with slight exception, it was published on Saturday of each week until Cobbett's death in 1835. Among the great mass of people it became the most powerful journal in England. And, although now largely forgotten except by historians who occasionally take a hasty glance here and there into its vast bulk of some 42,000 pages, it has left its impress on the most important newspapers of the twentieth century. For until Cobbett entered the field, there usually was no clear demarcation between news and editorial comment. The viewpoint of the paper was insidiously introduced through the selection and presentation of the news, and in anonymous, and often fictitiously signed, letters to the editor. Often what might appear to be a news story was such a hodgepodge of fact, opinion, and wishful thinking that the reader could not tell where one left off and the other began. To cite an amusing example, Richard Brinsley Sheridan, through use of tickets to his theatrical performances, prevailed on the papers to report his parliamentary speeches more extensively than those of his adversaries, and to insert "there was a loud cry of *hear! hear! hear!*" at points where he would have liked to have such reassurances from his listeners.[48] Further, until Cobbett appeared, the reader was given the news each day, but the relationship of one piece of news to another, or to something that had happened earlier, was left to the reader's recollection and imagination.

Cobbett was responsible for – if not the invention, at least the development, of – what is known in America as the editorial and in England as the leading article. His views were expressed in the *Political Register* in the form of open letters addressed to named individuals or groups of individuals and through a weekly column, often entitled "Summary of Politics," in which he reviewed and commented on the news reported in the daily papers. By these means he was able to state his own opinions in a straightforward manner (he signed these with his own name) and to draw together, in one article, the various materials bearing on whatever issue was being discussed, including anything that may have occurred in the past that was relevant to the issue. The extent of Cobbett's achievement was acknowledged, although in a curiously backhanded way, when *The Times,* in 1935, published its history: *"The Times* could and did learn from him [Cobbett] that the immediately powerful journalistic means of securing urgently needed measures of reform was to push forward the transformation of the newspaper paragraph into the leading article."[49]

When the *Political Register* commenced its career in January 1802, the issue of the day was still the relationship between Britain and France. Hostilities had ceased the previous October when a preliminary agreement of peace had been reached; but negotiations at Amiens were moving with painful slowness, and the definitive agreement was not finally signed until the end of March 1802. A general illumination in London was ordered at the end of the following month. Cobbett again refused to illuminate and again his windows were broken. "The poor Porcupine's windows have been smashed for not rejoicing as you and I do," wrote Henry Bankes to William Wilberforce; "he was not bound to rejoice, but he should have illuminated."[50] This time six of the assailants were taken by constables. Three proved to be government employees, two in the service of that branch of the government having a vested interest in newspapers, the post office. These two and one of the others were indicted and found guilty by a jury, who recommended them to the mercy of the court. Asked by counsel for the defendants whether he would join in the recommendation, Cobbett angrily replied: "Certainly not, Sir: I came here to ask for *justice* and not for mercy." Whether the result was justice or mercy is difficult to say. The three were fined a total of £70 and required to enter into recognizances to keep the peace for two years.[51]

This second assault on his premises did no more than the first to blunt Cobbett's outspoken criticism of the peace and its supporters. Hawkesbury's assurance, on signing the preliminary agreement, that "nothing was left to higgle about" showed that he knew little about negotiations and nothing about Bonaparte.[52] During the six months of higgling that ensued, the French managed to eke out a few more concessions. Cobbett was not only quick to call these to the attention of his readers, but went on to point out that the French were busily increasing their strength outside the treaty. They took over the Louisiana Territory from Spain, thereby acquiring nearly half of North America west of the Mississippi; they merged the separate states of

northern Italy into the Cisalpine republic with Bonaparte as chief of
state; they ordered the Swiss to adopt a constitution along French
lines and occupied a substantial part of the country.

While this French expansion represented serious threats to the
security and commerce of Britain, events within France itself, following shortly after the definitive agreement, drastically changed the
nature of the challenge from Cobbett's point of view. His opposition
to the French had been founded on his hatred of their mob rule and
their disrespect for religion. Now, within two months of the signing
of the treaty of Amiens in March 1802, Bonaparte was elected consul
for life, and formally welcomed to his court a representative of his
holiness Pius VII under a concordat reinstalling the Roman catholic
church in France. Almost overnight the atheism that had characterized French life for the past decade was replaced by established religion. And the rule of the rabble, which Pitt had once denominated
"the mortal enemy of all government," was replaced by the dictatorship of a man whom Pitt had called "the child and the champion of
jacobinism." Cobbett perceived that this was the end of libertarian
doctrine in France: "The mortal enemy of all government will be
destroyed by the very man who has been its principal supporter. The
child and the champion of jacobinism will murder his mother, and in
so doing will rid the world of a monster which has threatened its
destruction."[53] This conclusion was not shared by all those who had
been associated with Cobbett in his campaign against Jacobinism. The
phrase "Jacobin" continued in general use for years after 1802 to sig-
nify those out of favor with the various tory administrations that governed Britain. John Gifford's *Anti-Jacobin Review and Magazine* was
published under that name until 1821.

But Cobbett's holy war was over. His fight against Jacobinism,
which had begun so abruptly with the publication of *Observations on
Priestley* in 1794, ended with almost equal abruptness eight years later
with the creation of the Napoleonic dictatorship. From 1802 on, Cobbett turned his principal attention from the dangers of libertarian
doctrine imported from France to the purely domestic brand of problems relating to the governance of Britain, problems to which he
devoted the rest of his life.

8 · English justice

The partial, capricious cruel blows of despotism are much less injurious to the general and real liberties . . . than are any of those proceedings, by which tyranny is exercised under the names, and with the forms and appearance of law and justice.

WHILE THE ELEVATION of Bonaparte in 1802 to the position of dictator removed any threat to Britain from French political doctrine, it increased the threat to Britain from French military power and ambition. Cobbett continued to stress the rapacity of Bonaparte, the falsity of the peace, and the urgent need for adequate defense measures in preparation for the day war would be resumed. He was joined in this campaign by two French emigrants living in England who published papers in their native language: Jean Peltier, editor of *L'Ambigu* and a M Rignier, editor of *Courier François de Londres*. Bonaparte, in the habit of having foreign newspapers read to him while in his bath, was outraged by these attacks and ordered the French ambassador to lodge a formal complaint with Lord Hawkesbury, secretary for foreign affairs. This was done in July 1802.[1] A recent issue of *L'Ambigu* was specifically mentioned, although the ambassador made it plain that the complaint was directed "not to Peltier alone, but to the editor of the 'Courier François de Londres,' to Cobbett, and to other writers who resemble them." He claimed that "the perfidious and malevolent publications of these men are in open contradiction to the principles of peace."[2]

Following these representations, Spencer Perceval, the attorney general, filed an information charging Peltier with a libel on Bonaparte. Perceval personally conducted the prosecution at the trial held on February 21, 1803 before the chief justice, Lord Ellenborough, and a special jury.[3] According to Cobbett, "Lord Ellenborough and the Attorney-General both told the Jury, that if they did not find him guilty, we would have *war* with France!!!"[4] It took the jury "the space of a minute" to reach the obvious conclusion. The *Political Register* and the *Morning Chronicle* were alone among the London papers to protest against the proceeding as an interference with the freedom of the press; the others applauded the prosecution as necessary to preserve harmony between the two countries.[5] But Peltier was never brought before the court for sentencing; by May 1803 the two nations were again at war.[6]

The "peace" had lasted thirteen months after the signing of the definitive treaty of Amiens. It had been a hectic period for Addington and his cabinet. At first, they had bent every effort to cut costs by disbanding Britain's military forces. Lord St. Vincent, commander of the fleet at one of the great moments in English naval history (when the hitherto unknown Horatio Nelson became a national hero by a smashing victory over the Spanish navy off the coast of Portugal), now first lord of the admiralty, decommissioned ships and discharged seamen and dockworkers by the thousands. Soldiers and their officers were placed on half pay. The wartime income tax was repealed. All this had hardly been done when it became increasingly obvious that Cobbett had been right all along: the "peace" had been a fraud, and it was necessary to put the country back on a wartime footing. This proved a huge task; what had been saved by the initial cutbacks was now more than offset by the need to rearm in a hurry. Lord St. Vincent was bitterly attacked on all sides for his lack of foresight, although surely what he had been doing had the full acquiescence of the prime minister and the rest of the cabinet if not most of the press and the majority of the country's population. Those who had so enthusiastically acclaimed "Peace and Plenty" a few months before were now quick to condemn the government for its lack of preparedness.

To rekindle public enthusiasm for the war, the government released a 5,000-word paper entitled *Important Considerations for the People of This Kingdom* telling them "of the danger with which their property and their lives, their liberties, and their religion are threatened."[7] The tyrant Bonaparte had, "with the word *Liberty* continually on his lips, erected a despotism the most oppressive, the most capricious, and the most cruel that the Almighty, in his wrath, ever suffered to exist." Bonaparte hated and feared the example set by nearby Britain: "we must not remain free, lest they should learn lessons of freedom; we must destroy our ancient and venerable monarchy, lest they should sigh for a lawful and merciful king; we must not be happy, lest they should covet happiness; we must not speak, lest our voice should disturb the peace of Buonaparte; we must not breathe, we must cease to exist, because our existence gives umbrage to a man, who, from the walls of Acre, fled, in shame and disgrace, before a handful of Britons." Describing the barbarity of the French

IMPORTANT

CONSIDERATIONS

FOR THE

PEOPLE OF THIS KINGDOM.

PUBLISHED JULY, 1803,

And sent to the officiating Minister of every Parish

in England.

Printed by C. Rickaby, Peterborough-court, Fleet-street.

Important Considerations for the People of This Kingdom. Cobbett's anonymous rallying cry on the resumption of war against France in 1803 went to the minister of every parish in England under the royal seal. In 1809, when Cobbett was attacked as a renegade, he revealed that he was the author of the pamphlet

127

wherever their ambition had led them – in Italy, Egypt, Holland, Switzerland, and Germany – the paper ended with a stirring call to arms:

Singly engaged against the tyrants of the earth, Britain now attracts the eyes and the hearts of mankind; groaning nations look to her for deliverance; justice, liberty, and religion are inscribed on her banners; her success will be hailed with the shouts of the universe, while tears of admiration and gratitude will bedew the heads of her sons, who fall in the glorious contest.

The paper, bearing the royal seal, was sent to every parish church in England and Wales to be deposited on the pews, to be distributed in the aisles, to be posted on the church door. It was not generally known until 1809 that the author was William Cobbett.[8]

Bonaparte's invasion threats were seriously debated: When would the attempt be made? Would the French attack England directly or through Ireland, as they had done in 1797–8? The Irish rebels were so sure of French intervention that an uprising occurred in Dublin in July 1803, two months after the renewal of war. Viscount Kilwarden, lord chief justice, and his nephew were dragged from their coach and murdered, and several soldiers were killed, and although the insurrection was quickly put down (no French invasion was attempted), parliament passed legislation suspending the Habeas Corpus Act and declaring martial law in Ireland. The episode underscored Britain's lack of preparedness. Cobbett claimed that the appointees of Addington heading the Irish administration, though fully apprised of the likelihood of the uprising, had neglected to take the necessary precautions; that Ireland "is in a state of total neglect and abandonment."[9] This comment produced five letters from a Dublin correspondent who signed himself "Juverna," which were published in the *Political Register* from October to December 1803.[10] The letters suggested that the Earl of Hardwicke, the lord lieutenant of Ireland, had a head containing a "superabundant portion of particles of a very ligneous tendency" and that his qualifications as lord lieutenant (this being "his first *political* essay") were that he had "a good library in St. James's Square" and understood "the modern method of fattening sheep as well as any man in Cambridgeshire." Lord Redesdale, lord high chancellor, was also charged with inadequate qualifications for the task to which he had been assigned, having been nothing more than an "able and strongly built chancery pleader."[11] Somewhat ruder remarks were made about three other Irish officeholders: Mr. Justice Osborne, one of the judges of the king's bench; a Mr. Marsden, the undersecretary of state; and William Plunket, the solicitor general. It was apparent from other comments in the letters that the writer was no rebel; his complaint was that Addington had appointed incompetent, greedy, and, in some instances, dishonest officials to govern Ireland.

The "Juverna" letters became the foundation of both a prosecution for criminal libel brought by the attorney general, Spencer Perceval, against Cobbett as publisher and a civil action for damages brought against him by Plunket. The criminal action was tried in the court of king's bench, Westminster, on May 24, 1804, before the chief justice, Lord Ellenborough, and a special jury.[12] A number of distinguished individuals appeared as character witnesses on Cobbett's behalf: Robert Liston, former British minister to the United States; Lord Henry Stuart, secretary to the British legation under Liston; William Windham; Lord Minto, one of Windham's associates and presumably one of the original contributors to the fund for the establishment of the *Political Register*; Charles Yorke, home secretary; and John Reeves, printer to the king. They all testified that Cobbett was devoted to the king and the constitution. Liston, on cross-examination, admitted that Cobbett had "an ardent mind" and that he might be induced to libel a government "under which he was not living – always excepting his own."[13] The jury, after deliberating "about ten minutes," delivered a verdict of guilty, whereupon Lord Ellenborough imposed a fine of £500. The civil case brought by Plunket was tried two days later before Lord Ellenborough and the same special jury, which, after retiring for twenty minutes, returned with a verdict for the plaintiff, assessing the damages at £500.[14]

The cases were of far greater significance than might be reflected by the amount of damages assessed. The "Juverna" letters probably were libelous in a technical sense; that is, in a properly conducted legal proceeding, a properly constituted jury might reasonably have concluded that the language of the letters exposed all or some of the individuals to hatred, contempt, or ridicule, but it is probably even more likely that such a jury would have found for the defendant, or, in the event of a verdict for the plaintiff, only nominal damages would have been assessed. Damages of £500 in 1804 were far from nominal, representing about what the average farm laborer would earn over a twenty-five-year period. But Cobbett was the victim of a device which was an integral part of the corruption that existed in the government of the period. He was tried before a special jury, just as Peltier had been. And a special jury, particularly in Westminster and the county of Middlesex, was one made up of individuals who not only knew what was expected of them, but who were almost certain to do it. As a result, prosecution of a criminal action before a special jury almost always meant conviction.

The special jury had originally been intended to protect the parties at the bar when, as Blackstone put it, "the causes were of too great nicety for the discussion of ordinary freeholders."[15] It had gradually become a vehicle of oppression. The attorney general had a right to a special jury in a libel case.[16] The clerks charged with the duty of maintaining the panel of persons qualified to act as jurors identified those they considered suitable for a special jury by marking their names with "Esq." In the county of Middlesex there were roughly 400 persons so designated out of a total list of eligible jurors numbering about 4,000. The 400 lucky persons were paid a fee of a guinea each time they served and, according to Thomas Paine, an extra guinea if they found for the prosecution.[17] The full history of every "guinea man" and of his relationship with the government – whether he or any member of his family was pensioner or placeholder – was noted on the list, and continuance on the list was subject to good behavior. When a case was to be tried, forty-eight names out of the "Esqs." selected by the master of the crown office were presented to counsel for the two parties, and each was allowed to strike out any twelve of the names, an exercise which, in view of the manner of selection, was of extremely doubtful value to a defendant in any action brought by the government.[18]

The hearings in Cobbett's case provided a classic example of how the system worked, representing what Jeremy Bentham called "the grand modern edition of the grand star-chamber case *de libellis famosis*."[19] The criminal action against Cobbett was tried by the attorney general himself, who, after pointing out to the jurors that Lord Redesdale, one of the plaintiffs, was his brother-in-law, called upon them to contemplate the difference between the defendant and his distinguished relative: "Gentlemen, who is Mr Cobbett? Is he a man of family in this country? *Quis homo hic est? Quo patre natus?*"[20] In the civil case, Thomas Erskine, acting as counsel for the plaintiff (he had assisted Perceval in the criminal trial), explained to the jury that Lord Hardwicke was married to "one of his nearest relations."[21] Thus was the stage set: The cases represented a contest between persons of respectability and a man of no consequence.

The lord chief justice assisted in the prosecution. He was a notorious bully (one remembers Brougham's triumphant cry years later when he managed to put the old tyrant down), and on several occasions unnecessarily interrupted Cobbett's counsel, the distinguished whig barrister William Adam.[22] Although under the law the jury, and the jury alone, had the duty to determine whether the writings were libels, Ellenborough referred to them as such in his charge, adding: "when I call them libels I am anticipating your decision."[23] He defined a libel as anything that is "injurious to the feelings and happiness of an individual" or that "tends to the prejudice of any individual" or that means to imply that a man in high position is "ill-placed."[24] Bentham summed up these passages by saying: "if they mean anything, they mean this – viz. that it is a *crime* for *any man* to write anything which it happens to *any other man* not to *like*."[25] An unnamed "great orator and statesman" (presumably Windham) observed to Cobbett that if Ellenborough's statement of the law was correct, no writer could, with impunity, mention the name of any man unaccompanied by praise, for to name a man without praise might injure "his individual feelings."[26] It was not until 1825 that legislation was passed outlawing the special jury in the form faced by Cobbett and those other unfortunate individuals who happened to offend the feelings of some important government official.

The "Juverna" case did not end with the prosecution of Cobbett. The author of the letters proved to be Robert Johnson, justice of the court of common pleas in Ireland.[27] He was arrested there early in 1805, and after being denied the right of standing trial in Ireland, was carried off to England for a trial by Lord Ellenborough before one of his special juries.[28] Needless to say, Johnson was also found guilty. Instead of being brought up for judgment, he was allowed to resign, thereupon becoming eligible for a pension of £1,200 a year provided by law for judges of his standing.[29]

Cobbett's encounter with Lord Ellenborough occurred in May 1804, at a time when an important change of ministry was taking place. The month before, Addington had resigned under pressure, becoming Lord Sidmouth, and in May 1804 Pitt again took over as prime minister – a completely disastrous final effort terminating in his death twenty months later. The great issue of the day was still the war with France; it had caused Addington's downfall and proved to be Pitt's nemesis. Beginning with the resumption of the war in 1803, Bonaparte had accelerated his plans for an invasion of Britain. The threat dominated all thought in England. When discussing the next session of parliament in a letter to Windham, Cobbett was led to exclaim: "the *next!* will there be a next session?"[30] The attorney general, Spencer Perceval, writing to his brother-in-law, Lord Redesdale, at the end of December 1803, reported that the government had been fully convinced that the French had planned to invade on Christmas day, but that a storm had prevented their sailing: "we are certainly now to expect them the first time the weather permits."[31] There was reason for concern. Bonaparte demonstrated the seriousness of his intentions by assembling, in the newly enlarged French channel ports, over 2,300 invasion craft capable of carrying 167,000 fighting men.[32]

Addington, and then Pitt, proceeded to put the British navy back into wartime duty and to fortify the coastline. The blockhouses constructed to guard the Thames drew forth a comment from a reader of the *Political Register:*

> If *Blocks* can from danger deliver,
>> Two places are safe from the French;
>> The first is the mouth of the river;
>> The second the Treasury Bench.[33]

Then there was the huge task of raising the men by whom invasion could be repelled on land. The chief criticism of these programs related to the vigor with which they were being prosecuted and the character of the three-part army that was being created. The regular army, theoretically made up of volunteers who could be called on to serve in any part of the world, was encumbered by at least four other disabilities: Enlistment was for life, the pay of a private was a mere one shilling per day, discipline was severe, and the officers, who in most cases had purchased their commissions, were poorly trained.[34]

Despite the obvious need for a change in army structure, little change was made during the brief span of Pitt's second administration; as a result, enlistments for the regular army did not keep pace with losses through retirement and disability. Pitt had never taken much interest in the army, and now, seriously ill, much of his attention was devoted to the creation of a third coalition of land forces to bring down the French or, at least, to divert them from an invasion of Britain, and to the defense of his old friend Henry Dundas. Dundas for years had been king of Scottish patronage, controlling as many as thirty-nine of the forty-five Scottish votes in the Commons; he had been Pitt's political manager; and he had been Pitt's drinking companion – according to the painter Thomas Stothard, the two of them had finished off seven bottles of wine in a night.[35] During Addington's administration Dundas had been made Lord Melville; he was now first lord of the admiralty in Pitt's cabinet. Melville's ability to find places for ambitious countrymen linked his name with the seventy-fifth psalm: "For promotion cometh neither from the east, nor the west, nor from the south." The widespread complaints against Melville's predecessor, Lord St. Vincent, had resulted in an inquiry into the affairs of the navy by a five-man commission headed by Admiral Sir Charles Pole, member of parliament.[36] The commission did not limit the scope of its inquiry to the period of Lord St. Vincent's term of office, but almost certainly as the result of a tip by some informer, went back to the years 1784 to 1800 when Melville had been treasurer of the navy in the earlier Pitt administration. There they found a most amazing misuse of government funds. Melville's paymaster was a man named Alexander Trotter. Trotter, with Melville's knowledge, transferred government money aggregating over £8,000,000 from the Bank of England to his own account at the firm of Coutts & Co., where the government funds were mingled with the personal funds of Trotter and Melville. Trotter invested some of these mingled funds in securities for his personal account, various interest-free loans out of the funds were made to Melville, some of the funds were used for "private emolument," some of the funds were applied to unnamed "delicate and confidential transactions of government," and some of the funds were used for navy purposes.[37] Although it was alleged that all the government funds were finally restored (without interest), the exact state of the accounts could never be determined, since Trotter and Melville, by a formal written document executed after the start of the inquiry, had agreed "to cancel and destroy all the vouchers or other memorandums and writings" relating to the transactions.[38]

The nature of the findings of the commission became the subject of gossip beginning shortly after Trotter's testimony in June 1804, but the details of the story were not released until the following year. In February 1805, Cobbett wrote: "The Commission had already laid ten reports before parliament; the last is looked for with much anxiety by the public. It is said to be of so interesting a nature, that a great personage has thought it worthy of his particular perusal."[39] The text of the tenth report appeared in the *Political Register* of 30 March 1805. The commissioners described the difficulties they had encountered in getting the facts, not only because of the lack of records but because witnesses had resorted to the fifth clause of the act establishing the commission, which provided that "no person shall be compellable to answer any question . . . which may . . . tend to criminate such person or to expose such person to any pains or penalties."[40]

The tenth report immediately pushed all other news aside. The Pitt papers, the *Morning Post,* the *Morning Herald,* the *Sun,* the *Oracle,* and the *Courier,* defended Melville. The *Political Register,* along with the *Morning Chronicle* (a Fox paper) and *The Times* (an Addington paper) – "with a degree of talent and zeal that does them great honour" was the way Cobbett phrased it – "espoused the cause of the nation."[41] In the House of Commons, Samuel Whitbread, a Fox whig, gave notice of his intention to seek a vote censuring Melville, and on April 8, 1805 introduced a series of twelve resolutions, the first of which dealt with the history of parliamentary regulations concerning the handling of navy funds.[42] In the debate on this, Pitt made a speech of several hours, urging that all action on the tenth report be deferred until after a further inquiry could be made by a select committee. This being opposed by Fox, Pitt moved the previous question, thereby closing the debate and forcing an immediate vote on the first of Whitbread's resolutions. Much to Fox's surprise (he had predicted the defeat of the motion), the vote was split evenly, 216 to 216.[43] This left Melville's fate up to the speaker, Charles Abbot, who was thought to lack "dignity in his manner and appearance."[44] But his dignity of character was adequate to the occasion. "Amid a scene long remembered as one of the most striking that have ever been witnessed within the walls of the House of Commons," Abbot explained that he "could not in conscience do otherwise," and then cast his vote with those leading the attack against Melville.[45] Fable has it, though fable is probably wrong, that in the tumult that followed, Pitt was seen pressing his hat on his head to conceal the tears trickling down his cheeks.[46]

Whitbread's proposed resolutions of censure were then carried without division, including one characterizing Melville's conduct as "a gross violation of the law and a high breach of duty." Melville immediately resigned his cabinet post, and his name was stricken from the privy council. But that was not an end to the matter. Whitbread on June 13, 1805 moved for Melville's impeachment, whereupon Nathaniel Bond, one of Addington's oldest friends, moved an amendment providing that Melville be criminally prosecuted in the court of king's bench. Whitbread's motion lost by 195 to 272, but Bond's amendment passed by 238 to 229.[47] Melville was to be turned over to Lord Ellenborough and one of his special juries. Thirteen days later, when the attendance in the House had shrunk by over a third (many of the independent country members had gone home), the last decision was reversed by a vote of 166 to 143 – Lord Melville was not to be tried before a judge and jury, but in impeachment proceedings before the House of Lords, which included "seventy or eighty members . . . who had been exalted to their seats during the administration of which Lord Melville made a part."[48]

Pitt did not live long enough to see the outcome of the impeachment proceedings against Melville. He died on January 23, 1806 at only forty-six years of age and at the lowest point in his long career, filled with bitterness over Melville's disgrace and the frustration of his own final effort to create one more coalition of powers against the French. For Pitt, shortly after resuming the post of prime minister in 1804, had sent out envoys to Russia and Austria with offers of British subsidies. Pitt was warned by Cobbett in the *Political Register* and by Fox in parliament that he was bringing pressure on his allies prematurely; that they were not ready to face Bonaparte.[49] The warnings came to nothing. The inevitable result was obscured, for a moment, by Nelson's great victory at Trafalgar on October 21, 1805. But five weeks later Bonaparte defeated the combined Austrian–Russian

armies at Austerlitz, and Pitt's third coalition, for all practical purposes, had come to an end. The news of the battle was brought to Pitt
in December 1805, six months after the commons, acting on the tenth
report, had adopted its vote of censure against Lord Melville. "We
can get over Austerlitz," Pitt bravely told Huskisson, "but we can
never get over the Tenth Report."[50]

A month later Pitt was dead. Within two weeks, a new ministry had
been formed by Lord Grenville. This was the "ministry of All the
Talents," a combination of men of disparate views designed, it was
thought, to unify the country so that it might most effectually carry
on the war against Bonaparte.

Melville's impeachment proceeding, attended by Cobbett with his
wife and two children, was the most sensational event that occurred
during the relatively short life of the new ministry.[51] The House of
Lords proved to be a more congenial atmosphere than Lord Melville
might have encountered in Lord Ellenborough's court, as he was
acquitted in June 1806 on all ten of the charges brought against him,
the closest vote on any of the charges being 83 to 53.[52] Lord Chief
Justice Ellenborough, as a member of the House of Lords, voted
guilty on six of the ten charges. "I think," wrote Lady Bessborough,
one of Melville's admirers, "Ld. M. far from clear'd in a manner I
should like were I him," while a statement by the Marquis of Buckingham to his brother, Lord Grenville, made three weeks after the
acquittal suggests that Melville was "saved" by Grenville.[53] How, we
do not know, although perhaps the clue is suggested by our knowledge that the number of peers voting on the impeachment charges
was less than half of those qualified to vote, and that among those not
voting were Grenville and nine of the peers in Grenville's cabinet.

9 · "The system"

It is the system, the vermin-breeding system, that I, for my part, am at war with.

SIX YEARS had now elapsed since Cobbett's return to England. In that interval he had seen three changes in administration: in 1801, the resignation of Pitt after serving as prime minister for seventeen years and the succession of Henry Addington; in 1804, the reshuffle when Addington went out and Pitt came back in; and in 1806, following the death of Pitt, the creation of the ministry of All the Talents headed by Lord Grenville. The events accompanying these changes destroyed many of Cobbett's illusions both as to men and as to institutions.

When Cobbett was 3,000 miles away in America, Pitt had been the Great Statesman. He had entered office in 1784 "untainted in character, spotless in life . . . a saviour of society, who would cast the money-changers out of the temple of Government."[1] His very name, Cobbett stated, was "regarded as a sort of charm or spell sufficiently potent to protect us against all the demons of corruption."[2] Pitt's conduct at shorter range was a serious disappointment. Cobbett's admiration, gradually cooling, finally turned into hearty dislike. In July 1802 Pitt was still "among the greatest."[3] A year and a half later, in December 1803, when England was once more at war with France, Cobbett stated that although Pitt might "do much" as a member of a new administration, "this storm never can be weathered with Mr Pitt at the *helm*" – a totally new system of "politics and of political economy" was required.[4] By September 1804, the ministerial papers accused Cobbett of having finally deserted Pitt. "But to desert," Cobbett replied, "a man must first be enlisted, and if I might be said to be enlisted, it was in the cause of which I regarded you as the champion; and not in your personal service."[5] Pitt's acceptance of the questionable terms of the peace in 1801, after having opposed any peace with France in 1799, was the first incident to shake the pedestal, but since this occurred before July 1802, we must look elsewhere for a full explanation of Cobbett's change in views. And there were many incidents that cast doubts on Pitt's character.

According to Pitt's own account, he had resigned in 1801 because that good protestant, George III, was bitterly opposed to the introduction of legislation that would eliminate some of the legal disabilities imposed on Roman catholics. But, as Cobbett later pointed out, this alleged high-mindedness of Pitt did not prevent his return to the same office three years later, when he was willing to promise that he would never again revive the catholic issue.[6] Cobbett thought too that the 1801 transfer of the government from Pitt to his undistinguished friend Addington, with the concurrent transfer of Pitt's following in parliament (Pitt rarely attended in person during the first two years of Addington's ministry), was a private deal purely for Pitt's convenience, without regard to the desires or needs of the nation.[7] In November 1802 Cobbett wrote:

we saw twenty bills of great importance passed without twenty members in the House ... We saw a poor, tame, spiritless set of men, following the minister of the day, let him be who or what he would; we saw Mr Pitt making a conveyance of their support as if it had been his property in fee simple; we saw – we saw enough to wish never to see the like again.[8]

Before Pitt was through, Cobbett saw more things he did not like. In 1803, after several years of seeming indifference to the conduct of government, Pitt returned to join the attack on Addington and his cabinet. He rebuked them for their "tardiness, langour and imbecility," and declared them "incapable" of any energetic plan for the defense of the country.[9] Once he had regained his position as prime minister in May 1804, the alleged inadequacies of the members of Addington's cabinet did not prevent him from inviting half of them to join his own.[10] Pitt claimed that he would have preferred to have Grenville, Windham, and Fox in his ministry, but that the king had adamantly refused to accept Fox, while Grenville and Windham refused to take office without him. Pitt's credibility, in Cobbett's mind, was once again brought into question when, on the creation of the ministry of All the Talents in 1806, the king accepted Fox as secretary for foreign affairs.

Finally, the hearings on Lord Melville's conduct revealed not only that Pitt had been warned by an official of the Bank of England that large amounts of government money were being improperly transferred to a private bank, but that Pitt himself had been personally involved in some of the unorthodox methods of dealing with such funds. He had surreptitiously made an unrecorded loan of £40,000 of government money to two hard-pressed bankers, Pitt supporters in the House of Commons.[11] When this was disclosed, Pitt's friends passed a bill rendering him immune from any liability on account of the transaction. Cobbett thought that Pitt deserved censure more than Melville, and that Pitt's efforts to protect his friend were really efforts to protect himself. A shocked Cobbett wrote: "I blush to think of the pages, and I might say the volumes, perhaps, that I have written in praise of his talents and his qualities, but particularly his *financial skill* and his *purity!*"[12] So shocked was Cobbett that he took the strand of Pitt's hair with the gold filigree "W.P." that had been given to his small daughter and, despite her tears, threw it on the fire. Symbolically, the locket proved not to be real gold.[13]

These incidents by themselves would have provided an adequate explanation for Cobbett's changed views. But there were other matters which were probably of even greater significance, and they related to Cobbett's conception of the government of Britain. In his view, the well-being of the nation depended on a hereditary monarch advised by a ministry made up of men of great talent and high birth, completely unselfish, independent of public popularity on the one hand and of the monarch on the other.[14] William Windham was, in Cobbett's way of thinking, an ideal minister; he was rich and of good family, hence independent. Independence was an essential element in Cobbett's personal life; it was, likewise, according to his thinking, the root of good government. He was therefore strongly opposed to the use of "pensions and places" to support the administration.[15] Anyone in government who might want something other than the good of the nation was suspect. Cobbett hated to see bankers, merchants, and contractors in parliament. He would have preferred to exclude all men engaged in any business or profession.[16]

Pitt's system was completely antithetical to that of Cobbett. Despite the romantic view of Pitt as a figure divorced from the grubby side of politics, his parliamentary majority, after he first took office in 1784, was due to the diligence and largesse of John Robinson as patronage secretary.[17] Thereafter, Pitt's continuation in office was assured by the invaluable assistance of George Rose, who, as secretary of the treasury, used the patronage of the crown on Pitt's behalf, "with all the licentiousness and partiality of private property."[18] This included not only grants of money, but the creation of peers for the purpose of attaching boroughmongers to Pitt. Pitt's return to office in 1804 was accomplished with the credit built out of such patronage and with the backing of both Rose and Lord Melville, Melville himself controlling thirty-odd votes in parliament through his responsibility for patronage in Scotland.[19] In brief, Pitt's support derived from the wholesale use of pensions and places, and involved close association with bankers, merchants, and contractors, as disclosed in the Melville inquiry. Cobbett was concerned by Pitt's affection for the sinking fund, and particularly the practice of borrowing every year (frequently at higher interest rates than the initial debt) in order to make deposits to the fund with the attendant commissions, bonuses, and discounts to the bankers on what was borrowed – costs which could have been avoided simply by discontinuing the deposits.[20] The amount that had to be borrowed every year was increased by Pitt's habit of overstating the expected revenues and understating expected expenses, so that year-end deficits were inevitable.[21] The periodic borrowings provided opportunities for rewarding friends. Partisans of the government were given "slices" of a loan: "as the scrip, as it used to be called, was always directly at a *premium,* a bargain was always made with the loan-monger that he should admit certain favourites of the Government to have certain portions of scrip, at the same price that he gave for it."[22] The individual given such a "slice" never made any investment or took any risk; he was automatically given the amount of premium for the scrip assigned to him. This was a convenient way of taking care of friends of the government.

Pitt's system also involved the award of high positions in government to untried men without family. Pitt's friend Addington, son of a physician, fell into that category. And Addington, as if in imitation of Pitt, also surrounded himself with "climbers." Cobbett disliked them; a climber could not afford to be independent; his job was at the whim of his superior, and it was essential to hold on to the job. The more favors he accepted, the more obligated he became. Cobbett frequently repeated Swift's words that climbing is performed in the attitude of crawling.[23] Pitt's protégé George Canning, whom Cobbett regularly referred to as "The Upstart," fulfilled Cobbett's conception of how a climber behaves. Canning, the son of an actress of soiled reputation, entered parliament when he was twenty-three through the favor of the prime minister. He soon had a pension for life, and saw to it that pensions for life were granted to his sisters.[24] As treasurer of the navy in 1804 he allegedly hindered the commission's inquiry into Melville's conduct; as member of parliament he defended Pitt's role in the affair.[25] Would Canning resign when Addington (one of Canning's pet hates) was asked to join Pitt's cabinet? – "As well might you ask puss to part with her whiskers and her claws," responded Cobbett.[26] William Huskisson, another of Pitt's young men, was as objectionable as Canning. When he was thirty-one years old he was given a pension for life; he owed his seat in parliament to the government, and his qualification for that seat was provided by Alexander Davison, the enormously rich government contractor who was twice thereafter jailed, first for election bribery and later for falsifying vouchers in dealing with the government.[27] Lord Hawkesbury, born Robert Banks Jenkinson, fell into the same proscribed class. Although he later served as prime minister for fifteen years, he had little more to offer than "a respectable mediocrity of talents."[28] He was first attacked by Cobbett for his 1801 peace with France, but there were grounds for Cobbett's distaste more eloquent than this. Hawkesbury, like his father, who had been made Earl of Liverpool for a lifetime of loyal government service, was a perennial officeholder, doubly subservient because of his fear of losing office. When he became a pensioner at thirty-six on accepting the wardenship of the Cinque ports worth £3,000 a year, Lord Sheffield declared that "the Jenkinson craving disposition will revolt the whole country."[29] In 1802, while Cobbett was still an admirer of Pitt, he had written: "We think it probable, that Mr Pitt may again be minister, and if he should we hope he will perceive and avoid the evil consequences of surrounding himself with *low* and *little* men."[30] Cobbett had in mind the Cannings, the Huskissons, the Hawkesburys, and, of course, the Roses.

Addington had never held any appeal for Cobbett. He was created by Pitt, and was commended neither by family nor by demonstrated talents of a high order. He was believed, said Cobbett, to be a very *honest* man, "but what is that? Honesty alone is not a recommendation for a footman, and shall it be for a first minister?"[31] Addington's appearance, which was not impressive, reminded his detractors of his descent from a mere doctor of medicine. He was described by Lord Rosebery as having "the indefinable air of a village apothecary inspecting the tongue of the State."[32] The whig wit James Hare, happening to see Addington after it was announced that he was to be prime minister, was thrown into "such a fit of laughter that he laugh'd the whole way from the Horse Guards to the Stable Yard, and was oblig'd to sit down on a bench in the park to rest."[33]

Addington's performance in office was in the Pitt tradition; it did nothing to raise him in Cobbett's estimation. The members of Addington's administration were enlisted largely from his own family and former school friends at Cheam and Winchester.[34] Conventional in all things, even in the worst of them, Addington conferred on his son, a Winchester schoolboy, the clerkship of the pells, a lifetime sinecure worth £3,000 a year, and for himself, at the outset of his service as prime minister, accepted from the king a large house in Richmond Park, which in Cobbett's view constituted a waiver of his independence. Cobbett made sure that this would not be forgotten; the Addington government became the "Richmond Park Ministry."

Addington saw to it that Henry Dundas was made a peer (Lord Melville), thereby assuring himself of the Scottish votes in Dundas's pockets. After the general election of 1802, in which the ministers had announced that they would use "no influence or interference whatsoever," the *Political Register* published a letter from one of Cobbett's readers which pointed out that in Kent the government influence was "openly and systematically exerted at every contested election"; places and employments of all kinds were offered to electors, contracts were promised, dockyard employees who voted against the government candidate were dismissed, overage and disabled pensioners lost their allowances.[35] Government funds on deposit at the banking firm of Coutts & Co. were withdrawn because the head of the firm, Thomas Coutts, was father-in-law of Sir Francis Burdett, a candidate for Middlesex in opposition to the government choice.[36] In 1805 Addington, newly elevated to the peerage as Lord Sidmouth, entered Pitt's cabinet (despite the abuse he had suffered from Pitt the year before) but left a few months later when a cabinet post for his brother-in-law was refused by Pitt.[37]

What a twentieth-century historian refers to as Pitt's "disorderly" mind, Cobbett saw as something less attractive.[38] He thought that many of the individual actions taken by Pitt, and also by Addington, were rather stupid: The peace of Amiens, in which both were involved, was an outstanding example. He was probably quite genuinely surprised to discover that great men could be guilty of what he thought of as such gross errors in judgment. But it is likely that he was even more surprised by the web of corruption that appeared from top to bottom of their administrations, and which he regarded as an essential element of the Pitt system. It is difficult to recreate what Cobbett saw, because most of those living at that time who were writing letters and journals seemed so sublimely unconscious of it. Forty years before, Horace Walpole had declared after a series of British successes during the Seven Years' war: "We have been as victorious as the Romans and are as corrupt."[39] Walpole was referring to the illegal devices used to secure election to parliament. By the beginning of the nineteenth century, these devices were taken for granted. Parliamentary seats were openly offered for sale in the advertising columns of respectable London newspapers. The whig editors of the *Edinburgh Review* defended the practice on the ground that it provided "constitutional balance" by enabling the crown and the peers to be represented in the House of Commons.[40] But the corruption that began with parliamentary elections did not end there.[41] Once the members had arrived at the House of Commons, their voting was assured, in many cases, by government favors given or anticipated: pensions, honors, contracts, the granting of crown tenancies at less than their market value, appointments and promotions for the member or for his relatives or his friends.[42] Appointment to office was not according to any simple principle: The remnants of the aristocratic tradition espoused by Cobbett were mingled with the romanticism of friendship and the pragmatism of staying in power. And the "appointments" were not limited to the top political spots or even to what is now reserved to the civil service. The major opportunities for "respectable" employment were all favors within the granting or withholding of the government.[43] "The government employs and pays all, and it receives all. There is a chain of dependence running through the whole nation, which, though not everywhere seen, is everywhere felt. There is not one man in one thousand who does not feel the weight of this chain. Army, navy, church, the law, sinecures, pensions, tax offices, war and navy offices, Whitehall, India-house, Bank, contract, job, &c. &c. Who is there, who is not himself, or who has not a son, a brother, or some relation or other, employed and paid by, dependent for bread upon, the minister of the day?"[44] The result, according to Cobbett, was that "Weak and base, but cunning creatures, have long usurped and possessed whatever the public had to bestow upon talents and integrity, whether in church or in state, whether in the law, or in any other of the other higher walks of life."[45]

Not unexpectedly, these weak and base creatures conducted the affairs of government in a manner consistent with the methods by which they had been appointed. While this type of misconduct was fostered by inadequate methods of fiscal control and accountability, the most powerful force for corruption was the attitude of acceptance that pervaded society: The hangers-on of government had become so accustomed to the smell of corruption that they no longer noticed it. It is impossible otherwise to explain the practice by which army officers routinely mulcted their soldiers, and army quartermasters as routinely mulcted the government; the use of naval ships to engage in trade for the personal account of their officers; the sale of church livings and the "heaping of benefices and dignities upon persons and families devoted to the ministry"; the fees exacted from spectators by the doorman in charge of parliamentary galleries; the "slices" alloted to government friends out of periodic loans; the appointment of government clerks on the understanding that they would remit part of their salaries to the officer appointing them; the kickbacks to officials supervising government contracts; the fraudulent overcharges by "respectable" government contractors; the special juries; the subsidized and managed press.[46]

The cause of the people has been betrayed by hundreds of men, who were well able to serve the people, but whom a love of ease and of the indulgence of empty vanity have seduced into the service of the bribing usurpers, who have spared no means to corrupt men of literary talent from the authors of folios to the authors of baby-books and ballads. *Caricature-makers, song-makers;* all have been bribed by one means or another. Gillray and Dibdin were both pensioned. Southey, William Gifford; all, all are placed or pensioned. *Play-writers, Historians.* None have escaped.[47]

The reviewers of books were often paid by the authors of books; others like Southey and Gifford held government pensions.[48] The official paid a salary to inspect canvas supplied to the government was the principal supplier of canvas; the man appointed to specify the drugs furnished to the army had a monopoly of the drugs purchased by the army – a monopoly that had been in the family for more than seventy years.[49] Not surprisingly, both canvas man and drug man were zealous supporters of the government.

It was this network of corruption, beginning at the top with the use of government money and favors to insure parliamentary majorities and running in various forms through the whole fabric of society: the clergy, army and navy officers, lawyers, civil servants, bankers and merchants, down to the poorest doorman who unlawfully exacted fees in the spectators' gallery – "forming the whole nation into a string of political mendicants, cringing to the minister of the day for a portion of that which he has drained from them in taxes" – that Cobbett called the Pitt system.[50] So deeply rooted was the system that the rare individual who tried to expose such practice ran more risks than those engaged in them.[51]

Pitt had been able to maintain his system through exceptional talents for which Cobbett, cynically, gave him full credit:

He had talents, and, of their kind, very great talents. All the merchants and manufacturers who ever approached him were struck with admiration of his talents. He, according to the vulgar saying, "knew their meaning by their gaping." He knew all their business better than they did. His quickness was astonishing. He was an incomparable accountant, a consummate clerk, and he was besides a matchless *debater.* To a fluency, a command of words, that, perhaps, no man ever equalled, he added a readiness of conception, an adroitness in parrying the force of an argument, a command of temper, political courage, at once a decorum and disregard of means, surpassing any man of whom we have ever heard. He was a showy and a shallow man; but, his talents were precisely of the right kind for the theatre on which he had to act, and all the machinery and tactic of which he understood and knew how to use better, and used with greater successes for his objects, than any man that ever lived. Here are an abundance of *talents*; but, they are not such as mark the GREAT MAN, a character, which, when we are speaking of statesmen or ministers, belongs to those only, whose wisdom is proved in *the benefit which their measures produce to their country.*[52]

Since 1803 Cobbett had been insisting on a change in the Pitt system, but little hope for change existed so long as the author of the system was in the full exercise of his talents.

In 1806, while Pitt lay on his deathbed at his house in Putney and a new ministry was in the making, Cobbett again took up the cry:

The change, to answer any good purpose, must be *radical*; it must include all; yea, underlings and all; there must be a clean sweeping out of all the dirt of twenty years' collecting; it must be such a change as will lead to, and very soon produce, a complete *change of system*, or I shall have no hope in it.[53]

To accomplish this, the new ministry should be made up of "public men who have distinguished themselves as enemies of corruption and of corrupt rulers."[54] Members of the old Pitt team, "the Hawkesburies, the Cannings and the Old Roses," must be kept out of office. The practice of granting pensions (in the first ten months after Pitt's return to office another burden of nearly £40,000 per annum had been laid on the nation) and of compromises and concessions "to obtain votes and secure majorities" should, Cobbett hoped, be brought to an end: "It is the system, the vermin-breeding system, that I, for my part, am at war with."[55]

The new cabinet, the ministry of All the Talents, was announced on February 2. Lord Grenville was first lord of the treasury. Windham was secretary for war and colonies. Fox, with whom Grenville and Windham had been cooperating since Pitt's return to office in 1804, was foreign secretary.[56] No one from Pitt's cabinet was included. Lord Sidmouth was to be lord privy seal, but any association with Pitt had been redeemed, in Cobbett's eyes, by Sidmouth's staunch stand against Melville's conduct. In the next issue of the *Political Register* Cobbett laid down a course of action for the new administration: "I have always thought, that the very first act of a new ministry should be, to form committees of inquiry in both Houses of Parliament, or a joint committee of the two Houses, wherein to make, and whence to promulgate, a true statement of the affairs of the country."[57] Following these inquiries, the people should be told "not only the truth, but the whole truth." Pitt for example, had made "an annual boast about the prosperity, the flourishing state of the country." The people should know that while Old George Rose, Pitt's dispenser of patronage for twenty years, was receiving £18,000 a year from the public purse, over a million individuals out of a total population of nine million were being supported by the poor rates; that there are "hundreds of thousands of the people of England who never taste any food but bread and vegetables, and who scarcely ever know what it is to have a full meal even of these"; and that the weekly wages of the agricultural worker were not adequate to cover the bare cost of food for himself and his family, much less pay for clothing, fuel, or house rent. Continuing, he added: "this terrible evil cannot be, all at once, removed; but . . . in order to convince the people that their situation is known to and felt by their rulers, the new ministry should make some specific declaration upon the subject; and that, with all convenient speed, they should adopt measures for relief."[58] Cobbett's proposed inquiries were not to be limited to this single subject of the poor, or even the finances of the nation, but were to cover all principal areas of national concern.

A person in Cobbett's position – anyone in that position *except* Cobbett – might reasonably expect some material benefit for himself as a result of the appointment of the new ministry headed by men whom Cobbett, almost single-handed, had supported since 1801. Cobbett's relations with Windham had been especially close ever since they had met on Cobbett's return to England. Windham had urged Cobbett to establish the *Political Register,* and he and his friends had put up most of the original capital. Windham had declared in open parliament that Cobbett deserved a statue of gold from his country for the services he had rendered in America.[59] The correspondence from Cobbett to Windham that has survived (Cobbett rarely saved letters sent to him) suggests that they wrote to each other, or met, about once a week. Their ideas on many subjects coincided completely; and there is reason to believe that Cobbett's admiration for Windham, which is clear from the correspondence, was warmly reciprocated by Windham. On being accused in the House of Commons of repeating the views of Cobbett, Windham declared: "I set a higher value upon the opinions of that other person than I have the presumption to set upon my own."[60] When, in 1803, Cobbett stated that in the event of invasion he intended "to go instantly into the army," Windham expressed the wish that "we could be somewhere together."[61] In 1806, when Windham became a cabinet minister, he offered to make Cobbett his undersecretary of state.[62]

Yet Cobbett immediately made it plain to Windham that although he wanted nothing for himself, there was one thing he did want: the dismissal of Francis Freeling, secretary of the post office, a warm admirer of Pitt and, according to Cobbett, guilty not only of a gross violation of law but the oppressor of Cobbett and "of every man connected with the press and not of the Pitt faction or race."[63]

The story was this: In November 1800, a few weeks after Cobbett

146

had launched the *Porcupine*, he asked about the means of sending the paper to subscribers in Canada and Nova Scotia through the post office. Freeling, as secretary of the post office, replied that the exclusive privilege of forwarding publications to America and the West Indies had been granted to him personally, as remuneration in addition to his salary of £1,200, and that the charge was five guineas a year per copy.[64] Cobbett asked whether Freeling would accept "a couple of guineas a year" for each of 397 customers if payment were to be made in advance. Freeling said that he would settle for three guineas each on that basis; he also "hinted that it would not be proper to make our contract known, lest other Printers should think themselves ill-used," and assured Cobbett that he thereafter would receive advertisements of the post office for insertion in the *Porcupine*. Cobbett decided against the arrangement; he said he was revolted by the proposed clandestine compact and that making such a deal would encourage the continuance of an abuse of office by Freeling. As a consequence, Freeling and his subordinates, Cobbett claimed, did their utmost to injure him. Packets of incoming newspapers from America, formerly delivered to Cobbett at 10s. 6d. per packet, were now presented at a charge of five or six guineas. Cobbett's *Porcupine* sent to domestic subscribers via the mails was being replaced en route with rival papers. In addition, he suffered along with all the other papers from the shakedown that occurred when the weekly dispatch of news from Hamburg arrived. The postal clerks took this in charge, translated it, and then insisted that each newspaper pay a guinea for the translation; otherwise the news was withheld.

A complaint setting forth these facts was sent by Cobbett to the postmaster general, Lord Auckland, in June 1801.[65] Not having received any answer, other than what he regarded as a formal acknowledgement, Cobbett published the complaint in the *Political Register* for November 27, 1802, and reprinted the article in a pamphlet that went through several editions.[66] The publication of the complaint was a result of still another strange activity of the postal clerks working for Freeling; in addition to their translation services, they were news vendors on their own account (some of them were also news printers and publishers), and in that capacity were circulating a newspaper called the *Argus* which Cobbett maintained contained "the most atrocious libels upon the British government, and upon His Majesty himself."[67]

Cobbett's request for action against Freeling, made shortly after the new ministry took office in February 1806, was relayed by Windham to Lord Grenville, and was rejected by him. Two reasons seem to have been given: that Freeling's position was below the level usually affected on a change of ministry, and that Freeling had merely been "an over-active zealous officious partizan of an administration in which Ld Gren. had spent his life."[68] Grenville had not only spent much of his official life in cooperation with Pitt, but they were first cousins, and Grenville had married Anne Pitt, first cousin once removed of William Pitt. Grenville could not be expected to accept Cobbett's hatred of everything associated with the name of Pitt.

It has not been possible to provide an exact chronology of events: We do not know when Cobbett learned that his request had been turned down by Grenville; we know only that Cobbett wrote to Windham on February 10, 1806 stating his case against Freeling, and that five days later, on February 15, the *Political Register* published an article that was not flattering to the new prime minister.[69] It began with a fully warranted criticism of the designation of Lord Ellenborough, the chief justice, to a position in Grenville's cabinet – an unfortunate combination of executive, legislative, and judicial functions that succeeding prime ministers eschewed. Then Cobbett went on to a criticism of the personal conduct of Lord Grenville which, whether or not warranted, was certain to cause irritation: Grenville, while first lord of the treasury, was continuing to hold the incompatible job of auditor of the exchequer, to which a large pension was attached.[70] This was followed a few pages later by a franker analysis of Lord Grenville's capacities than most prime ministers like to hear, expressed in extremely patronizing terms: "I have certainly never pretended to represent him as a man of the very first rate abilities ... I have never thought of him as a man of great profundity, particularly in matters relating to political economy." These observations were hardly ameliorated by Cobbett's continuing egocentric remarks – in the tone of an elderly solicitor writing a character for one of his junior clerks – that, notwithstanding these deficiencies of Grenville, "I have always regarded him as a steady, a wise and an upright statesman."[71]

In view of Windham's known relationship with both Cobbett and the *Political Register,* this attack on Grenville must have been enormously embarrassing to Windham. Thus, a few days later we find Cobbett writing an explanation of his conduct to Windham, who had voiced his "serious displeasure" with the article:

With regard to the fact on the point of talents; that is a matter of mere opinion; and as to the motive of stating it, I will not disguise, either to you or to the world, that I was to begin preparing the public mind for a watchfulness over him, for a hesitation in applauding his measures relative to finance and other matters; and this because, I think, I clearly perceive, from the manner in which he has begun, and from the retention of so many of the Pitt sect about him and in every department within the reach of his influence, an intention, by no means equivocally indicated, to preserve, in spirit, at least, the accursed system, which I hope to see annihilated, and which, if not annihilated, I am fully persuaded will annihilate the liberties of the people first, and next the independence of the country.

Then, getting to what perhaps had most rankled:

Besides, Sir, there really does appear to me, and I cannot help saying it, something like inconsistency in attaching any degree of importance to my promulgated opinions, at the very time that my opinions communicated in private seem to be looked upon as entirely unworthy of notice; an instance of which last is strikingly afforded in the fate of my application with regard to Freeling.[72]

This episode spelled the end of the Cobbett–Windham friendship. Five days later (February 28, 1806) Windham wrote in his diary: "Came away in carriage with Fox; got out at end of Downing Street, and went to office, thence to Cobbett. Probably the last interview we shall have."[73] But the relationship concluded on an angrier note. The *Political Register* of March 1, after mentioning a complaint Cobbett had received from a "most respectable private correspondent," reiterated what Cobbett had said about Grenville in the earlier article (coupled with the suggestion that a treasury defalcation had occurred in the past because Grenville had not even "done the trifling business which his office of auditor required of him"), and took a high stand on his inalienable right to express his own opinions: "I have acted under a conviction that the promulgation of my opinion with regard to Lord Grenville would tend to the public good." This was followed by a long denunciation, expressed in Cobbett's haughtiest style, of those persons who are in "the habit of estimating the pretensions of men by the length of their purse, the mode of their garments, and the grace of their bow."[74] Windham took this as a personal reference, whereas Cobbett intended it as a rebuke to Grenville's nephew, Lord Temple, who had spoken slightingly of him.[75] The breach was inevitable, but nonetheless sad. Windham and Cobbett were remarkably compatible for individuals of such different backgrounds. But Windham, a decent, honorable man, was able to accept the realities of politics in his time. Cobbett never was.

The Freeling incident and two others that took place in the succeeding few months did much to set the pattern for Cobbett's future. One of these, already chronicled, was the acquittal of Lord Melville in the impeachment proceedings before the House of Lords in June 1806. The other, also in June 1806, involved a parliamentary by-election at Honiton in Devon. Before this, Cobbett had had some slight previous experience with parliamentary elections. In the general election of 1802 he had taken part in the government opposition to Charles James Fox, leading French sympathizer in parliament, who was standing for Westminster, the largest and most hotly contested urban constituency in England.[76] In a letter to Windham, Cobbett described the nature of his opposition to Fox, which, even at this date, emphasized sinecures and pensions rather than the old Jacobin issue:

I have taken a crowd of people to vote against him, and have published a handbill and a large placard, entitled "The Fox and the Geese", in which amongst other things, I have told the Geese to look into the reports of Parliament, where they will find that this man of *independence,* this enemy of *burthensome taxes* and of *placemen* and pensioners, has been a *sinecure placeman* from his childhood. The subject is popular, it is easily comprehended, and it is *new.* It has raised a great clamour, and though it came too late to have any material effect as to numbers of votes, it annoys him most furiously. He knows not what to say in reply to the blackguards, who cry out, and spare not, "No sinecure placemen, Charley!"[77]

Fox, as Cobbett had expected, was successful. So too was another French sympathizer at the general election of 1802: Sir Francis Burdett, candidate for Middlesex in opposition to the government nominee, William Mainwaring, banker and chairman of the Middlesex bench of magistrates. However, petitions claiming improprieties during the election were filed by both sides. After the passage of two years, while Burdett sat in the House, a select committee declared that Mainwaring had been the victor, but found him guilty of having illegally treated some of the electors, thereby becoming incapacitated to serve. A new election was ordered, in which Mainwaring's son took his place as the government candidate.[78]

By the time the new election was held in July and August 1804, Cobbett had become attracted to Burdett because of the attacks he had made in parliament on government corruption, particularly his criticism of the increasing cost of the civil list – that million-pound-a-year grab bag out of which grants were made to gain ministerial support.[79] Burdett, like Windham, had the attributes of independence Cobbett thought ideal for politics: he came from an ancient family and had money, but was engaged in no business or profession. His election slogan was, appropriately, "Burdett and Independence."[80]

The opposition to Burdett, in contrast, represented the dependence on government that Cobbett so heartily disliked. More than 400 illegal votes of Mainwaring senior had come, Burdett claimed, from the obsequious minions of the ministry: "the prebendaries of Westminister, with a long train of servants and pensioners, all the officers and placemen of the courts of Chancery, King's Bench, Common Pleas and Exchequer." The supporters of Mainwaring junior were of the same character:

The greater part of those persons by whom that gentleman was put forward, and by whom also the expenses of his election were defrayed, are known to be dependents upon, or expectants of, the ministry. They are, for the greater part, contractors, persons holding places or pensions during pleasure, and who are, of course, more strongly and immediately attached to the minister of the day than to the general interests of the people or of the throne.[81]

The principal charge levelled against Burdett in the 1804 election was that he was "disloyal," a convenient demagogic label for someone who disagreed with the ministers at any time during the long war with the French. The only evidence of disloyalty was Burdett's former Jacobin leanings, which, Cobbett pointed out, had no significance in 1804 when the importation of libertarian ideas had ceased to be a danger: "The tide has turned: from popular enthusiasm it has run back to despotism."[82] Cobbett was nettled by the smugness of Mainwaring's rich supporters – by the implied assumption in their attitude that *they* represented the honest, patriotic and loyal interests of the country. "I call none of their rights or virtues in question," wrote Cobbett, "am, in no sense of the word, the assailant, but stand purely on the defensive, and beg leave to presume that I ought not to be regarded as a disaffected person merely because I do not live upon the public money." This pert sarcasm was followed by some typical Cobbettian heresy:

Neither is the fact of their superior riches, acquired so suddenly as they are, an argument so convincing with me as it appears to be with many persons. There is something quite preposterous in the course of reasoning which it is fashionable to pursue upon this subject. When you express your surprize, and can hardly restrain your indignation, at seeing a broker, a contractor, a placeman, or speculator of any description, start all at once from the dunghill to a coach and four, with half a score grooms and footmen at his heels, you are told that his rise is a proof of his merit. For my part, I generally draw an exactly opposite conclusion, and in this I adhere to the rules not only of reason but of the law, which teaches us to suspect of demerit and even of dishonesty, those who exhibit signs of a sudden increase of their pelf, and which go so far as to authorize the magistrate to call upon such fortunate persons to render an account of their acquirements.[83]

More than 5,600 votes were cast during the election. Mainwaring had won by five votes if only those were counted that had been cast by the official closing time, i.e. 3 P.M. of the fifteenth day of polling, whereas Burdett had won by one vote if account were taken of the electors still waiting to vote at that time, a condition created, according to Cobbett, by the invariable practice of Mainwaring's supporters "to object indiscriminately to all votes tendered for Sir Francis Burdett in the afternoon of each day's poll."[84] The sheriffs declared Mainwaring the victor, but this was set aside early in 1805 by the findings of a select committee of the House of Commons, and Burdett took his seat in parliament. This was reversed by further proceedings in the House of Commons, terminating in February 1806 when Mainwaring was declared the lawfully elected candidate.[85]

Cobbett saw enough during the election – the ministerial support through government dependants, the demagogic propaganda, the huge cost (Burdett spent an estimated £56,000 to £100,000 in the two elections), the polling techniques, and the parliamentary review of challenged decisions – to strengthen his suspicions of what he had chosen to call the Pitt system.[86] Even the triumphal carriage in which victorious candidates were traditionally drawn home from the hustings by the "delirious populace" was a fraud: more often than not they were professionals hired at the standard rate of thirty shillings for the group.[87] In Honiton, only a few months after the last of the steps in the Burdett case, Cobbett had occasion to add further to his stock of suspicions.

The Honiton vacancy of 1806 arose when Cavendish Bradshaw, the holder of the seat, accepted an appointment as teller of the exchequer in Ireland, "by means of which he will draw into his own pocket some thousands a year" out of the public purse.[88] Bradshaw indicated that he would be a candidate for the vacancy created by his own resignation, and Cobbett announced that he would run against Bradshaw, having failed in his efforts to prevail on other independent men to do so. Cobbett offered the electors a pledge of a type never heard of before: "whether you elect me or not, I never, as long as I live, either for myself, or for, or through the means of, any one of my family, will receive under any name, whether of salary, pension or other, either directly or indirectly, one single farthing of the public money." And Cobbett was not finished with his pledge: "But, Gentlemen, as it is my firm determination never to receive a farthing of the public money, so it is my determination equally firm, never, in any way whatever, to give one farthing of my own money to any man, in order to induce him to vote, or to cause others to vote, for me."[89]

The week after Cobbett had offered his extraordinary pledge in the pages of the *Political Register,* he went to Honiton to be prepared for the election beginning on June 9, 1806. He was accompanied by Colonel William Bosville, a rich and jolly London bachelor, who provided transport in his own coach and four. The day following Cobbett's arrival another potential candidate appeared. It was young Lord Cochrane, aged thirty-one, one of the British navy's most dashing figures – yet in society "a mild, very gentleman-like, agreeable man" – who, before finishing his career at sea, was to serve as admiral of the British navy and as commander-in-chief of the navies of three other countries fighting to free themselves from foreign despots.[90] Cochrane, having just returned from a voyage, had read of Cobbett's search for an independent candidate, and had decided to run at Honiton. Cobbett immediately stood aside when Cochrane took the pledge that he would never accept any sinecure or pension or the grant of any public money, or ask or receive any such for any person dependent on him.[91]

Cobbett knew before starting for Honiton what any opponent of Bradshaw would be up against, and he was under no illusion that his stand could be successful: "*Success* is out of the question in *this* case; but the *example* will be of great utility, and, to end in good time, one must begin in good time."[92] In an attempt to dissuade Cobbett from making the trip, Bradshaw had sent him a message which Cobbett, with evident relish, repeated to the Honiton electors gathered on

"Posting to the Election." In November 1806 Burdett made a further (and final) attempt to win a Middlesex seat. This detail from Gillray's cartoon shows Burdett (arms raised) on his way to the hustings in a donkey cart with Horne Tooke and Colonel Bosville. Cobbett in the rear of the cart beats the drum with the *Political Register* in one hand and "inflammatory letters" in the other. James Cobbett thought this picture of his father "very like him." (JPC, p. 26)

June 9. The message (denied by Bradshaw) was that "nothing but *money* would do at Honiton, that he had given you six guineas each for the last election, and was to give you two guineas each for this election," which, Cobbett added, "I am exceeding sorry to have heard confirmed since my arrival in this place."[93] Cobbett also asserted that Bradshaw had said, standing in the entrance to the House of Commons, that the Honiton electors "were the most corrupt rascals in the world."[94]

Considering these facts and the Cobbett-sponsored pledge which Cochrane had taken, it is little wonder that Cochrane lost by 259 to 124. But rollicking Cochrane had his fun. He had known in advance what the result would be: "I always votes for Mister Most," one of the electors plainly told him. After his defeat was announced, Cochrane sent the town crier through Honiton with the announcement that ten guineas would be given to all those who had voted for him. "Notwithstanding the explanation that the ten guineas was paid as a reward for having withstood the influence of bribery," wrote Cochrane, "the impression produced on the electoral mind by such unlooked-for liberality was simply this – that if I gave ten guineas for being beaten, my opponent had not paid half enough for being elected; a conclusion which, by a similar process of reasoning, was magnified into the conviction that each of his voters had been cheated out of five pounds ten." The strategy paid off quickly enough, for at the general election held four months later, Cochrane won over Bradshaw. Not a single question was asked about payment until after the election was over. When the question was then put to Cochrane, he replied, "Not one farthing!"[95]

Cobbett had not waited for the voting in the first Cochrane–Bradshaw contest, but before leaving Honiton he talked with many of the electors in order to learn, at first hand, the workings of the bribery system. The electors hid behind the subterfuge that there was no bribery: "They take a certain sum of money each according to their consequence, their degree of influence, and their services to their candidates respectively; 'but this' they say 'comes in the shape of a reward after the election, and therefore the oath may be safely taken'." Many of those accepting payment contended that the money is "absolutely necessary to enable them to live . . . and that from election to election, the poor men run up scores at the shops, and are trusted by the shopkeepers *expressly upon the credit of the proceeds of the ensuing election*." Others relied on the sophistry that the members of parliament took good care of themselves, so the electors "had a right to do the same if they could." Traditionally, the politicians ascribed the evil to the cupidity of the electors, but to Cobbett the greater fault was that of the corruptors – "those who expose the poor and miserable to the temptation of selling their votes."[96]

The Honiton election, coming on top of Cobbett's other experiences, proved a turning point, possibly the most important turning point, in his career. He had entered politics in Britain thinking that the structure of government was close to perfection; that any imperfections were attributable to the wrong man in power or to mistakes in judgment. If Pitt could only replace Addington! If Grenville could only replace Pitt! – these were typical of his earliest thoughts. Then he gradually concluded that replacing Pitt was not enough; it was necessary to change Pitt's system. This, in turn, gave way to still another thought: that what he had called "Pitt's system" was not personal to Pitt, or to Addington, or to Grenville – it should more properly be called "the system," for it was the way government was conducted in England.

At the very outset of the newest ministry, when issues concerning alleged peculations and other misconduct in India were being debated, Cobbett called upon Grenville and his colleagues to pursue these issues vigilantly:

There must, I again repeat it, be no flinching; no partiality; no endeavour to smother the demands of justice; for, if there be, this ministry will be no better than the last; the people will think, and not without reason, that all public men are alike; that they have one set of principles for place, and another set for opposition; and thus will all confidence in the whole of the present race of public men be for ever destroyed.[97]

A few weeks later, after the ministry was settled in office and nothing had been done on the India issue, Cobbett again pleaded for an inquiry: "Give it us, or give us back for ever all the confidence we have at any time reposed in you."[98]

But it soon became plain that Grenville had no intention of setting his back against the corruption of the preceding administrations. The India inquiry was rejected despite the serious charges brought against the Marquis Wellesley as governor general. Cobbett's suggestion that committees be established to determine the true state of affairs in other important aspects of public life was ignored. Despite Pitt's involvement in the Melville affair, his debts were paid; he was eulogized, and honored with a public funeral and an expensive monument. Melville was let off by the House of Lords. Pitt's man Freeling and his postal clerks, and the many other Freelings and their clerks, were allowed to carry on without change. Grenville's brother, the Marquis of Buckingham, continued with his sinecure worth over £30,000 a year, which he had held since he was eleven years old, and Grenville's own tenacious hold on the auditorship of the exchequer (requiring him to "audit" his own accounts) demonstrated that the ministry of All the Talents did not intend to do away with all sinecures. The nonentity Cavendish Bradshaw, who held his seat in parliament through bribery, was given a well-paying place in the Irish exchequer, assuring Grenville of one more faithful vote in the Commons. The discharge of a clerk in the barrackmaster general's office after he had exposed the corruption in his department caused Cobbett to cry out: "The men I wished to see in power, are in power, and yet has this thing taken place."[99]

It was not the discharge alone that outraged Cobbett. He was shocked by the high-handed way in which the ministry met the issue when it was raised in parliament. The man who brought the barrack corruption to light, Richard Bateman Robson, an independent member of the Commons, had been immediately squelched by Sir Henry Petty, the twenty-six-year-old chancellor of the exchequer, whose brilliant speaking had marked him out as a natural successor to Pitt and Fox. Cobbett had had enough of brilliant speakers. He angrily declared:

The fact is, that the mere knack of making speeches, the mere knack of twirling off strings of sentences, is no mark whatever of superiority of mind; but is, very frequently, a mark of the contrary; heads, like other things, being in general, empty in proportion to the noise they make. . . . Let us be no longer thus amused, then; let us no longer be the sport of this sort of *brotherhood* amongst the pretenders to superiority of mind. Let us ask for the *proof* of their superiority.

The "brotherhood" was a kinship derived not from a jointly held concept of the best interests of the country, but from a jointly held view of personal advantage: What Cobbett had observed in action was "the *brotherhood of placemen by trade,* who, whether *in* or *out,* will always support the abuses and corruptions that exist."[100] There was nothing to choose between the ins and the outs; they stood together to defend the existing system. This is the reason why he had proposed to stand for election at Honiton. And it is the reason why, when he left Honiton in June 1806 after seeing the cancer that had taken hold in that beautiful valley, he exclaimed: "the more I reflect upon what I have now seen with my own eyes, the more firm does my conviction become, that this is the cause of all our calamities and our dangers, and that it is not, as Blackstone vainly imagines, to be removed by the laws *now in existence.*"[101] By mid 1806 Cobbett had definitely made a break with the past. From thenceforth his principal work has to promote those changes in the laws which he thought necessary to create a decent government devoted to the interests of the people.

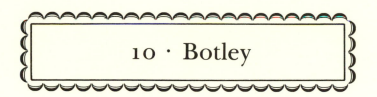

10 · Botley

I was resolved that, as long as I could cause them to do it, my children should lead happy lives; and happy lives they did lead.

"BOTLEY is the most delightful village in the world," wrote Cobbett in 1805. He had discovered this Hampshire village, five miles east of Southampton, on a holiday trip with his family the year before, when they had spent several weeks there in lodgings.

It has everything, in a village, that I love, and none of the things I hate. It is in a valley, the soil is rich, thick set with wood; the farms are small, the cottages neat; it had neither workhouse nor barber nor attorney nor justice of the peace ... "Would I were poetical", I would write a poem in praise of Botley.[1]

In this village, population about 600, Cobbett decided to settle. He bought a house there in July 1805: "large, high, massive, red, and square" with about three acres of lawn and gardens sweeping down to the Hamble river where salmon in plenty could be netted fifty yards from the door.[2] A rented house at 15 Duke Street, London, was given up, and the Cobbett family – father, mother, and four children, the eldest ten years old, the youngest two years old – moved to the country; not only to the country, but to a spot so far in the country "as to render a going backward and forward to London, at short intervals, quite out of the question."

Thus was health, the greatest of all things, provided for, as far as I was able to make provision. Next, my being always at home was secured as far as possible; always with them to set an example of early rising, sobriety, and application to something or other. Children, and especially boys, will have some out-of-doors pursuits; and it was my duty to lead them to choose such pursuits as combined future utility with present innocence. Each his flower-bed, little garden, plantation of trees; rabbits, dogs, asses, horses, pheasants and hares; hoes, spades, whips, guns; always some object of lively interest, and as much earnestness and bustle about the various objects as if our living had solely depended upon them. I made everything give way to the great object of making their lives happy and innocent. I did not know what they might be

Botley House. Cobbett's house at Botley, Hampshire, about five miles east of Southampton, acquired by him in 1805

in time, or what might be my lot; but I was resolved not to be the cause of their being unhappy then, let what might become of us afterwards.[3]

Cobbett had firm views on the education of children, as on every other subject that comes to mind. In many respects his views anticipated those espoused by Maria Montessori nearly a hundred years later: The child's initiative was developed through individual freedom of action, while sense perception and coordination were improved by work and sports. Cobbett believed that children naturally want to learn; everything was effected "without scolding, and even without command."[4] Cobbett himself was fond of book learning and, "knowing well its powers," wished the children to share his fondness. But he was opposed to any type of outward pressure. On wet days, in long evenings, the children (eventually there were seven – four sons and three daughters) gathered together:

A large, strong table, in the middle of the room, their mother sitting at her work, used to be surrounded with them, the baby, if big enough, set up in a high chair. Here were ink-stands, pens, pencils, india rubber, and paper, all in abundance, and every one scrabbled about as he or she pleased. There were prints of animals of all sorts; books treating of them: others treating of gardening, of flowers, of husbandry, of hunting, coursing, shooting, fishing,

158

planting, and, in short, of every thing with regard to which we had something to do. One would be trying to imitate a bit of my writing, another drawing the pictures of some of our dogs or horses, a third poking over Bewick's *Quadrupeds,* and picking out what he said about them; but our book of never-failing resource was the French Maison Rustique, or Farm-House, which, it is said, was the book that first tempted Duquesnois (I think that was the name), the famous physician, in the reign of Louis XIV, to learn to read. Here are all the four-legged animals, from the horse down to the mouse, portraits and all; all the birds, reptiles, insects; all the modes of rearing, managing, and using the tame ones; all the modes of taking the wild ones, and of destroying those that are mischievous; all the various traps, springs, nets; all the implements of husbandry and gardening; all the labours of the field and the garden exhibited, as well as the rest, in plates; and, there was I, in my leisure moments, to join this inquisitive group, to read the French, and tell them what it meaned in English, when the picture did not sufficiently explain itself.

When my business kept me away from the scrabbling-table, a petition often came, that I would go and talk with the group, and the bearer generally was the youngest, being the most likely to succeed.

What need had we of schools? What need of teachers? What need of scolding and force, to induce children to read, write, and love books?[5]

When Cobbett's fourth child, James, reached the age of fourteen, his father wrote:

You have now arrived at the age of fourteen years without ever having been bidden, or even advised, to look into a book; and all you know of reading or of writing you owe to your own unbiassed taste and choice. But while you have lived unpersecuted by such importunities, you have had the very great advantage of being bred up under a roof, beneath which no cards, no dice, no gaming, no senseless pastime of any description, ever found a place. In the absence of these, books naturally became your companions during some part of your time; you have read and have written because you saw your elders read and write, just as you have learned to ride and hunt and shoot, to dig the beds in the garden, to trim the flowers and to prune the trees.[6]

This self-education at home was the only schooling the children had except for the relatively short periods the three eldest spent in small schools when they were young, some French lessons, and a brief tutoring in Latin the older boys later received at home from a displaced catholic priest.[7] Yet the eldest child of Cobbett, Anne, was capable of acting as his amanuensis by the time she was only thirteen years old, and later became both an author and a publisher.[8] The four Cobbett sons (William, John, James, and Richard) all became lawyers; three were admitted as barristers, while the fourth and youngest, Richard, founded the distinguished firm of Manchester solicitors still practicing there today under the name of "Cobbetts."

The scorn felt by Cobbett for the kind of learning commonly forced on children is evident in his account of a recitation delivered by the small son of a neighbor:

I remember, on one occasion, a little pale-faced creature, only five years old, was brought in, after the feeding part of the dinner was over . . . to treat us to a display of his wonderful genius. The subject was a speech of a robust and bold youth, in a Scotch play, the title of which I have forgotten, but the speech began with, "My name is Norval: on the Grampian hills my father fed his flocks . . ." And this in a voice so weak and distressing as to put me in mind of the plaintive squeaking of little pigs when the sow is lying on them. As we were going home (one of my boys and I), he, after a silence of half a mile perhaps, rode up close to the side of my horse, and said, "Papa, where be the Grampian hills?" "Oh," said I, "they are in Scotland; poor, barren, beggarly places, covered with heath and rushes, ten times as barren as Sherril Heath." "But," said he, "how could that little boy's father feed his flocks there, then?" I was ready to tumble off the horse with laughing.[9]

Cobbett taught his children charity by being charitable. He would often take a child with him on his trips away from home; after a large breakfast, an allowance for a noon meal would be set aside – this to be given to some needy person on the road – and the child and father would forgo a regular meal until suppertime.[10] He taught his children to be abstemious by his own practice of getting up from the table when he was still hungry, by rarely drinking anything stronger than wine and little of that. He was neat in his person and in his work. When wearing knee breeches he was never, except once when he was ill, seen by his children outside his bedroom with them untied, the strings hanging down. His study was "kept strait and in order, no confusion." What few papers he had (and they were few) used to be folded, endorsed, and tied up neatly. His writing was neat, and his "very scratching out itself was always neatly and thoroughly performed."[11]

Cobbett taught his children to be industrious by being industrious himself. "I never spent an idle week, or even a day, in my whole life."[12] He believed in the adage of the country people that an hour's sleep before midnight was worth more than two after midnight.

To teach the children the habit of early rising was a great object; and every one knows how young people cling to their beds, and how loth they are to go to those beds. This was a capital matter; because here were industry and health both at stake. Yet, I avoided command even here; and merely offered a reward. The child that was down stairs first, was called the Lark for that day; and, further, sat at my right hand at dinner. They soon discovered, that to rise early, they must go to bed early; and thus was this most important object secured, with regard to girls as well as boys. Nothing is more inconvenient, and, indeed, more disgusting, than to have to do with girls, or young women, who lounge in bed: "A little more sleep, a little more slumber, a little more folding of the hands to sleep." Solomon knew them well: he had, I dare say, seen the breakfast cooling, carriages and horses and servants waiting, the sun coming burning on, the days wasting, the night growing dark too early, appointments broken, and the objects of journeys defeated; and all this from the lolloping in bed of persons who ought to have risen with the sun.[13]

The industry urged on his children by Cobbett was not to make them rich; it was to make them happy.

... as every sensible father must know that the possession of riches do not, never did, and never can, afford even a chance of additional happiness, it is his duty to inculcate in the minds of his children to make no sacrifice of principle, or moral obligation of any sort, in order to obtain riches, or distinction; and it is a duty still more imperative on him, not to expose them to the risk of loss of health, or diminution of strength, for purposes which have, either directly or indirectly, the acquiring of riches in view, whether for himself or for them.[14]

Although Cobbett was in need of money throughout most of his life, there have been few men to whom riches meant as little or who have been more generous with what they had. He turned out his pockets to reward a young journeyman carpenter who had risked his life to rescue a stranger's child from the hooves of a team of horses.[15] When he returned to England in 1800 he found his brothers "far from being in easy circumstances," and gave them a lift as well as making provision for some of their sons, out of the money he had brought with him to start business.[16] He later bought his easygoing brother Thomas a small farm and stocked it for him.[17] He sent four of his young nephews off to school. He never higgled over prices, never attempted to beat anybody down.[18] When his printers suggested that they would have to raise their prices if they granted a requested increase in pay to their employees, Cobbett urged them to go along with the increase.[19] His laborers at Botley were, he claimed, paid at least a quarter more than the laborers employed by the rich men of the area.[20] The practice in Hampshire and in much of the rest of England at the time was to pay farm laborers less than the amount necessary for a man and his family to live on, and to provide such supplementary allowances from parish funds as were needed for the bare survival of the worker and his family. This practice, known as the Speenhamland system, had been adopted by employers because of their fear that if they raised wages to cover the increased cost of living due to the inflation that occurred during the Napoleonic wars, they would be unable to lower them when prices fell back to their previous levels. Cobbett hated the Speenhamland system because of the indignity and unfairness of compelling a hardworking laborer to live on charity. He paid his own workers a living wage (at the same time, he was contributing to the parish poor rates, which made up the deficiencies in the wages of his neighbors who followed the Speenhamland system): "I take care that every man who works for me has the means of having one good meal of *meat* in every day, and a pot or two of beer once or twice a week."[21] He also paid them during periods of bad weather and illness when they were unable to work.[22] He was fond of commanding a number of men working in a field, giving orders in the style of an officer to his soldiers, in the winter often standing out in the cold with them until he was blue in the face.[23] He treated his workers with decency, allowing them the same freedom of conversation and unrestrained familiarity as were permitted to the children of the family. "In short," wrote Cobbett, "I do not believe, that, in the whole world, there is one man more completely happy in family and in those under his authority than I am . . . In my house we know of no such thing as blue-devils (which, by-the-bye, are much worse than black devils); we know of no lowness of spirits; we are always sober, always industrious, always up early in the morning; and, like the Quakers, we are *never gay,* and therefore, we are *always cheerful.*"[24] One of Cobbett's laborers told Alexander Somerville that he would never wish to serve a better master.[25] And Henry Hunt declared that Cobbett's employees "were always treated with the greatest kindness by him."[26]

These practical lessons in good living obviously depended as much on the mother as on the father. William Cobbett's Nancy was "an excellent woman and much respected by many *very* genteel people," wrote an American staying with the Cobbetts in 1801 shortly after they had returned to London.[27] Thomas Moore, who thought that Cobbett was "contemptible" for his reform activities, found to his surprise that Mrs Cobbett was "a quiet, good sort of woman."[28] Mary Mitford wrote that Nancy was "a sweet motherly woman, realizing our notion of one of Scott's most charming characters, *Ailie Dinmont,* in her simplicity, her kindness, and her devotion to her husband and her children."[29] Beyond such occasional comments, what we know of Mrs. Cobbett is chiefly derived from her husband's writings, and they confirm that she was an excellent woman, as well as a devoted wife and mother:

I had a partner that never frowned, that was never melancholy, that never was subdued in spirit . . . that fortified me, and sustained me by her courageous example . . . just as cheerful, and just as full of caresses, when brought down to a mean hired lodging, as when the mistress of a fine country house with all its accompaniments; and, whether from her words or her looks, no one could gather that she regretted the change.[30]

The industrious thirteen-year-old girl cleaning out the washing tub (or teakettle) on a wintry morning quite naturally became the industrious wife:

Till I had a second child, no servant ever entered my house, though well able to keep one; and never, in my whole life, did I live in a house so clean, in such trim order, and never have I eaten or drunk, or slept or dressed, in a manner so perfectly to my fancy, as I did then.[31]

Whenever Cobbett had to leave the house hurriedly with his books and papers scrambled about, he returned to find them arranged in the proper order, and the room freed of the effects of his and his ploughman's dirty shoes.[32] Once when Cobbett arrived home after midnight with his friend Peter Finnerty, they found that

She was up, and had a nice fire for us to sit down at. She had not committed the matter to a servant; her servants and children were all in bed; and she was up, to perform the duty of receiving her husband and his friend. "You did not expect him?" said Finnerty. "To be sure I did," said she; "he never disappointed me in his life."[33]

If we can assume – which the evidence suggests – that when Cobbett in 1829 wrote a generalized description of everything desirable in a wife, he used Nancy as the prototype, then we know more about her. We know that she spoke quickly and distinctly in a clear voice; that she walked with a brisk step and somewhat heavy tread, her feet coming down with a hearty good will; and that she preferred the useful and durable to the showy.[34] We also know that she was steady and careful – far more cautious than her famous husband. And since the only adverse criticism we have of Nancy Cobbett was the rumor (or was it only gossip?) that she had difficulty keeping her help, perhaps we may ascribe this to an overzealous attention to William Cobbett's precept that the wife must be "well acquainted with the character and general demeanour of all the female servants."[35]

Theirs had been a true love match; after they had been married more than thirty years, Cobbett wrote: "one hair of her head was more dear to me than all the other women in the world."[36] Yet love to Cobbett was no namby-pamby affair; no nonsensical compliments, no hanging trinkets and baubles on the object of his love. And above all, no dangling about at the heels of his wife.[37] She "ought to be heard, and patiently heard; she ought to be reasoned with, and, if possible, convinced" – a wife's judgment of men was often better than that of her husband, and "ought not to be set at naught without great deliberation" – but in the last resort, the man must be master.

As to matter of little comparative moment; as to what shall be for dinner; as to how the house shall be furnished; as to the management of the house and of menial servants: as to those matters, and many others, the wife may have her way without any danger; but when the questions are, what is to be the calling to be pursued; what is to be the place of residence; what is to be the style of living and scale of expense; what is to be done with property; what the manner and place of educating children; what is to be their calling or state of life; who are to be employed or entrusted by the husband; what are the principles that he is to adopt as to public matters; whom is he to have as coadjutors or friends; all of these must be left solely to the husband; in all these he must have his will; or there never can be any harmony in the family.[38]

Cobbett denied that this represented tyranny.

Am I recommending disregard of the wife's opinions and wishes? Am I recommending a reserve towards her that would seem to say that she was not trust-worthy, or not a party interested in her husband's affairs? By no means: on the contrary, though I would keep anything disagreeable from her, I should not enjoy the prospect of good without making her a participator.[39]

It would be quite wrong to read Cobbett's assertions about the husband's masterful role as an indication that his own wife accepted them as stated; the probability is that most of the items enumerated represented subjects on which one or more connubial battles had been fought during the thirty-seven years that elapsed between the date they were married and the date Cobbett wrote the statement above. Nancy Cobbett was lovable, but she was no tame pussycat. There is much to suggest that she had a mind of her own. She favored sending the children off to schools: "we must all have something to plague us," wrote Cobbett in 1809, "and my plague is my wife's taste for what is damned foolishly called education." Despite Cobbett's objection to "the hardware which women put on their persons," Nancy wore some of such hardware. She read (or, more properly, had read to her) books written by Hannah More although Cobbett condemned that lady as "the Old Bishop in petticoats."[40] Her ideas on politics and financial matters were more conservative than those of her husband, and it seems probable that she was not unwilling to let him know when she disagreed with him. For this reason, as time went on, Cobbett found more and more of his activities "disagreeable" as that word was used in the phrase "I would keep any thing disagreeable from her." In the period 1805 to 1809 he kept from her, for a time at least, his breach with Windham, certain of his business ventures, and some of his involvement in parliamentary elections.[41] "Talk not *here*," Cobbett wrote to John Wright in 1806, "about any *business* or *electioneering*. Be on your guard, suffer nothing to be drawn from you."[42] On another occasion, speaking of his "pecuniary concerns," Cobbett explained that "She has her own [notions] about such matters which cannot be altered . . . I cannot blame her anxiety; but as I cannot remove it, it's better not to awaken it."[43]

Cobbett does not seem to have thought of removing his wife's anxiety by forgoing the activities that caused her to be anxious. It did not take Cobbett long to make up his mind on a subject, and once he had done so, there was little chance of anyone changing it. According to Cobbett, a man's affection for his wife was not to be measured by his willingness to give in to her judgment, but by what he called "acts of real goodness to her": by assisting her in taking care of the babies, by spending his leisure time in her company, by preferring her presence and conversation to that of any other woman, by "a daily and hourly confirmation" of the fact that he valued "her health and life and happiness beyond all other things in the world."[44] To illustrate, he told this story about one of her early confinements:

I began my young marriage days in and near Philadelphia. At one of those times to which I have just alluded, in the middle of the burning hot month of July, I was greatly afraid of fatal consequences to my wife for want of sleep, she not having, after the great danger was over, had any sleep for more than forty-eight hours. All great cities, in hot countries, are, I believe, full of dogs; and they, in the very hot weather, keep up, during the night, a horrible barking and fighting and howling. Upon the particular occasion to which I am adverting, they made a noise so terrible and so unremitted, that it was next to impossible that even a person in full health and free from pain should obtain a minute's sleep. I was, about nine in the evening, sitting by the bed: "I do think," said she, "that I could go to sleep now, if it were not for the dogs." Down stairs I went, and out I sallied, in my shirt and trousers, and without shoes and stockings; and, going to a heap of stones lying beside the road, set to work upon the dogs, going backward and forward, and keeping them at two or three hundred yards' distance from the house. I walked thus the whole night, barefooted, lest the noise of my shoes might possibly reach her ears; and I remember that the bricks of the causeway were, even in the night, so hot as to be disagreeable to my feet. My exertions produced the desired effect: a sleep of several hours was the consequence; and, at eight o'clock in the morning, off I went to a day's business which was to end at six in the evening.[45]

Both father and mother loved their children. Nancy insisted on suckling her babies, despite the pain it caused her.[46] The children were never left to servants for a single hour. The burdens of tending them were shared by husband and wife. The noise of his children never disturbed Cobbett:

Many a score papers have I written amidst the noise of children, and in my whole life never bade them be still. When they grew up to be big enough to gallop around the house, I have, in wet weather, when they could not go out, written the whole day amidst noise that would have made some authors half mad. It never annoyed me at all. But a Scotch piper, whom an old lady, who lived beside us at Brompton, used to pay to come and play a long tune every day, I was obliged to bribe into a breach of contract.[47]

The children were "duly and daily washed, when well, in cold water from head to foot." They squalled, of course, and while they squalled, the presiding parent sang:

The moment the stripping of the child used to begin, the singing used to begin, and the latter never ceased till the former had ceased. After having heard this go on with all my children, Rousseau taught me the philosophy of it. I happened, by accident, to look into his *Emile*, and there found him saying that the nurse subdued the voice of the child and made it quiet by drowning its voice in hers, and thereby making it perceive that it could not be heard, and that to continue to cry was of no avail. "Here, Nancy," said I (going to her with the book in my hand), "you have been a great philosopher all your life without either of us knowing it."[48]

The aura of happiness at Botley was captured by Mary Mitford's description of a party given there around 1806, when the house was full of happy guests:

The house had room for all, and the hearts of the owners would have had room for three times the number. I never saw hospitality more genuine, more simple, or more thoroughly successful in the great end of hospitality, the putting everybody completely at ease. There was not the slightest attempt at finery, or display, or gentility. They called it a farm-house, and everything was in accordance with the largest idea of a great English yeoman of the old time. Everything was excellent – everything abundant – all served with the greatest nicety by trim waiting-damsels; and everything went on with such quiet regularity, that of the large circle of guests not one could find himself in the way.

At this time William Cobbett was at the height of his political reputation; but of politics we heard little, and should, I think, have heard nothing, but for an occasional red-hot patriot, who would introduce the subject, which our host would fain put aside, and got rid of as speedily as possible. There was something of *Dandie Dinmont* about him, with his unfailing good humour and good spirits – his heartiness – his love of field sports – and his liking for a foray. He was a tall stout man, fair, and sunburnt, with a bright smile, and an air compounded of the soldier and the farmer, to which his habit of wearing an eternal red waistcoat contributed not a little. He was, I think, the most athletic and vigorous person that I have ever known. Nothing could tire him. At home in the morning he would begin his active day by mowing his own lawn, beating his gardner, Robinson, the best mower, except himself, in the parish, at that fatiguing work.[49]

At the time of Miss Mitford's description of Botley, Cobbett was not yet a farmer. His holdings were limited to the three acres or so of lawns and gardens surrounding the house. Here he found a modest outlet for his insatiable love of growing things.

Few persons excelled him in the management of vegetables, fruit, and flowers. His green Indian corn – his Carolina beans – his water melons could hardly have been exceeded at New York. His wall-fruit was equally splendid, and, much as flowers have been studied since that day, I never saw a more glowing or a more fragrant autumn garden than that at Botley, with its pyramids of hollyhocks, and its masses of china-asters, of cloves, of mignionette, and of variegated geranium.[50]

The garden as so described by Miss Mitford (accurate except for the "mignionette," which Cobbett despised) was far from sufficient to occupy all the spare time of this enormously energetic man.[51] He took to coursing with his usual enthusiasm: acquired greyhounds, taught his boys to run through ploughed fields and coppices, went to coursing meetings with George Mitford, Mary's rakish father, and with other coursing addicts.[52] "I was yesterday at Meon Stoke, [where] we had some very fine coursing. We found 5 hares . . . There was one large greyhound dog; but my little bitches beat him hollow. They go like the wind. They have verified my old observation: that it is with dogs as it is with horses, the slenderer the make, the fleeter the pace."[53] In two successive years, 1805 and 1806, Cobbett joined local farmers in sponsoring single-stick competitions at Botley, which brought strong-armed, thick-skulled combatants "from all the Western Counties on this side of Cornwall":

This is an exercise that requires great strength and very great fortitude. The players use a stick three-quarters of an inch in diameter, 2½ feet long, and having a basket hilt to protect the hand. They are stripped to the shirt; and

William Cobbett hunting mug by Grainger (Worcester), given to Cobbett in 1820 by reformers of Coventry. The other side of the neck shows the gridiron

the object is to break the antagonist's head in such a way that the *blood may run an inch*. The blows that they interchange, in order to throw one another off their guard, are such as require the utmost of patient endurance. The arms, shoulders, and ribs are beaten black and blue, and the contest between two men frequently lasts for more than an hour. Last Whitsuntide there was a match at Bishops Waltham, where one of the players, feeling that he had a tooth knocked out, and knowing that if he opened his mouth the blood would be perceived, *swallowed both blood and tooth,* and continued the combat (with two others driven from their places in his gum) till he obtained the victory. And this only for a *prize of a guinea!*[54]

The first prize at the Botley competition held on October 11, 1805 was "Fifteen Guineas and a Gold-laced Hat." In the following year the prize was increased to twenty guineas plus the hat. "A fine day, and a company of people not less than six thousand in number. The whole of the village was full. Stages, in the form of amphitheatres, were erected against the houses, and, perhaps, seats let to the amount of 30 or 50 pounds! Every gentleman round the country was here."[55]

Cobbett, on principle, favored all "manly sports" that developed hardiness and tended to prepare men for "deeds of bravery of a higher order," in opposition to what he saw as the current trend toward effeminacy.[56] He thought duelling absurd; it could not decide the question of honor that was supposedly at issue – it was like "trying orthodoxy in religion by walking blindfolded over red-hot plough shares."[57] But Cobbett and his erstwhile friend Windham, himself an amateur pugilist, defended boxing, wrestling, and even bull-baiting, against the attempts, largely stimulated by methodists, to outlaw these sports along with "two-penny hops and gingerbread fairs" and other forms of public merrymaking indulged in by the lower orders.[58] Cobbett and Windham argued that the English tradition of settling disputes with fists was vastly superior to the stabbings and poisonings prevalent on the continent.[59] To the contention that less vice would be engendered if the farm laborer read good books rather than engaged in animal amusements, Cobbett replied:

as to the ploughman, sitting down to read his good book, after his labour is done, the idea never could have found its way into the mind of any one who knew what a ploughman was. Take a thousand ploughmen, set them down to their good books, after their day's work is done, and, in less than ten minutes, the whole thousand will be asleep. Animal amusement is the only amusement that such men *can* enjoy.[60]

Between his own animal amusements, Cobbett occupied himself with improvements to the house and grounds at Botley. Only the best of the Duke Street furniture, including the two mahogany tables and the looking glasses, were sent there; much of the balance was sold, as it would have been "a disgrace to the house."[61] At the instance of Mrs.

Cobbett, a pair of secondhand silver chamber candlesticks "with an extinguisher to each," was acquired.[62] The walls were hung with £500 worth of pictures bought from Colnaghi on credit terms "as long as that of a Lord or a Prince." Dominic Colnaghi told of Cobbett coming into his shop and "ordering to be packed up the whole of those covering one side of a large shop." Included were a number of engravings from Claude; colored sporting prints of dogs, dead game, coursing, and racing; the Duke of Newcastle out shooting on his pony; Stubbs's horses; Salvator Rosa's landscapes; portraits of celebrated men, particularly admirals and generals; "Lord Carlisle's Earth-stopper"; and a set of four prints of rural sports by William Woollett.[63] Cobbett contracted to have the grounds at Botley enclosed by a great brick wall, eight feet high; a portico was added; and other changes were made to the house itself. Some of these were "necessary to make Mrs. Cobbett like to live here; which, again, was necessary to happiness."[64] Cobbett's own happiness, aside from that derived from his family and his writing, was tied to the land. Almost from the first he had been anxious to extend his holdings: "If we buy upon mortgage, or in whatever way, it will be good."[65] Within three months after acquiring the Botley house, he bought his brother the small farm called Cock Street, six miles away at Droxford, and this transaction was hardly completed when he began negotiations for the purchase of a farm for himself. By May 1806 he had arranged to buy Fairthorn farm, approximately 260 acres, at a price of £11,000 "under a solemn promise of secrecy until September next." It is not clear when he took possession, but most of the financial demands resulting from the purchase seem to have fallen in 1807. In the next year he purchased 87 acres, mostly woodland, for 3,000 guineas, and Raglington farm of about 270 acres for £11,000. In 1809 he acquired some other small lots for £375.[66] The total of these land purchases, including the house and the small farm for his brother, came to over £27,000, and since Cobbett had no realizable assets of substance, the properties must have been heavily mortgaged.[67] This burden was lightened to the extent that Cobbett was able to sell timber growing on the land, but his debt was almost certainly between £20,000 and £25,000, on which interest alone would have amounted to £1,000 annually.[68] This was not his only need for current funds, since he immediately set under way a series of extensive capital improvements in the form of fences, hedges, ditches, workmen's cottages, and other buildings. At the same time, he was stocking the farms and buying equipment. Instead of trying to meet these varied demands for cash by setting aside the maximum acreage for the production of grain, which would provide immediate return at war-inflated prices (wheat was bringing 89s. a quarter in 1805 and 97s. in 1809, as contrasted with 54s. in 1798), he elected to utilize much of his land in the long-term project of growing trees.[69] The neighbors were amused by the "little bits of twigs" Cobbett began to plant. Mrs. Cobbett complained that he was "burying the money in the land."[70] But he was not to be deterred; his calculations showed that over a period of ten years, far more could be made by tree farming than by the more usual annual crops. "What I *lay out* is not spent . . . what is done now is worth forty times as much as the same thing some time hence."[71] Yet, even if the figures were correct, a deferral of income from farming – while expenditure continued – required either a great deal of capital (which Cobbett did not have) or a steady and substantial flow of income from some nonfarming source.

In Cobbett's case, his nonfarming income was limited to the profits from the *Political Register*. This had started in January 1802 with a circulation of less than 300 copies, but by the end of 1803 had exceeded 4,000 and was still growing.[72] Late in 1803 Cobbett had embarked on an entirely new publication: *Cobbett's Parliamentary Debates*, the origin – the "onlie begetter" – of the official report of parliamentary proceedings known today as Hansard.[73] The working editor and part proprietor of the *Parliamentary Debates* was John Wright, the former Piccadilly bookseller who had published Cobbett's works while he was still in America.[74] Wright had failed in 1802, but he was a man of considerable talent and quickly proved his usefulness after joining Cobbett in the following year. He was, according to Cobbett, "one of the cleverest men in England. He is a good scholar, writes well, has great good taste."[75] Wright not only edited the *Parliamentary Debates* but eventually took over almost all responsibility for the *Political Register* itself, except that of editor, which Cobbett never relinquished. Wright's duties increased as Cobbett's activities continued to expand. In 1805 he published a 1,300-page volume entitled *Cobbett's Spirit of the Public Journals*, consisting of articles on political subjects that had appeared during 1804 in English and American newspapers, plus a half dozen articles from French and Irish papers. In 1806 a much larger undertaking, which took fifteen years to complete, was initiated: *Cobbett's Parliamentary History*. Here, as in the case of the *Parliamentary Debates*, Cobbett and Wright were nominally coeditors, but the primary burden of the work fell on Wright. This 36-volume publication was a compilation of the available records of the political proceedings that had occurred between 1066 and 1803, when the *Parliamentary Debates* began. And then, in 1809, Wright with Cobbett and Thomas Bayly Howell (who did most of the work) commenced the publication of what is now known as *Howell's State Trials*, a collection of famous actions for "high treason and other crimes and misdemeanours," a 33-volume series requiring eighteen years to finish. Cobbett had the genius to see the need for these standard works – the *Parliamentary Debates* (or Hansard), the *Parliamentary History,* and *Howell's State Trials* – and to retain the men capable of fulfilling the undertaking.

It was Wright's appearance on the scene that made it possible for Cobbett to move to Botley; he rapidly became Cobbett's trusted man of business who could carry on the affairs of a London enterprise with an absentee owner and editor-in-chief. Cobbett looked to Wright not only to run the office and get the *Political Register* and other publications through the press, but to correct his grammar and spelling, to check his Latin, to censor objectionable passages, and to run all sorts of errands for the Cobbett family. The *Satirist,* a monthly magazine devoted to the flagellation of radicals, referred to Wright as "the poor devil who now corrects Cobbett's bad English, edits his Parliamentary History, brushes his coat, puffs him in the coffee-houses and debating shops, and does all his other dirty work."[76]

Not the least of these other duties was that of securing the necessary funds to support both the London business and Cobbett's activities at Botley. Nearly every letter from Cobbett (and he wrote once a week, frequently more often) contained some reference to money matters, with a demand for immediate action:

I have provided 500 pounds for a few days; but, the rest must be got somehow or other by you.

If Bagshaw can rake together £200 by the 10th I have secured the rest (until the money comes from Ireland) from Mr. Hughan.

Bring £40 at least with you – Indeed, as much as you can; for I have several things to pay here.

I enclose a Bill at 14 days for £320 which is the only way I could send it in, but I hope your Mr. Bagshaw will have no difficulty in getting it discounted in time to take up the Bill which is due on the 4th.

Tell me, by return post how much, at the most, we can possibly raise by notes.

I have received *thirty pounds* from you, which will be all I want, until my departure, which will be next Saturday; but, you must send me *ten pounds* to reach me, without fail, on *Friday* next.[77]

To meet these demands, Wright had available a steady and growing income from the *Political Register*. In June 1806 a total of 4,750 copies was being printed, which, assuming a 15 percent return on sales, would produce around £1,000 annually – no mean sum in 1806, but hardly enough to meet Cobbett's outlays.[78] The circulation almost certainly continued to grow, but even at a substantially higher level, say 8,000 (no exact figures are available), the profits would not seem adequate to cover all requirements.[79] The *Spirit of Public Journals* published in 1805 was a commercial failure and was not repeated in the following year; its loss increased the need for funds from other sources. The other serially issued projects, although successful over a long period, probably contributed nothing to current profits.[80] As a result, Wright was constantly exercised to meet the heavy demands made on him for cash. The system he followed, which may have been common enough at the time, was this: The major production costs were for paper and printing. These were purchased on extended credit – the paper from Cobbett's friend Swann, and most of the printing from the firm of Cox & Baylis or, after 1808, from T. C. Hansard. The primary outlet for the sale of the Cobbett publications was the newsman Richard Bagshaw, whose name appears as publisher of the *Political Register* and most of the other works issued by Cobbett. Bagshaw was regularly requested to accept bills of exchange drawn for periods as long as eighteen months in advance.[81] These were discounted by Wright to provide ready cash.[82] As a result, Cobbett was drawing on future profits in addition to current profits, and these were diminished by the interest charges reflected in the discount. Although this stretched Cobbett's commercial credit as far as it could go, it did not represent the limit of his borrowing, for he was able to, and did, secure numerous loans from friends upon no other basis than friendship.[83] Such a scheme could survive only so long as things ran smoothly; the whole structure was sure to come down in an instant if there were a fall in the volume of business or a decrease in profit margins or a loss of confidence or a decline in the lenders' means or some other untoward event that would impel anyone in the chain of credit to refuse to continue the practice.

Cobbett tended to be a pessimist – or perhaps we should say a realist – in the field of politics, but an optimist – or should it be a romantic? – when it came to his own affairs. In both he was headstrong, often impetuously plunging ahead on an initial impulse without much deliberation, and nearly unstoppable once under way. "Nothing so false as figures" was a favorite Cobbett saying, and yet we find him writing in 1807: "What I have done to this house &c. is so much of property transmuted. The plan which I gave £935 for will, next year, be worth £4,000."[84] He had had a number of experiences in personal matters since arriving in London that would have sobered a less optimistic man. The bookshop at its expensive Pall Mall address had failed.[85] The newspaper *Porcupine* had failed.

I embarked upon my own bottom, and, it is well known, that my enterprise was unsuccessful. The difficulties which this gave rise to are not to be described. I was saved from utter ruin by a friend, and, it is right, that all those who are good enough to set any value on my labours, should be informed, that that friend was Mr. Penn, who, from the knowledge he had acquired with respect to me, took me by the hand the very week that I came to England; most kindly inquired into my circumstances; and, when I stood in need of his aid, most liberally gave it me. I have wanted, and have found, other friends too; but Mr. Penn I shall always regard as my preserver.[86]

The crisis in which John Penn had acted as preserver occurred, presumably, in 1801 or 1802. But this was not the end of Cobbett's financial problems. He was unable to pay a note for £100 when it came due early in 1804.[87] He had to borrow in October 1804 to meet the judgment in the "Juverna" cases.[88] In the same year, he was called on to pay another large sum on account of his old Pennsylvania litigation. The recognizances of Benjamin Davies and Richard North executed on Cobbett's behalf in 1797 were declared forfeit in actions brought by the attorney general of the state, J. B. McKean, son of Cobbett's nemesis. As a result, in 1804, Cobbett reimbursed Davies and North for the $2,400 they had been forced to pay on their recognizances.[89] When he bought a suit of clothes that year, he explained that he had done so "lest people should take me for a heathen philosopher, upon the maxim that the arses of such gentlemen are always to be seen through their pocket holes."[90] In 1805 there were the losses occasioned by the unsuccessful *Spirit of the Public Journals*.

Cobbett had also engaged in a number of speculations outside the publishing field about which we know very little; but what little we do know suggests that they were not always profitable: "If the business has been a torment to you, it has been no less so to me," wrote Cobbett in 1806 to a fellow speculator.[91] Although nearly always pressed for funds, he was never long subdued in his enthusiasm for some new venture. "These pecuniary pinches give me great uneasiness at times," he declared in 1807 in the midst of another contemplated land purchase, "but they will cease before it be long."[92] Such occasional fits of uneasiness had no observable influence on his conduct.

One may wonder why, in the circumstances, Cobbett allowed himself to become so heavily indebted. Some of the elements we know; others we can only guess at. We know that Cobbett saw the economic advantage of buying land on mortgage during a period of heavy inflation such as was occurring during the Napoleonic war: "money every day depreciates, and while the nominal rent of the land must increase, that of the mortgage cannot."[93] We also know that he was anxious to make provision for his family and, in his middle forties with nothing saved up, felt some urgency in the matter: "unless I do it now, I lose years of my life, which it is now too late to do."[94] Finally, we know that Cobbett liked land not only for the things that it could grow, but perhaps even more for the less tangible benefits: the right to hunt, the right to vote, the right to run for parliament, and that inestimable blessing available to a nineteenth-century landowner, "weight in the county."[95] For these several reasons he wanted to buy as much land as he could. There is still the question why he went as far as he did; why he was not content with half the land at half the risk, or less. The answer seems to be (and this is the guesswork) that while he was occasionally uneasy about temporary shortages of funds, he did not see the long-term risk as particularly threatening. He was again at one of the high points of his career, and was surrounded by powerful new friends who paid homage to him. Lord Cochrane, Lord Henry Stuart, Lord Folkestone, and Lord Dorchester visited Cobbett at Botley, as did Dr. Samuel Parr (the whig Dr. Johnson), James Blomfield, future bishop of London, and Sir Richard Phillips, the rich London alderman. Lord Temple, Lord Clanricarde, and Lord Northesk invited Cobbett to course on their estates.[96] It is difficult at this distance to recognize the enormous power wielded by Cobbett. As early as 1802 or 1803 he was given credit for making, or, if not making, for breaking, ministers. We find the Earl of Dartmouth writing about "that fellow Cobbett whose damnable productions excite in my mind a weekly succession of rank indignities" and made him fearful that Addington might be forced out of office by Cobbett's attacks on him.[97] According to Cobbett, when George III in 1804 visited Old George Rose at Cuffnells, not far from Botley, he said, the moment he entered the house, "Where is my friend Cobbett's paper?"[98] John Horne Tooke had declared that Lord Grenville's party owed more to Cobbett "than to all other men living," and Cobbett agreed.[99] He had confidence in himself and created confidence in others to a rare degree. One of his sons wrote the following note twenty years after his father's death:

He had a great influence over every body about him; & inspired inferiors with awe. – Like Bonaparte: *"sauve moi, Napoleon"*. Those who looked up to him thought he [could do] any thing; & his manner of dealing with circumstances showed that he felt that himself . . . Also he inspired confidence in circumstances of difficulty, & had a way of speaking of undertakings that made others fancy him capable of every thing he resolved on. – Equally attached (or won) by affection, and subdued by fear. – His manner, when about to set to at any active pursuit, was full of resolution: stamping his feet as he got up, and calling out "Now, then!"[100]

Cobbett's confidence in his ability to sustain his acquisitions at Botley, despite the heavy indebtedness they entailed, was simply another manifestation of his irrepressible confidence in himself.

11 · Westminster elections

> There are, and, I think, every day's experience proves it, no parties in England now, answering at all to the description of Whigs and Tories. The motives of such parties have ceased to exist; the very elements for forming them are no more. No man calls himself a Tory; and, if there are some few, who call themselves Whigs, it is because they are dupes, or deceivers.

COBBETT'S EXPERIENCE up to the middle of 1806 (his visit to Honiton had occurred in May of that year) had produced three principles: that the government of Britain was fundamentally corrupt; that there was nothing to choose in this respect between a government of tories or one of whigs; and that the corruption could not be removed "by the laws now in existence." Since Cobbett was never a revolutionary, it followed that corrective laws could be effected only through the election of new members of parliament not attached to either of the two great parties.

At that time, the House of Commons consisted of 658 members: 489 elected in England, 100 in Ireland, 45 in Scotland, and 24 in Wales.[1] Of the English total, 80 members represented the forty counties.[2] These were elected by the "40 shilling freeholders"; that is, the adult male protestants owning property that would yield forty shillings or more per annum clear of all charges and deductions, a standard fixed in 1430 during the reign of Henry VI.[3] Although the changes in the value of money over a 300-year interval would suggest an increasingly democratic franchise, as a practical matter those nominated in the counties were nearly always the uncontested choice of the landed gentry, and to a lesser degree the aristocracy, of the area.[4] The remaining 409 members elected in England were (except for the 4 representing the two universities) returned by 203 boroughs on an antiquated distribution which gave no representation to the rapidly growing city of Manchester, while the pigsties of Appleby and the deserted "green mound" that constituted Old Sarum each sent 2 members to parliament. In only 22 of the 203 boroughs was the electorate over a thousand.[5] The right to vote in the boroughs, large as well as small, varied widely from one place to another depending on local tradition.[6] The majority of the boroughs were regarded as the property of proprietors who could either nominate a member or sell the seat, sometimes for as much as £5,000 for a single parliament.[7] In those boroughs where there was no proprietor, the votes of the individuals holding the franchise brought the current market price, which might be from £1 to £100 per person.[8] Since the voting was open and recorded in poll books subject to public scrutiny, a voter could require a substantial inducement to proclaim his opposition to a candidate favored by his landlord or his customers or any of the powerful interests in his neighborhood.[9] Money was not the sole means of getting votes or of forestalling votes that might go to an opponent; local patronage and entertainment were common persuaders. And then there was the practice of "shopping," by which voters were locked up and kept dead drunk until the day of election.[10]

Anyone without a patron seeking a seat in the House of Commons had to have a fat purse; even uncontested elections could cost hundreds of pounds, while one only moderately contested could cost from £2,000 to £6,000.[11] Where there was a contest, the cost could be ten times higher. The ministry, in order to insure its majority, was the largest purchaser of seats in the Commons. In 1807, it "bought up all the seats that were to be disposed of at any price."[12] The outright purchase of seats was not, however, the only hold the minister in power had over the House membership. There was a great floating vote in parliament that transferred itself almost automatically from one ministry to the next – some of the shift reflecting pure loyalty to whatever government was in power, and some reflecting the ability of that government to confer benefits on its followers. Thus, before the Duke of Portland became prime minister in 1807, his party in the House of Commons could muster a bare sixty votes; immediately afterwards, and before a general election could be held, they had a majority.[13] Instead of the minister following the parliamentary vote as today, the parliamentary vote followed the minister. In the period 1783 to 1830, no cabinet ever resigned as the result of a defeat in the House of Commons.[14]

Various attempts have been made to express in numbers the undemocratic character of the parliament at this period. Charles Grey in 1793 had presented a petition stating that 154 individuals returned 307 members of the lower house.[15] Sir Francis Burdett in 1806 claimed that nearly half the whole of the House of Commons consisted of persons who held government posts or government pensions.[16] Representation of the great bulk of the people of Britain was a fiction only. Bishop Horsley probably expressed the view of most of the upper classes when he said that he "did not know what the mass of the people in any country had to do with the laws, but to obey them."[17] The names of "tory" and "whig" had, by nearly general consent, lost all significance: the differences between the two parties were more a matter of history and theory than of practice. There was a small governing class which took turns in governing.

For an independent – someone outside the aristocracy or landed gentry who was unwilling (or unable) to buy a seat or to be beholden to a patron who would provide one for him — the only access to parliament was through one of the electoral districts where there was no proprietor and where the number of voters and their status permitted them to exercise a modicum of independence. Two of the most obvious opportunities were the county of Middlesex and the borough of Westminster, that huge aggregation of shops and homes on the abbey's lands from Temple Bar to Kensington Palace, and from Oxford Street to the Thames. In both of these there was a wide franchise. Middlesex had polled nearly 6,000 voters; Westminster had polled over 12,000.[18] In Middlesex the radical John Wilkes had been three times elected in 1769 and three times excluded by action of the House of Commons, but was finally allowed to serve when elected for the fourth time in 1774, whereupon he became a rather respectable member of parliament. Middlesex was also where Sir Francis Burdett had been twice elected at huge cost and twice unseated by the House of Commons. In the borough of Westminster, the whigs and tories had an economical arrangement, common throughout England, by which the two seats were divided between them. Fox had been the whig member since 1780. In July 1806 it became known that Fox was critically ill, and whether it was because of that or because a dissolution of parliament and a general election were being talked about, Cobbett began a series of open letters "To the Electors of the City of Westminster" that continued for more than a year. The first of these was published on August 9.[19] The motto at the head of the *Political Register* of that date was a quotation from Rousseau: "The English are free only forty days, once in seven years; and, the use, which they then make of their freedom, shows that they desire to be enslaved all the rest of their lives."[20] The electors of Westminster, Cobbett pointed out, unlike the electors of boroughs where the members were small or were dependent on one or two rich men, were in a position to be independent. They did not need to concern themselves with "the interest of such or such a nobleman" or with the electors' customers, whose trade "when compared to the weight of taxes, brought down upon them from the want of real representatives, is as a farthing to a pound!"

The possessor of the elective franchise is the holder of a trust; he acts not only for himself, but for his country in general, and more especially for his family and his children. To violate his trust, or to neglect the performance of what it imposes upon him, is, therefore, not merely an act of baseness, not merely a degradation of himself, but a crime against others.[21]

Cobbett added that it was not his intention to offer himself as a candidate "unless it shall be found that no other man in the kingdom has the public spirit" to do so on principles that will assure the electors against the loss of their freedom.[22]

Five weeks later Fox died. A by-election to select a replacement was immediately called. Rumors flew about that the candidates would be Earl Percy, the twenty-one-year-old son of the Duke of Northumberland, and the fifty-five-year-old Richard Brinsley Sheridan – whig politician, wit, onetime dramatist, theater owner, prosecutor of Warren Hastings, spendthrift, and dissolute drinking companion of the dissolute Prince of Wales – at the moment serving as treasurer of the navy.[23] Sheridan had been in parliament since 1780 as a representative of Stafford, with five to six hundred electors, half of whom were prepared to sell their votes for five guineas each.[24] As a representative of Westminster he would be in a stronger position to succeed Fox as leader of the opposition in parliament. Cobbett's Letter II stated:

As to the candidates, who have offered themselves to you, at this time, I could have wished, that either one or the other had explicitly pledged himself never, in his whole life, to touch, either by himself or his relations, one farthing of the public money. But, since neither of them has done this, your choice, if no new candidate offers himself, must be influenced by other considerations and it appears to me, that the very first consideration is, that of preventing your city from becoming, as to all practical purposes, *a mere family property*, handed over from one Lord to another Lord, just like a private estate, with all the game and deer thereon feeding and being. I beg you to reflect, only for one moment, upon the shocking degradation of being thus transferred.[25]

By the time this statement was being read in the *Political Register*, Sheridan had appeared at a meeting called by his friends at the Crown and Anchor tavern, and had stunned the audience by declaring that he would not stand because to do so would be contrary to the wishes of his deceased friend [Fox], as it might mean "disturbing the peace of the city," and he therefore recommended the election of Lord Percy.[26] Cobbett sensed what the politicians of the day called a "job." A ministerial paper had hinted that Sheridan would lose his place in the government if he opposed the son of the powerful duke. Cobbett concluded that an even worse sin was involved: that Sheridan from the first was "in concert" with the duke's son, and that Sheridan's candidacy was "for the purpose of preventing any other candidate from coming forward . . . until it should be too late."[27] While there is considerable question whether that had been Sheridan's original intention, it seems to have been the way things worked out.[28] The electors attending the meeting at the Crown and Anchor unanimously rejected Sheridan's recommendation of Percy, who, according to Charles Greville, was "an absolute nullity, a bore beyond all bores," and appointed a committee to locate other potential candidates.[29] But at that late date (Cobbett's tentative offer was overlooked) no one could be found who was willing to run.

Cobbett's Letter IV savagely attacked Sheridan, claiming that at best he had abandoned the people of Westminster for selfish reasons. The right to sit for Westminster had been decided by the whig politicians, not by the voters.[30] But Cobbett had something to say to them too: "for, though I am convinced, that you have been miserably duped, I have seen but in very few of you a disposition to resent the duplicity; and you appear to me to be just as ready and willing to be duped tomorrow as you were yesterday." What particularly galled Cobbett was that Percy, now elected without contest on October 7, was "chaired" by the mob in a style traditionally reserved for conquering heroes, an action which Cobbett rather unfairly imputed to the whole body of the Westminster electorate:

excuse me, if I ask you what consolation you now feel from reflecting upon "the chair, with a velvet cushion," in which the Lord was carried round Covent-Garden and along the Strand; excuse me, if I should ask you what a taste has been left by his beer and the orts of his table, which we are told he so generously bestowed upon you; excuse me if I ask you whether you remember how the high-blooded Sire sat smiling at the window, as the news-papers tell us, while you, like beasts of burden, were carrying the son upon your shoulders, and if I reproach you with worse than beastly unreasonableness if you complain of burdens hereafter.[31]

Percy's victory was short-lived. Within less than three weeks, parliament was dissolved, and a general election was set for November.[32] The by-election of October 1806 proved to be only the first round of a three-round bout.

The second round took place a month after the first. The regular party candidates at the general election for Westminster were Sir Samuel Hood for the tories and Richard Sheridan for the whigs. Hood was an obviously popular choice. He was no politician; he had spent his life in the navy, and in September 1806 had lost an arm fighting against the French. The independent candidate was a Cobbett protégé, James Paull, son of a tailor, a strange, fiery little man who, although only thirty-six years old, had allegedly made a fortune as a merchant in India. He had purposefully returned to England late in 1804, bought a seat in parliament for the borough of Newton, Isle of Wight, in June 1805, and proceeded to bring charges against the

"Triumphal Procession of Little Paul the Taylor upon his new Goose." As portrayed by Gillray, the procession is led by the rich Colonel Bosville, scattering coins. Horne Tooke follows, leading a goose with the head of Sir Francis Burdett. Paull, dressed as a tailor, rides on the back of the goose. Cobbett brings up the rear, blowing a trumpet

governor of India, Marquis Wellesley, for malfeasance in office. Cobbett had met Paull through Windham and had secretly, at Windham's instigation, drawn up charges against Wellesley.[33] Cobbett encouraged Paull's efforts to obtain a parliamentary hearing on the charges and defended him against the allegations that he was "a mere adventurer," asserting that Paull was "a man far beyond the reach of the political corruption of the times" and one on whom "the public may safely rely."[34] Shortly after publishing this panegyric, Cobbett began to have some private qualms about Paull, who was headstrong and would not always accept Cobbett's advice. "Paull is going on like the devil," Cobbett wrote to Wright in June 1806, and a month later declared that "Paull is too fond of the Bond Street set, has too great a desire to live amongst the great."[35] Nevertheless, Cobbett remained an admirer of Paull's objective of exposing government corruption, entertained Paull at Botley, used Paull's parliamentary postal franks, and was one of Paull's warm supporters at the meeting at the Crown and Anchor tavern on October 30, 1806 when Sir Francis Burdett announced Paull's candidacy.[36]

The polling began four days later, on November 3, allowing little time for preparation. Paull's backers made a brave beginning. "On Monday, the 3rd instant," wrote Cobbett, "Mr Paull proceeded from

"View of the Hustings in Covent Garden" by Gillray. The candidates at the November 1806 election for Westminster: Admiral Hood (who turns away to hide his smiles at Sheridan's embarrassment); the dissipated Sheridan, shocked and angered by the unfriendly crowd; and James Paull, who leads the assault on Sheridan: "the sunk, the lost, the degraded Treasurer." Samuel Whitbread stands between Hood and Sheridan. Cobbett, Burdett, and Bosville are on Paull's left

his house to the hustings in his barouche and four, accompanied by Sir Francis Burdett, myself and some other friends; Colonel Bosville in his coach and four following."[37] That a tailor's son should aspire to a seat in parliament was the subject of a great deal of humor among those supporting Sheridan; a stage from Drury Lane was brought to the hustings at Covent Garden with four tailors at work, a live goose (symbol of the tailor), and several cabbages (symbol of the tailor's meager diet).[38] The caricaturist James Gillray commemorated the event with three cartoons ridiculing Paull's small size, his undistinguished ancestry, and his enthusiastic but motley supporters.

Cobbett stayed at Paull's house throughout the fifteen days of voting, and every day stood by him at the hustings. When the polls closed on November 19, the recorded vote was Hood, 5,478; Sheridan, 4,758; and Paull, 4,481.[39] That the newcomer Paull was within 300 votes of the total polled by the veteran Sheridan was only a small part of the story. Paull had been well ahead during the first several days of polling; the whigs then made a deal with the tories by which all Hood voters would be urged to cast their second vote for Sheridan.[40] Thus, looking at the single votes cast, Paull had 3,077 against 1,033 for

Hood and 955 for Sheridan. An even more significant portent was that the independents had, for the first time, made a start at building an organization manned by local middle-class constituents. Westminster businessmen like a Mr. Hewlings, feather merchant, became personally involved in getting out the vote among their fellow electors.[41] The next time, wrote Cobbett on December 27, 1806, they "will not come inexperienced to the contest," and the next time, he asserted, "is at no great distance." Seeing that the ministry of All the Talents was laboring under great difficulties and must soon give way, Cobbett called for "another opportunity of trying our principles," expressing confidence that the big porter brewer, Colonel John Elliot, one of Sheridan's chief supporters, "will find those principles a good deal stronger and more pure than his porter."[42] Cobbett's instincts were right about the longevity of the ministry of All the Talents. Before another six months had passed, the ministry had gone down, and another general election was called. Thus May 1807 saw the third round of the battle for Westminster that had started eight months earlier, in October 1806. Cobbett's journalistic efforts between round two and round three were devoted principally to showing that an independent candidate should be returned by the large middle-class electorate of Westminster: the old whig party hack Sheridan was grossly inadequate, and, indeed, no one with attachments to the elite ranks of the regular parties – either the ins or the outs – could be expected to interest himself in the needs of the great mass of people.

Cobbett had been at war with Sheridan for a long time. Sheridan was one of the old whig Opposition to which Windham belonged when Cobbett had returned to England in 1800.[43] But politics to one side, it is hard to imagine the abstemious Cobbett finding much attractive in the purple-cheeked, red-nosed jester that Sheridan had become in his middle years.[44] Cobbett saw at an early date that Sheridan's speeches in parliament, although technically brilliant, were extremely shallow and frequently not all his own. They were a collection of "the strayed thoughts of others . . . a foundling hospital of wit."[45] Sheridan played to the gallery, waiting safely on the sidelines until he saw the moment for a demagogic declamation in high oratorical style: "you hunt not in the pack; but while others are steadily engaged in the chase, you are beating about for yourself; always taking care, however, if the day prove fortunate, to come in amongst the first and most noisy at the death."[46] Sheridan was what the politicians of the day called "versatile": "so ready have you been to broach sentiments, so bold have you been in advancing them, and so long have you passed with impunity through an endless maze of inconsistencies, that, it is by no means wonderful if you do not take the trouble to recollect, during one debate, any thing you have said in a former one."[47] These are a tiny sample of the unpalatable truths Cobbett had levelled at Sheridan over the years.[48] Now, in preparation for the general election of May 1807, Cobbett stepped up the campaign: one prong of the attack was directed at Sheridan personally. He was receiving the £5,500 a year attached to the sinecure post of treasurer of the navy although, according to Cobbett, he had never rendered any public service, however small, at any time of his life. Sheridan's son Thomas, "of whom we have never heard but in the circles of pleasure," was receiving, while living in England, £2,000 a year as mustermaster of Ireland in addition to his pay as captain of a regiment serving overseas.[49] Since Sheridan "came into the receipt of the public money," he had abandoned all the fine promises he had made during the years he was in opposition.[50] Sheridan's notorious evasion of his creditors (a seat in parliament exempted him from arrest) was dramatically portrayed by Cobbett in an incident that had occurred at the hustings during the November election. Sheridan had declared to the crowd that although he generally admired Cobbett, he condemned his proposal to levy a tax on the interest paid on the national debt, since this would constitute "breaking faith with the public creditors".

. . . which words were hardly out of his mouth when the air rang with a shout of indignant surprise; and this unusual clamour, in which every voice had been strained to its utmost, being followed by a short interval of comparative silence, a man, from the middle of the crowd, in a very distinct voice, uttered the following words: *"hear! hear! hear! Sheridan; Richard Brinsley Sheridan,* DETESTS BREAKING FAITH WITH CREDITORS!" which words were echoed and re-echoed through every part of the immense multitude collected in Covent Garden and the adjoining streets and houses.[51]

Cobbett was confident that his taunts had struck home.

He [Sheridan] may disguise his feelings from some people, but he cannot from me. No hare, with a half a mile of naked downs before her, and a brace of my Lord River's best greyhounds at her heels, ever cocked her ear with more anxious solicitude than he will, on Saturday night, to hear the contents of this Register. I speak this, not to his shame, but in his commendation, it being the act of an enemy to represent him as so callous as not to feel what I have said, and what I shall say, of him.[52]

We can be sure that Sheridan, accustomed most of his life to the applause of the press, was dispirited by this type of psychological warfare, to which there was no adequate reply.

From a long-term point of view, a more significant line of attack taken by Cobbett was against the thesis that only the wellborn were entitled to participate in governing the country. Cobbett, at the high point in his tory career, had noted a new element at the 1802 election for Middlesex: "It is not, as heretofore, a contest between such a gentleman and such a gentleman; but between the high and the low, the rich and the poor. In many places, at least, almost all the rich are on one side, and all the poor on the other."[53] Cobbett saw the explosive nature of this class issue and took full advantage of it here. Sheridan and his supporters had boasted of their high blood, and they made no effort to conceal their contempt for Paull, descendant of a tailor.[54] Sheridan's bumptious son declared that Paull was so base that he (the younger Sheridan) might "raise him in the estimation of society by kicking him out of it."[55] More explosive material was offered by one of Sheridan's principal backers, who stated that he would have the names of Paull's voters published "that none of them might ever be admitted into gentlemen's company."[56] These claims were used by Cobbett as a two-edged sword. Richard Sheridan's father had been an actor, and playactors, Cobbett pointed out, had been bracketed by Pope with pimps: "Unelbow'd by a Flatt'rer, Pimp, or Play'r."[57] The Duke of Northumberland, possibly motivated by such considerations, refused to allow his son, Lord Percy, to stand for Westminster with Sheridan.[58] As the second edge of the sword, Cobbett mentioned that there were perhaps 10,000 tailors in Westminster (not all, of course, entitled to vote), and it was this group – the tailors, the small merchants, the main body of the electors of Westminster – to which Cobbett appealed when he spoke of the "contumely and insolence of our 'high-blooded' opponents at Westminster, and that foul combination there formed against the exercise of the undoubted rights of the people, a combination avowedly founded upon the arrogant and unjust allegation, that, on account of our low birth, we were unworthy of any public influence or trust." He continued:

May we not be permitted to ask, too, where, in the history of the last eighteen eventful years, the superior wisdom and courage and virtue of "high-blood" had discovered itself in a manner so decided and so conspicuous as to warrant the doctrines held forth by our haughty and supercilious adversaries at Westminster? Yes, surely, we may ask, whether any one will now venture to maintain, that none but "high-blooded" men are capable of defending the honour and the territory of their country?[59]

Approaching the same subject again and again, Cobbett drove home the point that the voters must no longer allow their choice to be dictated by the ruling classes. They must no longer allow themselves to be "treated as persons too low and insignificant to be heard in public."[60] The roles should be reversed; "the supporters of Mr Sheridan were formed by nature, or by habit, to be *ruled by us* . . .

though they happen to be upheld by a state of things calculated to favour them, I hope there are none amongst us so base as to believe, that it is, from that fact to be concluded, that they are our superiors . . . From the beginning to the end of the contest, they discovered, in all they said and in all they wrote, a total want of foresight and of talent, an inherent, an hereditary, and incorrigible stupidity.[61]

It is notable that in Cobbett's appeal to the electors he unambiguously identifies himself with the group he is addressing. It is: *"our* low birth," "may *we* not be permitted to ask," "ruled by *us."* This identity of interest was one of Cobbett's great strengths. For not only did he understand those who were not highborn and believe in them, but they in return – recognizing the identity of interest – understood him and believed in him, and gradually absorbed the confidence that he exuded.

In this interim period preceding the May 1807 election, Cobbett said a great deal about Sheridan, but relatively little about the independent candidates. Paull obviously wanted to run again, but Cobbett was increasingly uneasy about him. Cobbett had disagreed with the filing of a petition on Paull's behalf to upset Sheridan's victory.[62] A second petition, filed by Paull himself, accusing Sheridan of tampering with Paull's witnesses proved to be a boomerang when the House found, in March 1807, that the petition was "false and scandalous."[63] This finding did not directly affect Paull's integrity (since he seems to have been taken in by information furnished to him by a scoundrel married to Sheridan's illegitimate daughter), but it was another blot on Paull's discretion and on his appeal as a candidate.[64] Cobbett wanted the independents to nominate Sir Francis Burdett, and him alone. He wrote to Paull and to Lord Cochrane (a rumored candidate) suggesting that they stand aside for Burdett.[65] In the event, no one proved tractable. Burdett said that he would permit his name to be brought forward, but would not make any effort himself, even to appearing at the hustings. A small committee of independent Westminster voters decided to back both Burdett and Paull.[66] "What can those fools mean by putting up Mr Paull, except for the purpose of vexing Sir F. Burdett's friends?" Cobbett wrote to Wright early in May 1807. "What a mortifying thing it must be to Mr Paull to see the votes he will get!"[67] Cochrane too decided to run. Sheridan was the official whig candidate, and John Elliot, the porter brewer who had backed Sheridan in the November election, became his running mate as the official tory candidate, making a total of five contenders.

The polls were to open on May 7 for the usual fifteen-day period. Cobbett's editorial in the *Political Register* for May 2 contained an endorsement of Paull written in Botley on April 30: if it had not been for Paull, there would have been no election in November 1806; but for him, Westminster would have been a "close borough." Paull would "set about the pursuit of public robbers." He had, to the highest degree, the virtues of "firmness, industry, and perseverance."[68] Cobbett had written this endorsement reluctantly. While he felt able to praise Paull's firmness, industry and perseverance, he doubted Paull's judgment. Yet he thought Paull deserved support for his vigorous efforts to gain a hearing on the charges of malfeasance brought against the Marquis Wellesley. He also felt that Paull had been treated shabbily by the House of Commons during the hearing on his election petition. "They bullied Paull," wrote Cobbett to Wright, quickly adding, as a comment on his feckless associate: "however, what a cursed thing it is to have more sail than ballast."[69]

Cobbett's position was clarified by the events of May 2. On that date Paull fought a duel with Burdett, and both were seriously wounded – it was thought that Paull's wound might prove fatal. The Westminster committee decided to support Burdett alone.[70] In the next issue of the *Political Register* (May 9) Cobbett expressed his regret that "Mr Paull is no longer in a state to be thought of as your representative," adding that he had always believed that Burdett was the fittest man to represent Westminster, that this belief was known to Paull, and that Cobbett was sure that Paull, at any time, would have resigned his pretensions in favor of Burdett.[71] "If you succeed in causing Sir Francis Burdett to be returned to parliament," wrote Cobbett the following week, "you will have done more for the country, in the space of fourteen days, than has been done for it, during the last hundred years."[72] Cobbett's open support of Burdett still left him with another difficult decision. He had become friendly with Lord Cochrane since the Honiton election the year before, and yet Cobbett was opposed, on principle, to the election of army or navy officers to parliament on the ground that the requirements of their professional duties during the continuing war against France were inconsistent with attending meetings in parliament, and that such officers were too much under the control of the ministry of the day, since appointments, promotions, and demotions were crown prerogatives. With this reservation, Cobbett warmly commended his friend, assuring his readers that Cochrane would zealously discharge his trust if elected.[73]

Cobbett did not attend the election in person, intending to go to London in the event of a victory. He wrote Wright on May 17, 1807, a week before the close of the polls:

it seems to me, that I have done the wise thing all through. It would never have done to have to defend myself against the charge (however false) of having deserted Paull, when it was found that no one would vote for him. And yet it was difficult not to attack his opposition to Sir Francis' election. I think I have done what was best. I have left neither side just grounds for complaint. I am in hopes *both* our friends will be chosen.[74]

"Election Candidates; or the Republican Goose at the Top of the Pole." The republicans' victory of May 1807 is portrayed by Gillray. Burdett tops the candidates
(despite the injury received in the Paull duel, realistically depicted), followed by
Cochrane with a reform cudgel provided by Cobbett. Sheridan, dressed as harlequin, struggles near the bottom, and Paull falls headlong

As Cobbett hoped, both Burdett and Cochrane were elected, giving Cobbett "the greatest pleasure I have ever felt in my life" – possibly one of the greatest surprises as well, since he had confidently predicted that "the contest would be useless if Sir Francis Burdett would not come forward in person."[75] The votes were Burdett 5,134; Cochrane, 3,708; and Sheridan, 2,615.[76] Sheridan was more than a thousand votes behind Cochrane, despite the fact that Elliot withdrew on the eleventh day, presumably to help Sheridan, since at the time he withdrew Elliot had nearly three times as many votes as Sheridan.[77] Paull had declined the contest early in the polling.

The Westminster election was a great victory, not so much because of the particular individuals who won, or those who lost, but because the regular party candidates, the representatives of the governing class, were beaten by the people governed, and the latter had been able to do it on an expenditure of less than £800. "This election," wrote Cobbett in the *Political Register* for May 30, 1807, "is the beginning of a new era in the history of parliamentary representation."[78]

As soon as Burdett had sufficiently recovered from the wounds suffered in the duel with Paull, he was "chaired" through Westminster in a grand cavalcade along streets "crowded so as to leave not a foot of vacant ground." The order of the procession, published some days before, began: "Marrowbones and Cleavers, four and four. Four trumpets on Horseback," and included bands, boy buglers, the high constable on horseback, the electors of the Westminster parishes marching four by four, Sir Francis Burdett "In a Grand Car, drawn by four Grey horses," followed by "Horsemen, four and four. Carriages to close." Among the latter was the coach and four of Colonel Bosville with William Cobbett.

When we arrived at Covent Garden we found all the low buildings in the middle of the square so loaded with people that the chimney tops were hidden from our view: hundreds were sitting or standing upon the roofs and ridges of the houses round the square, and, upon a moderate computation, there could not be less than one hundred thousand persons, who here saw the procession at one and the same time.

Two hours and a half after the procession began at Sir Francis's home on Piccadilly, it ended at the Crown and Anchor tavern in the Strand, where 2,000 persons, paying twelve shillings each, joined the celebration meal and responded to the jubilant toasts. A half million in all, Cobbett estimated, had participated in the event at one time or another, yet not a single act of violence was committed, contrary to the expectations of the authorities, who had been dismayed at the thought of the people electing a candidate of their own choice. Thus the troops guarding the palace and offices at Whitehall had been doubled. The local regiments of regular soldiers were called out in the morning and kept in arms throughout the day. The horse artillery were kept harnessed in St. James's park to draw the cannon if they should be needed to cope with the unruly crowds. Volunteer corps were summoned to muster "with fixed flints." Cobbett, with typical cynicism, remarked on "how happy" the officers of these troops must have been to find that the people "could chair their representative, legally and virtuously chosen, and return to their houses, without requiring to be shot at!" Delicately chaffing the Duke of York, commander-in-chief of the army, for the "motherly care" he had taken of the lives of the king's subjects, Cobbett made one of those extraordinary leaps, so characteristic of his writing, from the current subject to a country scene:

The ground, in which my habitation stands, consists of about three acres, the greater part of which is in grass. In this grass, and at about forty yards from my door, a skylark chose as the place to build her nest. Never having before seen one of these naturally shy birds fix its breeding place so near to a house, and having been so much delighted with the singing of the old bird, we delayed the mowing of the grass a little longer than we otherwise should have done, in order to give the young birds time to get fledged. When we saw them out of the nest, the mower was set to work; but, not without some fear as to the fate of the brood, I requested him to begin at the part most distant from the nest; but (and the fact is a very curious one) my fears were soon completely removed; for he had not cut the third swarth, when the old larks, skimming up in the air, taking a turn over his head, and perceiving where unto his operations tended, flew back in great haste, carefully collected their young ones all together upon a little mound, and having so done, they gave me a farewell chirrup, and away they flew into my neighbour's field. –"There!" said I to myself, "is an instance of tenderness and of foresight of danger, equalled only by our consummate Commander in Chief!" – How happy, then, must that royal person have felt on Monday night, upon finding that there was no need for those precautions, which he had so laudably taken, and that the several corps of troops had nothing to do but to go back quietly to their barracks, and return their ammunition into the magazines, there to be kept until wanted to kill those bloody-minded villains, the French, who, were they to become masters of our country, would, doubtless, establish an accursed military despotism.[79]

For years afterwards, a Grand Reform Dinner was held annually at the Crown and Anchor to commemorate the election of May 1807. Many individuals shared in the victory. The Westminster committee that nominated Burdett, made up largely of the middle-class amateurs who had gained their first experience in the November 1806 election, were an important element in canvassing the electors. They were stimulated by one of their number, the industrious, self-educated master tailor Francis Place – a lover of "quiet power"; an extreme egotist like most reformers – who, working largely behind the scenes, developed into one of the leading forces for reform during the first half of the nineteenth century.[80] But there were other elements at work in addition to the Westminster committee: Cochrane, not sponsored by the committee, polled enough votes to be elected. Cochrane campaigned as one "entirely unconnected with any of the great parties in parliament," as a friend of reform and as opposed to placemen and pensioners in parliament – all favorite Cobbett themes.[81] It is also probable that the destruction of Sheridan, who never again offered himself for election in a major constituency, was a significant factor.[82] It was two months after the Westminster election of May 1807 and one month after the chairing of Burdett that Francis Jeffrey, writing in the *Edinburgh Review,* declared that Cobbett "has more influence . . . than all the other journalists put together."[83]

12 · Reform and reformers

I wish to see the poor men of England what the poor men of England were when I was born.

THE MEMBERS OF PARLIAMENT returned at the general election of May 1807 included a fair number who at one time or another had professed themselves friends of reform. One of the most notable of these was the whig Charles Grey, who, in 1792, 1793, and 1797, had introduced motions in the House of Commons calling for changes in the laws relating to parliamentary elections and for a more equitable distribution of seats.[1] The bill proposed in 1797 would have made parliaments triennial (in substitution for the seven-year maximum then prevailing); would have done away with the rotten boroughs, giving increased representation to the counties and the new urban constituencies; and would have granted the right to vote in the towns to every householder and in the counties to every copyholder and leaseholder paying a minimum annual rental, in addition to the already eligible freeholders.[2] Although Grey's motion was defeated, it was supported by the vote of more than ninety members – a number that seemed astounding a few years later when the enthusiasm for reform had shrunk to near nothing as a result of the imminence of French invasion, the threat of rebellion in Ireland, and the repressive measures adopted by the Pitt government beginning in 1797. Windham's rhetorical question: "What, would he recommend you to repair your house in the hurricane season?" was the short answer of those opposing reform in the 1790s; and the high winds, it seemed, never ceased blowing in the years that followed.[3]

Lady Holland, who did not like Grey, claimed that he had raised the reform issue only "because it would be more peculiarly distressing to Pitt than any other he could bring forward."[4] Whether or not Lady Holland's accusation was correct, it seems likely that many of those who were willing to support reform at that time did so to gain popularity or to bring their own party into power, rather than to purify the government. This thought is reinforced by Grey's suggestion that reform was needed because the House of Commons (of which he had been a member in opposition since 1786) had neither "watched the conduct of the minister" nor "been a faithful guardian to the public purse."[5] Further, Grey, as well as nearly all his adherents, lost his ardor for reform after 1797, and did not resume it until the vigorous public agitation that occurred thirty years later.

During the first ten years or so of the long interim period – say, from 1797 to 1806 or thereabouts – the cause of parliamentary reform was kept alive by John Cartwright, former major of the militia, a respectable descendant of an old Nottinghamshire family, who had been a persistent but gentlemanly and sometimes boring agitator for reform since 1780. In October 1805, when Cobbett's articles in the *Political Register* alternated between the Melville scandal and the conduct of the war against France, Cartwright wrote to Cobbett expressing his esteem for Cobbett's energy, his independent spirit, and his "indignant warmth against peculation," and enclosed a few essays "written to serve our injured country."[6] It seems likely that these were some of Cartwright's articles that had been previously published, rather than anything for insertion in the *Political Register*; in any event, nothing that can be identified with Cartwright appeared in Cobbett's paper during 1805. It was not until March 1806, shortly after Cobbett's break with Windham, that Cartwright's name was mentioned in that publication. Then Cobbett applauded the major's recently published book, *England's Aegis,* in which he argued that an adequate defense of England could not rest on a professional army, but must depend on the wholehearted support of a free people who treasured their liberty under a just and tolerant government.[7] Thereafter, Cartwright became a frequent contributor to the *Political Register* in the form of letters to the editor. Cartwright was friendly with Sir Francis Burdett and with Francis Place, the tailor turned political adviser, and often dined with Place, "eating some raisins he brought in his pocket, and drinking weak gin and water."[8]

Paull had disappeared after his duel with Burdett, and in 1808 took his own life. Cartwright, Place, Burdett, and Cobbett – all of whom played an important part in the Westminster elections of 1806–7 – were to remain for many years the principal agitators for reform.[9] To this central core, two lesser names must be added: Lord Cochrane, who continued as a member for Westminster until 1818; and Lord Folkestone, another friend of Cobbett's (he stood as godfather to one of Cobbett's daughters), who served in the House of Commons from 1801 to 1828, when he succeeded his father as Earl of Radnor.[10] Henry Hunt – later notorious as "Orator" Hunt – began to take an interest in the political scene about the time of the Westminster elections of 1806–7, but remained relatively obscure until about 1816.[11]

The parts played by the seven individuals named were quite different. Cartwright and Cobbett were the only writers in the group, and Cartwright, whose writing was not particularly distinguished, was never a journalist. At this stage of his life (he was sixty-seven in 1807) he wrote letters to newspaper editors and not much more. Place's activities were principally behind the scene, and he gradually attached himself to the philosophical reformers, Jeremy Bentham and James Mill. Cobbett (until Hunt came along nearly ten years later) was the only exciting public speaker of the seven. Burdett spoke well ("all grace and music," wrote Disraeli) but limited his speeches to parliament and meetings of his constituents, while Cobbett, and subsequently Hunt, who began speaking to their neighbors, later stumped the country. This appeal to the people was regarded in many quarters as in bad taste; as late as 1886 Queen Victoria was critical of Gladstone for speaking to public audiences outside his own constituency. Cobbett bore the additional stigma of journalist, a degrading profession in an age when a gentleman's letters to the press were ordinarily signed "Junius" or "Verax" or simply "A British Observer." Cobbett not only did all the writing that is ordinarily recognized as his, but also prepared motions and speeches for Burdett (who was lazy) and as well, it is believed, for Cochrane and Folkestone. Gillray's cartoon of the Westminster election of 1807 showed Cochrane with a cudgel labelled REFORM and the words "lent to him by Cobbett." Folkestone's dependence on Cobbett was derided in the *Satirist:*

> Of my little Lord Folkestone 'twas once shrewdly said,
> But for Cobbett he'd scarce know his heels from his head.[12]

Even among so small a group as the four reformers constituting the core of the movement, it was difficult to reach agreement regarding the reforms that should be supported on the single issue of parliamentary representation. The closest thing to a consensus was the proposal that Burdett submitted to the House of Commons in 1809, by which the right to vote would be given to freeholders, householders, and others subject to direct taxation; equal electoral districts would be established based on population; and parliament would be brought back to "a constitutional duration."[13] These proposals, Cobbett stated, were "precisely that which I wish for" (Cobbett and Burdett had met in Oxford two weeks before the program was made public), but they probably did not go as far as Place and Cartwright would have liked.[14] The issue Burdett put before the House of Commons was not whether his specific suggestions should be accepted but whether the House would in its next session "take into consideration the necessity of a reform in the representation." Even on this narrow issue, Burdett was unable to collect more than fifteen votes.[15]

The changes in parliamentary representation put forward by Burdett were, for Cobbett, only a means to an end. He had a much broader view of the changes that were ultimately necessary in the government: "Of what has been denominated *Parliamentary Reform*, I have always disapproved," wrote Cobbett in March 1806, "because I never could perceive, in any one of the projects that were broached, the least prospect of producing a *real reform.*"[16] This was written prior to his disappointment with Grenville's ministry of All the Talents, when he still believed that the more important changes – the real reforms – would be effected by a new set of ministers willing to uproot "the Pitt system." Cobbett's expectations were justified by the makeup of Grenville's cabinet, which included not only Cobbett's friend William Windham, the principal supporter of the *Political Register,* but also Fox and Charles Grey, who for twenty years or more had been the verbal champions of reform and enemies of corruption. Their failure, once in office, to make any effort to clean up the government convinced Cobbett that parliamentary reform was an essential. Without it, without a different body of men in parliament, the other needed reforms could not be accomplished.

Viewed historically, Cobbett's ideas on the real reforms that were needed stemmed largely from his ultra-tory days. In 1802 he had warned of the "subserviency of statesmen to the views of money-lenders" and attacked sinecures and pensions except when granted for exceptional public service.[17] In the following year he declared that the national debt should be "annihilated"; denounced the sinking fund, whose alleged purpose was to reduce the national debt; and opposed the bank restriction law permitting the Bank of England to suspend payment in specie and to substitute paper money.[18] In 1804 he pointed out that the poor rates and number of poor had increased with the increase in enclosures.[19] When bread – the chief sustenance of the working class – rose from 8¼d. to 14d. between August and December 1804, Cobbett asserted that the rise was not due solely to the poor harvest but was attributable, in part, to the effect of paper money in a time of dearth and to the corn laws, which provided a bounty for grain exported from England.[20] Early in 1805, Cobbett claimed that the poor of the country, constituting one-eighth of the entire population, were worse off than the slaves of the West Indies, and that the number of paupers was related to the huge increase in interest on the national debt "drawn from the labour of the people and given to the loan-jobbers and other makers of, and dealers in, paper money."[21] A few weeks later he wrote that "ever since the system of taxation began in this country, the imposers of taxes have constantly professed to tax the rich as much, and the poor as little, as possible; and at the end of a hundred years' taxing, the rich are richer and the poor poorer than ever." Such was the result because "all taxes, be they what they may, must finally fall upon labour, labour being the only source of the means of paying taxes."[22]

Thus by February 1805 Cobbett had laid the platform on which his later broad-scale reform program was founded. He became a reformer by the same process that had earlier made him a reactionary. He had attacked the Jacobins because of their disregard for law and religion, which led, in his opinion, to bloodshed and misery. Now he attacked the governors of England because of their profligacy, dishonesty, and indifference, which had led, in his opinion, to the creation of more than a million paupers out of a nation of nine million.[23]

Some of the incitement to corruption within the House of Commons itself was apparent on the surface. Individuals who bought seats in parliament frequently hoped to recoup the cost out of public funds. Members holding government places and pensions were expected to support expenditures brought forward by the party in power. Hence Cobbett urged the enforcement of the laws which prohibited the sale of seats; the termination of sinecures and pensions, except those which had been granted for exceptional public service; and the enactment of legislation to exclude placemen and pensioners from the House of Commons, except (as he shortly added) the five or six "principal servants of the King, who have, every day, statements to make to the House."[24]

And, when I talk of sinecures and pensions, I do not confine myself merely to what is called the place and pension list, but extend my view to the sinecure and pension-list of the *East-India Company,* to that of the *Colonies,* to that of the *courts of law,* and several others, *all* of which sinecures *are paid by the people of this country.* – The army and navy contracts is the next branch; the barrack department the next; and the enormous sums paid out of army and navy money to persons who perform little or no service. – But, how is this to be accomplished? Restore the law for *excluding placemen and pensioners from the House of Commons,* and the whole will be accomplished in a year. This is the root of all the evil; this, and this alone it is that renders our situation dangerous.[25]

As the quotation itself suggests, corruption at the top was not the only problem. There was also a constant bubbling up of questionable actions from the lower levels of government and, everywhere, evidence of a great quantity of inefficiency. The members of the two great parties seemed to view the expenditure of public funds with the dispassion of dancers in a minuet, "Their hair so nicely powdered and their gloves so genteely drawn off from one hand at a time, while they occasionally press their delicate fingers upon the table, and gracefully bow to the honourable gentlemen on the other side."[26] Because of lack of adequate reports, it was not possible for the average member of parliament, much less anyone outside, to learn how the public money was being spent. Information that one would think was readily available, such as the amount of interest paid by the government to the Bank of England, then privately owned, was not published, and the ministry successfully refused to produce it in parliament.[27] Millions were voted when "not an account; not a single estimate, not a voucher of any kind, whether as to receipt or expenditure, was yet before the House."[28] The ministry of the day, through its parliamentary majority, could gain approval of any financial proposal it put forward. Bills of importance passed with twenty members present or even, on occasion, to the "yawnings of a House of half a score."[29] Cobbett could recall no instance when a ministerial bill to spend money had been rejected.[30] The House of Commons had abandoned its traditional "power of the purse."[31]

While there was little that took place in the Commons that escaped his attention, Cobbett concentrated his efforts on government outlays of a potentially embarrassing nature – such as the emoluments of the "younger branches of the royal family" and the pensions and sinecures granted to the great and nearly great[32] – and to those two categories of expenditure which alone constituted nine-tenths of the budget, namely, the armed forces and the national debt. The waste in the army and navy was notorious. Admiral Markham had stated publicly in 1804 that the cost of the navy could be cut by a third; Cobbett thought that army as well as navy expenditures could be halved "if all waste was as effectually prevented as it might be."[33]

Over a third of the total cost of government was attributable to the national debt – a subject that became a lifelong bête noire for Cobbett. In the period 1793–1801 Pitt created debt in the amount of £334 million, for which the government had received only £200 million in cash: instead of issuing £100 of debt at par, with interest of 5 percent, it issued £100 of debt at 60 with interest of 3 percent on the face value.[34] Thus the holder received not only an effective interest rate of 5 percent on what he had invested, but also would receive, when the debt was discharged or redeemed, a capital gain of 40 points. The transactions raised a host of questions: Was the money wisely spent?[35] Should it have been raised by increasing current taxes, rather than by borrowing?[36] If the borrowing was proper, was the discounting necessary? To what extent was the total debt the result of hidden profits going to the bankers, brokers, and government insiders?[37] Should the debt which was purchased with inflated paper money be paid off by the government in gold? These were questions Cobbett explored at one time or another.[38] And then there was the terrible sinking fund: Pitt had undertaken to buy back a portion of the debt each year and deposit it in the sinking fund. The original idea had been to support the sinking fund out of tax surpluses and thus annually reduce the total debt outstanding. But the continuation of the war prevented such a surplus, so each year the government borrowed more than it needed for its current requirements in order to keep up the payments to the sinking fund. Each new borrowing entailed commissions and related expenses, and since the new borrowing could be at a higher interest rate than the debt outstanding, the process, with rare exception (if any), increased the burden on the nation instead of reducing it. Hence the debt snowballed, for there were not only the new borrowings to meet the requirements of the sinking fund, but further borrowings to pay the interest on previous borrowings. By 1805 the interest on the national debt was £29 million – "a sum equal in amount to the whole of the annual expenditure of the French empire."[39] If that amount were applied to the needs of the poor, there would be no paupers in England. Cobbett spoke constantly of "annihilating" the national debt, which to him meant anything from taxing the interest on the debt to disavowing it completely, but all the more drastic methods of annihilation seem to have been premised on the assumption that they would be applied only if necessary to save the nation.[40]

To Cobbett, the tax burden arising from the heavy interest was only one of several reasons why the national debt was an evil. Of equal importance was that the financing of government expenditure through debt, coupled with the substitution of paper money for specie, beginning in 1797, produced a substantial "depreciation of money" – what a later age, looking at the obverse, would call inflation.[41] Beyond the usual hardships this inevitably entailed, it now brought a special wrench to the farmers of England, who found that many of their landlords, in face of rapid inflation, would no longer grant long-term leases. But farmers compelled to cultivate upon the tenure of a single year could not afford to invest money in improvements – a development almost immediately recognized by the authorities on the subject as "the greatest impediment to the agricultural industry of the country."[42]

This was not the end of the consequences of the national debt. There was also the social and political disruption caused by the availability of an investment that would yield 5 percent, nearly twice the 3 percent return ordinarily derived from landownership.[43] The landed gentry could nearly double its income by giving up an often lonely life in the country and joining other indolent fundholders living in London. This had grave consequences to those left behind. The millions of people of agricultural England looked not to London for their leadership either in peace or in war, but to the local landed gentry, the bone and marrow of the country; they lived among the people, they worshipped with them, played with them, shared good times and bad with them; they administered the laws; they were the representatives of the people in parliament.[44] Now they were being seduced from their critical role in the life of the country by a rising new class, the moneymen of London, those who managed the funds and profited by the trade that rapidly developed in the various types of securities becoming available.[45] The moneymen were the obvious purchasers of the country estates. The gentry, by selling, increased their income; the moneymen, by buying, increased their social standing. Government contractors, manufacturers, merchants, and nabobs followed the moneymen. All the changes which brought in the new faces were not voluntary. The economic pressures of the period – heavy taxes and rapid inflation succeeded by rapid deflation – often forced out the traditional owners. Cobbett claimed that in one county with about 200 pretty considerable mansions belonging to noblemen or gentlemen, only 44 were still in the hands of the families that had been in possession thirty years before.[46] The ancient bond between landlord and farmer that had existed for generation after generation was suddenly severed; the farmer found himself paying rent to a demanding absentee landlord with whom he had nothing in common.[47] It became usual to employ bailiffs. "Scotch bailiffs, above all, were preferred, as being thought harder than any others that could be obtained."[48] When agriculture flourished during the Napoleonic wars, many farmers developed expensive tastes: They rode afield wearing scarlet hunting jackets; they wore "shining boots, white cravats, and broadcloth coats instead of spatterdashes, red handkerchiefs, and smock-frocks"; they drank imported wine instead of home-brewed beer; they bought pianos, and their daughters took French lessons; they added dining rooms to their houses, and their workers no longer ate with the farmer "at the long oak table, three inches through, at which the whole family sat." The farmers' wives became grand ladies: "when 'twas dame and porridge, 'twas real good times; when 'twas mistress and broth 'twas worse a great deal; but when it came to be ma'am and soup, 'twas d—d bad."[49] Smaller farms began to disappear because of enclosures and advantageous offers made by those anxious to expand their holdings. Cobbett claimed that "three farms have been turned into one within fifty years."[50] The smaller farmers thus dispossessed became laborers. The agricultural revolution, like the industrial revolution, moved to larger units of production and to the separation of owner from manager and manager from worker. The personal relationships that had formerly existed in agriculture were largely destroyed. The "shallow fool," wrote Cobbett,

cannot duly estimate the difference between a resident *native* gentry, attached to the soil, known to every farmer and labourer from their childhood, frequently mixing with them in those pursuits where all artificial distinctions are lost, practising hospitality without ceremony, from habit and not on calculation; and a gentry, only now-and-then residing at all, having no relish for country-delights, foreign in their manners, distant and haughty in their behaviour, looking to the soil only for its rents, viewing it as a mere object of speculation, unacquainted with its cultivators, despising them and their pursuits, and relying, for influence, not upon the good will of the vicinage, but upon the dread of their power. The war and the paper-system has brought in nabobs, negro-drivers, generals, admirals, governors, commissaries, contractors, pensioners, sinecurists, commissioners, loan-jobbers, lottery-dealers, bankers, stock-jobbers; not to mention the long and *black list* in gowns and three-tailed wigs. You can see but few good houses not in possession of one or the other of these.[51]

Locke had said that "it is labour indeed that puts the difference of value on everything," and such a concept seems to be at the heart of Cobbett's hatred of those who did not perform what he thought of as labor: "the Jews," "the Jew-like," and the "Jewish Christians," i.e. the bankers and brokers and moneylenders, regardless of religion; the quakers – "worse than the Jews" – who speculated in crops purchased from the farmer before harvest; and the "nabobs" who came back to England with the plunder of India with which they too bought land being vacated by the gentry.[52] This group, particularly the moneymen and the nabobs, fuelled corruption in government by bidding for seats in parliament and then using their influence there for legislation that promoted their own interests. Another new class living on the labor of others were the tax assessors and collectors – Cobbett claimed there were 150,000 – who were engaged to enforce the taxes that had recently been imposed: "Would that Buonaparte could see them all, gentle and simple, noble and plebeian, drawn out on Salisbury plain (for no other place could exhibit them at one view); for he must be something more than mortal not to be dismayed at the sight."[53] The methods of this formidable host, Cobbett claimed, inspired "disguise, insincerity, suspicion, fraud and ill-will," producing a decline in both morality and public spirit.[54] Thus, the creation of the national debt – a device designed to ease the demands on current taxpayers by spreading the burden over future years – had become in Cobbett's eyes a leading force for social and political upheaval of the most corrosive nature.[55] To the citizen of the twentieth century who has lived so long in the tiger's cage that he no longer fears the tiger, Cobbett's never-ending strictures on the public debt and paper money seem to be near-madness. It is only after observing the full implications for the agricultural England of nearly two centuries ago that one can grasp the significance of Cobbett's campaign for the "annihilation" of the national debt, his attacks on paper money, and what he meant when he wrote that "When the funding system . . . shall cease to operate upon civil and political liberty . . . parliament will . . . reform itself."[56]

Cobbett was not alone in his extreme views on this subject. The philosopher and historian David Hume, writing a half century before Cobbett, had foreseen the public debt as inevitably creating "poverty, impotence, and subjection to foreign powers." He had written about the encouragement that debt gives "to an useless and inactive life" and to the increase of bribery and corruption. He had solemnly declared that "either the nation must destroy public credit, or public credit will destroy the nation."[57]

Although these secondary consequences of the debt were never far from Cobbett's mind, the main thrust of his attacks at this period was directed to the tax burden itself, which fell principally on articles of consumption. True, there was an income tax from 1798 to 1802 and again from 1803 to 1816, but this mild imposition, which never exceeded 10 percent, produced less than one-quarter of the total tax yield.[58] The consumer articles taxed directly included candles, salt, sugar, soap, tobacco, shoes (leather), tea, beer. "Are not bread and milk and butter and cheese and meat taxed? Yes, and that too very heavily in the taxes on land, houses, windows and income."[59] A laborer with wife and several children, earning from seven to twelve shillings a week, was, according to estimates at the time, paying from one-quarter to one-half of his earnings in tax![60] While these estimates appear high, there can be no doubt that the taxes were burdensome.[61] Cobbett claimed that they were *the cause* of the misery of the laboring class, although he often enough cited other elements which led to the distress of the poor.[62] There was, for example, the Speenhamland system by which farm laborers' wages were admittedly kept below subsistence level, making their survival depend on the generosity of local poor law commissioners.[63] "When I see a great farmer," wrote Cobbett, "I know that he has from 40 to 100 poor wretches of *paupers*, or of *half starved labourers*, at home."[64] And there were at least six pieces of legislation, some of which have already been mentioned, that were condemned by Cobbett as inimical to the interests of the poor: the acts by which more than three million acres of common and waste lands were enclosed in the period 1741–1801, lands on which the poor had traditionally pastured their cattle and gathered their fuel;[65] the Combination Acts of 1799 and 1800 making it a criminal offense for workers to act collectively;[66] the act of 1797, extended at various times, suspending payment in specie by the Bank of England, which stimulated inflation through the issue of unlimited amounts of paper money;[67] the corn laws, which kept up the price of bread, the chief item in the workman's diet, by forbidding the import of foreign grain at low prices and by providing a bounty for British grain that was exported;[68] the game laws, which prevented a starving man from taking a hare, even on his own land, unless he had a freehold estate of £100 per annum, so that fifty times as much property was required to kill a hare as to vote for a member of parliament;[69] the law of settlement, by which a laborer could be sent back to his home parish if he ever became a charge, for no matter how short a period, in another parish in which he was working.[70]

Over and over again, each time in slightly different words, he drove home his point:

a labouring man, in England, with a wife and only three children though he never lose a day's work, though he and his family be œconomical, frugal and industrious in the most extensive sense of those words, is not now able to procure himself by his labour a single meal of meat from one end of the year unto the other.[71]

Cobbett's objectives for the laboring man were modest. "I wish to see the poor men of England what the poor men of England were when I was born," he wrote in 1807.[72] Those who claim that Cobbett was looking for the restoration of a golden age are talking nonsense. The quoted words themselves establish that Cobbett never had the slightest notion that the poor should be made rich.[73] "Well do I remember," wrote Cobbett, harkening back to what he thought were good times, "when old men, common labourers, used to wear to church good broad-cloth coats which they had worn at their weddings." In those days "every poor man brewed a barrel of ale to be drunk at the lying-in of his wife, and another to be spent at the christening of the child." The laborer had household goods consisting of "his clock, his trenchers and his pewter plates, his utensils of brass and copper, his chairs, his joint stools, his substantial oaken tables, his bedding." Coats for Sunday wear that were forty years or so old; home-brewed ale for festive occasions; pewter and oak – these, and enough to eat, a fire to sit by, and a dry roof, were the ingredients of Cobbett's vision of what the poor men of England had when they were "well off" fifty years before, and what they might again hope for.[74]

Plainly, even this modest goal was not attainable under the existing economic structure, which was founded on the assumption that a worker should receive no more than what was necessary for survival – the same assumption that dictated the amount of food allowed to a workhorse.

Would you have no soul of them all earn a penny more than what is barely sufficient to maintain life? Would you have them to be, in effect, slaves from the cradle to the grave? Of what avail is it for a man to be industrious, if his industry will neither enable him to lay something up in store, nor enjoy a day of leisure or recreation? What motive had he to keep from the parish list, if he be certain, that a cut in the hand in whetting his scythe, will make him a pauper?[75]

With these words Cobbett urged the gentlemen of England – those who talked of "love of country, of public spirit" – to do as he did, to pay their laborers a decent sufficiency. "I cannot endure the idea of a labourer's receiving regularly, while he and his family are all in good health, a part of his subsistence in the character of a pauper."[76] Cobbett thought it ludicrous for rich men like George Rose and John Curwen to suggest savings banks for the poor laborer when it was apparent that he did not even have enough to satisfy the present wants of his family.[77] Cobbett did not visualize a richer country, but only one in which there was a more equitable distribution of the necessities of life. "England would be what it formerly was: a less *splendid* and more *happy* land." To Cobbett, a champion of human dignity, decent wages meant more than enough to eat; they meant personal freedom. He wanted the laborer to be allowed to manage his own affairs entirely in his own way. He was against philanthropy of any kind, either to provide support to the worker or directed at his morals, religion, or education.[78] He resented the phrase "lower classes" and its implication that the poor were less worthy.[79] He was outraged by the proposal of Malthus that the poor workman should defer marriage until he was able to maintain a family without parish assistance, that he should "be taught that the laws of nature had doomed him and his family to starve." Cobbett thought that this "laws of nature" argument was completely answered by Charles Hall's claim that the average working man produced six to eight times as much as his family consumed, but the rest was taken from him by those who produced nothing.[80] And, Cobbett asked, why should not the restraint apply to the clergy, who were supported by the rest of the population, and why not to the holders of pensions and sinecures, such as the family of Old George Rose, who received more than

£11,000 a year out of public money?[81] In a broader view, the issue was simply whether there was to be one rule for the poor and another for the rich – an issue to which Cobbett had a lifelong sensitivity. Why was it, Cobbett asked, that the widow of an officer killed in service received a pension, but a widow of a private soldier received nothing?[82] When Sir Samuel Romilly committed suicide after the death of his wife and was permitted a Christian burial on a finding of "temporary mental derangement," Cobbett pointed to the young bootmaker of Manchester who hanged himself after his rejection by the girl he loved and was buried in a hole by the highway with a stake driven through his body. "Justice and law are mere mockery; they are merely insulting words," wrote Cobbett, "unless they be impartially administered."[83]

Cobbett was not, as some have believed, against teaching poor children to read, but he thought the ABCs a poor substitute for food, and used this issue, with tongue in cheek, to castigate both the corrupt press and the corrosive influence of writers who promoted lower-class servility or superstition.[84]

The *utility* of reading consists in the imparting knowledge to those who read; knowledge dispels ignorance. Reading, therefore, naturally tends to enlighten mankind. As mankind become enlightened, they become less exposed to the arts of those who would enslave them. Whence reading naturally tends to promote and ensure the liberties of mankind. "How, then," you will ask, "can you object to the teaching of the children of the ignorant to read?" But, Sir, when we thus describe the effects of reading, we must always be understood as meaning, the reading of works which convey *truth* to the mind; for, I am sure, that you will not deny, that it is possible for a person to become by reading more ignorant than he was before.

It was taken for granted that what children read after they had been taught "will be calculated to give them *true notions,* and will inculcate the principles upon which men ought to be governed." But in the vast majority of English newspapers the new pupil "will find falsehoods upon every subject of a public nature; praises of all those who have power to hurt or reward; and base calumnies on all those, who, in any degree, make themselves obnoxious to power." Equally false doctrine appeared in the tracts of Hannah More and other believers in abject acquiescence for the lower classes, who glorified "the religious mouse, who lived upon dropped crumbs, and never, though ever so hungry, touched the cheese or bacon on the racks or shelves." Thus Cobbett sarcastically concluded that teaching the children of the poor to read would do more harm than good.[85]

Cobbett's preoccupation with the problems of the laboring man was one of the principal distinctions between him and the other reformers active in the period immediately following the Westminster elections of 1806–7. This was seen by one of the wise men of the time, James Mill, who wrote of Cobbett in 1808:

He has assumed the patronage of the poor, at a time when they are depressed below the place which they have fortunately held in this country for a century, and when the current of our policy was to depress them still farther. At a time, too, when every tongue and every pen seemed formed to adulation, when nothing is popular but praises of men in power, and whatever tendency to corruption might exist, receives in this manner double encouragement, he has the courage boldly to arraign the abuses of government and the vices of the great. This is a distinction which, with all his defects, ranks him among the most eminent of his countrymen.[86]

The approach taken by Cobbett was anticipated by Thomas Paine, who declared in Part II of the *Rights of Man,* published in 1792, that the millions wasted on government were more than sufficient to redress the wretchedness of the poor.[87] But almost immediately after making this assertion, Paine had left England and faded into relative obscurity, while Cobbett was preaching each week to thousands of readers. Cobbett used many of the same facts as Paine and reached many of the same conclusions, but they disagreed on both causes and remedies. Paine believed that revolution was necessary to improve the lot of the poor; the monarch and aristocracy must go and property must be redistributed by a stiff graduated estate tax that became confiscatory above a yearly value of £23,000. In contrast, Cobbett believed in changes by constitutional means only. He accepted the monarchy and aristocracy.[88] He at first opposed even a flat-rate income tax because it checked "industry and economy," but later went along with a graduated tax – not, however, to reshape society, but to raise needed revenue.[89] Cobbett thought that the national debt was a principal cause of the impoverishment of the laborer and should be annihilated, while Paine thought that it served to keep alive a·capital useful to commerce. Unlike Paine, who believed that the government should assist the poor by monetary grants for each child in a poor family, Cobbett believed that the need of such families should be met in the first instance by increasing their earnings rather than by subsidy. If such increased earnings were not forthcoming, then society had an obligation to provide the necessities of life. Unlike Paine, who was a deist and eagerly looked forward to a revolution in the religious system, Cobbett was attached to the religious principles of the church of England. He was, however, outraged by the worldly conduct of its clergy, and gradually came to favor both a repeal of the acts of parliament that had established the church by law, and the use of the nonreligious property of the church to reduce the national debt, leaving the church of England in much the same status as the dissenting churches: "I object not to its communion, but to the application of its temporalities."[90] Cobbett was not a revolutionary. He had no desire to create a brave new world. He wanted only to correct, by lawful and peaceful means, some of the evils in this one.

Not all of Cobbett's spleen was vented on those subjects that directly affected the poor. He had an interest in, and a view on, nearly every matter that came to his attention, and in many instances his views would appear to justify the commonly held conclusion that the side he took on any issue was largely dictated by his desire to assume the unpopular position. Thus, although he had a healthy protestant attitude toward the pope ("that old sodomite," he called him in a letter to Wright), he took the tolerant and humanitarian view on catholic emancipation: the proposal to relieve the Roman catholics of the United Kingdom from the existing legal restrictions which prevented them from voting for members of parliament, serving in parliament, or holding top staff positions in the army and certain government offices.[91] This was primarily an Irish problem – there were only 60,000 Roman catholics in England at the end of the eighteenth century – and Cobbett defended the proposal on the ground that it would make the Irish more satisfied with their lot (hence less of a defense problem) and would induce more of the Irish to enlist in the army, which badly needed recruits. Cobbett's concern for the Irish went far beyond the narrow issue of what was popularly known as catholic emancipation; he wanted to see the whole oppressive system of governing Ireland changed.[92] In contrast, Cobbett at first took an intolerant and inhumanitarian view of Negro slavery, finding support for the practice in the Bible, in the inferiority of the blacks, in the commercial needs of the West Indies, and in a demonstration that the black slaves of the Caribbean were better off than the white slaves of Britain. But by 1808 he had somewhat relented: "If the thing *can be*, I shall be glad to see the blacks as free, in every respect, as the whites."[93] There is, however, an ambiguity in that statement which was almost certainly intentional. Cobbett claimed that the Negroes were better fed, better clad, and less hardly worked than the laborers of England. West Indian slaves were sometimes flogged, but so were English soldiers, sailors, and militiamen: "I myself," declared Cobbett, "have seen hundreds of men flogged, and are not negroes flogged for just the same, or exactly similar offences?" Cobbett asserted: "I hold all slavery in abhorrence," and he never used sugar, coffee, or rum because they were the produce of slavery. Although West Indian merchants found comfort in some of Cobbett's statements on the subject of slavery, they were barbs more probably intended for Wilberforce and his "amis des noirs" who wept for the blacks 5,000 miles away and voted for the oppression of the impoverished English on their doorsteps; who moved not a finger to save Cobbett from prison when he condemned the flogging of militiamen at Ely.[94]

Cobbett startled many of his readers with his conclusion that "commerce" – i.e. foreign trade – was of no value to a country.[95] His articles called "Perish Commerce" claimed that the production devoted to foreign trade could be diverted to production for domestic trade without any loss to the nation.[96] Cobbett also contended that the British colonies were more of a burden than benefit (considering the cost of conquest, defense, administration, and subsidies), a view that Turgot had endeavored to promote in France.[97] His arguments on most of these topics were presented with surprising persuasiveness. Looking over the range of the subjects and the positions he took on them, one is left with the impression that his motivation in many cases was not so much that of taking the unpopular positions as of exposing the hypocrisy of his opponents: the high-church fellows at the university with their snug livings who opposed Catholic emancipation; Wilberforce and the other evangelicals in parliament known as the "Saints" who declaimed against the evils in the West Indies and ignored the sores at home; the rich London merchants who talked of "patriotism" at their elaborate turtle dinners, but were thinking of commercial profits; the nabobs, Englishmen of quite ordinary talents who went out to India for a few years and came back rich.

The gusto with which Cobbett made these exposures and those relating to his more usual topics of corruption and inefficiencies in government will explain why the chancellor, Lord Eldon, wrote as he did to his brother, Sir William Scott: "As to Cobbett, I am quite out of patience about those who will take in his paper; but I observe that all my friends, in short everybody one knows, abuse him, but enjoy his abuse, till he taps at their own door, and then they dont like the noise he makes – not a bit of it."[98]

13 · Cobbett versus Perceval

The little talent I have lies in the way of plucking and tearing to pieces.

ONE OF THE DOORS at which Cobbett noisily tapped more than once was that of Spencer Perceval, chancellor of the exchequer in Lord Portland's cabinet from 1807 to 1809 and prime minister from 1809 to 1812.

Perceval, second son of a second marriage of Lord Egmont, was a lawyer who had entered the government after ten years of private practice. He served a year as solicitor general before becoming attorney general in 1802, and, not surprisingly, his income from private practice kept pace with his rising importance as a public official, growing from £1,800 in 1801 to nearly £10,000 in 1804. Perceval's home life would have been a model even in Victorian times. He was a good husband of a pretty wife and a good father of a family of twelve children. Among friends he was known for his sweet temper, his engaging manners, his sprightly conversation, and his generosity. He was devoutly religious, and this, with the other qualities mentioned, gave him every reason to think of himself as a good man.[1] And so he was. In public life he was good too in nearly every respect. He was honest; he worked hard; he was a loyal and conscientious servant of the king; he was quick-witted, and despite his small size – Lord Eldon called him "little P" – he was an effective debater in the House of Commons. But he had one great failing as the leader of a nation: He totally lacked breadth. Brougham ascribed this to Perceval's unfamiliarity with any learning outside the law, except for the usual classical education of an English youth. "Of views upon all things the most narrow," Brougham ponderously wrote, "upon religious and even political questions the most bigoted and intolerant, his range of mental vision was confined in proportion to his ignorance on all general subjects."[2] Cobbett in his forthright style stated that Perceval was "short, spare, pale-faced" – his pale face accentuated by the black clothes he habitually wore – a "hard, keen, sour-looking man . . . with no knowledge of the great interest of the nation, foreign or domestic."[3]

Brougham and Cobbett were, no doubt, biased; yet regardless of where one turns for facts, Perceval remains one of those insubstantial, shadowy prime ministers of the first third of the nineteenth century: Addington, Perceval, Liverpool, Goderich – unrealizable figures when placed beside Pitt, Peel, Wellington, Gladstone, or Disraeli.

Perceval had entered Cobbett's life in 1804 when, as attorney general, he had acted as chief prosecutor in the "Juverna" case, but this episode seems to have created no fixed animosity on Cobbett's part. Between 1804 and 1807, when Perceval became chancellor of the exchequer, Cobbett had applauded Perceval for his efforts to mitigate the evils caused by the widespread practice of the clergy of residing away from their livings, employing underpaid curates to perform their duties.[4] Over half of all church livings worth more than £150 a year were held by nonresidents who rendered no service in the parish to which they had been appointed.[5] But, evenhandedly, the *Political Register* had mentioned aspects of Perceval that Cobbett did not admire: Perceval was a follower of the "squandering Pitt" and a patron of the shady Trotters, Davisons, and "thousands of their like."[6] In dealing with the orders in council of the preceding ministry, Perceval "seemed to have lost sight of every thing but . . . instant injury to the enemy without the least consideration as to the consequences with regard to ourselves."[7] And there were Perceval's sinecures. When he was twenty-two months old, "in consideration of the good and faithful service already performed," he was granted a reversion (in succession to his eight-year-old brother) to the office of registrar of the court of admiralty, worth about £12,000 a year. In 1791 (he was then twenty-nine) he was appointed surveyor of the meltings and clerk of the irons, worth something more than £100 a year –small at the Perceval level of society, but more than twice the pay of a clerk in the stamp office and about three or four times the gross annual earnings of the average laborer of the period.[8]

The creation of Lord Portland's ministry at the end of March 1807 and the elevation of the former attorney general to chancellor of the exchequer and leader in the House of Commons was a danger signal that Cobbett immediately recognized. He wrote to Wright saying that after the May general election was over, "I shall set about writing sober essays of *exposure*. Quote from official documents, state the bare facts, and lament, as I most sincerely do, the inevitable consequences."[9] A few days later he wrote:

I am this week engaged upon a most important and interesting discussion, on a letter to Perceval; and, I am resolved, that with this letter, I will begin a new *manner* of expressing myself. I see the fangs of law open to grasp me, and I feel the necessity of leaving no hold for them, and even no ground for silly cavillers, upon the score of coarseness or violence.[10]

The letter to Perceval appeared in the *Political Register* of May 16, 1807. It was restrained and dignified; if any fault could be found, it was the slightly patronizing air implicit in the letter form of editorial. "It is generally believed," wrote Cobbett, that, "as to all concerns and relationships of private life, it would be difficult to find a better man than yourself; and in this belief, I sincerely join."

As to public concerns, as there requires but very little more, in a minister . . . of this country, than strict honesty, a clear understanding, common powers of convincing others, industry such as is necessary in common life, love of country, and resolution to do that which the constitution demands, I should have no doubt of your being fit for the situation, were I not afraid, that the lures of ambition and your want of intrinsic political weight, may possibly drag you along, step by step, in the paths wherein your predecessors, for twenty three years past, have invariably trodden. That you would not voluntarily join in those deeds of corruption, which are such a disgrace to the government and the country, and which have, at last, brought the latter to the brink of ruin, political as well as pecuniary, I believe; but, when a man has once staked his fortune upon the maintenance of any principle or any party, and particularly if he has persuaded himself that to maintain the same is for the public good, he is very apt to yield to the solicitations of those by whom he is surrounded, and, when the necessity occurs, to regard the end as sanctifying the means.

After this exceedingly mild vote of confidence, Cobbett immediately expressed, with a high degree of percipience, what most concerned him about the new minister:

I do not believe, that for the love of the thing, you would wish to see your country bent down under an inexorable tyranny; but, I may think, and I do think, that you are too much of the opinion, that fear, and not love, is the principle by which we are to be governed, and . . . that your reliance, for the maintenance of the governing powers, is much more upon coercive than persuasive means.[11]

Cobbett's letters to Wright reflected this concern: "That one should live in this state of jeopardy every hour is mortifying enough; it is, indeed, a political hell."[12] Wright's duties included that of censorship: "I have sent you the Major's letter for insertion; but, if you should find any passage too strong, pray weaken it; for it would not suit me to be shut up."[13]

Cobbett's new manner did not lead him to avoid issues; but he tried to be more factual and to eliminate abuse and extreme accusations. When Perceval was granted another sinecure, that of chancellor of the duchy of Lancaster worth £4,000 a year and "having attached to it a good deal of church patronage," Cobbett mentioned the grant without apparent rancor.[14] He could not resist the temptation, however, when the issue of recruiting 38,000 men for the army was raised, of mentioning that one year's income from the sinecure held by Lord Arden, Perceval's brother, together with those of a handful of others (including the Grenvilles), was equal to the cost of raising the men who were needed.[15] Cobbett's principal measure on the sinecure issue was exerted behind the scenes through his new friend, Lord Cochrane, who, immediately after the convening of the parliament, made a motion (almost certainly motivated by Cobbett, if not actually written by him) calling for the appointment of a committee to report on the sinecures, pensions, and places enjoyed by members of the present House of Commons, or their wives, children, and other relations.[16] This was modified, at Perceval's instance, to provide that the report, instead of particularizing members of parliament, would include all sinecures, pensions, and places with the exception of the army and navy, which Cochrane had wished to include "because of the manner in which he had observed commissions to have been disposed of in the latter service."[17] But even with this exclusion and some other defects that Cobbett pointed out, the report when completed in 1808 was a forward step in the reform movement. It was the first attempt to provide the public with complete information on the covert workings of one aspect of the system, and became the basis for much of the agitation by Cobbett and other reformers in the years to follow.

The whigs, who were now the outs, and the friends of Pitt, who were now the ins, greatly simplified Cobbett's program of exposing corruption by exposing it themselves in a series of recriminating debates on their respective corrupt practices in the election just past.[18] "An old poacher is said to make the best of gamekeepers," commented Cobbett with amusement, observing that there seems "on the two sides, to have been a pretty equal balance of jobs."[19] Nor was it necessary for Cobbett to do much to propagandize the illegal purchase and sale of parliamentary seats. During the election month, May 1807, the London daily papers carried advertisements – Cobbett counted fifty-seven of them – blatantly offering to buy or sell such seats along with such other marketable commodities as government positions and church livings.[20] The *Courier,* a ministerial paper, jubilantly reported that three of the members of the outgoing cabinet (Grey, Windham, and Petty), who at one time had represented large constituencies, found it necessary to "sneak in for rotten boroughs."[21] Cobbett twitted Perceval on the obvious inconsistency between the admission that such infamous practices existed and his party's abuse of Sir Francis Burdett for calling attention to the practices.[22]

The new ministry was also charged by Cobbett with having misled the public on the issue of catholic emancipation. Grenville and his friends had gone out of office because of the unwillingness of the king to accept a modest relaxation of the restrictions against catholics, which they had put forward in the belief that it would facilitate military recruitment in Ireland.[23] The tories had campaigned at the general election on a "no-popery" platform, a platform of much demagogic appeal but one hardly justified by the innocuous legislative change that had been proposed. Even on this issue Cobbett remained calm. He stated his belief that the change would not have accomplished its objective, but that if even a much more drastic relaxation were to be adopted, which he advocated, there was no more reason to fear popery than there was to fear witchcraft.[24] Although he was willing to credit the ultrareligious Perceval with sincerity "in his alarms upon this score," Cobbett made it plain that the party to which Perceval belonged could not be so credited.[25] The new administration became known, among its enemies, as the "no-popery ministry," in contrast to the equally sarcastically named "no-peculation ministry" that had gone before.

The other great issues of 1807–8 related to the prosecution of the war. Since the defeat of the Austrians in 1805 and the collapse of Pitt's third coalition, the British had been sitting on the sidelines, preparing to resist an invasion attempt and blockading France by sea while Bonaparte expanded his power on the continent. Suddenly, in August 1807, without declaring war, a strong British naval force made a surprise attack on neutral Denmark. After a brief defense, Copenhagen surrendered, and the Danish fleet was carried back to England before Bonaparte could act. The whig opposition condemned this bold stroke as immoral, but Cobbett vigorously defended it: "This enterprize was really well conceived and well executed," wrote Cobbett, later declaring that if the ministers did not deserve being impeached for what they had done, they would have deserved impeachment for not doing it.[26] But that was not the end of the newly found energy. The Danish enterprise of 1807 was followed in 1808 by the first victory in years by a British army against the French. In November 1807 a French army had crossed Spain, entered Portugal, and captured Lisbon without a fight. A few months later the Spanish king surrendered his rights to the throne, and the French now seemed to be masters of Spain as well as Portugal. But the great mass of the Spanish people, unwilling to be thus transferred, had rebelled. A swell of sympathy for the Spaniards spread across England, and British forces were sent there and to Portugal. Late in the summer of 1808, in the midst of good news from Spain, where the rebels had shown surprising strength, came even more astounding news from Portugal. There, in mid August 1808, the French under Junot were decisively defeated at Vimeiro by Arthur Wellesley, the future Duke of Wellington. When the story reached England at the end of the month, the country went wild with joy at this proof that the armies of Bonaparte were not invincible. Cobbett, seeing the impact this could have on the rest of the world, wrote in the *Political Register*:

The victory, though not more glorious to the nation, is, in this as well as in other parts of its consequences, near and remote, of far greater importance to us than the victory of Trafalgar, which gave no new turn to the war, excited no great degree of feeling in the nations of Europe, and did not, in the least, arrest the progress of the French arms or diminish their fame or that dread of those arms which universally prevailed.[27]

Two weeks later joy was replaced by rage. The nation learned, to its dismay, that almost immediately after Wellesley's victory a treaty had been signed at Cintra by which the victors agreed to transfer the defeated French army with all its equipment and plunder safely out of Portugal and into France. The bells of churches in England were rung muffled, as upon occasions of public mourning.[28] Cobbett reflected the common view of the Cintra convention when he wrote to Wright: "both our admiral and our general ought to be hanged."[29] Three days later Cobbett expressed his certainty that "Wellesley has been the *real* author of all the mischief."[30]

Cobbett had a deep distaste for Wellesley's older brother Richard (Marquis Wellesley), being convinced that as governor general of India, Richard Wellesley had been guilty of the crimes charged against him by James Paull. Some of this distaste was transferred to the young brother, who was a part of Richard Wellesley's Indian administration.

Cobbett also thought that Arthur Wellesley was arrogant, a trait he was quick to detect in others. Thus while Cobbett was predisposed against the future Duke of Wellington, he was far from alone in his criticism of the Cintra convention and his demand for a public inquiry. A number of petitions to the king for an investigation were stimulated by Cobbett and those closely associated with him: the petition from the City of London had been moved by "that very public-spirited and excellent man" Robert Waithman, a Cobbett admirer and friend.[31] That from the county of Berkshire reflected the activity of Lord Folkestone, who had been working closely with Cobbett for six years.[32] Cobbett mentioned a move for a petition from Essex, where Holt White, Cobbett's solicitor, was a man of much importance and worked in cooperation with Montagu Burgoyne, a reform candidate for parliament in 1810.[33] And finally, a petition was submitted from

Hampshire, in which Cobbett was personally active, going to Winchester for the county meeting with Peter Finnerty and about twenty farmers "of the first reputation and property hereabouts."[34] A tory opponent, writing a dozen years later, provided an eyewitness account of Cobbett:

I myself never saw this extraordinary character but once – It was at a county meeting in Hampshire . . . He is perhaps the very man whom I would select from all I have ever seen if I wished to shew a foreigner the beau ideal of an English yeoman. He was then, I should suppose, at least fifty years of age; but plump, and as fresh as possible. His hair was worn smooth on his forehead, and displayed a few curls, nut-brown then, but probably greyish by this time, about his ears. There is something very firm and stately in his step and port – at least there was so in those days. You could see the serjeant blended with the farmer in every motion of his body. His eye is small, grey, quiet, and good-tempered – perfectly mild – You would say, "there is a sweet old boy – butter would not melt in his mouth." He was dressed the day I saw him, in brown coat, waistcoat, and breeches, all of the same piece – a scarlet underwaistcoat, a drab great-coat hanging wide, and fastened before by a "flying strap", top-boots of true work-like pattern, and not new, but well cleaned (another relic probably of his camp-habits,) – he had strong grey worsted gloves, and a stout ash plant in his hand. If he had not been pointed out to me by one who knew him, I should probably have passed him over as one of the innocent bacon-eaters of the New forest; but when I knew that it was Cobbett, you may believe I did not allow his placid easy eye and smile to take me in.[35]

It was at this Winchester meeting that Cobbett learned – possibly for the first time – his power to hold a large audience. "I *alone* was able to equal in votes the whole of the Whig party in this county," he later wrote to Wright.[36] He put down a would-be heckler in classic style: "I fixed my eye upon him, and pointing my hand down right and making a sort of chastising motion, said, 'Peace, babbling slave!' which produced such terror amongst others that I met with no more interruption."[37] Cobbett's speech, attended with much "laughter and applause," shouts of "go on, go on," and an occasional "bravo, bravo," was not limited to the point directly at issue – the need for an inquiry on the Cintra convention – but dwelt on the £23,000 in sinecures held by the Wellesley family; the £254,000 paid annually to the 291 generals in the British army; the £12,000-a-year sinecure of the apothecary general of the army, a resident of Hampshire; and the fact that the Duke of York, despite his failure as a commander at the Helder in 1799 and his disgraceful capitulation there, was receiving £50,000 a year, which was "equal to the poor's rates of 125 parishes and the assessed taxes of 146 parishes."[38] Such forthright talk was a new thing at a Hampshire county meeting. "I have had letters from all parts of the county beseaching me to persevere," said Cobbett in a letter to Wright.[39]

In response to the great public clamor, a court of inquiry was established, but it was not to Cobbett's liking. It was a private investigation, and the report, issued in December 1808, completely cleared Wellesley. The court of inquiry found that his superior, Sir Harry Burrard, had vetoed Wellesley's pursuit of the defeated French force because the British were short of cavalry and cannon, and although the court formally cleared Burrard, he never assumed another command in the field. Cobbett, allowing his prejudices to get in the way of a fair assessment, declared: "The cause of this disgraceful event appears to me to be the design of Wellesley to have to himself all the honour that was to be achieved, and the desire of Sir Harry Burrard to thwart him in that design."[40] To the comment in the report that no further military proceeding (i.e. court-martial) was necessary because "zeal and firmness" had been exhibited by all those under inquiry, Cobbett remarked that "The court might as well have reported that they found Sir Arthur Wellesley and his associates to have been excellent psalm singers."[41] Then, having vented his personal spleen, he offered an observation that probably reflected the view of most of the people in Britain:

An army that cost for the last year, upwards of *twenty millions of pound sterling* out of which above *four millions* went for *ordnance;* such endless trains of horses and waggons and equipage of all sorts; a country full of barracks and magazines and laboratories; every town full of soldiers and horses; the drum and the trumpets stunning us, and the country shaded with clouds of military dust from April to October; and with all these means, with all this warlike parade and bustle and clutter and expense before our eyes, are we, in good earnest, to be quieted, by being told, that our army of 35,000 men failed to capture 14,000 Frenchmen for the want of *horse* and *artillery,* and that, too, in a country where, it is notorious, all the people were our friends, and all the enemies of the French? If so; if we really are thus to be quieted, it matters very little who are our commanders, who are our rulers, or what either of them do. Tell us not that the horses were at Chichester or at Cork, and that the cannon were at Woolwich. What is that to us? They should have been where they were wanted. It was the business of some of you to see that they were there. You had a thousand ships of war at your command; the transports for the year will cost us two millions of pound sterling; you might have shipped off one half of the whole nation in the ships at your command; and now you tell us a whining story about want of horse and artillery. What are your bickerings to us? What is it to us, who amongst you are to blame? . . .

It is quite beneath us; it is to assist in abusing and cheating ourselves, to enter at all into the squabbles between ministers and generals. It signifies not a straw to us who is to blame. The blame, where there is any, is amongst them; and we have a right to complain, and to expect redress.[42]

The court of inquiry had condoned the Cintra convention by a vote of four to three, but this did little to dispel the widespread belief that it had been a sad mistake, or to correct the impression that the British general staff, with its 6 field marshals and 291 generals costing £254,000 a year, under the command of the Duke of York costing £50,000 a year, was not an efficient instrument for fighting a major war.[43]

To complicate matters further, during the time the Cintra convention was in the forefront of the news, another affair affecting the British army was quietly building up behind the scenes to produce an added burden to Perceval's role as leader of the House of Commons. The *Political Register* of August 6, 1808 contained the strange comment that "There is ONE SUBJECT, which, *at this moment,* engages the attention of every man, who is conversant with public affairs" – but, Cobbett added, it was a subject no one dared write about.[44] The following week, the question was raised as to why the Duke of York, as commander-in-chief of the armies in Spain and Portugal, was not sent there.[45] The same question was moved up to first position in the next issue of the paper:

Of all the subjects, which, for some time past, have engaged the attention of the public, no one has excited an interest so general and, to all appearance, so deep, as the talked-of appointment of the Duke of York to take command of the army destined to act in Spain and Portugal. Not to the inns, the coffee-houses, the marts, the malls, and the settled gossiping houses has the conversation upon this subject been confined. It has entered into all private circles; it has been a standing dish at the dinner and tea-table; men stop each other in the street to talk about the Duke of York's going to Spain; the eager Londoner stops, even in his way to the 'Change, to ask whether it really be true that the Duke of York is going to Spain; nay, in the very church-porches of the country, among the smock-frocked politicians, whose conversations, as to public matters, seldom went beyond the assessed taxes, you see half a score faces thrust almost to the point of contact, in order to know "for zartin if the Duke of Yark be a gooen to be zent to Spain."[46]

An odd anonymous pamphlet, also issued in August 1808, contended that both of the parliamentary parties were hostile to the duke.[47] Nothing further was written on the subject until October 22, when the following paragraph appeared at the end of Cobbett's weekly "Summary of Politics":

I cannot help pointing out to the attention of the reader, a pamphlet, just published, under the following title: *"An Appeal to the Public and a Farewell Address to the Army,* by Brevet Major Hogan, *who resigned his commission, in consequence of the treatment he experienced from the Duke of York, and of the system that prevails in the army, respecting promotions."* This, I scruple not to say, is the *most interesting* publication that has appeared in England for many years. It should be read by every individual in the nation. Oh, what a story does this gentleman tell! What a picture does he exhibit! What facts does he unfold! If *this* produce no effect upon the public, why, then, we are so base and rascally a crew, that it is no matter what becomes of us. We are unworthy of the name of men, and are beneath the beasts that perish.[48]

Very briefly, the major had applied for a promotion and had put up the prescribed payment, in accordance with the official requirements then in force. After the passage of three years during which forty officers junior to Hogan had been promoted, he had requested a personal interview with the Duke of York. At the interview he told the duke that he had been advised that he could get the promotion for about half the official rate by means of "low intrigue." But the duke showed no interest in hearing more about the accusation, although Hogan was "prepared with ample evidence to satisfy his highness, that such proceedings were going on daily as were disgraceful to the character of the army."[49]

The pamphlet telling this story was published on October 15, 1808, and went through the first two editions in eight days. The subject that had previously been little more than gossip was catapulted into the open on January 20, 1809, when Gwyllym Wardle, member of parliament for Okehampton in Devonshire, gave notice that a week from that date he would submit a motion in the House of Commons relative to the conduct of the commander-in-chief with respect to the granting of commissions, the making of exchanges, and the raising of levies for the army. As though there were not enough already to criticize, four days before Wardle's notice England suffered another great military loss. On January 16, Sir John Moore, commander of the British forces in Spain, died at Corunna as his troops scrambled to safety aboard a waiting British fleet, leaving behind their cannon, their horses, their stores, their brave leader, and 5,000 of their comrades who had been captured or killed by the enemy.

To Cobbett, nearly all these developments were added proof of the need for reform, and each event had a reform lesson. The guerrilla uprising in Spain, for example, viewed by Whitehall as an effort to expel Bonaparte, was seen by Cobbett as an effort of the Spanish patriots to reform their government; in that guise it was used by him as a thinly veiled attack on conditions in Britain. His articles in the *Political Register* on Spain in midsummer 1808 claimed that the Spaniards were "waging a war against bribery and corruption and peculation much more than against Buonaparte"; that they were fighting for "*a representation of the people*; and also for a *reform of abuses,* including, of course, not only an examination into the conduct of peculators, but the condign *punishment* of those infamous wretches, who have so long revelled in luxury upon the fruit of the people's labour";

and that not only was Spain "a nation . . . capable of defending itself without a royal family and a civil list," but that no effort was made to defend the Spanish royalty, nor did the people bestir themselves until the king and prince "were safely gone" from the country.[50] Each of these comments contained its own message, but perhaps the overriding message was in one of the earliest of the articles: "All the kings that have been pulled down have been represented to us as being adored by their subjects. Will kings and princes never take warning? Will they never profit from experience? Will they go on believing in none but their parasites?"[51] When Cobbett endorsed the standards the Spaniards might be expected to apply in filling the top army posts, the Duke of York was not far from his mind:

Commands in the army will not be bestowed upon silly boobies, by way of bribe to their fathers, or other relations; and, I trust, that mothers and wives and sisters and she-cousins and kept-mistresses will have very little to do in the appointing of generals and other officers. But, above all things, the Spanish patriots should be advised to take care not to appoint for the commander of their army, a notorious stinking coward, a fellow the history of whose campaigns would be the reverse of the old proverb, and whose motto might be, "one pair of heels is worth two pair of heads".[52]

The Prince of Wales (whose father, George III, was now seventy years old) seems not to have been overlooked. In choosing a leader, the people of Spain should take "a man of sense, and of *real* virtue"; they would be well advised to pick a cobbler "in preference to a prince, who should be a notorious fool or profligate, or, perhaps both."[53] And there were comments that might refer to almost any one of the sons of George III: "The man, whose time is spent amongst drunkards and harlots and players and musicians, naturally and necessarily becomes base in every sense in which the word can be taken."[54] These were strong words when applied as Cobbett almost certainly intended them to be applied, but under the circumstances, who would be willing to come forward and say, "He was referring to *me*"? Cobbett managed to get by with this attack without any noticeable reaction from anyone in the government, although he may have been adding to the already large stock of resentment standing against his name. Unfortunately for him, the issues that came to a head in 1809 did not lend themselves to a similar type of oblique assault.

The big issue of 1809 arose out of Wardle's charges against the forty-six-year-old Duke of York. They were, in the main, that army commissions had been sold by Mrs. Clarke, mistress of the duke from about 1803 to 1807, and were currently being sold through a London office acting as agent for the duke's latest mistress, a Mrs. Carey.[55] Two days after Wardle had made his motion in the House, Cobbett –

who had been charged with being a Jacobin conspiring to destroy the government for pointing out abuses of the type cited by Wardle – exploded with delight at the thought of the exposures certain to follow: "This is an admirable fellow. I will perform a pilgrimage to see him. Oh! the damned thieves! 'A Jacobinal conspiracy!' Damned, hell-fire thieves!"[56]

On February 1, the House of Commons, resolving itself into a committee of the whole, began taking testimony, and for the next six weeks virtually all the time of the House was devoted to this subject. Mrs. Clarke was the principal witness. She proved clever and pert, and, to many of the members of the House, convincing.[57] There could be no doubt that she had been the duke's mistress and that she had accepted money, not only for army commissions, but for any of the other favors the duke was believed capable of producing, including, in one case, the right to preach to the king. The sole question was whether the duke knew, or should have known, what she was about.[58] Even the *Courier,* which was regarded as a ministerial paper, refused to follow the party line: "We are sure," that paper declared on March 10, "that there is not a man in London who, during the time Mrs Clarke lived with the Duke, had not heard rumours of such influence." When, on March 17, 1809, the House voted on Perceval's resolution that "there was no ground to charge his royal highness with personal corruption, or with any connivance at the corrupt and infamous practices developed in the evidence," there were 278 ayes and 196 noes, a margin of only 82.[59] The duke resigned as commander-in-chief on the same day, and presumably he terminated his relations with Mrs. Carey, although there had never been time to consider Mrs. Carey's business activities during the hearings themselves.[60]

Wardle had entered parliament in 1807. Until he brought his charges, he was unknown to Cobbett and, apparently, to the other reformers. However, Sir Francis Burdett seconded Wardle's motion for the inquiry, and Lord Folkestone took an active part (too active, it later appeared) in Wardle's support. Cobbett at Botley tried to help by sending suggestions to Wardle, Burdett, and Folkestone.[61] The defense of the duke fell principally on the king's servant, the former attorney general, Spencer Perceval. He was assisted by members of his cabinet and William Adam, a member of parliament who had served for years as legal adviser to the Duke of York.[62] One can be reasonably sure that Perceval's assignment was not one he greatly relished. Even under more congenial circumstances, to be an advocate in a case in which one is sitting as judge is not a completely comfortable role, but here, wholly apart from the duke's possible culpability for the irregular sale of army commissions at cut rates, the

"A Private Examination." Mrs. Mary Anne Clarke, ex-mistress of the Duke of York, being "examined" by Wardle with the assistance of Burdett and Folkestone. The latter, holding up Burdett, declares: "Cobbett stands by me and I'll support you." Cobbett, towering over the others, holds up Folkestone, saying: "Talk of Portland Stone – I say theres nothing like Folke Stone." To the left little Perceval ("I perceive all") throws the light of truth on the lady, while John Fuller, of Rose Hill Park, Sussex and member of parliament, blasts her with a bellows. Burdett shields Mrs. Clarke with a Whitbread ale barrel. Samuel Whitbread had taken a prominent part in supporting Wardle in parliament. The picture on the wall is labelled "Distant View of Newgate & Pillory"

immorality implicit in the duke's relations with the principal witness must have made it a profoundly distasteful defense for a man like Perceval to undertake. And Cobbett, who rarely gave an opponent the slightest benefit of any doubt, made Perceval's position even more unpleasant by emphasizing all those aspects of the case that Perceval himself would have found most unattractive. Cobbett called attention to Perceval's cross-examination of a Miss Taylor, who had testified to a conversation between the duke and Mrs. Clarke.[63] Perceval had forced Miss Taylor to admit that she was an illegimate child and that her mother had been imprisoned for debt, although these facts appeared doubtfully relevant to either her testimony or her credibility. Wilberforce, a moral man whose good opinion meant something to Perceval, thought Perceval guilty of "brow-beating" the witness.[64] And to make matters worse, Cobbett mounted a highly successful public subscription campaign on Miss Taylor's behalf, claiming that she had been ruined by "having been *compelled* to give evidence, and to make a full exposure of all her connections and acquaintance."[65]

If one accepts Cobbett's version of the case, the Taylor episode was a matter of poor taste or bad judgment or, at its worst, heartlessness on the part of Perceval. One of the other charges Cobbett levelled against Perceval came perilously close to an allegation of dishonesty. The incident had all the complications and surprises of cheap fiction. On February 4, three days after the start of the hearing, Perceval was advised that a Captain Sandon (who had been involved in some of Mrs. Clarke's shady transactions) had in his possession a note allegedly written by the duke to Mrs. Clarke in which his royal highness disclosed his knowledge of a request made by Mrs. Clarke on behalf of one of her clients. Thus the note was of critical importance in answering the single open question; namely, was the duke aware of the traffic in which Mrs. Clarke was engaged? The duke assured Adam, who in turn told Perceval, that the note was a forgery. On the following day Perceval heard that the note had been destroyed, and he thereupon quietly passed on the story to a few influential members on both sides of the House, but not a word was said to those engaged in the prosecution.[66] The facts seemed extremely damaging to the duke's traducers: a paper purporting to implicate the duke had been forged and then destroyed before the wickedness could be demonstrated to the world. Perceval and his colleagues decided to withhold this devastating material until it could be most effectively used. The obvious place would have been on cross-examination of Sandon and Mrs. Clarke, but when they testified on February 10 neither said anything about such a note. Wardle ended his presentation on February 16, and still the note had not been mentioned. Perceval was then in the unenviable position of having to admit that he had been sitting through the whole case with some undisclosed information relevant to the points at issue. There was no other way out, since his secret had been disclosed to select members of the whig opposition at a time when he looked forward to confronting the witnesses with their criminal handiwork. So, on February 16, Perceval made his confession. If the information he was about to disclose had been improperly withheld, Perceval began, it was entirely his fault. He then told the House what he had told a few select members sometime before: about the discovery of the note, the declaration by the duke that it was a forgery, and its destruction.[67] Sandon became Perceval's scapegoat. When he had testified he had said nothing about the note or its destruction; therefore, according to Perceval, he had suppressed this important feature in his evidence.[68] When Sandon was recalled, he proved to be a consummate liar, but it was discovered that the note had not been destroyed, and when it was produced and examined by a series of experts (the duke did not choose to appear) the majority indicated it to be in the duke's handwriting.[69] Obviously Perceval could not be held responsible for whatever prevarications, if any, may have been resorted to by the duke, but Perceval was plainly responsible (far more than Sandon) for the withholding of evidence. His fumbling answers and his repeated apologies are persuasive testimony to his evaluation of his own conduct. Consider, for example, this vacuous and confusing explanation offered by Perceval:

> I might be permitted to add, that, feeling there was a considerable degree of awkwardness in the appearance of being backward to bring forward at the earliest period a fact so important as this fact was, we did think that our own honour would hardly be safe, unless we made a communication not only of the fact, but of our determination to produce it in the manner in which we did.[70]

Cobbett's great talent for picking out the weak points in an opponent's case was never more clearly demonstrated than in this instance when he drew together the facts relating to the Sandon episode and spread them out fully in the *Political Register* for all to see. During the debates that followed the hearings, there was no letup in Cobbett's campaign against Perceval. The *Political Register* for March 11, 1809 carried as its motto: "That they may do evil with both hands earnestly, the prince asketh, and the judge asketh for a reward; and the great man, he uttereth his mischievous desire: so they wrap it up."[71] In the following week, to accompany Perceval's speech in defense of the duke, the motto described the sinecures held by Spencer Perceval and his brother, Lord Arden.[72]

One must not conclude from what has been said that Cobbett's great objective was to get the Duke of York removed. "I do not care a straw about the matter," he wrote before the final vote, "unless the dismission were accompanied with measures, which should *effectually* prevent similar corruptions in future; and, as no such measure appears to be in agitation, I think it of no consequence whatever to the nation, whether the Duke be dismissed or whether he remain."[73] While this almost certainly is an exaggerated statement of his feelings, it is plain that his principal motive was the disclosure of corruption for the purpose of inducing or forcing reform. And the reform he wanted was directed not at getting the duke to spend his nights at home with the duchess, but at improving the quality and reducing the cost of the army by replacing a system of corruption and favoritism with one based on merit. For the existence of such corruption and favoritism was patent. The son of Mrs. Jordan, mistress of the Duke of Clarence, had been made a cornet at fourteen.[74] One of the Malings, a witness in the Duke of York inquiry, became a captain without ever having been on military duty.[75] The son of William Adam, legal adviser to the Duke of York, was a lieutenant colonel at twenty-one:

[I]s it possible, that the other officers, Captains old enough, perhaps, to be his father, and who have every fair claim to prior promotion, can cordially submit to the command, and, occasionally, to the *reproof,* of a boy of twenty-one? What would Mr Adam say, if he had to plead before a *judge* of twenty-one years of age?[76]

And apart from the loss of morale among fellow officers, there was also the welfare of the rank and file to be considered: "Is it not shocking, that the *backs* of hundreds of our brave countrymen should be committed to the power of a wretch, who has been base enough to purchase that power with a bribe to a kept-mistress?"[77] Just as their backs depended on being fairly treated, their lives, as well as the survival of the country, depended on their being wisely led. General Sir Thomas Picton six years later said: "Nine French officers out of ten can command an army, whilst our fellows, though as brave as lions, are totally and utterly ignorant of their profession. D—n it, sir, they know nothing. We are saved by our non-commissioned officers, who are the best in the world."[78]

The other great reform Cobbett pursued was equal treatment of rich and poor. It was outrageous, he thought, that the common soldiers should be flogged for even minor infractions of rules, and that their superiors in rank, regardless of their shortcomings, rarely met with even the mildest punishment:

Partiality even in the distribution of *favours,* when those favours are paid for by the public, is mischievous and hateful enough; but, not one millionth part so mischievous and so hateful, so detestable in the eyes of every just man, and of virtue, as partiality in the distribution of *punishments.* It is mortifying enough in all conscience to see the parasite pampered with the means of rewarding the meritorious; but to see the great villain braving the laws, while the petty are hanged in chains, is what no man can bear without feeling a desire to see overturned, torn up from the foundation, utterly destroyed and scattered to the winds, the whole of the system and fabric of that government, where [whence?] such partiality has proceeded.[79]

It was this irate feeling about partiality, perhaps, that caused Cobbett, at the outset of the inquiry on the Duke of York, to conclude that regardless of the consequences he must no longer exercise restraint over his attack on abuses: "I must stand the brunt. No flinching would either be honourable or politic," he put in his letter to Wright on February 2, 1809 as he completed the first of his angry articles on the inquiry. Continuing, he declared: "In short, my mind is made up to proceed as I have done, and to defy prosecution."[80] During the six weeks of hearings and debate, the sales of the *Political Register* kept pace with Cobbett's rising invective; there was no flinching.[81]

14 · Perceval versus Cobbett

Not only must every man, who thus puts himself forward, *expect* to have his character and actions inquired into, but they *ought* to be inquired into and publicly discussed.

EVEN AFTER the Duke of York had resigned and the case against him was regarded as over, Cobbett continued week after week his attacks on Spencer Perceval. In the issue of the *Political Register* for April 8, 1809 the motto and a portion of the text were devoted to one of Perceval's less distinguished victories as attorney general.[1] In 1802 he had prosecuted Philip Hamlin, a half-crazy tinman who naively wrote to the prime minister (Addington) offering to pay £2,000 if he were appointed surveyor of customs at Plymouth. Perceval had coldly thrust aside Hamlin's plea for consideration of his family, declaring that the issue was not one of personal feelings, but of public justice. Hamlin had been fined £100 and sentenced to three months in jail. This had ruined his business, Cobbett claimed, and Hamlin died shortly after his release from prison. Not a pretty tale to be tied to the name of a good man; it was a tale Cobbett repeated a half dozen times during the next three months.[2]

During April and May 1809, Perceval offered several additional targets to his growing inventory of vulnerable points. An investigation initiated earlier in the year showed that directors of the East India Company, who were sworn not to sell company appointments, were in the practice of giving writerships to their relatives and friends, who in turn sold them for as much as £3,500 each.[3] Several clergymen were implicated in the transactions, and in one instance a writership was traded for a church living. The committee report described one arrangement by which a writership was to be exchanged for a seat in parliament: Lord Clancarty wanted a seat in parliament; Lord Sligo was willing to sell one for about £3,000. Lord Castlereagh, secretary for war and colonies, offered to give Clancarty a writership which was to be sold to a Mr. Ogg for something over £3,000. "Lord Castlereagh did not know Ogg, Lord Clancarty did not know Ogg, Lord Sligo did not know Ogg; but Ogg was to get the Writership, Sligo was to get the money, and Clancarty was to get the seat."[4] The details were handled by a pair of commission agents in the business of arranging such transactions. The deal fell through for reasons that are not entirely clear, so that no part of the arrangements was ever consummated. When a motion of Lord Archibald Hamilton charging Castlereagh with a gross violation of his duty as servant of the crown was negatived by a vote of 216 to 167, a substitute resolution was adopted with the support of Perceval, declaring that since "the attempt of Lord Viscount Castlereagh to interfere in the election of a member has not been successful, this House does not consider it necessary to enter into any criminal proceedings against him."[5] Cobbett pounced on this point with Cobbett-like ferocity: "now, Englishmen, who have been taught so highly to prize impartial justice," compare this decision with that of Philip Hamlin, the Plymouth tinman, whose "attempt, observe, *was not successful,* any more than that of Lord Castlereagh!"[6]

This appeared in the *Political Register* of May 6, 1809. In the same issue was an article on a motion of Lord Folkestone for the appointment of a committee to inquire generally into the corrupt disposal of offices. This too had been opposed by Perceval, who declared that "it was not the punishment of past offences, which we should so ardently seek as remedies and preventatives of such abuses." Once again Cobbett hauled out the Hamlin case:

Good; but, how came we to hear nothing of this, Sir, when you prosecuted Hamlin, the Tinman of Plymouth, who had seen hundreds and thousands of advertisements of places under government for sale, and who was so ignorant a man, that when the *warrant* went down for apprehending him, he took it to be the *patent* for his place? How came we to hear nothing of this doctrine then, Sir, when you demanded his punishment in the name of PUBLIC JUSTICE, and when the judge pronounced sentence upon him for the sake of *example*?[7]

The *Political Register* of May 6, like all issues of Cobbett's paper, was published on a Saturday. On the following day, Sunday, May 7, Perceval took a copy of the *Political Register* with him when he called on the speaker of the House, Charles Abbot, a fellow barrister and legal scholar. What occurred at the meeting is recorded in Abbot's diary for that date:

He thought Cobbett had at last committed himself in his paper upon the House of Commons vote, for rejecting Lord Folkestone's motion for a Committee to inquire into the sale of all places in the State, &c, but, when he showed me the paper, it did not so strike me that the libel was more violent than what all the Opposition papers contained every day; nor was such as could usefully be proceeded upon.[8]

It is not difficult to see at this point the inevitable outcome of Cobbett's heightened campaign against corruption. For, of course, matters could not end with his comment on Folkestone's motion. Each week produced more causes that had to be attacked. On May 11 William Madocks, member for Boston, charged Perceval and Castlereagh with corrupt practices in a new case involving a parliamentary seat: Mr. Quintin Dick had bought a seat at the borough of Cashel from the treasury. When the Duke of York issue arose, Dick decided to vote against the duke, but was told by Lord Castlereagh he must vote for the government or resign his seat, and he resigned. Madocks charged Perceval "as being privy [to] and having connived" at the transaction, and stated that he would "engage to prove by witnesses at your bar" the truth of his allegations if the House would permit him to call them.[9]

Madocks was never given the opportunity of calling the witnesses, because his motion was overwhelmingly defeated by a vote of 310 to 85. George Ponsonby, leader of the whigs in the House, expressed the view of many when he stated that since the sale of seats had become "as glaring as the noon-day sun," it would be unfair to single out Perceval and Castlereagh as the victims.[10] Cobbett's old friend William Windham, representing the more conservative whigs, argued that the elements labelled "corruption" by the reformers were an essential part of the constitution (an argument urged by the *Edinburgh Review* in 1807), while others of his persuasion claimed that those who condemned corruption "did not sufficiently distinguish between corruption, properly so called, and the influence which property would always have in every well regulated society."[11] What may have been the predominant view was expressed by the foreign secretary, George Canning, who resented the rising tide of criticism expressed in public meetings and petitions: The time had come, said Canning and his followers, to oppose any type of "popular encroachment" on the rights of parliament – a practical application of Bishop Horsley's opinion that the people had nothing to do with the laws but obey them.[12] To similar effect was the contention that the purpose of the reformers was "to level down all public men to their own very humble state."[13] When, in the early hours of May 12, the vote on Madocks's motion took place, "there was heard, from all quarters and corners of the House, the exclamation: 'a *stand*, a *stand!*' 'It is,' exclaimed many voices at once, 'high time to make a stand against popular encroachment'."[14] This view, which had been urged by Canning in debate, explains in part why Madocks's motion drew only 85 votes as compared with the 167 votes secured by Hamilton's motion three weeks before. "Popular encroachment" was in the air, and Cobbett had done much to put it there. In mid April he and his friends in Hampshire, farmers and tradesmen, had requisitioned a county meeting, an activity traditionally reserved to the nobility and gentry, and had put through resolutions thanking Wardle and his supporters in the Duke of York proceeding in defiance of a statement of the ministers that they would oppose any vote of thanks to Wardle if moved in the House of Commons.[15] Similar resolutions from all over England (Cobbett published about fifty of them in the *Political Register*) poured in to parliament, often complimenting members who had supported Wardle and condemning those who had not. Such popular comment on the conduct of members of the House was regarded by many as sheer impertinence. The other element that may have caused a decline in the reform vote was the position that had been urged by Sir Francis Burdett at a public meeting of reformers held at the Crown and Anchor tavern on May 1, 1809 attended by eleven to twelve hundred diners, with thousands more assembled outside.[16] This was the meeting at which Burdett discussed the need for parliamentary reform. The program he submitted to the House a month later included nothing startling: Freeholders, householders, and others subject to direct taxation should be given the right to vote; equal electoral districts should be established; parliaments should be limited to a "constitutional duration." What was startling was Burdett's suggestion at the Crown and Anchor meeting that "Reform ought to commence in a message from the King to the House of Commons recommending to that body to purify itself." To the shocked *Times,* this aspect of Burdett's proposal would make parliament a "mere organ of the Crown": "The King, who can now only summon, prorogue, and dissolve Parliament, might, under this new system, if ever he should meet with an untractable House of Commons, say, 'Gentlemen, new-model yourselves, I am not content with the principle upon which you are at present constituted.' "[17] It is difficult to know whether this argument or any of the other arguments brought forward at the time represented true motivations or were only makeweights, but we do know that "a stand, a stand!" became the order of the day. This, plus the events that were shortly to unfold concerning Cobbett, Wardle, and Folkestone, put a brake on the reform movement that would last for a long time.

The last bit of reform momentum was expended in early June 1809 when the House passed what had become a semiofficial government bill to end the sale of seats in parliament. Even that advance, which stigmatized conduct that was already clearly illegal, was approved by a margin of only fifteen votes and would have failed entirely if it had not been for a strong lecture delivered to the House by the Speaker, Charles Abbot, who declared that "To do nothing is to do everything. If we forbear to reprobate this traffic we give it legality and sanction."[18] After finishing the speech, Abbot sent his handwritten copy to Cobbett for publication in the *Political Register,* where it was reproducèd in full.[19] Although Cobbett, as usual, thought the bill was too mild, Abbot's action confirms the conclusion that Cobbett's propaganda had been one of the primary factors that led to the passage of the bill; and, in practice the act put an end to the advertising of seats. It also probably reduced, although not entirely eliminating, the outright purchase and sale of seats.[20] Cobbett was eager to have everyone appreciate that this was only a tiny part of the whole program: "we want a Reform, not to consist of a statute to prescribe whether our rights should be *sold, swapped* or *given* away, but that shall restore those rights to us, their owners."[21]

The "stand" made by the government and its friends was not limited to a stiff-backed attitude toward remedial legislation. It began to manifest itself in a more aggressive form that was not entirely new to Cobbett. Attacks in pamphlets and in the columns of rival journals had been a feature of Cobbett's life since the start of his journalistic career in Philadelphia. When he returned to England in 1800 he immediately fell out with what he then thought were the Jacobin papers, and, as his politics changed, he picked up new rivalries. At the end of the peace of Amiens in 1803 he so bitterly complained of the lack of preparedness in the British navy that Lord St. Vincent, first lord of the admiralty, sponsored the establishment of a new paper, the *Standard,* "for the sole purpose of vindicating Government against the vile charges of Cobbett and other miscreants of his description."[22] The *Edinburgh Review,* founded in 1802 by Sydney Smith, Francis Horner, Henry Brougham, and Francis Jeffrey – all whigs – as a magazine of literary criticism, became irrevocably stamped as a political publication in 1807 when it attacked Cobbett in an article written by Jeffrey at the instigation of Brougham, who was handling the whig press campaign in the general election of that year.[23] After the reference to Cobbett's enormous influence previously quoted, Jeffrey devoted twelve pages to Cobbett's inconsistencies (his shift from conservative to reformer), and another twenty pages to Cobbett's "pernicious and reprehensible" doctrines. Jeffrey stoutly contended that the House of Commons as then constituted adequately represented "all the different opinions" in the country and reflected the "balance of the constitution," since it contained persons who had obtained their seats through the crown and through the influence of the "peers and great families," as well as those chosen "in consequence of their reputation or popularity with the majority of their electors." The final third of the *Edinburgh Review* article consisted of a strange reversal from the middle section, with a long list of dangers which concerned Jeffrey, almost identical with those Cobbett had been complaining of, and ending with the admission that the legislature had "recently exhibited some strange and alarming appearances." The *Edinburgh Review* attack on Cobbett pleased many people, but the principles at the core of Jeffrey's article – the arguments that the king and nobility should be represented in the Commons to provide constitutional balance, and that there was no need for reform – were disavowed in the *Edinburgh Review* itself within eighteen months after they had been urged against Cobbett.[24]

Much more serious trouble for Cobbett developed from a monthly magazine called the *Satirist,* which began publication in October 1807.[25] Its first issue declared that it was devoted to "the present servants of the crown" and proposed, if necessary, to defend them. The founder and proprietor until 1812 was George Manners, a person of some mystery.[26] That he had a connection with the government may be implied from his appointment as British consul in Boston, Massachusetts following his newspaper career. Defending the servants of the crown *Satirist*-style meant a constant flow of scurrility and innuendo of the lowest order directed against anyone in opposition to the ministry, ranging from Windham to Brougham among the whigs and, more obviously, Cobbett and all those associated with him. This included the "long-nosed triumvirate," that is, Burdett, Folkestone, and Wardle ("remarkable," claimed the *Satirist,* "for long bows and long noses"), as well as the lesser lights among the reformers.[27]

In November 1808 the *Satirist,* after accusing Cobbett of inconsistency (using material that had appeared the year before in the *Edinburgh Review* and adding certain references taken from the *Porcupine*), alleged that he had been a British spy in America, and that Cobbett's animosity to Pitt arose because Pitt had refused to dine with him despite Windham's urgings.[28] In the December 1808 issue the *Satirist* claimed that Cobbett had been a "deserter."[29] When Cobbett answered by printing a copy of his honorable discharge, the *Satirist* of February 1809 produced an abbreviated account of the court-martial of 1792 – which, so far as the general public was concerned, had lain forgotten in the war office records for nearly twenty years.[30] According to Manners, editor of the *Satirist,* Cobbett had maliciously preferred foul but groundless charges against officers of his regiment; he "deserted and went over to France" before the trial; and the officers against whom the charges were made had been fully cleared.[31] The article added that Cobbett's discharge from the army had been scandalously granted by a traitor, Lord Edward Fitzgerald, "as the price of meditated treachery." Manners not only had access to the war office files, but he also knew what was going on in the village of Botley – possibly through the vicar there, the Reverend Richard Baker, who had been a Cobbett supporter up to early November 1808, but who seems to have had a falling out with Cobbett shortly after that time.[32] Thus the April 1809 issue of the *Satirist* carried a story about Cobbett's alleged tyrannical treatment of one of his employees, a boy who had run away and whose mother and brother had been falsely arrested at Cobbett's request.[33] The story appeared under the heading "Another Instance of William Cobbett's Mild and Humane Disposition."

All these charges had been made by the *Satirist* before May 7, that Sunday on which Spencer Perceval had met with Charles Abbot to see whether Cobbett could be jailed for libel, but they probably were noticed only by the arch-conservatives who read that publication. Closely following the meeting of May 7, the charges attained national notoriety. On May 17 the *Courier* ran an article about Cobbett's inconsistencies, and several days later a pamphlet appeared entitled *Elements of Reform, or an Account of the Motives and Intentions of the Advocates for Parliamentary Reformation by William Cobbett, Proprietor of the Political Register*. The pamphlet was dedicated to the liberal whig Samuel Whitbread with "the sincere wish" that nothing might prevent Whitbread and "those illustrious Patriots, Sir Francis Burdett, Lord Folkestone and Mr Wardle" from "hanging together for the benefit of the Nation." The text consisted of Cobbett's strongly expressed statements in opposition to reform dating back to 1802 and earlier.

Cobbett's answer to the *Elements of Reform* in the *Political Register* of May 27 was short in Cobbettian terms (six pages), with some very sensible observations:

The doctrine of *consistency*, as now in vogue, is the most absurd that ever was broached. It teaches, that, if you once think well of any person or thing, you must always think well of that person or thing, whatever changes may take place either in them, or in the state of your information respecting them. For instance, if you praise a man to-day, and, to-morrow, receive proof of his long being a thief, you must continue to praise him. Where is the man, who has not changed his opinions of men as well as of things?

The truth is, that, as to opinions, no man is to be blamed for a change, except there be strong reason to conclude that the change had proceeded from *a bad motive;* or, rather, that it is not a real, but a pretended change, for the purpose of something selfish or wicked.[34]

Within two or three days after this answer was published, Cobbett was assaulted by a more troublesome charge in another pamphlet which laid out in agonizing detail what the *Satirist* had briefly touched on several months before. The new pamphlet was entitled *Proceedings of a General Court Martial Held at the Horse-Guards, on the 24th and 27th of March, 1792, for the Trial of Capt. Richard Powell, Lieut. Christopher*

Seton, and Lieut. John Hall, of the 54th Regiment of Foot; on Several Charges Preferred against Them Respectively by William Cobbett, Late Serjeant-Major of the Said Regiment. [35] The cover of the pamphlet placed in juxtaposition two statements. The first was taken from a letter Cobbett had written to Sir Charles Gould, judge advocate general, on March 11, 1792: "If my accusation is without foundation, the authors of cruelty have not yet devised the tortures I ought to endure. Hell itself, as painted by the most fiery bigot, is too mild a punishment for me." The second sentence was from the finding of the court-martial on March 27, 1792: "The said several Charges against those Officers respectively are, and every part thereof is, totally unfounded."

The *Satirist* hailed the publication with a long account headed "Cobbett's Death-Blow." [36] The pamphlet consisted of papers on file at the war office reprinted without editorial comment. The facts seemed to speak for themselves: Cobbett had brought serious charges against his superiors; instead of supporting the charges, he had left the country; the men charged had been acquitted. So eloquently did they speak that the original 2s. 6d. issue was quickly succeeded by an edition at one-fifth the price. Cobbett acknowledged the pamphlet with a short statement dated June 1 in which he said that "the Government (for it is hard to conceive that any body could have done it without its consent) appears to have sanctioned" the publication of the documents; that he would not have noticed the thing at all if the whole of the papers had been published; and that in his next double number (they ordinarily were issued every four to six weeks) he would give a full account of the matter. This statement appeared in the issue of the *Political Register* dated June 3. [37] Six days later, the ministerial paper the *Courier* began a series of letters directed at Cobbett signed "Anti-Scoundrel." The first of these, featured on the front page of the *Courier* in space ordinarily reserved for advertisements, demanded that Cobbett either admit that he had brought false charges against his superior officers or make a flat denial of the accusations. [38] A second "Anti-Scoundrel" letter on June 15 claimed that Cobbett was being evasive in letting several issues of the *Political Register* go by without an answer. "Why, let me ask you again and again, did you not vindicate your honour and honesty in either of your two next numbers?" [39] The *Courier* had interests to serve other than those of the public. In 1809 its editor, T. G. Street, had accepted £2,000 in return for a promise to support the Perceval ministry. [40]

Cobbett's apologia, when it appeared in the *Political Register* of June 17, began with the accusation that the personal attacks on him, based on events that had taken place almost twenty years before, represented an effort by "the associates in corruption" to avoid the charges

Cobbett had brought against them. They had threatened to disclose the court-martial story when Cobbett was attacking Pitt and Melville in 1805–6, and Cobbett challenged them to do it then. Now, Cobbett contended, they had spent "not less, perhaps, than ten thousand pounds" (certainly an exaggeration) on the pamphlet, sending hundreds and thousands of copies into Hampshire. "The robbers, as they have come down from London in their carriages, have brought with them whole bales, which they have tossed out to all whom they met or overtook upon the road."[41]

Cobbett's affirmative answer rested on one major point; the account of the court-martial contained in the pamphlet omitted twenty-two out of twenty-seven letters that Cobbett had written to the government, and particularly those which showed that the secretary at war, Sir George Yonge, despite the assurances he had given Cobbett at the outset, had failed to secure the books of account, and that the judge advocate had refused to grant a discharge to Corporal Bestland, who was an essential witness in the event any alteration had been made in those books.[42]

Cobbett's answer did not convince his enemies, as "Anti-Scoundrel" made clear in further letters published in the *Courier*.[43] Even Cobbett's friends thought he could do better. Wright urged him to print the twenty-two missing letters, but Cobbett argued that it was internally evident that the letters had been suppressed and that, although he was willing to show the letters in his possession to Sir Francis Burdett or to Peter Finnerty or any other friend, "I cannot condescend to do this to the public; indeed it is impossible. They must believe me, or let it alone."[44]

Cobbett had still not reached the end of his troubles. As the *Satirist* had implied, an action for assault and false imprisonment, in which damages of £1,000 were claimed, was brought against Cobbett and two others (the constable and tything man of Botley) by William Burgess, pauper brother of Cobbett's youthful employee, and on July 20 Cobbett and his codefendants, without offering any evidence, were found guilty as charged, and damages were assessed at £10, of which Cobbett paid one-third.[45] The publisher of the court-martial pamphlet sent a reporter to Winchester to take down the proceedings in shorthand. From this was produced a third pamphlet: *Cobbett's Oppression!! Proceedings on the Trial of an Action between William Burgess, a Poor Labouring Man! and William Cobbett, the Patriot and Reformer!!* The day after the trial the walls in London were covered over with large bills proclaiming "Oppressions of Cobbett" and "Cobbett, the Oppressor of the Poor."[46] The London papers gave great prominence to the story. In the *Morning Post* of July 22 it nearly filled the columns

reserved for news, displacing the French bulletin on the defeat of the
Austrians at Wagram.[47] Yet Cobbett wrote to Wright with his usual
confidence: "As to the *Winchester trial,* you shall see that I will turn *it*
to good account."[48]

Cobbett's version, however, is not particularly appealing to a twentieth-century ear.[49] At that time, it was illegal for a servant in husbandry to leave his master without a quarter's warning, unless on a showing of reasonable cause before a justice of the peace.[50] Jesse Burgess,
a carter boy sixteen years old, had been hired on the specific understanding that he would get up in the morning when Cobbett did, that
is, at 5 A.M. Jesse worked for Cobbett for several months, then left
without notice after reprimands for coming to breakfast before he
had cleaned the stable, and for lying in bed beyond the agreed hour.
When the boy refused to return, Cobbett swore out a warrant for
him. The lad was arrested and brought back to Botley, where he was
taken to the Dolphin, a public house. He had been accompanied, voluntarily, by his mother and older brother William. This was the first
act of the drama. In the second act, the boy "escaped" from the Dolphin; the mother and brother started out for home; the constable and
tything man in hot pursuit failed to find the boy, but took the mother
and brother into custody and returned them to Botley. After being
held nine hours they were released on the promise that they would
bring Jesse before the magistrates in Southampton on the following
Monday. This seems not to have happened; but a fortnight later he
was apprehended by the Botley constable and taken to Southampton,
where, after a hearing before the magistrates at which he had the
opportunity to justify his conduct (by showing any ill-usage to which
he had been subjected), he was found guilty and sent to prison. The
boy's older brother, William, initiated the action for false imprisonment. Cobbett, who claimed he had played no part in the apprehen-
sion of the brother (or mother), was made codefendant with the constable and tything man, and hence, under the law then prevailing, he
and his codefendants were disqualified from testifying on Cobbett's
lack of participation.

Cobbett was extremely defensive about his involvement in the
affair. He produced facts showing that he was a good employer: he
paid substantially more than his neighbors, and his men had been
with him for long periods. He justified the measures he had pursued
by pointing to the prevalence of a fraudulent practice in which a
worker, having induced the farmer to provide him room and board
during the winter when there was little to do, would depart as soon as
good weather returned; the custom of the country to enforce the law
against deserting servants; and the general utility – indeed, "the

duty" Cobbett owed to the farming community – of setting a good example so that others would not "set contracts at nought" or "make agreements with fraudulent intention." Cobbett's defense included the claim that the charge of false imprisonment was a concocted affair. This view was stimulated in Cobbett's mind, if not confirmed, by the appearance of two barristers of some distinction on behalf of the pauper plaintiff (who, though employed, was receiving poor relief and as a pauper was entitled to free counsel); by the assertion of one of these barristers at the hearing that Cobbett was an advocate of reform; by the early involvement of the *Satirist* in the matter; and finally by the fact that a Winchester lawyer told Cobbett's attorney: "take care what you are about, for it is determined to crush him."[51] Cobbett made much of the scale of the efforts being expended for this purpose:

I find, that, for more than two months past, more space has been occupied with ME, than with the Emperor Napoleon, the Archduke Charles, and Sir Arthur Wellesley, all put together; and, I could almost venture to assert, that, during that time, there have been, in various ways, not less than from *twenty to thirty thousand* pounds expended upon publications against me . . . In short, when compared to the defeating of me, the defeating of Buonaparte appears to be considered as a mere trifle. His fearful, his terrific success, really seems to have been overlooked during the tide of joy excited by the damages of £3. 6s. 8d. obtained against me at Winchester; and, all that appears to have been wanting, was, the firing of the Park and Tower guns.[52]

Near the end of this pamphlet barrage came the news that the government had decided to proceed against Cobbett for criminal libel. There appears to have been no public announcement, but by July 22, 1809 Cobbett knew that such a prosecution was under way, and he knew that the charge was based on an article that had appeared in the July 1 issue of the *Political Register*.[53] The principal subject in that issue was a review of the session of parliament which had ended earlier in the week. The emphasis was on the part played by the "Tinman's Prosecutor" in the cases relating to the charges against the Duke of York, the barter of an East India writership for a seat in parliament, and the resignation of Quintin Dick, who could not in good conscience hold his seat and vote against the ministry. Once again there was the suggestion, only slightly veiled, that Perceval had endeavored to cause the destruction of the duke's note in Sandon's possession; once again the story of Perceval's prosecution of Philip Hamlin was repeated.[54]

Certainly it is not wonderful, in the light of these circumstances, that another wholly unrelated article was found in the issue of July 1 on which the charge of criminal libel could be based. This pertained to the flogging of five local militiamen at Ely, an incident reported by the *Courier* in the following words:

The Mutiny amongst the local militia which broke out at Ely, was fortunately suppressed on Wednesday, by the arrival of four squadrons of the German Legion Cavalry from Bury, under the command of General Aukland. Five of the ring-leaders were tried by a Court Martial, and sentenced to receive five hundred lashes each, part of which punishment they received on Wednesday, and a part was remitted. A stoppage for their knapsacks was the ground of complaint that excited this mutinous spirit, which occasioned the men to surround their officers, and demand what they deemed their arrears.[55]

Cobbett's comments on this news reflected several of his prejudices. First, he hated the German mercenaries, because he felt that their presence in England represented a potential threat to civil liberties.[56] Second, he believed strongly that expanding the rights and liberties of the people, rather than repressing them, was essential to the defense of the country, since men fight best for what they love. Finally, he disliked the use of flogging for maintaining military discipline. Cobbett began his article with the sarcasm that "useful employment" had finally been found for German troops, namely, as "the means of compelling Englishmen to submit to that sort of discipline, which is so conducive to producing in them the disposition to defend the country, at the risk of their lives." Then he exploded:

Five hundred lashes each! Aye, that is right! Flog them; flog them; flog them! They deserve it, and a great deal more. They deserve a flogging at every meal-time. "Lash them daily, lash them duly". What, shall the rascals dare to *mutiny*, and that, too, when the German Legion is so near at hand! Lash them, lash them, lash them! They *deserve* it. O, yes; they merit a double-tailed cat. Base dogs! What, mutiny for the sake of *the price of a knapsack!* Lash them! flog them! Base rascals! Mutiny for the price of a goat's skin; and, then, upon the appearance of the *German Soldiers,* they take a flogging as quietly as so many trunks of trees! – I do not know what sort of place Ely is; but I really should like to know how the inhabitants looked one another in the face, while this scene was exhibiting in their town. I should like to have been able to see their faces, and to hear their observations to each other, at the time. – This occurrence at home will, one would hope, teach *the loyal* a little caution in speaking of the means, which Napoleon employs (or, rather, which they say he employs), in order to get together and discipline his Conscripts. There is scarcely any one of these loyal persons, who has not, at various times, cited the *hand-cuffings,* and other means of *force,* said to be used in drawing out the young men of France; there is scarcely one of the loyal, who has not cited these means as proof, a complete proof, that the people of France *hate Napoleon and his government, assist with reluctance in his wars,* and would *fain see another revolution.* I hope, I say, that the loyal will, hereafter, be more cautious in drawing such conclusions, now that they see, that our "gallant defenders" not only require physical restraint, in certain cases, but even a little blood drawn from their backs, and that too, with the aid and assistance of *German* troops.[57]

This is the language which formed the basis of an information filed by the attorney general, Sir Vicary Gibbs, against the editor (Cobbett), the printer (T. C. Hansard), and the publishers (Richard Bagshaw and John Budd) of the *Political Register*. At first, Cobbett seems to have panicked at the thought. Despite his calm assurance to Wright that the trial would be "a *very good* thing for me," he inserted a strange recantation in the *Political Register* of 29 July:

Those . . . who, at Ely, and elsewhere, have quelled the spirit of mutiny amongst the Local-Militia, are certainly entitled to the thanks of the country. No one can be pleased to see his countrymen flogged; but, when, as in this case, they have *voluntarily* entered, and that, too, for the sake of *a bounty,* I say, as I said before, "flog them", if they do not abide by their bargain, and strictly obey their officers.[58]

This is the sole public recognition that an information was being prepared. Privately, it was discussed in hushed tones between Cobbett and Wright. The latter, apparently, explored with John Reeves (an old friend of Cobbett's who, as king's printer, was on good terms with the party in power) what might be done to modify the decision of the attorney general to proceed against Cobbett. To this move, Cobbett replied on August 18, 1809:

I am fully prepared for the *worst,* and therefore, am no longer under any *anxiety.* I would rather be gibbetted than owe my life to the intercession, such as you speak of, and such as I am afraid you *half-solicited.* I told you to keep very *quiet.* Say nothing at all about the matter to any one. Ask no questions; and only be sure to tell me precisely what you hear. I am not afraid of them.[59]

Thereafter matters moved surprisingly slowly. It was not until November that Cobbett began to collect material for his defense, which he had resolved to undertake himself despite the importuning of his friends. He called on Wright to obtain for him such things as the attacks on him in the past six months by "the ministers, or their partisans"; the libels written by Canning and the other authors of the *Anti-Jacobin*; the names of the writers hired or paid by the government; the criticism of "eminent men against *an army* of foreigners" in England.[60]

The delay that took place in Cobbett's case may in part be accounted for by the doubts concerning the ability of the Portland ministry to continue in office. The war against Bonaparte had not gone well. Hopes rose when Arthur Wellesley advanced from Portugal into Spain and, according to his dispatches, defeated the French at Talavera in July 1809; but within a matter of days he was in full retreat toward the Portuguese border, leaving 1,500 wounded soldiers behind him.[61] At almost the same time, a British expeditionary force under the command of Lord Chatham had landed on the Dutch island of Walcheren, but was never able to reach its objective of Antwerp. Instead, it had to creep back to England after the loss of thousands of men to malaria.[62] The news from the two fronts was being gloomily studied in London in late August 1809 when the Duke of Portland, who had been prime minister in name only since his designation in 1807, suffered a stroke and resigned on September 12, 1809. Spencer Perceval's problem of creating a new government was complicated by Canning's refusal to serve under him; by the duel fought between Canning and his fellow cabinet member Lord Castlereagh over Canning's scheming to get Castlereagh removed from office; and by the refusal of the whigs Grenville and Grey to come into the government.[63] But despite all this, "little P" finally won out. By October 1809 he was prime minister in name as well as in fact – although it was commonly thought that the shaky structure could not last long.

As time went by and no further move was made by the attorney general, Cobbett's optimism increased. This was stimulated by the independence demonstrated by a jury who refused to accept the ruling of Judge Mansfield in an action brought against one of Cobbett's friends, Henry Clifford.[64] By January 1810, Cobbett was so confident that he did not care whether the government went ahead with the action against him or dropped it: "I really do not know which I ought to wish for: a trial or a nolle prosqui . . . I am, really, rather indifferent about the matter," he said in a letter to Wright.[65] His confidence was further increased in March 1810 by the success of James Perry, editor of the *Morning Chronicle*, in an action for seditious libel tried before Lord Ellenborough and a special jury: "We have all . . . drunk Mr Perry's health," said Cobbett in a letter to Wright. "I made even little Suzan [aged 3] lisp out the words."[66] There seems to have been the belief among Cobbett's friends that the action against him had been dropped.[67]

It is possible that in the hurly-burly of events Cobbett was forgotten, or if not forgotten, set aside for more pressing matters. His writing on most subjects was as saucy as ever, with one notable exception: all references to the Plymouth Tinman disappeared from the *Political Register*. Perceval was hardly mentioned at all. Perhaps the government was satisfied that Cobbett's ardor had been permanently dampened by the pendency of the attorney general's action, the pamphlet campaign of 1809, and the continuing asaults from the *Satirist*, which had been joined in October 1809 by still another subsidized paper, *Blagdon's Weekly Political Register*, an obvious imitation, in both name and appearance, of Cobbett's publication.[68] If so, this misconception was corrected by Cobbett's involvement in another of the sensational events that characterized the history of early-nineteenth-century England.

The story begins in February 1810 when Charles Yorke, a friend of Perceval, moved to close the gallery of the House during the debate on the Walcheren expedition. Windham supported Yorke with some abusive comments on the corruption of the press and its employees who reported debates in the House.[69] John Gale Jones, a surgeon–apothecary–reformer, announced a public debate on the subject, asking "which was the greatest outrage upon the public feeling, Mr Yorke's enforcement of the Standing Order to exclude strangers from the House of Commons, or Mr Windham's recent attack upon the liberty of the press?"[70] At Yorke's instance, Jones was brought before the House and imprisoned in Newgate for contempt. His cause was taken up by Sir Francis Burdett, who moved for Jones's release on March 12, 1810, urging that the House had no power to imprison Jones without a trial. Twelve days later the *Political Register* printed a letter entitled "Sir Francis Burdett to His Constituents; Denying the Power of the House of Commons to Imprison the People of England." The letter claimed that the treatment of Jones was in derogation of Magna Carta and the laws of the land, and must be resisted

because, should the principle, upon which the Gentlemen of the House of Commons have thought proper to act in this instance, be once admitted, it is impossible for any one to conjecture how soon he himself may be summoned from his dwelling, and be hurried, without trial, and without oath made against him, from the bosom of his family into the clutches of a jailor.[71]

Charles Abbot's diary for the next day reads:

After church went home with Perceval to see Cobbett's last paper, containing Sir Francis Burdett's letter to his constituents, denying the power of the House of Commons to imprison other than its own members.

Perceval proposed to move, on Tuesday next, to commit Sir Francis Burdett to the Tower, and to order the attendance of Cobbett. N.B. The latter was not done.[72]

As a result of the debate that followed, Cobbett became quite sure that he would be called before the House, and he advised Wright that "If they call me before them, I shall say, that, as the speaker himself sent me *his* speech to publish, I, of course, thought it right to publish the speech of any member of the House, especially when he put his name to it."[73] As Abbot's postscript indicated, Cobbett's attendance was not ordered. There was a better way of getting at him. Three weeks after the publication of Burdett's letter, Cobbett's communications to Wright reflect renewed activity by the attorney general on the long-pending libel action against Cobbett.[74] "You surprise me much in the information that the prosecution against Mr Cobbett is not dropped," wrote James Swann, Cobbett's paper supplier, to Wright on May 21, 1810.[75] And this time there was no doubt about it: The charge against Cobbett, after nearly a year's hibernation, was assigned for trial on June 15.

No change, however, was made in Perceval's plans for Sir Francis Burdett. In the early hours of April 6, after an all-night debate, Perceval succeeded in getting an almost evenly divided House of Commons to vote for Burdett's commitment to the Tower. By this time an enormous public interest had been aroused in the issue. An outraged London mob took over the capital for the three days following the action in the House. The arrest of Burdett on April 9 and his removal to the Tower, accomplished only through the use of a great assemblage of troops, constitutes one of the most dramatic episodes in the evolution of civil liberties in Britain.[76] Fact and fiction, in unknown proportions, are mingled in the story that has been handed down of the defiance shown by the authorities of the City of London toward the parliamentary officials; of the offer by Lord Cochrane to provide gunpowder to blow up the government forces threatening Burdett's house in Piccadilly; of the ultimate entry of those forces and the arrest of Sir Francis as he read Magna Carta to his son. Perceval won the contest of strength, but that is all. The episode confirmed Burdett as the hero of the people and, equally, Perceval as their enemy. When Burdett was finally released from the Tower after the prorogation of parliament on June 21, the event produced an undeclared public holiday: "People came over from Ireland and Scotland to see the sight."[77] Crowds in the thousands and tens of thousands filled the streets: "Knife-grinders, ballad-singers, butchers boys, journeymen and labourers of all descriptions, ardently joined in the spontaneous, though somewhat unpolished, festivity; and every thing announced a sort of popular jubilee!"[78] There was disappointment among the people when Burdett chose to leave the Tower by water, instead of participating in the planned triumphal procession from the Tower to Piccadilly, but the crowds made the best of the holiday.[79]

In 1819 Cobbett revealed that the document which sent Burdett to the Tower and made him the darling of the people had been written by Cobbett himself.[80]

15 · Into Newgate

Another trial before that villainous judge is ruin, if not death.

COBBETT'S TRIAL for seditious libel on June 15, 1810 had some ominously familiar aspects: once again it was the court of king's bench, Chief Justice Ellenborough, and one of the government's special juries. Once again the attorney general personally conducted the prosecution, but this time that office was filled by Sir Vicary Gibbs. Spencer Perceval now stood in the wings. The current attorney general was "a little irritable, sharp-featured, bilious-looking man," sometimes known as "Vinegar Gibbs," much addicted to the use of the ex-officio information which permitted the attorney general, on his own initiative, to start a criminal action against any individual, thereby depriving him of the protection which the common law intended to provide by requiring indictment by a grand jury after testimony under oath.[1]

The court was crowded at an early hour. "The subject itself was sufficiently interesting, but the circumstance of Mr Cobbett's making his own defence, added the motive of curiosity to that of public spirit."[2] If the crowd had come to witness a courtroom drama, they were sadly disappointed. The efficient government libel machine rolled over Cobbett like the Juggernaut. After reading Cobbett's article to the jury, Gibbs stated that the charges of cruelty and injustice were unfounded: The men "rose in actual mutiny," they committed "dangerous breaches of the public peace," and the law by which they had been punished was "mild in its progress, mild in its conclusion." He assured the jurors that while the author of the article "will of course be heard patiently," it was his "serious, decided, personal opinion" that the article was libelous.[3]

Cobbett did not meet these issues head on. He began with a long reply to the calumnies levelled against himself in the press. Possibly he thought this was necessary to counter prejudices held by the jury, or possibly he had expected Gibbs to begin with these charges and was not sufficiently flexible to rearrange his argument. He spent even more of his time attacking the use of German troops in England. When Cobbett did get to the points made by Gibbs, he asserted that the affair at Ely was not a real mutiny (the men had not taken up arms against their superiors), that it was nothing more than a squabble, and that the men involved in the squabble were not regular troops but were local militia – "young fellows, probably in smock frocks, just taken from the plough, and ignorant of that subordination that is practised in the army." His indignant complaints against what had occurred were not intended to overturn the government, but were for the purpose of correcting the evils he perceived: the extreme punishment and the use of foreign troops to enforce such punishment; and "if I do express this indignation which I feel, in somewhat of angry language, are you, upon that account, to presume that I am guilty of deliberately wishing and contriving to subvert the government of the country?"

The representatives of government conducting the trial answered this question in the affirmative. Ellenborough refused to allow Cobbett to show that his comments on the treatment of the militia at Ely were no harsher than the comments made by members of parliament on the treatment of regular British troops at Walcheren. And Gibbs assured the jury that when it came time for Ellenborough to address them, "his Lordship would tell them, whether the object of this paper was not to create general discontent, and defame and vilify these who had legally entered into service of this country."[4]

The chief justice's charge fully vindicated the prosecutor's prediction: "how a squabble with their Officers could be considered as any other than an act of mutiny, and of the most dangerous sort too, was beyond his conception." The character of Cobbett's article, Lord Ellenborough told the jurors, was clear beyond doubt, "it being the confident certainty and full conviction of my mind, that this is a most seditious libel." The special jury, which under the law was charged with the responsibility of deciding whether or not there was a libel, had been well selected. What was there left to decide? Without leaving the box, they dutifully parroted the lord chief justice. The trial had taken three hours and a half from start to finish.

Looking at the trial from the advantage of nearly 200 years of hindsight, one sees that Cobbett made a major error in tactics. He would have been far better off, at least on paper, if he had said nothing about his calumniators or about the desirability of maintaining German troops in England, but had concentrated on the argument that he was a lifelong enemy of cruelty and injustice, of which the affair at Ely was a shocking example.[5] Although Cobbett touched briefly on the youth and inexperience of the men and the mild nature of their remonstrance, he would have found further support along these lines in the *Times* account of the incident, published more than a week before his article appeared. According to *The Times,* the men who had complained of the "stoppage for their knapsacks" – causing a shortage of food – "had come from some distance . . . had received no pay for some days during which some of them were half starved," and while they had "put all their officers under arrest," they had "been otherwise peaceable." *The Times* called for a government inquiry into the "cruel neglect" of the militia and deprecated the manner of quelling "the insurrection" with German troops, "a body of which our Constitution allows us to know nothing."[6] Although not as vituperative as Cobbett, *The Times* raised all the main points raised by Cobbett and made the same objections, but no legal action was initiated or threatened against that paper.

By not focusing his efforts on these facts, Cobbett played into the hands of the prosecution. One listening to Cobbett's argument and Gibbs's reply would have thought that the main issue in the case was whether German troops were brave or cowardly, not whether a writer should be sent to prison for condemning the cruelty and injustice of laying 500 lashes on the backs of half-starved lads asking for something to eat.[7] Cobbett was guilty of another lapse. In the uncongenial atmosphere of Lord Ellenborough's court, he seems to have forgotten one of his most effective defenses. He had a bundle of letters written to him by distinguished persons, Lords Grey, Castlereagh, and Grenville included, "respecting matters inserted or to be inserted in the Register, all laudatory," which he had planned to read in court to show that "he was not the man described either in the information or by the attorney general in his speech, but a loyal subject." These were never mentioned.[8] Skilled trial counsel would hardly have made the same mistakes, but they probably could not have changed the result.[9]

Not Perceval alone, but the government at all levels had scores to settle with Cobbett. He had condemned the celebration of the king's jubilee on October 25, 1809, a day set aside to commemorate the fiftieth year of the reign of George III.[10] What reason was there to rejoice? asked Cobbett. During that period the national debt had been increased from £90 million to £700 million; the number of paupers had increased from 200,000 to 1,200,000; America had been lost following the capture of a whole British army at Saratoga and another at Yorktown. At the moment of celebration thousands of British soldiers were sick and dying at Walcheren; thousands more wounded had been left behind a retreating British army in Spain; and the French, who dominated the European continent, threatened to invade the country. The junior members of the royal family had also come under attack by Cobbett: He opposed increases in their hand-some allowances and inveighed against the public display of their mis-tresses.[11] He thought the royal family should pay taxes like everyone else.[12] The influential leaders of the opposition, as well as the mem-bers of the cabinet, were constantly under Cobbett's flail. And the chief justice now presiding at his trial had been told by Cobbett, in a letter addressed "To the Right Honourable Lord Ellenborough" pub-lished by the *Political Register* in September 1808, how he should inter-pret the law of libel.[13]

There is no reason to conclude, therefore, that the outcome of Cob-bett's trial before Lord Ellenborough in July 1810 would have been changed whatever Cobbett might have said or whatever might have been said on his behalf, but he at least could have spared himself some indignities if he had employed a lawyer instead of attempting to defend himself. Ellenborough was a tartar under all circumstances. Here he three times interrupted Cobbett's presentation with objec-tions which Cobbett, untrained in the law, had no way of answering or circumventing. While the report of the trial is silent on whether Ellenborough may also have employed his well-known talent for rid-icule, he could easily have applied further pressure on Cobbett with-out saying a word, for when the judge laughs, it generally follows that the jury and the audience and the lawyers laugh too. This may explain in part the account of Cobbett's performance given by Francis Place:

He made a long defence, a bad defence, and his delivery of it and his demeanour were even worse than his matter. He was not at all master of himself, and in some parts where he meant to produce great effect he pro-duced laughter. So ludicrous was he in one part that the jury, the judge, and the audience all laughed at him. I was thoroughly ashamed of him, and ashamed of myself for being seen with him.[14]

This version, written by Place years later and after a falling out between Place and Cobbett, very possibly exaggerates the degree of failure. But failure it surely was. Cobbett himself was crushed, for the moment, by his own performance. He rushed from the courtroom and immediately set off for Botley.[15] In close pursuit came a tipstaff to seize him personally and bring him back to London to give bail.[16] Then he was permitted to return home to await formal judgment and sentence.

Back again at Botley, Cobbett was enveloped in gloom. Dependent on him were a wife and six children from three to fifteen years old, with another on the way. In addition, he had dependent on him, for almost everything, "nearly twenty children" besides his own.[17] He had no liquid assets. Everything he owned was either invested in the 600 acres of farmland in the neighborhood of Botley or, seventy miles away, in the publishing venture at London. Both of these enterprises were operated with borrowed money. From someone (whom, we do not know) came the suggestion that Cobbett could escape a prison sentence if he closed down the *Political Register*. Within ten days after the end of the trial he decided on this course.[18] He abjectly wrote a farewell article to appear in the final issue, scheduled for June 30, in which he announced not only that he would discontinue the *Political Register* but that he would never, so long as he lived, publish or contribute to any newspaper or similar publication.[19] This renunciation and a statement of his claims to indulgence at the hands of the government were turned over to John Reeves, Cobbett's old friend who was king's printer. Reeves's letter of June 27 to Cobbett reported that he had given the papers to Charles Yorke, first lord of the admiralty, who was to see "what can be done on the subject, with Mr Perceval." Reeves added that there were "two chances" – one with the government and one with the court: "If the Government should feel themselves so circumstanced that they cannot hold their hand, but must direct the Attorney-General to proceed according to his notice, on Thursday, you will still have the benefit of your measure, in the eyes of the Court. No doubt, they will take such a sacrifice into consideration."[20] Reeves's letter, received by Cobbett the next day, Thursday, June 28, rekindled the old fires. "No," he declared in a letter he immediately sent off to Wright, "I will not sacrifice *fortune* without securing *freedom* in return." But as he wrote these words he decided that even the assurance of freedom was being bought at too high a price, and resolved to withdraw the proposal made to the government. "I would *rather* be called up than put down the Register," he added. Although it was still a week away from the date of judgment, he refused to await Perceval's decision. Wright was ordered to take the farewell article out of the issue to be published that Saturday (now only two days away) unless he had already heard, prior to the receipt of Cobbett's message, that he was not to be brought up. Reeves was to be told immediately of the change in plans.[21] To make certain that Cobbett's message had not miscarried, Peter Finnerty, visiting at Botley, was hurried off to London to confirm what Cobbett had stated in his letter.[22] All this was done, and the proposal withdrawn, before the government decision (if one was ever made) was known.[23]

Once this resolution had been taken, Cobbett felt better for it. "I shall be with you, in good spirits, on Wednesday night," he told Wright as he prepared to leave for London and the court session at which judgment was to be entered.[24] "I cannot send you any money. I am obliged to leave with Mrs Cobbett all I can get."[25] Thereafter the

powerful hand of government closed over him. When Gibbs prayed
for judgment against Cobbett on July 5, he declared that the libel of
which Cobbett was guilty was of "much darker and blacker hue" than
any that had previously been before the court, since it "went to subvert society itself."[26] Cobbett was remanded to the King's Bench
prison and four days later was sentenced to be imprisoned in Newgate
for two years and fined £1,000.[27] Before being released from prison,
he was to enter into a recognizance "to keep the peace" for seven
years, under bond in the amount of £3,000 and with two sureties in
the amount of £1,000 each – imposing, in layman's terms, an additional fine of £5,000 in the event Cobbett misbehaved at any time
during the seven-year period.[28] Thus he was condemned to remain
under the thumb of the government for a total of nine years. How
thoroughly one's exterior may mask what lies within is recorded by
The Times: "Mr Cobbett appeared not much affected by the sentence;
his deportment during its delivery was unembarrassed – he left the
Court with a smile on his countenance."[29] Cobbett's joint defendants
in the libel action, the publishers Richard Bagshaw and John Budd
and the printer T. C. Hansard, did not contest the attorney general's
information. Although Cobbett told the court that none of the other
defendants "had anything whatsoever to do with the offensive publication," they were all given prison terms, the publishers two months
each and the printer three months.[30]

Cobbett was immediately carried off to Newgate – a sinkhole of
depravity and mismanagement like most English prisons of the
period – where he was placed in a common cell with a miscellaneous
lot of inmates. He was able to ransom himself by arranging to pay a
turnkey five guineas a week for an unfurnished room in the prison.[31]
One of a group of Cobbett's friends who had followed him to
Newgate hurried home and brought back "bedstead, chairs, tables,
bedding, and every thing," then put together the bedstead and made
up the bed.[32]

Nancy Cobbett was with her husband in London, and was at
Newgate within a half hour after he had been taken there, but the
children had remained at Botley in the care of her sister:

The tears of the postman, a rough and hardy fellow who had lost an arm in
the military service, prepared my daughter for the news. The three boys were
in the garden hoeing some peas. My daughter called the eldest to tell him
what had been done. He returned to the others, and they hearing their sister
cry, asked him what was the matter. He could make them no answer, but,
pulling his hat over his eyes, took up the hoe in a sort of wild manner and
began to chop about, cutting up the peas and all that came in his way. The
second took hold of him, and seeing his face bathed with tears, got, at last, an
account of what had been done to a father, who had never given either of
them a harsh word since they were born.

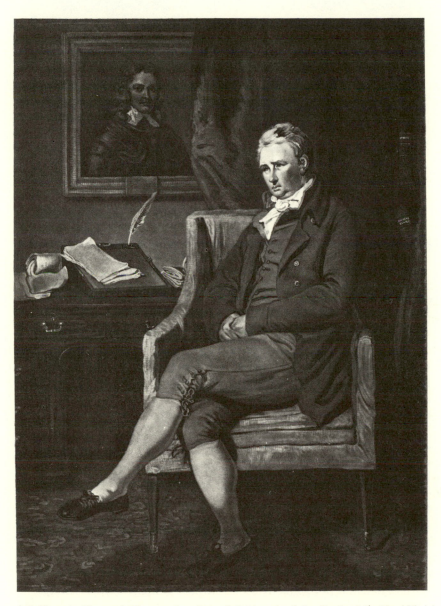

Cobbett in Newgate. Crayon drawing of Cobbett by John Raphael Smith, with picture of John Hampden on the wall. Cobbett's son James thought that this portrait "gives the exact attitude in wh. he wd. sit when meditating. Like him in figure & exact to his dress. But the air of seriousness in his face has too much of the crabbed, & not sufficient of the full & florid in complexion. When in that attitude, & in thought, his countenance always seemed to me to be the most remarkably expressive of gravity that I ever saw; the most perfect living picture of deep thought." (JPC, p. 26)

. . . the youngest could not, for some time, be made to understand what a *jail* was; and, when he did, he, all in a tremor, exclaimed, "Now I'm sure, William, that Papa is not in a place *like that!*"

By that very night's post I got a letter from my daughter and one from my eldest son, and he concluded his in these words: "I would rather be now in the place of my dear Papa, than in that of those who have sent him to prison." I wrote them back for answer, that I was very well; that imprisonment would not hurt my health; and concluded by saying, "be you *good children,* and we shall all have ample revenge."[33]

The feelings of those who had "sent him to prison" were recorded by Cobbett in an article written years later. Perceval and his brother-in-law Lord Redesdale, meeting at the portal of Westminster Hall just after the verdict of guilty had been announced, "shook hands and gave each other joy." Charles Adams, member of parliament, said that Cobbett should have been flogged himself.[34]

Within a few days after Cobbett had been lodged in Newgate, his situation there was greatly improved through the intervention of an admirer, Matthew Wood, sheriff of London and Middlesex, who saw to it that Cobbett was moved from the prison to the adjacent house of the keeper, a Mr. Newman.[35] For twelve guineas a week in rent, and another eight guineas a week in fees, he was, at length, comfortably housed in a sitting room and two bedrooms at the top of Mr. Newman's house, quarters previously occupied by Alexander Davison, the enormously rich contractor (friend of Nelson and of various members of the political establishment and entertainer of royalty) who had been convicted in 1808 of defrauding the government.[36] The coziness of the accommodations was tempered by the view, which looked down upon the place of execution. "Blinds were drawn down, but we heard what was going on."[37]

For the next two years, the top floor of Mr. Newman's house became the headquarters for the family, for the operation of the Botley farm, and for the conduct of Cobbett publishing ventures. One or two of the children at a time, turn and turn about, stayed with Cobbett in his rooms. The two eldest boys, when there, spent a few hours a day learning French from an abbé who lived in Castle Street, Holborn. Their mother came up to London every two or three months.[38] To avoid having a child born in a felon's jail, or be absent from the scene at the time of the birth,

My wife, who had come to see me for the last time previous to her lying-in, perceiving my deep dejection at the approach of her departure for Botley, resolved not to go; and actually went and took a lodging as near to Newgate as she could find one, in order that the communication between us might be as speedy as possible; and in order that I might see the doctor, and receive assurances from him relative to her state. The nearest lodging that she could find was in Skinner street, at the corner of a street leading to Smithfield. So that there she was, amidst the incessant rattle of coaches and butchers' carts, and the noise of cattle, dogs and bawling men; instead of being in a quiet and commodious country-house, with neighbours and servants and every thing necessary about her. Yet, so great is the power of the mind in such cases, she, though the circumstances proved uncommonly perilous, and were attended with the loss of the child, bore her sufferings with the greatest composure, because, at any minute she could send a message to, and hear from, me. If she had gone to Botley, leaving me in that state of anxiety in which she saw me, I am satisfied that she would have died: and that event taking place at such a distance from me, how was I to contemplate her corpse, surrounded by her distracted children, and to have escaped death, or madness, myself? If such was not the effect of this merciless act of the government towards me, that amiable body may be well assured that I have *taken and recorded the will for the deed,* and that as such it will live in my memory as long as that memory shall last.[39]

Regular communications with Botley were maintained through means of a hamper which shuttled back and forth between there and Newgate.

This hamper, which was always, at both ends of the line, looked for with the most lively feelings, became our *school.* It brought me *a journal of labours, proceedings,* and *occurrences,* written on paper of shape and size uniform, and so contrived, as to margins, as to admit of binding. The journal used, when my son was the writer, to be interspersed with drawings of our dogs, colts, or any thing that he wanted me to have a correct idea of. The hamper brought me plants, bulbs, and the like, that I might see the size of them; and always every one sent his or her *most beautiful flowers;* the earliest violets, and primroses, and cowslips, and blue-bells; the earliest twigs of trees; and, in short, every thing that they thought calculated to delight me. The moment the hamper arrived, I, casting aside every thing else, set to work to answer *every question,* to give new directions, and to add anything likely to give pleasure at Botley. *Every* hamper brought one "letter", as they called it, if not more, from every child; and to *every* letter I wrote *an answer,* sealed up and sent to the party, being sure that that was the way to produce other and better letters; for, though they could not read what I wrote, and though their own consisted at first of mere *scratches,* and afterwards, for a while, of a few words written down for them to imitate, I always thanked them for their *"pretty letter";* and never expressed any wish to see them *write better;* but took care to write in a very neat and plain hand *myself,* and to do up my letter in a very neat manner.[40]

As is so often the case, this account (written years after the event) is a slightly romanticized version of what actually occurred. We know that while Cobbett was in prison he wrote at least one painfully tart response to his eldest son, William, complaining that "Your letters of late have been so full of blunders, so full of self-contradictions, so full of bad spelling, so full of blurs, and they have been so unsatisfactory in their contents, that really, at last, I am got to hate to see them come."[41] But William, unlike the other children in the family, was a lifelong problem to his demanding father, and, on occasion, his non-Cobbettian conduct was conveniently overlooked.[42] Thus, with this exception, the hamper was an unmitigated source of delight when opened at Newgate.

When it returned to Botley it contained not only Cobbett's answers to the family messages, but also his instructions concerning the operation of the farm: "all orders, whether as to purchases, sales, ploughing, sowing, breeding; in short, with regard to every thing."[43] These orders were scrupulously detailed. The exact dimensions of the new farm gates that were to be built, including the type and size of the wood to be used (even the copse from which the wood was to be cut), with carefully drawn illustrations, were set forth in Cobbett's written directions.[44] Precise instructions were given for the determination, to the nearest pound (to be written "in *words* and *not in figures*"), of the amount of chaff and turnips fed to the sheep each day.[45] These orders were read aloud to the farm laborers at Botley by young William, twelve years old, or by his brother John, ten years old, who rode off each morning to see what the men were doing (Fairthorn farm was a mile from the house, Raglington three miles) and to report this to Newgate with any comments from the workers.[46] Thus Cobbett's orders were often accompanied by his responses to issues previously raised by the men:

Tell Master Robinson, that, if it will take a *week* for 3 carts to carry about 40 loads of dung *ten hundred yards* (for it is no more), it is high time to leave off keeping teams. – Each team ought to go *15 times* in a day, and I expect that they will do it, and there is not, at most more than 2 *days work.*

You say that Master Robinson says that I have laid out *a month's* work. – What have I laid out?

1. Dressing Harfield's field.
2. Carrying one load of dung to Hurchetts.
3. Carrying the dung into Barn Close.
4. Carry the manure from Roe Ash Green into the Home Mead.

I expect this to be done *in less than a week;* and if it is not, I shall be very much disappointed.

Fifteen times a day from Curbridge Common to Barn Close is only about 18 miles a day for the horses.

Let the horses be well fed when they work.[47]

Concerned about a sedentary life at Newgate, Cobbett adopted a spartan program to keep himself fit. Rising at 6 A.M. in the winter, and even earlier in the summer, he went onto the roof of the prison and exercised there with dumbbells, going through the motions of farm work (digging, raking, mowing) as well as various military maneuvers, until he was in a sweat. He would go back to his rooms, wash and shave in cold water, and put on clean linen, to be ready at eight o'clock for a breakfast of tea and a one-penny roll. For his mid-day dinner he ate a whiting or a single mutton chop and perhaps a little vegetable, but nothing else – no pastry or cheese. He took noth-ing between the midday meal and breakfast. Those of the family who were with him had to be content with one chop also, but they were allowed to "make up" with pies and puddings.[48] Outside visitors were offered "beef stakes and porter. I may vary my food to mutton chops, but never vary the drink."[49]

Work began as soon as breakfast was over. The work that immedi-ately faced Cobbett after breakfast on July 10 following his first night in Newgate prison was the issue of the *Political Register* for that week, scheduled to be published four days away, on July 14. There had been no break in the publication of the *Political Register* on account of the trial; there had not even been a hint of the short-lived proposal to wind it up, but in three out of the last four issues Cobbett's contribu-tion (on which its circulation depended) had been limited to brief notes explaining his preoccupation with the matters pending before the court. With the issue of July 14 Cobbett resumed the editorial chair. The motto he chose for this issue suggested that he had no intention of being completely downed by his situation: "Sir Walter Raleigh wrote his History of the World in a prison; and it was in a prison that Cervantes wrote Don Quixote."[50] The article that fol-lowed, and its sequence a week later, the last Cobbett would write about the trial for two years, dealt with the statement made by Sir Vicary Gibbs on July 5 as a part of his prayer for judgment. Cobbett singled out for criticism several assertions made by Gibbs, including his statement that Cobbett's punishment should be severe because the article in question, and everything Cobbett wrote, was for "base lucre." If the punishment were light, other libelers would be willing to run the risk in order to "make a fortune" and to "amass wealth." Cobbett pointed out that the charge of writing for "base lucre" could be made against any author: Milton and Swift and Addison received money for their works, and Pope more than all these together, although he wrote with more severity than Cobbett. Even bishops sold their writings, not excluding their sermons. (Cobbett almost certainly was thinking of the writings and sermons published by Bishop Law, Lord Ellenborough's father.) Lawyers sold reports of cases and other writings. (Gibbs had published two of his own speeches in 1795.) The appellation "base lucre" does apply, Cobbett claimed, "When a man bargains for the price of maintaining such or such principles, or of endeavouring to make out such or such a case, without believing in the soundness of the principles or the truth of the case" and "whether

Instructions from Newgate to Botley. Cobbett's instructions for the building of a farm gate illustrate his unusual attention to detail and his intimate knowledge of the subject – characteristics that were manifested in whatever, large or small, captured his interest

Stroud

The gates, if still you will see there will require to a new one, they are to be of the usual width, and stand exactly five feet high, to range with the tops of the hedges — They are to be made of poles. — The post to be Oak Tops, or Kittens. — The hinges to be good well twisted withes for the present; and the fastening a good well twisted withe to go over the back head of the gate and the head of the shutting post, both of which must be left about 6 or 8 inches longer, higher than the fence for that purpose. — The bars must not be more than about 6 or 7 inches asunder at bottom, and they may grow wider as they approach the top. — The Lower Bar is to be about 6 inches from the ground. — The following sketch may be some guide. I suppose. — The poles the bars to be 2 inches and a half through. The gate is 9 feet wide. — The poles to be shaved Alder, cut in the Alder gully at Lochlans.

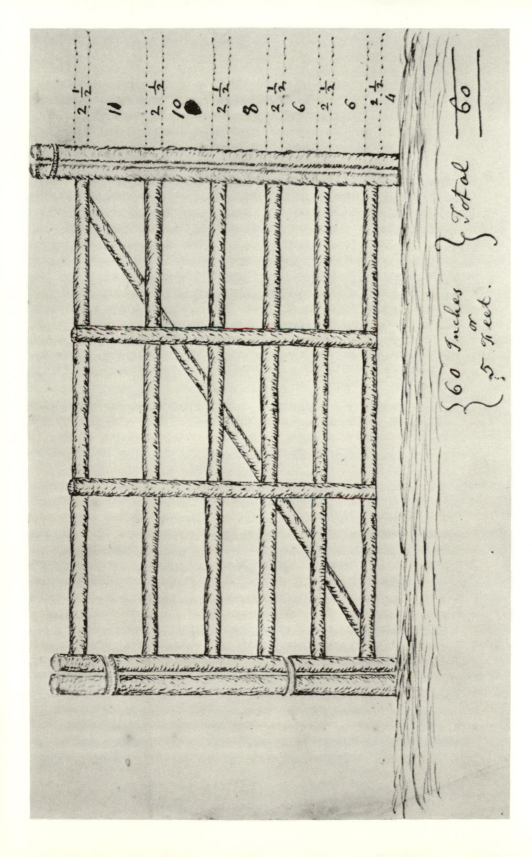

2 ½
11
2 ½
10
2 ½
8
2 ½
6
2 ½
6
2 ½
4

60 Inches ⎫ Total
   or   ⎬ ——
5 Feet. ⎭ 60

he works with his tongue or his pen."[51] (Gibbs, when in private practice, had defended the radical reformers Thomas Hardy and Horne
Tooke against charges of treason; now as attorney general he was
leading the attack against the reformers.)

Cobbett went on to show that, of all writers for the press, the words
"base lucre" were least applicable to him. He had never accepted compensation to insert or suppress an article; in America he had rejected
offers of payment by the British minister; he had refused two services
of plate "tendered for the successful exertion of his talents"; he had
turned down the offer of the *True Briton* newspaper. Cobbett denied
that he had made a fortune or amassed wealth as Gibbs implied. But
if he had, "what right would any one have to reproach me with the
possession of it?"

I have been labouring seventeen years, since I quitted the army. I have never
known what it was to enjoy any of that which the world calls pleasure. From
a beginning with nothing I have acquired the means of making some little
provision for a family of *six children* (the remains of *thirteen*) besides having,
for several years, maintained almost wholly, three times as many children of
my relations. And, am I to be reproached as a lover of *"base lucre"*, because I
begin to have a prospect (for it is nothing more) of making such a provision?
And, am I now, upon such a charge, to be stripped, in one way or another, of
the means of making such provision? Was it not manly and brave for the
Attorney General, when he knew that I should not be permitted to answer
him, to make such an attack, not only upon me but upon the future comfort
of those, who depend upon me for support?[52]

After reading this article, Swann wrote: "I was very glad to see by the
last Register that Mr Cobbett's spirit is by no means cowed."[53]

No, not cowed, but it is surprising that he was not, for his situation
was one that would have extinguished a less fiery spirit. On top of the
indignity of being imprisoned and the physical constraints which that
entailed, Cobbett's incarceration had precipitated a crisis in his
already shaky financial affairs. To the undiminished cost of maintaining a family and a farm at Botley there were added the twenty guineas
a week for accommodations at Newgate and the £1,000 fine. But of
even greater immediate concern was his loss of credit. Previously
acquiescent creditors (his friend James Swann was an exception)
became impatient, if not desperate, to have their accounts paid:
"every one to whom I owed a shilling, brought me sighs of sorrow
indeed; but, along with these, brought me his bill."[54] Rejecting offers
of a public subscription to help meet these demands (he did accept a
cheque for £1,000 from Colonel Bosville and was advanced £2,000 by
Sir Francis Burdett), Cobbett turned to more basic solutions.[55] He
decided that he must terminate his involvement in the three ancillary
publications: the *Debates,* the *Parliamentary History,* and the *State Trials.*
These were all serially issued; they sold slowly, so that a large stock of

the earlier volumes had to be warehoused; and each year more money had to be laid out for the new volumes being published. Wright was the working editor of the *Debates* and of the *History*, and supervised the publication of the *Trials*. He and Cobbett were, in effect, partners; Wright received no salary for this work (or for what he did for the *Political Register*), but by oral agreement was to receive two-thirds of the profits from the *Debates* and half of the profits from the *History* and the *Trials*. In the meantime he was allowed an advance of four pounds a week to be applied against the profits of the three named publications.[56] He lived with the Cobbetts in their house in Duke Street until they gave it up in 1805; thereafter he rented rooms in a house in Panton Square.[57]

Within three months after the trial, Cobbett arranged to sell his own share in the three-venture partnership to John Budd, who had been involved in all of Cobbett's publishing activities as bookseller and bookbinder, and had been a joint defendant with Cobbett in the libel case. Budd thus took over one-third of the unsold volumes of the *Debates* and half the unsold volumes of the other two publications, as well as the same fractional interest in the copyrights to these works.[58] At the same time, Cobbett proposed a formal transfer to Wright of the latter's share in the volumes and copyright; all that remained was to agree on the financial terms, since Cobbett had laid out all the money expended on the ventures. Wright proposed a lump-sum settlement by which he would pay Cobbett £500. To assess this proposal, Cobbett asked for a statement showing receipts and disbursements for the publications.[59] When this was not forthcoming, the two men began to wrangle (by January 1811 Cobbett was referring to Wright as "this damned fellow"), and Cobbett refused to negotiate further until he could see the accounts in detail. Since Wright claimed that he did not have them, Cobbett insisted on reconstructing the accounts from the books of the papermaker Swann, the printer Hansard, the binder Budd, the booksellers Bagshaw and Budd, and whatever records the two quarrelling parties had kept. In 1808 Cobbett had declared that their accounts were such as "the devil himself would never unravel," and between 1808 and 1811 nothing had been done to improve the quality of the records; there were just more of them.[60] Thus two days a week for four months were spent on the reconstruction project.[61] But even after this was completed, and a "Book of Works" had been produced, no agreement could be reached. The two parties disagreed and their solicitors disagreed, so in the summer of 1811 the issue was submitted to a chancery lawyer, William Cooke of Lincoln's Inn, for final decision.[62] After more wrangling and more explanations, Cooke found that Wright was indebted to Cobbett for £6,630 and must indemnify Cobbett for outstanding notes in the amount of £1,500.[63] This occurred in December 1811. From that point on, the records are even less explicit than before. What seems to have happened was this: Wright was given two years to pay the award, Cobbett's interest being secured by a mortgage given by Wright on the stock of books and copyrights to which he was entitled.[64] Thereafter, Hansard brought the enterprises back into a single ownership by purchasing the interests of both Budd and Wright in the copyrights and in the huge stock of books, estimated at more than 35,000 volumes.[65] Wright joined Hansard's organization and continued to work on the *Debates* and the *Parliamentary History,* while Howell, the editor of the *State Trials,* took over that publication as proprietor by arrangement with Hansard.[66] Hansard and Cobbett quarrelled, and it seems probable that Cobbett finally settled his claim against Wright for something less than the arbitrator's award. If he had received the whole amount of the award, he could have done no better than break even; as it was, he almost certainly suffered a substantial loss on the three publications. The dates, even the order, of these events are obscure, but the last *Political Register* printed by Hansard was the issue of March 28, 1812. Thereafter Cobbett sent his work to another printer, which would suggest that matters had come to a head about that time, but provides no clue as to when they were finally settled.[67]

As one might expect, the dispute between Cobbett and Wright led to a lifelong enmity. It also produced a great number of stories that continue to circulate in two rival versions, the most damaging of which (from Cobbett's point of view) was Wright's claim that when he failed in business in 1802, Cobbett, a creditor, had enticed him to Peel's coffeehouse, where he was arrested and taken to prison.[68] Cobbett claimed that he had given bail for Wright and that the committal was made with Wright's acquiescence for the purpose of protecting him against other creditors. During one of the wrangling sessions of 1811, when Wright asserted this claim in Cobbett's presence, Cobbett allegedly produced a bill made out by Wright's solicitor, acknowledging the fact that the committal was with Wright's knowledge and consent, whereupon, according to Cobbett, those who had just heard Wright assert his claim were struck with "horror," and the sight of this irrefutable proof "appeared to be too much even for the nerves of Mr Wright."[69] He could say nothing.

For all practical purposes, the Cobbett–Wright association ended shortly after Cobbett entered Newgate. Wright had once seemed a necessity to the publication of the *Political Register.* Now that Wright had been cast loose, Cobbett demonstrated that he was quite capable of carrying it on alone.

Notes

~~~~~~

Abbreviations

Add. MSS. – British Library, Additional Manuscripts

Anne – "Account of the Family" by Anne Cobbett (Nuffield xv)

DNB – Dictionary of National Biography

ER – Edinburgh Review

JPC – Recently discovered notebook entitled "Memoranda relating to Life & Times of Cobbett" dated "Manchester, July 6, 1855. J.P.C." (estate of General Sir Gerald Lathbury)

JPC Memoir – "A Memoir of William Cobbett by James Paul Cobbett" (70-page manuscript) with introduction dated "Manchester October 1, 1862" (Nuffield xiv)

No. 1 Correspondence – Recently discovered notebook entitled "No. 1 Correspondence from 14 Jany. 92 to 24 Sepr. 1793" containing copies of Cobbett's correspondence relating to the 1792 court-martial and the original of his discharge from the army. At some point, pp. 69–74 of the notebook were removed, and thus all correspondence after March 1792 is missing

PRO – Public Record Office

QR – Quarterly Review

Susan – "Additional Notes" written by Susan Cobbett relating to family affairs (Nuffield xvii)

WR – Westminster Review

Various other documents held in the Nuffield College library are identified by the numbers assigned to them in M. L. Pearl, *William Cobbett: A Bibliographical Account of His Life and Times* (London 1953), pp. 223f.

The Cobbett children are identified in the notes by their Christian names alone: Anne, William junior, John, James, Ellen, Susan, and Richard. Their mother, Anne Reid Cobbett, is referred to as Nancy.

The writings of Cobbett are referred to in the notes by short titles alone. Their full titles and information about their publication are given in the Cobbett bibliography that follows the notes.

Introduction

1 Mary E. Clark, *Peter Porcupine in America: The Career of William Cobbett, 1762–1835* (Philadelphia 1939), p. 166n; *Edinburgh Review* x (July 1807), 387; Spencer Walpole, *A History of England from the Conclusion of the Great War in 1815* (London 1890) 1:267; 85 *PR* 775.

2 *Times*, June 20, 1835.

3 *The Holland House Diaries 1831–1840*, ed. A. D. Kriegel (London 1977), p. 309; William Hazlitt, *The Spirit of the Age: or Contemporary Portraits* (2nd ed., London 1835), p. 333.

255

4   39 *PR* 867; 40 *PR* 826; 42 *PR* 234.
5   30 *PR* 362.
6   11 *PR* 15.
7   35 *PR* 486; *Westminster Review* I (Jan. 1824), 7.
8   16 *PR* 115.
9   See ch. 12, n. 50.
10   15 *PR* 816.
11   41 *PR* 588–9.
12   *Works* I:173; *Advice,* para. 14.
13   *Works* VII:63.
14   Donald Winch (ed.), James Mill, *Selected Economic Writings* (Edinburgh 1966), p. 90.

1. Youth

Motto: 83 *PR* 411. See also 36 *PR* 25.

1   *Year's Residence* vi, para. 8.
2   C thought he had been born on March 9, 1766. His children decided, after his death, that he had been born in 1762. 88 *PR* 707. However, by 1862 James Cobbett was fairly certain that the correct date was 1763. JPC Memoir, pp. 33–4. This date was independently confirmed by E. I. Carlyle in *William Cobbett: A Study of His Life as Shown in His Writings* (London 1904), p. 303, and since then has been generally accepted. The original *DNB* entry using 1762 was later corrected to 1763.
3   Daniel Defoe, *A Tour through the Whole Island of Great Britain* (2 vols., Everyman ed.) I:142.
4   Anne, p. 12.
5   *Works* IV:31; 70 *PR* 236.
6   *Works* IV:33; JPC, pp. 70–1. C's father (1738–92) and grandfather (1701–60) were both George Cobbett. His father had a small piece of land near Manley Bridge, about a mile and a half south of Farnham.
7   *Works* IV:34; 78 *PR* 212; 88 *PR* 460. 52 *PR* 144: "It was a boast of my father, that he had three boys, whose ages put together made only that of a man of thirty, who did as much work as any man of thirty."
8   81 *PR* 729; *Woodlands,* para. 32.
9   *Works* IV:34–5; Anne, p. 1; JPC, p. 72. According to Tom Cobbett, he and his brothers had attended a school in Farnham conducted by a Mr. Newman. JPC, p. 70. Perhaps this is what C refers to at 81 *PR* 729: "I was, indeed, attempted to be sent to a day-school . . . but never did I acknowledge schoolmaster to be my master."
10   76 *PR* 689. See also 66 *PR* 355.
11   *Works* IV:30–2, 36; 31 *PR* 715. The manufacture and use of such rushes is described in *Cottage Economy,* paras. 194–7. C's father also burned peat which C helped cut on Bagshot Heath. 31 *PR* 717.
12   *Rural Rides,* 41 (44 *PR* 20–1).
13   81 *PR* 513–15. See also 11 *PR* 232.
14   42 *PR* 514: "from about twelve years of age, I resided in or near the place but very little."
15   59 *PR* 773.
16   36 *PR* 23.
17   Anne, p. 3; JPC, p. 70.
18   52 *PR* 411; 80 *PR* 781. See also 16 *PR* 652.
     The saying about the devil and the good tunes is usually attributed to Rowland Hill (1744–1833).
19   Anne, p. 2.
20   Anne, p. 3; *Works* IV:37–9. See also 32 *PR* 1097.

21 *Works* IV:40–1.
22 *Works* IV:42. According to the account of his son James, during the time C was working for Holland he translated Voltaire's *Candide,* which he renamed "Cunegonde, or All for the Best." JPC, pp. 1, 38. Yet other evidence suggests that C did not learn French until after he enlisted in the army.
23 *Works* IV:43.

2. The soldier's friend

Motto: 12 *PR* 522.

1 C always kept February 4 "in recollection." *Year's Residence,* para. 20, entry for Feb. 4, 1818.
2 *Corn,* para. 159; 33 *PR* 481. The Philadelphian Mathew Carey wrote in 1799 that C had a "carotty head and Drawcansir face." Pierce W. Gaines, *William Cobbett and the United States 1792–1835: A Bibliography with Notes and Extracts* (Worcester, Mass. 1971), p. 195. Freneau spoke of C's "red foxy scalp." Clark, *Cobbett,* p. 111.
  His hair turned gray and then white at a relatively early age. C wore spectacles (presumably only for reading) before he went to America in 1817. 48 *PR* 78.
3 *Works* IV:44.
4 When C visited Hull in 1830 he suggested that they would have been better advised to erect a statue to Andrew Marvell than to William III. 69 *PR* 521.
5 *Works* IV:34, 44–5; *Advice,* para. 44. See also 34 *PR* 259. At another point C credits Benjamin Garlike, future British envoy to Denmark, with the initial stimulus to his study of grammar. 32 *PR* 1098–9.
6 *Works* IV:44; Debbieg entry in *DNB.*
7 *Works* IV:45–6.
8 71 *PR* 658; 67 *PR* 99.
9 15 *PR* 901; 32 *PR* 1099; *Advice,* para. 39.
10 15 *PR* 387.
11 15 *PR* 901.
12 82 *PR* 155; *Corn,* para. 3; 68 *PR* 509. C's manuscript is now at Yale University. Letter to Windham, Dec. 6, 1805, Add. MSS. 37853, fol. 191: "after long application to reading and drawing plans, particularly by night, I used sometimes to reel with giddiness, nearly to falling."
13 15 *PR* 913. See also *Corn,* para. 184.
14 32 *PR* 1100–5; *Corn,* para. 183. According to the first reference, "I had the Appendix completed in rough draft in two days and one night. Having the detail before me the Report was short work and the whole was soon completed." In the second reference the work "cost me about thirty nights."
15 See 38 *PR* 230, in which C describes his notion of feminine beauty while speaking of Queen Caroline; but presumably his remarks applied to Nancy.
16 *Advice,* paras. 94, 95. Nancy claimed that she was scrubbing out a teapot on that frosty morning rather than a washing tub. JPC Memoir.
17 8 *PR* 521. C here speaks of £140 as his savings up to 1792. Elsewhere he suggests that they amounted to 200 guineas. 15 *PR* 903. See *Advice,* para. 95.
18 15 *PR* 902. See also 8 *PR* 580.
19 *Corn,* para. 182. A defunct spring in Fredericton was sometimes called "Cobbett's well" by local historians, but the facts on which the mythology is based (i.e. that C wooed Nancy in Fredericton) are so wild that the story can only be regarded as evidence of C's pervasive reputation. Gerald Keith, "The Legend of Jenny's Spring," *New Brunswick Historical Society Collection,* no. 18 (1963).
20 15 *PR* 903.
21 Fitzgerald endeavored to persuade C to stay in the regiment, promising him a commission if he would do so. If C had not been getting married and had

remained in Fitzgerald's regiment "he wd certainly have followed him to the end."
Anne, pp. 15–16.

22 *Works* IV:47; 15 *PR* 46. The original of the discharge is included in No. 1 Correspondence.

By 1805 C had magnified the words "good behaviour" and "services" rendered
to the regiment that appeared in the discharge to "constant good behaviour" and
"great services." 8 *PR* 521. See also *Corn*, para. 182.

23 *Advice*, para. 96; *Political Censor*, Sept. 1796, p. 60. 69 *PR* 469: "Billy."

A half century later only 50.5 percent of the women being married were able to
sign the register. George Boyce, James Curran and Pauline Wingate (eds.), *Newspaper History from the Seventeenth Century to the Present Day* (London 1958), p. 42.

24 There are four principal sources of information regarding the court-martial: C's
account in 1809 (15 *PR* 903f); the war office files in the Public Record Office (WO
1/1051, 1053; WO 72/15) and Pitt's papers (PRO 30 8/124); No. 1 Correspondence;
and *Proceedings of a Court Martial* as set forth in n. 31 below.

The petition to the king was accompanied by a letter to Yonge dated Jan. 14,
1792. PRO WO 1/1051, fol. 273. The PRO files do not include C's original petition
naming four officers but only the redrafted petition.

25 Letter to Yonge, Jan. 22, 1792, PRO WO 1/1051, fol. 261.

26 C's gloss on p. 1 of his copy of redrafted charges. No. 1 Correspondence.

27 Letters to Yonge, Feb. 10 and 15, 1792, PRO WO 1/1051, fols. 247, 249.

28 Letters from Gould, Feb. 23 and Mar. 2, 1792, and letter to Gould, Feb. 25, 1792,
PRO WO 72/15. Letter to Pitt, Mar. 7, 1792, PRO 30 8/124.

29 Letters from Gould, Feb. 23, Mar. 9, 15, 17, and 19, 1792, and letters to Gould,
Mar. 11, 16, and 19, 1792, PRO WO 72/15.

C had previously consented to a proceeding limited to such part of his charges
as "His Majesty shall for the present think proper to refer for Examination." Letter to Yonge, Feb. 15, 1792.

30 Letter to Gould, Mar. 19, 1792, PRO WO 72/15; 15 *PR* 915.

31 *Proceedings of a Court Martial Held at the Horse Guards on the 24th and 27th of March
1792, for the Trial of Capt. Richard Powell, Lieut. Christopher Seton, and Lieut. John Hall
of the 54th Regiment of Foot on Several Charges Preferred against Them Respectively by
William Cobbett, Late Serjeant-Major of the Said Regiment &c.* (London 1809), pp. 18–
27 (PRO WO 72/15).

32 Ibid. pp. 29–32.

33 The history of the 1809 publication is told in ch. 14.

34 C claimed that he and Lane were friends. Lane had been the captain who had
enlisted C, and "he had always shown great kindness towards me." 15 *PR* 907.

The stories told by C and Lane are inconsistent, and the two bits of information
provided by C are self-contradictory; hence the text represents a guess as to what
actually occurred.

Charges were lodged against Lane by his fellow officers for having consorted
with C, and in his response to the war office dated April 30, 1792 he stated that he
had visited C on March 19 to "demand an explanation" from C for presuming to
send a number of soldiers to Lane who had claims for "donation money," and that
this was the only connection he had with C after the latter had brought charges
against the other officers. PRO WO 1/1053.

In the public statement C made in 1809 he said that when he *returned* from
Portsmouth after his trip there on March 20, Lane then told him that the soldiers
had been brought up from Portsmouth "to swear that at an entertainment given
to them by me before my departure from the regiment, I had drunk 'the destruction of the House of Brunswick.'" 15 *PR* 906.

In what was presumably C's contemporaneous entry relating to the incident, he states that he discovered the opponents' strategy on March 20, the day following his meeting with Lane. No. 1 Correspondence (Nuffield).

35 15 *PR* 905. In C's letter to Pitt he stated that "the commanding officer at the regiment has suffered many of the books to remain unsecured; that is to say, in the hands of those whose interest it was to alter them."

36 15 *PR* 906. C's 1809 statement says that he had "solemnly engaged not to have recourse" to Bestland's testimony unless "he was first out of the army; that is to say, out of the reach of the vindictive and bloody lash."

In 1810 a corporal who accused his colonel of defrauding soldiers of shoes (and was unable to obtain a conviction) was sentenced to receive 1,000 lashes. 18 *PR* 146.

No copy of C's letter from Fratton appears either in the Public Record Office or in No. 1 Correspondence. C proposed in 1832 that soldiers testifying before a court-martial "ought to be discharged before they be examined." 77 *PR* 99.

37 No. 1 Correspondence.

Body and Philpot had been named as witnesses by C.

38 *Soldier's Friend,* pp. 9, 17.

39 4 *PR* 238–9; 8 *PR* 517, 522, 545.

40 76 *PR* 725; 82 *PR* 774.

41 C used the same line from "The Traveller" at 15 *PR* 359. See also 10 *PR* 449; 12 *PR* 865.

42 Letter from Lane, Apr. 30, 1792, PRO WO 1/1053.

Part II of Thomas Paine's *Rights of Man,* reputedly published in England on February 16, 1792, contains the sentence: "As soldiers have hitherto been treated in most countries, they might be said to be without a friend" (Penguin ed., p. 290). C makes it clear that he read Paine's book immediately after it was published. 8 *PR* 523. Perhaps not too much emphasis can be placed on this circumstance, since in C's petition to the king, written a month before the supposed publication date of Paine's book, he says: ". . . where shall the poor soldier find a Friend? – I am sure I hear your Majesty's gracious answer – *He shall find a Friend in me.*"

43 *Works* IV:49; Anne, pp. 3–4.

While Anne's notes state that C planned to establish a school at Farnham, C told an American audience that he had determined, even before he left the army, to settle in the United States. *Works* IV:50.

44 Susan to John, Sept. 30, 1835; *Works* IV:51. C's recollection in 1828 that the trip "lasted . . . part of September, the whole of October, and part of November" is in error. *Corn,* para. 158. They were in New York before the end of October. *Works* IV:48. By November 2 they had gone from New York to Philadelphia and from there to Wilmington.

3. Joseph Priestley

Motto: *A Little Plain English,* preface, p. 6. See *Manchester Lectures,* p. 74: "I . . . had been pushed into politics in America by the violence of the Americans against England."

1 Washington to General Knox, cited in Samuel Eliot Morison, *The Oxford History of the American People* (New York 1972) II:33.

2 Adrienne Koch, *Adams and Jefferson: "Posterity Must Judge"* (Chicago 1963), p. 37, citing Charles Francis Adams (ed.), *The Works of John Adams* (Boston 1850–6) IX: 563–4.

3 John Marshall, *The Life of George Washington* (Fredericksburg 1926) IV:481.

4 Edmund Burke, *Reflections on the Revolution in France . . .* (London 1795), pp. 118, 248.

5   Morison II:50.
6   "Jefferson began referring to his friends as 'The Republicans' in 1791." Ibid. p. 60n.
     Jefferson's party later dropped the name "republican" and called themselves "democrats." During the period covered by this chapter, the names "republican" and "democrat" were more or less interchangeable and are here so used. The modern Republican party in the United States was formed in 1854.
7   Ibid. p. 50.
8   John C. Miller, *Alexander Hamilton: Portrait in Paradox* (New York 1959), pp. 344–7.
9   The Cobbetts had landed in New York but proceeded almost immediately to Philadelphia. *Works* IV:48.
10   Short to Jefferson, Aug. 6, 1792 (Library of Congress).
11   John to Susan, Oct. 7, 1835 (Nuffield). Relatively little is known of Garlike. He served in Berlin, St. Petersburg, and Copenhagen, and was given an honorary D.C.L. by Oxford University in 1810.
12   8 *PR* 521.
13   Lord Edward Fitzgerald, born the same year as C, had spent his youth in France and later became an enthusiastic supporter of the French revolution. He joined the Society of Friends of the People in April 1792 and was cashiered from the British army for attending a revolutionary banquet in Paris in October of that year. He was arrested in 1798 in the Irish rising and died in prison from wounds received at the time of his arrest.
     The *Satirist* of November 1808 (p. 339) states flatly that C did not get his letter of introduction through Fitzgerald.
14   Letter to Jefferson, Nov. 2, 1792 (Library of Congress).
15   Letter from Jefferson, Nov. 5, 1792 (Morgan Library).
16   John C. Miller, *The Federalist Era 1789–1801* (New York 1960), p. 33.
17   Howard Mumford Jones, *America and French Culture 1750–1848* (Chapel Hill 1927), p. 134.
18   *Works* IV:14; Esther Brown, *The French Revolution and the American Man of Letters* (New York 1951), p. 112.
19   *Works* I:114.
20   Charles Downer Hazen, *Contemporary American Opinion of the French Revolution* (Baltimore 1897), pp. 166–9. The "cleavers and knives" were less sanguinary than might appear, being a traditional feature of triumphal processions on both sides of the Atlantic. See, for example, 12 *PR* 1.
21   Gaetano Salvemini, *The French Revolution 1788–1792* (London 1954), p. 312.
22   Hazen, p. 183.
23   *Works* IV:10–11.
24   *Works* I:116.
25   *Works* VII:131.
     In 1821 C wrote: "Thus, in judging of the French Revolution . . . we are not to inquire what fooleries or violences were committed during its progress; but, we are to ask, *what has it produced in the end?*" 40 *PR* 1221.
26   Hazen, p. 176.
27   Ibid. pp. 176–7.
28   Ibid. p. 182.
29   Harry M. Tinkcom, *The Republicans and Federalists in Pennsylvania 1790–1801* (Harrisburg 1950), p. 77, quoting Alexander Graydon, *Memoirs*, p. 335.
30   Hazen, p. 186.
31   Jones, *America and French Culture*, p. 541.
32   Hazen, p. 216. See *Works* I:113.
33   Hazen, p. 164.

34 Ibid. p. 184, quoting C's *History of the American Jacobins* (Philadelphia, Nov. 1796), p. 15.

35 The grammar *Le tuteur anglais*, published in March 1795, was an enormous success. By 1861 there had been thirty-five editions. Gaines, *Cobbett*, p. 18; 82 *PR* 20. C had commenced the work in 1793. Letter to James Mathieu, Dec. 13, 1793 (Huntington). See also 33 *PR* 249-56.

36 *Works* v:41; letter to James Mathieu, July 19, 1793 (Huntington).

37 *Impeachment of Mr. Lafayette . . . Translated from the French by William Cobbett* (Philadelphia 1793).

38 *Impeachment*, p. 13.

39 *Impeachment*, p. 3.

40 *Impeachment*, p. 68.

     A few years later C sarcastically wrote of the proscription of Lafayette as "a blot scarcely perceptible in the constellation of virtues which the French Republic exhibited." *Works* I:98.

41 Salvemini, *French Revolution*, pp. 294-6.

42 *Impeachment*, p. 68.

43 Susan to John, Sept. 30, 1835 (Nuffield).

44 Letter to James Mathieu, Jan. 31, 1794 (Huntington).

45 Letter to Rachel Smither, July 6, 1794 (Nuffield).

46 Anon., *Observations on the Emigration of Dr. Joseph Priestley, and on the Several Addresses Delivered to Him on His Arrival at New York* (Philadelphia [1794]).

47 *Works* I:130-1.

48 *Works* I:132-4.

49 *Works* I:132.

50 *Works* I:153.

51 *Works* I:155.

52 *Works* I:157.

53 *Works* I:158.

54 *Works* I:161-2.

55 Letter to Mathieu, Dec. 13, 1793 (Huntington).

56 *Works* IV:53-4.

57 *Works* IV:54, 56.

58 Gaines, *Cobbett*, pp. 4-9. On all editions after the first, Bradford's name appears as publisher.

     The original version of *Observations on Priestley* was rather solemn stuff. Cobbett later added a five-page story of a farmer's bull, in which he poked fun at Priestley for his provocative Jacobinism, his preaching, and his experiments "bottling up his own f—rts, and selling them for superfine inflammable air." *Works* I:219.

4. George Washington

Motto: *Works* IV:117.

1 Morison, *Oxford History* II:61-2.

2 *Gazette of the United States*, June 9, 1794, p. 3.

3 Burke, *Reflections on the Revolution in France*, p. 226.

4 *Impeachment*, p. 74.

5 *Works* II:158, 165; Hazen, *Contemporary American Opinion*, p. 205.

6 Morison II:62-3.

7 Bradford Perkins, *The First Rapprochement: England and the United States 1795-1805* (Philadelphia 1955), pp. 44f.

8 Jones, *America and French Culture*, p. 530. On the British side it was also a "bad bargain," or so it was thought by Lord Hawkesbury, president of the board of trade, and by Charles James Fox. Perkins, pp. 4-5. In 1803 C said that he agreed

with Fox that "in some respects" the treaty was too favorable to the Americans, at the same time pointing out that certain of the terms of the Jay treaty were, from the British point of view, more advantageous than those in the British–Swedish treaty. 4 *PR* 723, 733.

9 *Works* II:56–7.
10 *Works* II:3.
11 *Works* II:7.
12 *Works* II:58.
13 Southern democrats who thought holding titles of nobility "vicious" and inconsistent with a republican form of government thought holding slaves "quite a different thing." *Works* II:48. The *Philadelphia Gazette,* voice of the democrats, in July 1794 printed "a list of Democrats, the great benefactors of mankind; among them are Marat and Jesus Christ." *Works* II:44n.
14 *Works* II:59.
15 *Works* II:30, 62, 63.
16 *Works* II:22, 59. "It was necessary for me to say something to disguise the fact that it proceeded from an *Englishman's pen.*" 15 *PR* 777.
17 *Works* IV:122.
18 Gaines, *Cobbett,* p. 13.
19 Clark, *Cobbett,* p. 28.
20 *Works* II:79.
21 *Works* II:89. Mrs. Rowson also was cousin of Anthony Haswell, editor of the *Vermont Gazette,* a democratic newspaper.
22 *Works* II:73. The source of this *nom de plume* has never been identified, but it would be typical of C to adopt a name that had been applied to him by someone in opposition.
23 *Works* II:86n. In the original version, the lady was not identified. Her name was added in a footnote introduced when *Works* was published in 1801.
24 *Works* II:56; III:348. A long anonymous pamphlet published in 1796 (presumably by James Callender) systematically assailed each of C's writings and defended the Swanwick name: *British Honour and Humanity; or, the Wonders of American Patience as Exemplified in the Modest Publications, and Universal Applause of Mr. William Cobbet.* Gaines, *Cobbett,* p. 180.
25 Henry van Schaack to Theodore Sedgwick, Jan. 30, 1797 (Massachusetts Historical Society). "Scrub" is the name of a man-of-all-work in George Farquahar's *The Beaux' Stratagem.*
26 *Works* I:113.
27 *Works* II:129n.
28 *Works* II:123.
29 *Works* II:152–3.
30 Perkins, *The First Rapprochement,* p. 32.
31 Albert J. Beveridge, *The Life of John Marshall* (Boston and New York 1916) II:116.
32 *Works* II:273, 275.
33 Washington to Hamilton, July 29, 1795, quoted in Beveridge II:120.
34 Gaines, *Cobbett,* p. 22. Washington's library at the time of his death included a copy of *A Little Plain English* and *A New Year's Gift.* P. C. Griffin, *A Catalogue of the Washington Collection in the Boston Atheneum* (Boston 1897), p. 49.
35 *Works* II:369–73; Perkins, *The First Rapprochement,* pp. 36–7; Morison, *Oxford History* II:67.
36 *Works* II:271–2.
37 *Works* II:373–4.
38 *Works* II:369.
39 Gaines, *Cobbett,* p. 30.
40 *Works* II:410–20, 460, 472.

41   Madison to Jefferson, Jan. 10, 1796. Gaines, *Cobbett*, p. 31, quoting Moncure D. Conway, *Edmund Randolph*, p. 347.

42   John A. Carroll and Mary W. Ashworth, *George Washington* (New York 1957), p. 336, quoting Shippen diaries (Library of Congress).

43   Ibid., quoting William Plumer papers (Library of Congress).

44   *Works* III:9.

45   *Works* III:14, 32, 39. The custom of answering the president's address, which was shortly abandoned in Congress, was borrowed from the practice of the British parliament.

46   *Works* III:81.

47   *Works* III:222–5.

48   *A Letter from the Right Honourable Edmund Burke to a Noble Lord* was published at Philadelphia in May 1796 with a preface by Peter Porcupine. In the preface C again warned the wealthy *sans-culottes* in America who depended on the stability of the government, yet were endeavoring to shake it to the ground. Gaines, *Cobbett*, pp. 49–50.

49   Ibid. pp. 34–41.

50   Beveridge, *John Marshall* II:150–1.

51   Ibid. p. 121.

52   Perkins, *The First Rapprochement*, p. 41.

53   Timothy Pitkin, *A Political and Civil History of the United States of America* (New Haven 1828) II:478.

54   Perkins, pp. 41, 42; *Annals of Congress*, 4th Congress, 1st session, 1291. In *Works* v:301 a French official is quoted as saying that the treaty was approved "by two votes only . . . and this was owing to a political error of our own government."

55   77 *PR* 647.

56   Gaines, *Cobbett*, pp. 4–34. In 1808 C wrote: "I agree . . . that every man should put his name to what he causes to be published." 14 *PR* 270–1.

57   *Works* IV:122.

58   *Works* v:361–2. According to a later account, C and Talleyrand met "frequently." *Porcupine*, Aug. 26, 1801. The meetings took place at the house of Moreau de St. Méry. 70 *PR* 429.

59   *Works* v:363.

60   Duff Cooper, *Talleyrand* (London 1952 repr.), p. 80.

61   *Works* IV:58.

62   Gaines, *Cobbett*, pp. 17–19.

63   Ibid. pp. 26–8.

64   68 *PR* 229; Clark, *Cobbett*, p. 37.

65   *Works* IV:128.

66   *Works* IV:3–4.

67   *Works* IV:11, 13; 8 *PR* 519. Three years after the battle, "thousands," according to C, still thought the French had won. *Works* v:288–9.

68   *Works* IV:5–6.

69   *Works* IV:20–1.

70   *Works* IV:114. C's father had died in 1792.

71   Allan Nevins and Frank Weitenkampf, *A Century of Political Cartoons: Caricature in the United States from 1800 to 1900* (New York 1944), p. 22. The print is described at *Works* IV:116–17.

72   *Works* IV:26–7.

73   *Works* IV:61, 63.

74   *Works* IV:25f. C claimed that it was republished in England at the request of Canning, then an undersecretary of state in Pitt's government. 15 *PR* 909.

75   The omission of the court-martial was later referred to by C as "a small chasm." 8 *PR* 521.

C's failure to mention his marriage may explain the subsequent charge that he had never married the young girl "who lived with him as his wife." C, who had strong puritanical feelings about such matters, testily countered by announcing that he had shown his marriage certificate to James Abercrombie, vicar of Christ Church, Philadelphia. Gaines, *Cobbett*, p. 181, quoting James Carey, *A Pill for Porcupine*; *Works* IV:120.

76 C's long-held view that Franklin was "a low, cunning, huckstering man" (53 *PR* 346) seems to have been due, in part at least, to C's contempt for Franklin's emphasis on self-interest, reflected in his advice on prudence and money-making.

77 *Works* IV:28.

78 *Works* IV:124.

79 *Works* IV:54–9.

80 *Works* IV:124.

81 *Works* IV:124–6.

82 *Works* IV:132–3.

83 Miller, *Alexander Hamilton*, p. 441; Morison, *Oxford History* II:68, 69. The phrase "entangling alliances" was Jefferson's, appearing in his inaugural address of March 4, 1801. *Inaugural Addresses of the Presidents of the United States*, House Doc. 540, 82nd Congress, 2nd session, 13.

84 *Works* IV:143–8.

85 *Works* IV:177–8.

86 *Works* IV:139, 140.

87 *Works* IV:211f. Since breaking with Bradford early in 1796 over *Prospect from the Congress-Gallery*, C had embarked on a series containing similar materials entitled the *Political Censor*, of which eight numbers were issued between March 1796 and March 1797.

88 *Works* IV:230–1.

89 *Works* IV:262–6.

90 *Works* IV:157.

91 *Works* IV:266.

92 *Works* IV:267. In 1822 C asserted that Jefferson's knowledge and talent at writing exceeded the sum total of all British diplomats for the last thirty years. *Collective Commentaries*, p. 74.

93 Gaines, *Cobbett*, p. 68; Ralph Adams Brown, *The Presidency of John Adams* (Lawrence 1975), p. 21.

94 Miller, *Alexander Hamilton*, p. 450.

95 Letter to David Stuart, cited in John C. Fitzpatrick (ed.), *The Writings of George Washington from the Original Manuscript Sources 1745–1799* (39 vols., Washington 1931–44) XXXV:360.

Washington's comment has traditionally (and erroneously) been assigned to C's "Letter to the Infamous Tom Paine" in the *Political Censor* for December 1796, which, however, was not published until January 24, 1797 – more than two weeks after Washington's letter to Stuart. Gaines, *Cobbett*, p. 70. See Moncure D. Conway, *The Life of Thomas Paine* . . . ed. Hypatia Bradlaugh Bonner (London 1909), p. 226; *Writings of George Washington* XXXV:360n94; Clark, *Cobbett*, p. 79; Gaines, p. 72. Griffin (*Catalogue of the Washington Collection*, p. 49) assumed that the comment related to *A New Year's Gift*, published a full year before Washington's letter.

5. John Adams

Motto: *Works* V:4 (Mar. 1797). Cf. prospectus of the *Anti-Jacobin; or, Weekly Examiner* (Nov. 1797): "To that freedom from partiality . . . by the profession of which so many of our Contemporaries recommend themselves, We make little pretension."

1 R. A. Brown, *Presidency of John Adams*, p. 25.

2 Morison, *Oxford History* II:70.

3 *Inaugural Addresses of the Presidents of the United States*, House Doc. 540, 82nd Congress, 2nd session, 7.

4 Charles Warren, *Jacobin and Junto* . . . (Cambridge 1931), p. 67, quoting *Aurora*, Dec. 23, 1796; Beveridge, *Life of John Marshall* II:161–3.

5 Paine's "Letter to Washington" was published in the *Aurora* on November 18, 1796.

6 *Works* III:397.

7 Paine's "Letter to Washington" quotes some language published by "Peter Skunk, or Peter Porcupine" (allegedly under the patronage of the "Washington faction") which Paine unconvincingly claimed was intended to lead to his execution by the French. Clark (*Cobbett*, p. 77) cites the May 1796 *Political Censor* as the source of the quoted language, but it cannot be found there. See also Conway, *Life of Thomas Paine*, pp. 200f.

8 *Works* IV:327–31. Paine's letter to Mr. Secretary Dundas of June 6, 1792 speaks of Washington as "more of a gentleman than any king." Thomas Paine, *The Political Works of Thomas Paine Complete in One Volume* . . . (London [1844]), p. 600.

   Years later C claimed that Paine's pen "much more than the sword of Washington" was responsible for the victory of the Americans. Address to the Electors of Preston (1826) (Fitzwilliam Museum).

9 Charles Francis Adams (ed.), *Letters of John Adams Addressed to His Wife* (Boston 1841) II:244.

10 *Inaugural Addresses of Presidents of the United States*, p. 8.

11 *Works* V:67.

12 James Brown Scott (ed.), *The Controversy over Neutral Rights between the United States and France 1797–1800* (New York 1917), p. 16.

13 *Works* V:376; VI:32.

14 Alexander de Condé, *The Quasi-War: The Politics and Diplomacy of the Undeclared War with France 1797–1801* (New York 1966), p. 124.

15 The original name of C's paper was *Porcupine's Political Gazette and United States Daily Advertiser*. The shortened name was adopted after April 22, 1797. Gaines, *Cobbett*, p. 77. From March 1798 through August 1799 C also published the *Country Porcupine*, consisting of extracts from *Porcupine's Gazette*. Gaines, p. 84.

16 *Works* V:4. Similar thoughts are expressed in the prospectus of the *Anti-Jacobin; or, Weekly Examiner*, the first issue of which was published on November 20, 1797.

17 *Works* V:37, 65, 103–4, 108.

18 *Works* V:373, citing U.S. Treasury Dept. circular dated Apr. 8, 1797, signed "Oliver Wolcott, Jun."

19 *Works* IV:308.

20 *Works* V:390.

21 Condé, p. 125.

22 Scott (ed.), *Controversy over Neutral Rights*, p. 17.

23 Letter to Mary Cranch in Stewart Mitchell (ed.), *New Letters of Abigail Adams* (Boston 1947), p. 152.

24 *French Arrogance*, pp. 9, 17, 28.

25 Gaines, *Cobbett*, p. 246.

26 *Works* VIII:318, 320.

27 *Works* VIII:320n; *Letters to Thornton*, p. 4.

28 Richard B. Morris, *Encyclopedia of American History* (New York 1953), pp. 128–9.

29 Bulmer Hobson (ed.), *The Letters of Wolfe Tone* [1821] (Dublin 1920), p. 46. Tone was a visitor in America from August 1, 1795 to January 1, 1796.

   In 1816 C declared that the Irish in America had "behaved very peaceably," surpassing in success the "emigrants from any other nation." 30 *PR* 557.

30 *Works* IX:114.

31 John Quincy Adams to Abigail Adams, June 27, 1798 in W. C. Ford (ed.), *Writings of John Quincy Adams* (New York 1913–17) II:323.
32 John C. Miller, *Crisis in Freedom* (Boston 1951), p. 98.
33 *Works* VIII:246–7. See also *Works* X:16, where C put the number of such villains at 50,000 in Pennsylvania alone.
34 *Country Porcupine*, Nov. 8 and 9, 1798, quoted in Miller, *Crisis in Freedom*, p. 55. In 1814 C claimed that the Sedition Bill was passed in the heat of the moment and was something Adams would not have thought of if he had not been surrounded by "Massachusetts Federalists." 26 *PR* 688.
35 Quoted by Miller, *Crisis in Freedom*, p. 92. While the total number of federalist papers (103) exceeded the total democratic papers (64), the reverse was true of those "strongly" supporting the two parties (19 to 48). David H. Fischer, *The Revolution of American Conservatism* (New York 1962), p. 131.
36 *Works* VI:420; A. P. Wadsworth, *Newspaper Circulations, 1800–1954*, Trans. Manchester Statistical Society (1955), p. 7.
37 *Works* VI:315; VII:19–20; IX:356. In 1814 C said: "I lived in Philadelphia about eight years, with every disposition to find fault with every thing that I saw, or heard of, that was amiss." 26 *PR* 655.
38 *Works* VIII:124.
39 *Works* VIII:34.
40 *Porcupine's Gazette*, Oct. 3, 1797, quoted in *Works* VII:228.
41 *Works* IX:25–6.
42 Letter to Thomas Boylston Adams, July 9, 1799 in Ford (ed.), *Writings of J. Q. Adams* II:433.
43 Letter to Abigail Adams, July 3, 1799 in ibid. II:430.
44 Letter to Mary Cranch, Mar. 13, 1798. See also letter to same, May 7, 1798, both in S. Mitchell (ed.), *New Letters of Abigail Adams*, pp. 144, 169.
45 Benjamin Latrobe to J. B. Scandrelle, Apr. 30, 1798 (American Philosophical Society).
46 Griffith J. McRee, *Life and Correspondence of James Iredell . . .* (2 vols. in 1, New York, 1949) II:465–6.
47 Gaines, *Cobbett*, p. 28.
48 Letter to William Gifford, June 28, 1799 (Yale).
49 Liston to Grenville, June 25, 1798 (National Library of Scotland).
   "The government have made me offers of their support, which I never accepted of." 15 *PR* 777. See also 36 *PR* 26; 30 *American PR* 5; 69 *PR* 454; 77 *PR* 647.
50 *Works* IX:246.
51 *Works* VIII:145, 162–5, 169–70.
52 Warren, *Jacobin and Junto*, pp. 81, 84.
53 R. A. Brown, *Presidency of John Adams*, pp. 73–4.
54 Ibid. p. 57. Years later C declared that Adams "did, yielding to the counsels of weak and violent men, push things very nearly to an offensive and defensive alliance with us." 26 *PR* 688.
55 Condé, *The Quasi-War*, pp. 126–8.
56 Scott (ed.), *Controversy over Neutral Rights*, p. 20.
57 Condé, p. 128.
58 *Works* X:149. On March 12, 1799, C wrote to T. J. Mathias, author of the celebrated *Pursuits of Literature*: "neither your aweful voice, nor that of an angel, were one to descend, can save America from another revolution!" Add. MSS. 22,976, fol. 212.
59 Miller, *Alexander Hamilton*, p. 493.
60 *Works* X:153n. But see XI:68.
61 *Works* X:48.
62 *Works* X:150. In 1816 C stated that Adams was "a wise and most excellent man; a

true lover of his country and of the cause of freedom in every country." 30 *PR* 538. See also 26 *PR* 688, 811–12.

63 Letter to James Lloyd, Jan. 1815 in C. F. Adams (ed.), *Works of John Adams* x:11.

64 Letter to John Turnbull, Sept. 10, 1800 in ibid. ix. "Fenno" was John Ward Fenno, who, in 1798, at age nineteen, had taken over the *Gazette of the United States* on the death of his father, John Fenno.

The electoral vote for president suggests a somewhat different story from that asserted by Adams. When he was elected in 1797 he received 71 electoral votes including 16 from Massachusetts, 12 from New York, and 1 from Pennsylvania. In the 1801 election he received 65 electoral votes. He retained all 16 votes from Massachusetts; he picked up 6 additional votes in Pennsylvania (where C and Fenno published their papers); but he lost all 12 votes from New York, the home state of Alexander Hamilton. Svend Peterson, *A Statistical History of American Presidential Elections* (New York 1963), pp. 12–13.

65 *Works* x:155. By 1801 C was convinced that Adams had thought of deporting him but had been deterred by the attorney general. *Works* x:155n. See also x:185n.

C later stated that Pickering was thought of as the great champion of the British cause in America, and that he had known him "very well." 20 *PR* 297, 397. But by 1814 C was referring to his erstwhile friend as "poor Timothy Pickering," one of the American "noblesse" and a traitor to his country, i.e. an opponent of the war of 1812. 26 *PR* 804, 811–12.

66 The official, Louis Otto, later French representative in England (see ch. 7), is quoted in E. Wilson Lyon, "The Directory and the United States," *American Historical Review* XLIII (Apr. 1938), 520. See also letter from John Adams to John Quincy Adams, Mar. 31, 1797 in C. F. Adams (ed.), *Works of John Adams* VIII:537.

6. Some personal feuds

Motto: 12 *PR* 522.

1 The original name of Bache's paper, the *General Advertiser*, was changed to the *Aurora* in 1794.

2 *Works* VII:332.

3 Letter to Mary Cranch in S. Mitchell (ed.), *New Letters of Abigail Adams*, p. 143; Liston to Grenville, June 25, 1798, quoted in Perkins, *The First Rapprochement*, p. 9; William Smith to Ralph Izard, May 23, 1797, quoted in V. B. Philips, "South Carolina Federalist Correspondence," *American Historical Review* XIV (1909), 788.

4 *American PR* XXX:4–5.

5 Albert C. Baugh, *A History of the English Language* (New York 1935), pp. 441–2.

6 Letter to Noah Webster, Feb. 6, 1797 (New York Public Library); *Works* V:143.

7 Ford (ed.), *Writings of J. Q. Adams* II:428–9.

8 *Works* VII:4n.

9 *Works* IX:29, 31.

10 *Works* XI:253n. See also Harry R. Warfel, *Noah Webster: Schoolmaster to America* (New York 1936), p. 160.

11 *Works* V:200.

12 Harry R. Warfel (ed.), *Letters of Noah Webster* (New York 1953), p. 148. See also Webster's letter to Timothy Pickering, July 17, 1798 in ibid. p. 182.

13 *English Grammar*, letter XXIII.

14 *Works* VI:4–5, 20, 35, 65, 76, 91; x:84–5, 188.

Mathew Carey, *A Plumb Pudding for the Humane, Valiant, Chaste, Enlightened Peter Porcupine* (1799) and *The Porcupiniad: A Hudibrastic Poem* (1799). Mathew Carey's brother James also wrote pamphlets attacking C. Gaines, *Cobbett*, pp. 181, 190, 193. The background of the Cobbett–Carey feud is given in *Mathew Carey: Autobiography*, Research Classics I (Brooklyn, N.Y. 1942), letters VI–IX, pp. 30–9.

15 The *Aurora* published letters written by "Robert Slender," pseudonym for Philip Freneau, in which C was gently mocked, along with other high federalists. See IV, V, VI, VIII, and XVIII in *Letters on Various Interesting and Important Subjects* by Robert Slender, O.S.M. (Philadelphia 1799). Freneau had some far more bitter things to say about C in his poetry.

   When C visited Philadelphia in 1818 he made a point of shaking hands with Carey and with William Duane, Bache's successor as editor of the *Aurora*.

16 J. H. Peeling, "Governor McKean and the Pennsylvania Jacobins (1799–1808)," *Pennsylvania Magazine* LIV:320, 354. A recent biographer portrays McKean as a complex man, "almost pathological in his insistence upon deference in his political and judicial capacities." G. S. Rowe, *Thomas McKean: The Shaping of an American Republicanism* (Boulder 1978), p. 403. See also pp. 228, 249, 304, 401.

17 William Vans Murray to J. Q. Adams, Dec. 3, 1799, quoted in Peeling, "Governor McKean," p. 320.

18 *Works* III:437; VI:80, 94n, 95n.

19 *Works* IV:365.

20 *Works* VI:329.

21 *Works* V:424; VI:123, 249f.

22 *Works* VI:241, 249, 273, 293.

23 Pickering to attorney general, July 24, 1797 (Massachusetts Historical Society).

24 Octavius Pickering and C. W. Upham, *Life of Timothy Pickering* (Boston 1867–73) III:399–400. Yrujo's letter was dated August 8, 1797. Yrujo and Sarah McKean were married on April 10, 1798.

25 *Works* VII:337; petition, Feb. 19, 1818 (Historical Society of Pennsylvania); undated memorial signed by Joseph Nancrede as attorney for C (Haverford).

26 *Works* VII:338–9.

27 *Works* VII:355–7; Blackstone IV:132, 150–1; John D. Lawson, *American State Trials* (St. Louis 1916) VI:677: McKean "forgot he was a judge, became an advocate, and in turn, libeled the prisoner at the bar."

28 Francis Wharton (ed.), *State Trials of the United States during the Administrations of Washington and Adams* (Philadelphia 1849), p. 329.

29 *Works* VIII:138.

30 *Reports of Cases Adjudged in the Supreme Court of Pennsylvania*: 3 Yeates 93, 94.

31 Ibid. 2 Yeates 352. Application for removal was made to the state court, whereas under later practice the application would be made to the federal court.

32 *Works* IV:361–2.

33 *Works* XI:250.

34 James T. Flexner, *Doctors on Horseback* (New York 1937), pp. 97–8, 102.

35 *Works* XI:259.

36 Flexner, p. 105. There was also great disagreement in the medical profession regarding the contagious nature of yellow fever. C's view that it was not contagious was confirmed by experiments in 1822 at Fort Royal, Martinique. 52 *PR* 294.

37 Carl Binger, *Revolutionary Doctor: Benjamin Rush, 1746–1813* (New York 1966), p. 229. Cf. Flexner, p. 102, where the claim is made that Rush *underestimated* the blood in the human body.

38 Rush's vanity accounted for his loss of Washington's friendship. A few months after Rush entered the army during the revolutionary war, he decided that Washington should be replaced as commander-in-chief, and sent an unsigned letter denouncing him to Patrick Henry, governor of Virginia, who forwarded it to Washington. Washington had no difficulty identifying the author, since Rush had almost concurrently written him a warm letter of regard. According to a third-hand report, Washington declared that he "had been a good deal in the world and seen many bad men, but Dr. Rush was the most black-hearted scoundrel he had ever known." Adams, however, thought Rush "one of the best of men."

39 Flexner, p. 57. See also Lyman H. Butterfield (ed.), *The Letters of Benjamin Rush* (Princeton 1951) i:lxi; David F. Hawke, *Benjamin Rush: Revolutionary Gadfly* (Indianapolis and New York 1973), p. ix.

40 Butterfield (ed.) i:lxv–lxxi. Rush's court-martial prosecution is described by Flexner, *Doctors on Horseback*, pp. 81–5.

41 *Works* iv:362.

42 *Works* vii:164–8. See also vii:194. *Gil Blas* by Le Sage, translated by T. G. Smollett in 1749, was widely read in the eighteenth century. A 1795 cartoon by Cruikshank, "Doctor Sangrado releeving John Bull of the Yellow Fever," portrays Pitt as Sangrado. The name was also applied to Henry Addington. M. Dorothy George, *English Political Caricature 1793–1832: A Study of Opinion and Propaganda* (Oxford 1959), pp. 14, 65. See also 3 *PR* 618.

43 Jared Ingersoll to Benjamin Rush, Oct. 20, 1797 (Historical Society of Pennsylvania), cited by Clark, *Cobbett*, p. 147.

44 2 Yeates 275. See n. 31 above.

45 During the summer of 1798 Philadelphia had another yellow fever epidemic, but C did not resume his attacks on Rush.

46 *Works* vii:370–2, 378–80, 382, 386–7. Bache's paper, before Spain became a French ally, had called the king of Spain an "infamous tyrant" and the Spanish people "slaves," the "most cowardly of the human race." *Works* vii:382.

47 *Works* vii:317.

48 *Works* vii:334.

49 *Works* x:190.

50 Roberdeau Buchanan, *The Life of the Hon. Thomas McKean, LL.D.* (Lancaster 1890), p. 85.

51 *Works* xi:365. C claimed that the "base and corrupt Judge contrived the means of postponing the cause seven times . . . till, at last, he found one [a jury] from which he was sure of a verdict." 54 *PR* 581–2.

52 Richard E. Welch, Jr., *Theodore Sedgwick, Federalist: A Political Portrait* (Middletown 1965), p. 200.

53 Letter to Edward Tilghman, Dec. 9, 1799 (New York Public Library).

54 J. A. Martin, *Martin's Bench and Bar of Philadelphia* (Philadelphia 1883), p. 23.

55 *Works* xi:287–8.

56 Burton A. Konkle, *Joseph Hopkinson 1770–1842* (Philadelphia 1931), pp. 6, 43, 82; *Works* xi:388.

57 Harper was condemned by C in 1814 as one of America's "noblesse," i.e. one who was opposed to the British–American war of 1812. 26 *PR* 804.

58 *A Report of an Action for a Libel, Brought by Dr. Benjamin Rush, against William Cobbett, in the Supreme Court of Pennsylvania, December Term, 1799, for Certain Defamatory Publications in a News-Paper, Entitled Porcupine's Gazette, of Which the Said William Cobbett Was Editor. Taken in Short Hand by T. Carpenter* (Philadelphia 1800), [2]; *Works* xi:370.

59 Martin, *Martin's Bench and Bar of Philadelphia*, p. 23; *Works* xi:287n.

60 William J. Dunham, "Mahlon Dickerson: A Great but Almost Forgotten New Jerseyan," *Proc. New Jersey Historical Society* lxviii (1950), 302.

61 14 *PR* 170.

62 *Works* xi:146–50, 277–86. See opinion of Dr. John Brickell, January 23, 1800, that bleeding made Washington's death speedy and inevitable. *Works* xi:279–80.

63 *Letters to Thornton*, p. 27. A letter dated October 15, 1800 from Harper to Rush in the possession of the Historical Society of Pennsylvania contains a pencilled note by Rush's son referring to Harper: "a friend of Dr. R's yet was the counsel for Cobbett. He said to Dr. R after the trial: 'I was obliged to say something for him'."

64 *Report of an Action for a Libel*, pp. [30–5].

    Harper charged C $60 for his services, "being the same charged" by each of C's other counsel. The quoted words have been misinterpreted to mean that Harper charged C nothing for his own services, but acted only as a collection agency for the other counsel. Letter to Harper, Jan. 20, 1800 (Rutgers); C. Rexford Davis, "William Cobbett: Philadelphia Bookseller and Publisher," *Journal of the Rutgers University Library*, Dec. 1952, pp. 16, 22.

65 *Works* XI:319n, 321–4.
66 Henry Adams, *History of the United States of America* (New York 1889–91) I:118.
67 *Works* XI:145, 296–7.
68 *Letters to Thornton*, p. 21.
69 Gaines, *Cobbett*, p. 77.
70 *Works* XI:137–40.
71 No. v of the *Rush-Light* was devoted to what, for C, was a gentle chiding of Joseph Priestley, ending with the request that Priestley, who continued to live in western Pennsylvania, return home to England and confess that America was not the land of free and happy people that he had once thought it to be. Although Priestley had been subjected to almost constant attack since 1794, he was still able to say of C: "At this time [May 1800] he is by far the most popular writer in this country, and, indeed, one of the best in many respects." J. T. Rutt, *Life and Correspondence of Joseph Priestley* (2 vols., London 1831–2) II:432.
72 *Works* XI:268–70; George W. Corner (ed.), *The Autobiography of Benjamin Rush* . . . (Princeton 1948), p. 96n35. "Cobbett the layman must be credited with a suggestion of scientific importance that never seems to have occurred to Rush the physician – or for that matter to any of his professional colleagues for another generation or so . . . Cobbett in his approach to clinical statistics proved himself a better epidemiologist than Rush." Butterfield (ed.), *Letters of Benjamin Rush* II:1217.
73 *Works* XI:221–2. "I condemn myself only for some harsh expressions which I made use of in speaking of their conduct and practice," wrote Rush in his memoirs, where he went on to explain that he was contending with the "most criminal ignorance." Corner (ed.), *Autobiography of Benjamin Rush*, p. 97.
74 *Works* XI:260.
75 *Works* XI:158.
76 *Works* XI:367; letter to Tilghman, Dec. 6, 1799 (New York Public Library).
77 *Works* XI:211. There seems to be fairly general agreement that "the trial was in some respects unfair and that the damages were excessive." Butterfield (ed.), *Letters of Benjamin Rush* II:1216. The combined total of all fines imposed against the eight defendants found guilty under the Alien and Sedition Acts was $2,505. Miller, *Crisis in Freedom*, pp. 102–222.
78 *Letters to Thornton*, p. 19 (almost certainly written on December 16, 1799 and hence misplaced by the editor); Clark, *Cobbett*, p. 164; letter to John Wright, Jan. 4, 1800, Add. MSS. 22906, fol. 5; letter to Edward Tilghman, Dec. 18, 1799 (New York Public Library).
79 C was arrested and immediately released on bail. Letter to Wright, Jan. 4, 1800, Add. MSS. 22906, fol. 5.
80 C claimed that the governor of the "province" of Canada (New Brunswick) was one of them. 4 *PR* 240. And see n. 81 below.
81 *Letters to Thornton*, pp. 24, 59, 71; Butterfield (ed.), *Letters of Benjamin Rush* II:1218n, quoting Livingston to Rush, July 16, 1801. According to C, Rush's lawyers took half as a contingent fee. The original proposal seems to have been a loan to C (*Letters to Thornton*, p. 35), but as early as February 1800 there appears to have been a move, in which John Ashley of Philadelphia took a leading part, to relieve C of the burden (ibid. pp. 50, 71, 72, 93, 96, 101, 111, 119; and esp. P.S. to letter of Feb. 19, 1800, p. 63). C stated that the money came from his countrymen in Canada and the United States (*Porcupine*, Nov. 3, 1800; 4 *PR* 240; 8 *PR* 525); from "some very worthy men in Canada" (32 *PR* 16); and from "public-spirited men

(chiefly *Scotchmen*) in Canada" (69 *PR* 453). See also Susan to John, Sept. 30, 1835 (Nuffield).

The *Westminster Review*, after C's death, claimed that "the agents of Great Britain in the United States" had contributed to the settlement. Oct. 1835, p. 465. Thornton almost surely contributed something and raised "other friends." *Letters to Thornton*, p. 111.

82 *Letters to Thornton*, p. 72.

83 Ibid. pp. 35, 71.

In 1817 C retold the story in a more appealing way: that the damages he had to pay "together with the consequences of it, actually deprived me of every shilling I had in the world, and sent me home upon a subscription, raised by some very worthy men in Canada." 32 *PR* 16.

84 *Works* XII:109–10.

7. The end of Jacobinism

Motto: Letter to Joseph Dennie, May 7, 1800 (Harvard).

1 *Letters to Thornton*, pp. 99–100.

2 Ibid. p. 101.

3 Quoted in E. P. Thompson, *The Making of the English Working Class* (Penguin ed. 1975), p. 199.

4 *Letters to Thornton*, pp. 103–4; Susan to John, Sept. 30, 1835 (Nuffield); letter to Wright, July 8, 1800, Add. MSS. 22906, fol. 9.

5 The first English edition of *A Bone to Gnaw*, issued in 1797, contained the subtitle *To Which Is Prefixed a Rod, for the Backs of the Critics . . . by Humphrey Hedgehog* – a pseudonym of John Gifford. Gaines, *Cobbett*, p. 15. While in America C had also received laudatory letters from a number of prominent pamphlet writers, including John Reeves, John Bowles, Sir Frederick Morton Eden, the Reverend Mr. Ireland (later dean of Westminster), and the Reverend John Brand. 69 *PR* 567.

The two Giffords, who had fallen out shortly before C's return to England, were often confused. According to the *DNB*, in 1800 William Gifford, on entering Wright's bookshop, was assaulted by John Wolcot ("Peter Pindar") for a review written by John Gifford. C, however, seems to suggest that William Gifford had committed the offense resented by Wolcot. 43 *PR* 581. See ch. 15, n. 69.

6 *Letters to Thornton*, p. 109; 32 *PR* 17. Others at the dinner with Pitt were Canning, Frere, and George Ellis. Frere later reported that "Cobbett behaved perfectly well." Lord Broughton, *Recollections of a Long Life . . .* ed. Lady Dorchester (London 1910 repr.) III:129. At another Hammond dinner the guests included Canning, Jenkinson (later Lord Liverpool), and William Huskisson. 45 *PR* 455; 56 *PR* 685; 58 *PR* 586. C also dined at Canning's house in Putney. 15 *PR* 777.

7 Letter to William Gifford, Nov. 4, 1799, PRO 30/8 124. After William Gifford's death, C wrote that he was a man of talent who was vicious only because he was ashamed of being servile to men in power. 65 *PR* 628–9; 69 *PR* 569.

8 Susan to John, Sept. 30, 1835 (Nuffield); Anne, p. 9.

9 *Boswell's Life of Johnson*, ed. A. Birrell (6 vols., London 1903) VI:189. See also Henry Brougham, *Historical Sketches of Statesmen Who Flourished in the Time of George III* (London and Glasgow n.d.) I:269–77.

10 *Letters to Thornton*, p. 105.

11 Philip Freneau, "The Royal Cockneys in America," in *The Poems of Philip Freneau*, ed. F. L. Pattee (3 vols., New York 1963) III:185.

12 8 *PR* 550; 18 *PR* 16 ("a share of the True Briton"); *Letters to Thornton*, p. 110. See also 32 *PR* 17; 77 *PR* 648. Sinecures held by government writers of the time are given in 69 *PR* 567–70.

13 8 *PR* 550; 32 *PR* 19; 43 *PR* 606.
14 32 *PR* 17. In 1830 C stated that he had "only about £500" when he arrived in London. 69 *PR* 454.
15 *Letters to Thornton*, pp. 110–11.
16 Dyckman papers (New York Historical Society, doc. 590 or 596). Possibly as a result of the death in 1802 of John Ward Fenno, to whom C had sold his New York bookshop, Morgan returned to the United States shortly after the Pall Mall shop had been opened. 8 *PR* 553. It was sold by C to E. Harding effective December 31, 1802. C and family moved to 15 Duke Street, Westminster, near the end of 1802.
17 *Works* I:22, 24, 16.
18 Quoted in E. P. Thompson, *English Working Class*, p. 517.
19 Compare *Bloody Buoy*, p. 226 and *Democratic Judge*, p. 62 with *Works* III:224, IX:367–8, and XII:151. C's changed view of Washington occurred prior to his departure from America and was possibly attributable to Washington's support of Adams's treaty with the French. See letter to Jonathan Boucher, Apr. 19, 1800 (Yale), in which C asserts that the world had been deceived as to Washington's character. Much later, C declared that Washington "on the whole . . . left no party any good reason to complain of him" (26 *PR* 688); that he was "one of the first of patriots" (27 *PR* 592); that he was "the greatest statesman that has been known in our day, and the very best civil ruler" (65 *PR* 731). With the passage of time, not only Washington but all the early American presidents were hailed as paragons of virtue. 66 *PR* 189.
20 *Works* I:3. Reeves, according to C, was "a really learned lawyer, and, politics aside, as good a man as ever lived." 69 *PR* 569. See also 70 *PR* 761.
21 *Letters to Thornton*, p. 111; 4 *PR* 582.
22 At an earlier date (presumably prior to the French bloodshed) Windham had been an enthusiastic republican. Broughton, *Recollections* III:138.
23 *Works* VII:103. See also 2 *PR* 763. Later, after C had shifted sides, he lost his admiration for Burke. See n. 33 below.
24 Wadsworth, *Newspaper Circulations*, p. 7. A great wealth of information on the circulation of newspapers early in the nineteenth century is given in the editor's introduction to *The Collected Works of Samuel Taylor Coleridge*, general ed. Kathleen Coburn (London and Princeton 1969–) 3: vol. I.
25 *History of "The Times": "The Thunderer" in the Making 1785–1841* (London 1935), p. 36.
26 Arthur Aspinall, "The Circulation of Newspapers in the Early Nineteenth Century," *Review of English Studies* XXII (Jan. 1946), 30. C claimed an average of ten readers for his weekly *PR*, many copies of which went to private subscribers. 4 *PR* 930.
27 *History of "The Times"*, pp. ix, 10–89, 120; letter to Windham [1803], Add. MSS. 37853, fol. 110; 1 *PR* 221; 2 *PR* 209; 8 *PR* 398; 10 *PR* 804, 807; 11 *PR* 234, 545–9; 12 *PR* 69, 77, 125, 129, 333; 33 *PR* 79–98; Arthur Aspinall, *Politics and the Press c. 1780–1850* (London 1949), pp. 66–192.
28 Aspinall, *Politics and the Press*, p. v.
      Henry Clifford, the legal writer, claiming that "almost the whole of the public press of that day was venal," demonstrated that it was possible to get an article published by paying five shillings to "one of the runners . . . for the papers." Henry Hunt, *Memoirs of Henry Hunt Esq. Written by Himself in His Majesty's Jail at Ilchester* (London 1820) I:543–4. See also 24 *PR* 358.
29 *History of "The Times"*, p. 33. There were a number of other newspapers representing commercial interests that had relatively slight influence on political issues. The *Morning Advertiser*, set up by London publicans, at one point had the largest circulation of any of the papers. Aspinall, *Politics and the Press*, p. 202n; 30 *PR* 676.

30 Aspinall, *Politics and the Press*, p. 206: "After 1805 *The Times* was completely independent." But this, presumably, refers only to financial independence, and even
here excludes government advertising, which *The Times* seems to have received
until around 1819. For an 1827 comment on press corruption see 62 *PR* 349–50.

31 H. R. Fox Bourne, *English Newspapers: Chapters of the History of Journalism* (London
1887) 1:221, 297–309; *Poetry of the Anti-Jacobin* ... with explanatory notes by
Charles Edmonds (2nd ed., London 1854), pp. 245–7. Government payments to
the *Courier* are referred to in *Collected Works of Coleridge* 3: vol. 1: cxxviii and Denis
Gray, *Spencer Perceval: The Evangelical Prime Minister 1762–1812* (Manchester
1963), p. 132. According to the latter, daily circulation around 1811 was: *Courier*,
5,800; *Times*, 5,000; *Morning Chronicle*, 3,500.

32 Lord Granville, Leveson-Gower (1st Earl Granville), *Private Correspondence 1781 to
1821*, ed. Countess Granville (London 1916) 1:329.

33 Add. MSS. 37853, fols. 12–13. The "swinish multitude," a phrase once used by
Burke, afterwards thrown up to him by adversaries to show his lack of sympathy
with The People, is here used cynically by one Burke admirer to another. In later
years C completely disavowed Burke's conservative philosophy, attributing it to his
government pension. See, for example, 22 *PR* 420; 30 *PR* 41.

34 *Letters to Hawkesbury*, pp. 6–8.

35 Ibid. pp. 17–18.

36 Letter of John Pershouse, Dec. 2, 1801 (American Philosophical Society).

37 The nine letters, combined with other material, were published in book form in
1802. "Of this production it was said by the celebrated Swiss historian, Muller, that
it was more eloquent than any thing that had appeared since the days of Demos-
thenes." *Morning Chronicle*, June 19, 1835.

38 *Letters to Hawkesbury*, p. 140.

39 Letter dated Oct. 24, 1801 (item 47, Sotheby's sale catalogue, London, Dec. 12,
1977).

40 Robert Southey, *Letters from England*, ed. Jack Simmons (London 1951), p. 73.

41 Beginning with the issue of October 15 the name of the paper was changed to the
Porcupine, and Antigallican Monitor, possibly reflecting C's sale of all or part of his
interest to John Gifford. See 4 *PR* 582. Gifford sold the paper to Redhead Yorke
and a Mr. Bateman late in November 1801. Letter to Windham, Nov. 24, 1801
(Add. MSS. 37853, fol. 17).
    The paper was called the *True Briton and Porcupine* from January 1 to April 3,
1802. Thereafter the *"and Porcupine"* was dropped.

42 Letter to Windham, Nov. 24, 1801, loc. cit. At another point C stated that he had
"sunk about £750 in the Porcupine." 8 *PR* 552.

43 *Porcupine*, Dec. 9, 1800.

44 32 *PR* 19–20. See also 8 *PR* 553. C's remarks were probably directed primarily to
the *Morning Post*.

45 In practice, every four or five weeks a double issue of 64 columns was published.
The price was the same.

46 32 *PR* 20. The contributors included two "private friends" of C's, not otherwise
identified, together with Windham and "eight other gentlemen of the New Opposition." 8 *PR* 553. Presumably, these were Dr. French Laurence, Gilbert Elliot
(later Lord Minto), Earl Spencer, Earl Fitzwilliam, and four Grenvilles: Thomas,
William, Lord Temple, and the Marquis of Buckingham. E. P. Smith, *Whig Principles and Party Politics: Earl Fitzwilliam and the Whig Party* (Manchester 1975),
p. 267.

47 This name was used from the start. Confusion has resulted from the fact that in
the first two years of publication the weekly parts were reprinted and bound
semiannually with an extended supplement. These four volumes were called *Cobbett's Annual Register*. Cf. M. L. Pearl, *William Cobbett: A Bibliographical Account of His*

Life and Times (London 1953), pp. 60–1. From 1817 to 1828 various minor changes were made in the original title. See Pearl, pp. 63–5.

Stanley Morison, in his review of the history of English newspapers, declared the *PR* "a first-class piece of up-to-date craftsmanship in printing." *The English Newspaper* (Cambridge 1932), p. 227.

48   4 *PR* 417, 737, 741. Wilberforce, after reading the glowing news accounts of one of Sheridan's drunken speeches, commented: "So true is what Cobbett said of his friendship to editors and reporters." Robin Furneaux, *William Wilberforce* (London 1974), p. 302.

49   *History of "The Times"*, p. 253.

50   R. I. and Samuel Wilberforce, *The Life of William Wilberforce* (London 1838) III:47.

51   1 *PR* 509–12, 671; 2 *PR* 60, 99–108.

52   1 *PR* 157.

53   1 *PR* 606, 671.

8. English justice

Motto: 7 *PR* 342. See also 19 *PR* 1199.

1   3 *PR* 1002. Bonaparte also complained directly to the British ambassador of "the abuse thrown out against him in the English public prints." 3 *PR* 1033, 1035. The French ambassador in London apparently offered to "prosecute their printer [who was writing against the British], if Addington will prosecute Cobbett." *Report on the Manuscripts of J. B. Fortescue, Esq. Preserved at Dropmore* (London 1892–1927) VII:131 (cited hereafter as *Dropmore Papers*).

2   The article in *L'Ambigu* was alleged to be an incitement to the assassination of Bonaparte, since it expressed a hope for his early "apotheosis." 3 *PR* 1232. Fox unfairly charged C with a similar offense for his statement – referring to Peltier and other French journalists in London – "were we Frenchmen we would not attack him with a pen." 2 *PR* 714–20. In 1818 C declared that the passage had been written by William Elliott; that he (C) had been approached by a Frenchman, Mehée de la Touche, with a plot to destroy Bonaparte but would have nothing to do with him. 33 *PR* 389–90.

3   3 *PR* 276, 1228.

4   Letter to Windham [Feb. or Mar. 1803], Add. MSS. 37853, fol. 68.

5   4 *PR* 445; 10 *PR* 585.

6   In February 1803 C had commenced the publication of a French version of *PR* entitled *Le Mercure Anglois de Cobbett* to be issued monthly; it was discontinued after a few issues. 3 *PR* 544; Pearl, *Cobbett*, p. 73.

7   4 *PR* 129–42.

8   15 *PR* 916; 71 *PR* 157. According to C, a phrase or two in the circular had been underlined by the prime minister. 15 *PR* 990.

9   4 *PR* 288.

10   4 *PR* 545, 586, 609, 801, 961. The manuscript had been handed to C "by a member of parliament; it had been certified to be true by a marquis and another member of parliament." 37 *PR* 1451.

11   4 *PR* 610, 612, 615, 616.

12   5 *PR* 801.

13   5 *PR* 850.

14   5 *PR* 859, 865, 894.

15   Blackstone III:357. The origin of the special jury and its extension to criminal prosecutions is described in Thomas Paine's "Letter to the Addressers on the Late Proclamation." Paine, *Political Works,* pp. 441–3.

16   Aspinall, *Politics and the Press,* p. 40.

17 Paine, *Political Works*, pp. 442–3. Lord Cochrane told parliament that persons paid to get on the special jury list and that if they displeased the judge care was taken to prevent them from serving again. 26 *PR* 38. The purity of special juries was defended by the then attorney general, Sir William Garrow. 26 *PR* 62–3.

18 19 *PR* 482; 22 *PR* 70.

19 Jeremy Bentham, *The Works of Jeremy Bentham*, ed. John Bowring (Edinburgh and London 1843) v:8on.

Henry Clifford was alleged to have said that "procuring and packing a special jury . . . was . . . invariably done in every political cause, where the crown was the prosecutor," hinting that this was a part of a more general venality that affected the bench and bar of the period. H. Hunt, *Memoirs* 1:474–5.

20 5 *PR* 834, 839. Lord Redesdale had urged that no action be instituted against C for the libel against him, but this seems to have been rejected by Addington and Eldon on the ground that it was a government issue rather than a personal matter. Perceval to Redesdale, Dec. 12, 1803 (Perceval papers).

21 5 *PR* 878.

22 Brougham's triumph occurred in 1814. Chester New, *The Life of Henry Brougham to 1830* (Oxford 1961), p. 160.

23 5 *PR* 858.

24 5 *PR* 854, 857. Four years later in a civil libel action brought by an author against a publisher criticizing his work, Ellenborough stated that "to repress just criticism would be extremely injurious to society" and, without saying so, completely disavowed the principle that a libel should be measured by the feelings of the one against whom the remarks were directed. 14 *PR* 167–8.

25 Bentham, *Works* v:107.

26 14 *PR* 161. The *Morning Chronicle* of May 24, 1804 had the courage to condemn Ellenborough's opinion.

27 The *DNB* article on John Philpot Curran states that C gave up Johnson's name. It seems more probable that C only gave up the manuscripts (37 *PR* 1451) and that the identification of the author was made by the government through the offices of "a Gentleman . . . from Ireland who . . . has not the least hesitation in pronouncing the manuscripts in question . . . were written by Mr. Justice Johnson." Perceval to Hawkesbury, June 20, 1804 (Duke).

28 *A Full and Faithful Report of the Proceedings in His Majesty's Court of Exchequer in Ireland, in the Case of Mr Justice Johnson, London, 1805, and Arguments of Counsel and Opinions of Judges in the Case of King v. Mr Justice Johnson, Court of King's Bench, Ireland* (Dublin 1805). 102 Eng. Reports 1412; 103 Eng. Reports 26.

29 9 *PR* 884; Perceval to Redesdale, June 10, 1805 (Perceval papers). The decision to pursue Johnson had been made at cabinet level. Perceval to Hawkesbury, June 20, 1804 (Duke).

30 Letter to Windham, Oct. 3, 1803, Add. MSS. 37853, fol. 94.

31 Perceval to Redesdale, Dec. 27, 1803 (Perceval papers).

32 Richard Glover, *Britain at Bay: Defence against Bonaparte 1803–14* (London 1973), pp. 100, 179.

33 3 *PR* 555.

34 R. H. Gronow, *Recollections and Anecdotes: Being a Second Series of Reminiscences . . .* (London 1863), pp. 210–11.

35 Holden Furber, *Henry Dundas, first Viscount Melville 1742–1811* (London 1931), p. 305, app. A; Samuel Rogers, *Recollections of the Table-Talk of Samuel Rogers . . .* ed. Morchard Bishop (London 1952), pp. 76–7.

36 7 *PR* 374.

37 7 *PR* 449–93. See 455, 456, 461, 463, 482.

38 7 *PR* 851, 877–8, 888–9.

39 7 *PR* 244.

40   7 *PR* 449, 481.
41   7 *PR* 554.
42   7 *PR* 546.
43   7 *PR* 550. Wilberforce's vote against Pitt on this issue has been cited as proof of
     his independence, but it could be cited with equal validity as proof of his desire to
     revenge himself on Dundas, who, in 1792, had sabotaged Wilberforce's motion for
     abolition of the slave trade by proposing it be accomplished "gradually." See R.
     Coupland, *Wilberforce: A Narrative* (Oxford 1923), pp. 164, 171, 299–301.
44   Granville, *Correspondence* 1:331.
45   *DNB;* Granville, 11:51.
46   Lord Rosebery, *Pitt* (London 1902 repr.), p. 250.
47   7 *PR* 927.
48   7 *PR* 973, 980, 983.
49   8 *PR* 714, 769, 865.
50   Rosebery, p. 251.
51   Anne, p. 22.
52   9 *PR* 985–7.
53   Granville 11:201.

9. "The system"

Motto: 9 *PR* 96. Cf. "The defect lies in the system." Thomas Paine, *Rights of Man* (Penguin ed. 1976), p. 284.

1   Rosebery, *Pitt,* p. 61.
2   8 *PR* 97.
3   2 *PR* 56.
4   4 *PR* 905. C's attitude toward Pitt had changed much earlier. In his letter to
     French Laurence of October 28, 1802 (Illinois), he calls Pitt a "miserable charla-
     tan" and refers to his "shabby tricks," and in December 1802 C made it clear that
     Pitt alone, without a radical change in the system, would not do. 2 *PR* 702–3.
        Had Pitt changed, or had his real character been revealed? When he first
     appeared on the scene, Paine and many others thought that "He gave symptoms
     of a mind superior to the meanness and corruption of courts." *Rights of Man,*
     p. 284. Wilberforce, looking at Hoppner's portrait of Pitt, painted near the end of
     his life, exclaimed: "a vile picture – his face anxious, diseased, reddened with wine,
     and soured and irritated by disappointments. Poor fellow, how unlike my youthful
     Pitt." Coupland, *Wilberforce,* p. 446.
5   6 *PR* 456–7.
6   Pitt's "want of firmness . . . inflicted an injury upon the empire, the evil conse-
     quences of which to this day are felt in the relations between England and Ire-
     land." David Plunket, *The Life, Letters, and Speeches of Lord Plunket* (London 1867)
     1:285.
7   4 *PR* 92.
8   2 *PR* 633–4.
9   7 *PR* 89–90.
10   Seven out of eleven of Pitt's ministry had been in Addington's. 7 *PR* 91.
11   7 *PR* 827, 866, 871, 879–81, 897, 963f.
12   7 *PR* 939.
13   Anne, p. 14.
14   2 *PR* 56. 14 *PR* 837: "they are both gentlemen of fortune and of respectable fam-
     ily; and, of such members of parliament ought to consist."
15   7 *PR* 597.
16   4 *PR* 739.

17 C. E. Fryer, "The General Election of 1784," *History* n.s. IX (Oct. 1924), 221.
18 Richard Pares, *King George III and the Politicians* (Oxford 1953), p. 125n, quoting Fox.
19 Furber, *Melville*, app. A.
20 5 *PR* 589; 11 *PR* 331. See also Steven J. Watson, *The Reign of George III 1760–1815* (Oxford 1960), p. 291.
21 7 *PR* 289.
22 *Manchester Lectures*, p. 95; 81 *PR* 785. *Collected Works of Coleridge* 4: vol. 1:lxviii: "there is reason to believe that various forms of stock-jobbing continued to be a regular Stuartian [editor of the *Courier*] perquisite of journalism." And see 42 *PR* 723: "it was common to let newspaper editors and clerks in offices have what was called a *slice of a loan*."
23 7 *PR* 32.
24 7 *PR* 510.
25 7 *PR* 655; 8 *PR* 103.
26 7 *PR* 28.
27 *DNB*; 2 *PR* 54, 67–71; 9 *PR* 243; 11 *PR* 108; C. R. Fay, *Huskisson and His Age* (London 1951), p. 42. Much later C wrote an interesting analysis of Huskisson's abilities. 82 *PR* 458.
28 Brougham, *Historical Sketches* II:171.
29 *DNB*.
30 2 *PR* 56.
31 Ibid.
32 Rosebery, *Pitt*, p. 230.
33 Granville, *Correspondence* I:320.
34 Philip Ziegler, *A Life of Henry Addington, First Viscount Sidmouth* (London 1965), pp. 19, 23.
35 4 *PR* 397, 412.
36 2 *PR* 164; 8 *PR* 8.
37 Ziegler, pp. 239, 241.
38 Richard Pares, *The Historian's Business and Other Essays* (Oxford 1961), p. 125.
39 Quoted by Lewis Namier, *The Structure of Politics at the Accession of George III* (2nd ed., London 1961), p. 158.
40 *ER* x (July 1807), 413–15.
41 ". . . being thus disciplined to corruption by the mode of entering into parliament, it is not to be expected that the representative should be better than the man." Paine, *Rights of Man*, p. 246.
42 Public property on Pall Mall leased to the Duke of Marlborough for £62 a year was re-leased by him for £3,000 a year. The Duke of Buckingham's house on Pall Mall was rented by him from the government for £15 a year to 1808, and thereafter for £54 a year. 44 *PR* 15; 45 *PR* 112.
43 Pares, *George III*, pp. 7, 17–26. "The post of Colonel of a Regiment is a sinecure in fact; and . . . you will not find twenty out of nearly two hundred, which are not in the hands of the Borough families. So it is with the staff." 32 *PR* 698. In the navy, young men of good family were advanced over the heads of thousands of more experienced officers. 50 *PR* 217–22, 257–92. "Out of every five young men called to the bar, four assume the character and garb for the purpose of obtaining employment under the government." 32 *PR* 771.
44 14 *PR* 585–6. In 1806, appointments to the army, navy, church, law, colonies, and home service were estimated at several hundred thousand with total annual emoluments of £20 million. *ER*, July 1809, p. 285, quoted by Arthur Aspinall, *Lord Brougham and the Whig Party* (Manchester 1927), p. 43.
45 9 *PR* 163. Men of influence secured clerical appointments for their sons, who "coolly and solemnly" declared that they were " 'moved and called . . . by the Holy

Ghost', when, they well know, all the while, that they are really called to the office, by the base corruption of their fathers!" 32 *PR* 789. See also 44 *PR* 342.

46 Some examples not previously noted: 7 *PR* 708n, 788–91, 809–10; 8 *PR* 21–3, 60; 9 *PR* 165; 10 *PR* 693, 749; 11 *PR* 108–17, 545–9. In 1804 the king told George Rose that he thought the press was being "remarkably well managed." George Rose, *The Diaries and Correspondence of the Right Hon. George Rose*, ed. L. V. Harcourt (London 1860) II:175.

For a treatise on the venality of the British quartermasters, see James Thomas Flexner, *States Dyckman: American Loyalist* (Boston 1980).

47 34 *PR* 980–1.

48 13 *PR* 873; 33 *PR* 679; 46 *PR* 21; 66 *PR* 61. The usual price of a reviewer, "as well known as that of bread or beer," was "half a guinea and a copy of the book itself." 34 *PR* 267.

49 16 *PR* 7; 14 *PR* 805–16; 16 *PR* 585.

50 6 *PR* 618. C became convinced that if Pitt had lived a few more months "he would have been routed from his office." 41 *PR* 399.

51 9 *PR* 897; 10 *PR* 85; 15 *PR* 322; 17 *PR* 398–9.

52 19 *PR* 43–4, part of an extended discussion of Pitt's talents and shortcomings beginning at p. 37. C's analysis appears extreme, but the essence of what he said is supported by the mature comments of Wilberforce, one of Pitt's oldest and closest friends, who regretted Pitt's failure to "govern by principle rather than by influence." Coupland, *Wilberforce*, pp. 325–6. Pitt's great oratorical skills, which C greatly admired, are brilliantly described at 33 *PR* 368–70.

53 9 *PR* 95. A French-American visitor to England in 1809–11 wrote: "its political institutions present a detail of corrupt practices ... and of personal ambition, under the mask of public spirit ... more disgusting than I should have expected." Louis Simond, *An American in Regency England ...* ed. Christopher Hibbert (London 1968), p. 166.

54 9 *PR* 143.

55 8 *PR* 105–17; 9 *PR* 96.

56 "Mr. Fox ... went into this coalition with great reluctance ... Mr. Fox told me so himself." 30 *PR* 521.

57 9 *PR* 164.

58 9 *PR* 168–70.

59 4 *PR* 229.

60 67 *PR* 327–8.

61 Letter to Windham, Sept. 27, 1803, Add. MSS. 37853, fol. 92; letter from Windham, Oct. 9, 1803, ibid. fols. 95–8.

62 56 *PR* 582; 64 *PR* 208; 77 *PR* 649; *Manchester Lectures*, p. 85.

63 Letters to Windham, Feb. 10 and 23, 1806, Add. MSS. 37853, fols. 211–12, 218–19.

C also wanted Windham to retain, as his undersecretary, Granville Penn, brother of C's "preserver," John Penn, referred to at 8 *PR* 551. Letters to Windham, Feb. 14, Mar. 2 and 9, 1806, Add. MSS. 37853, fols. 213, 223, 225; letter from Windham, Mar. 6, 1806 (Baring Bros. archives); Windham to Grenville, Feb. 16, 1806 in *Dropmore Papers* VIII:33.

64 Freeling, who had been a subscriber to the twelve volumes of C's *Works*, received over £3,000 a year from his overseas franking privileges. He seems to have had an interest in the *Sun* newspaper; he used the post office facilities to distribute anti-Cobbett material; and he encouraged the circulation of "no-popery" propaganda during the general election of 1807. Aspinall, *Politics and the Press*, pp. 23, 24n, 78, 87, 177–9.

Twenty years later the breach appears to have been mended. In 1827 C praised the quality of the postal service. 64 *PR* 611, 838. In 1829 a post office advertise-

ment appeared in the *Political Register,* but apparently only one. 68 *PR* 384.
The troubles of *The Times* with the corrupt post office are described in *History of "The Times",* pp. 96–108.

65 Add. MSS. 34455, fols. 393–409. It appears from the original complaint, although not from the version printed in *PR,* that C and Freeling were also in dispute over postal charges of some £9 for magazines sent to C in Philadelphia.

66 2 *PR* 673–86; Pearl, *Cobbett,* p. 71. Auckland's reply stated that the practice was of long standing, and that C had misconceived Freeling's "character & meaning." Add. MSS. 34455, fols. 417–19.

67 2 *PR* 607.

68 Letter from Windham, Mar. 6, 1806 (Baring Bros. archives); 73 *PR* 744.

69 9 *PR* 193–201.

70 9 *PR* 195–6. Parliament passed a bill permitting Grenville to hold the incompatible positions. See 11 *PR* 522.

71 9 *PR* 199. C's continuing grudge against Grenville was expressed publicly (e.g. 16 *PR* 428–32; 33 *PR* 598) as well as privately. See letters to Wright, Add. MSS. 22906, fols. 202, 272.

72 Letter to Windham, Feb. 23, 1806, Add. MSS. 37853, fols. 218–19.

73 *The Diary of the Right Hon. William Windham 1784 to 1810,* ed. Mrs. Henry Baring (London 1866), p. 460.

74 9 *PR* 314–20.

75 Letter to Windham, Mar. 9, 1806, Add. MSS. 37853, fol. 225.

76 C's attitude toward Fox is complicated by two elements: (1) C's changes in principles and, to a lesser extent, those of Fox and (2) C's inclination to distinguish Fox's liberal statements from his performance as a politician. C had so violently attacked Fox's Jacobin tendencies when Fox visited Bonaparte in 1802 as to "greatly hurt" Earl Fitzwilliam, one of the original contributors to the fund for starting the *Porcupine.* E. P. Smith, *Whig Principles,* pp. 267–8. C became an open supporter of Fox after he joined forces with Grenville and Windham in 1804: "Fox the friend of France had me for an enemy: Fox the enemy of France has me for a friend." Letter to Windham [Nov. or Dec. 1803], Add. MSS. 37853, fol. 103. See also 8 *PR* 656. In 1806 C turned against Fox for his acquiescent performance in the ministry of All the Talents, but in the same year, when C became concerned about the trend toward strong-arm government, he wrote to his business associate John Wright: "I hope Fox will live long yet; for, I am always afraid, that were he dead tyranny, sheer unmixed tyranny, would be let loose upon the land." July 30, 1806, Add. MSS. 22906, fol. 177. Thereafter C frequently spoke of his respect for Fox as a liberal: in 1810 ("his words will never die"), in 1811 ("always on the side of humanity"), and in 1822 ("hated by nobody; loved by a great many"). 18 *PR* 1092; 20 *PR* 454; 43 *PR* 573–4. But in 1816 C expressed his dislike of Fox's performance as politician ("lived and died a sinecure placeman and pensioner"). 30 *PR* 269. See also 31 *PR* 487, 645; 63 *PR* 525; 76 *PR* 807.

77 Letter to Windham, July 9, 1802, Add. MSS. 37853, fol. 43.

78 *Journals of the House of Commons* LIX:398 (July 9, 1804).

79 2 *PR* 1772–3; 6 *PR* 343–8.

80 6 *PR* 262. In 1802 C stated: "we detest and loath Sir Francis Burdett . . . for his . . . assertions respecting his and our sovereign," but defended Burdett's tactics as being less objectionable than those of the ministry (2 *PR* 151–2), and earlier stated: "we do not despair, notwithstanding present appearances, of seeing Sir Francis a . . . very loyal gentleman." 2 *PR* 90. C explained his 1802 position at 10 *PR* 748–54.

81 6 *PR* 261; 6 *PR* 339.

82 6 *PR* 334.

83 6 *PR* 340–1.

84 6 *PR* 290–4.

85 7 *PR* 400–6; *Journals of the House of Commons* LXI:35 (Feb. 10, 1806). See *Annual Register* for 1806, p. 369.

86 M. W. Patterson, *Sir Francis Burdett and His Times (1770–1844)* (London 1931) I:151; 10 *PR* 558.

87 H. Hunt, *Memoirs* I:544.

88 9 *PR* 833. The constitutional compromise of 1707 allowed a member of the House of Commons to accept a place under the crown but forced him to vacate his seat and stand for reelection. Pares, *George III*, p. 8.

89 9 *PR* 833–4.

90 Broughton, *Recollections* II:96. Cochrane's foreign service was in Brazil, Chile, and Greece.

91 9 *PR* 877f.

92 Letter to Denis O'Bryen [May 1806] (American Philosophical Society). See also letter to Swann, May 26, 1806 (Bodleian).

93 9 *PR* 880.

94 Ibid.

95 This is the story as told in Lord Cochrane's "autobiography" published in 1860, shortly before Cochrane's death. Thomas Cochrane, *The Autobiography of a Seaman by Thomas, Tenth Earl of Dundonald* (London 1860) I:179–81, 202–3. It was written at least in part by George Earp with the help of Cochrane's secretary, William Jackson, when Cochrane's memory was failing. In a debate in the House of Commons on January 29, 1817, Cochrane had asserted that he had paid the Honiton voters ten guineas each the time he was "first returned as a member to the House," and offered to show the bills and vouchers which he had for the money. Hansard, 1st ser. XXXV:92. See also 221 (Feb. 5, 1817) and XXXVI:600 (May 15, 1817). It is possible that the "bills and vouchers" were for the Honiton post-election dinner, which cost £1,200 and which Cochrane refused to pay for. Christopher Lloyd, *Lord Cochrane . . .* (London 1947), p. 85.

96 9 *PR* 970–1. See also 31 *PR* 806.

97 9 *PR* 145. See 15 *PR* 619.

98 9 *PR* 462.

99 9 *PR* 911.

100 9 *PR* 790–1. "We now know that the Pitts and Grenvilles and Foxes are all alike." 10 *PR* 229. Compare: "All this seems to show that change of ministers amounts to nothing. One goes out, another comes in, and still the same measures, vices, and extravagances are pursued." Paine, *Rights of Man*, p. 284. Because the whigs claimed to be the defenders of public liberty, C tended to blame them more for their inaction than he blamed the tories for their oppressive actions. See, for example, C's attacks on Earl Fitzwilliam and his son, Lord Milton. 34 *PR* 1006.

101 9 *PR* 972.

10. Botley

Motto: *Advice*, para. 282.

1 Add. MSS. 37853, fol. 177.

2 Mary Russell Mitford, *Recollections of a Literary Life* (London 1859), p. 199, where she mistakenly refers to the river as the "Bursledon"; 12 *PR* 13.

3 *Advice*, para. 283.

4 *Advice*, para. 290.

5 *Advice*, paras. 291, 293, 292.

6 *English Grammar*, letter I.

7 *Advice*, para. 290; 65 *PR* 511; Jeremiah O'Callaghan, *Usury* (London 1828), p. 25.

In 1804 William spent a month in a school at Twyford, while Anne was in a school at Winchester for a longer period. William, John, and Anne attended school in Bishop's Waltham in 1805–6, and the two boys were at Micheldever in 1807–8 and there or somewhere else in Hampshire in 1809.

8 Anne, pp. 13, 18, 23.

9 *Advice*, para. 283.

10 60 *PR* 175–6 (*Rural Rides*, p. 417).

11 JPC, p. 25; Anne, pp. 17, 18. In 1819 C said: "Before they imprisoned me I was now and then tempted to drink wine and spirits and water." 35 *PR* 12. In 1809 he had said that he drank no wine. 16 *PR* 99.

12 *Advice*, para. 293.

13 *Advice*, para. 292. C added the word "more" to each of the three phrases quoted from Prov. 24:33.

14 *Advice*, para. 287.

15 *Advice*, para. 178.

16 *Letters to Thornton*, p. 111.

17 Susan (Nuffield xvii:6).

18 16 *PR* 115.

19 16 *PR* 918; 36 *PR* 29.

20 16 *PR* 115.

21 18 *PR* 141.

22 16 *PR* 111–12.

23 JPC, pp. 26, 29.

24 16 *PR* 116. See also *Two-Penny Trash*, Oct. 1, 1830, pp. 83–5.

25 Alexander Somerville, *The Whistler at the Plough* (London 1852), p. 263.

26 H. Hunt, *Memoirs* iii:21–4. An analysis of C's farm account book suggests that he was "strict in his dealings, yet at most times kind and generous." M. L. Pearl, "Cobbett and His Men," *Countryman* xliv (Autumn 1951), 118.

27 Dyckman papers, doc. 561 (New York Historical Society).

28 Thomas Moore, *Memoirs, Journal and Correspondence of Thomas Moore*, ed. Lord John Russell (London 1856) ii:356, viii:86.

29 Mitford, *Recollections*, p. 200.

30 *Advice*, paras. 168, 217.

31 *Advice*, para. 161.

32 *Advice*, para. 92.

33 *Advice*, para. 176.

34 *Advice*, paras. 103–9.

35 Henry Hunt, who was disliked by Nancy, seems responsible for the accusation that she had difficulty with her help. H. Hunt, *Memoirs* iii:21; *Advice*, para. 115. C does ambiguously suggest that his wife "has made her servants humble," but perhaps this was the result of her breadmaking skills. Letter to Wright, July 28, 1805, Add. MSS. 22906, fol. 64.

36 *Advice*, para. 192.

37 *Advice*, paras. 165, 168.

38 *Advice*, paras. 189, 190. C had frequent occasion to respect his wife's better assessment of his coadjutors and friends. 36 *PR* 35.

39 *Advice*, para. 186.

40 Add. MSS. 22907, fols. 72, 164, 186; *Advice*, para. 109; 42 *PR* 188. See also 69 *PR* 711. In C's tory years he had been an admirer of the lady and she of him. Letter to Hannah More, Oct. 20, 1800 (Illinois). Presumably the children read aloud to their mother.

"When times are *smooth* she will contradict and blame me often enough," C wrote on Dec. 25, 1799. *Letters to Thornton*, p. 26.

41 Letters to Wright, Mar. 2 and 4, 1806, Add. MSS. 22906, fols. 51, 141.

42 Letter to Wright [Aug. 1806?], ibid. fol. 181.

43 Letter to Wright, Oct. 17, 1805, ibid. fol. 96.

44 *Advice,* paras. 165, 167, 189, 196. See also paras. 250–2.

45 *Advice,* para. 166.

46 *Advice,* para. 228.

47 *Advice,* paras. 256–8.

48 *Advice,* para. 257. Many of C's ideas about education seem to have been derived from *Emile,* although, as can be seen, he gives Rousseau little credit.

49 Mitford, *Recollections,* pp. 200–1. The red waistcoat mentioned by Miss Mitford and/or a red kerchief tied around the neck, noted by other observers, matched C's naturally florid complexion.

50 Ibid. p. 200.

51 Anne, p. 22.

52 Letter to O'Bryen, Dec. 31, 1805 (American Philosophical Society); Frank Swinnerton, *A Galaxy of Fathers* (London 1966), pp. 219f.

53 Letter to Wright, Sept. 28, 1806, Add. MSS. 22906, fol. 202.

54 Letter to Windham, Oct. 6, 1805, Add. MSS. 37853, fol. 184.

55 Letter to Wright [Sept. 1806], Add. MSS. 22906, fol. 187. The second tournament was held on September 18, 1806.

56 8 *PR* 200.

57 10 *PR* 991, 993, 1000, 1003; 11 *PR* 5; 16 *PR* 417.

58 1 *PR* 603, 626, 636, 667, 773; 2 *PR* 634; 5 *PR* 112; 8 *PR* 193, 371, 417, 442, 459; 9 *PR* 226, 364; 10 *PR* 269; 12 *PR* 485.

59 8 *PR* 195–200.

60 12 *PR* 485.

61 Letter to Wright, Dec. 25, 1805, Add. MSS. 22906, fol. 117.

62 Letter to Wright, Feb. 2, 1807, ibid. fol. 243.

63 Letter to Colnaghi, Jan. 13, 1808 (Illinois); JPC, p. 29.

64 Letter to Wright, Nov. 29, 1807 (Illinois). C also bought trees (limes, planes, and sycamores) twelve to fifteen feet high from a Brompton nursery, which he planted at Botley. *Woodlands,* para. 46.

65 Letter to Wright, Nov. 10, 1805, Add. MSS. 22906, fol. 102.

66 Susan's note of land bought by C (Nuffield xviii); letters to Swann, May 26, 1806 (Bodleian), Mitford, Apr. 22, 1808 (Illinois), and Wright, Apr. 23, 1807 and May 13, 1808, Add. MSS. 22906, fol. 277 and 22907, fol. 7.

67 JPC, p. 105; Susan's note of land bought by C (Nuffield xviii). The Cock Street purchase was financed in the first instance with promissory notes or discounted bills. Letter from Swann, Sept. 18, 1805, Add. MSS. 22906, fol. 78; letter to Wright, Sept. 20, 1805, ibid. fol. 80. In 1817 and 1820 the mortgages on the Botley property amounted to £16,000 or £17,000. *QR* xxi:136n; C's Statement of 1820 (Illinois); 32 *PR* 526.

68 Letter to Wright, Mar. 20, 1808, Add. MSS. 31126, fol. 34. Interest was limited by law to 5 percent, and that appears to have been the rate at which C borrowed. Letter to Swann, Sept. 18, 1805, Add. MSS. 22906, fol. 78. Discounting cost more than mortgaging "but was pleasanter in many respects." Letter from Swann, Sept. 22 [1805], ibid. fol. 81.

   C estimated that his timber sales amounted to £4,500. Statement of 1820 (Illinois).

69 C never planted more than thirty-one acres of wheat. In 1810 he planted only enough "for the consumption of my own house." 18 *PR* 939–40.

70 Anne, pp. 23–4. As early as 1807 C was importing seeds and young trees from America. Letter to Wright, Jan. 30, 1807, Add. MSS. 22906, fol. 242.

71 Letters to Wright, Oct. 22, 1807 (Illinois) and July 11, 1808, Add. MSS. 22907, fol. 24.

72 4 *PR* 929. Sales had reached 2,000 at January 1803. 3 *PR* 1.

73 The first number of the *Parliamentary Debates* was Dec. 3, 1803 (4 *PR* 800); the first volume was published in June 1804. Pearl, *Cobbett*, p. 76. In December 1810 C announced that thereafter the debates would be "published in parts." 18 *PR* 1228.

74 17 *PR* 203; Gaines, *Cobbett*, p. 15.

75 Letter to Hibbert, Dec. 29, 1805, Add. MSS. 22906, fol. 119.

76 Wright moved into C's house at 15 Duke Street in 1803 or 1804 and lived there with the family (and later alone) to the end of 1805, just prior to the time it was relinquished by C. The *Satirist* quotation appears in Edward Smith, *William Cobbett: A Biography* (London, 1878) II:110n.

77 The quotations are a small sample for 1806–7: Add. MSS. 22906, fols. 139, 157, 199, 204; Jan. 11, 1807 (Cornell); May 17, 1807 (Illinois).

78 Wright to Swann, June 30, 1806 (Bodleian) states that 4,750 copies are to be printed. C had previously ordered that 750 copies in excess of current sales be printed to "lay bye." Letter to Wright, Aug. 31, 1804, Add. MSS. 22906, fol. 20. The £1,000 of annual income is based on 4,750 copies at 6½d., i.e. sale price less stamp tax. Regular newspapers were allowed a 16 percent discount from the stamp price for torn and unsold numbers, but C was allowed only 4.9 percent. 15 *PR* 349.

79 By 1817 circulation had fallen to 1,600, but C claimed that his income from the *PR* was "never less than fifteen hundred pounds a year, I believe." 32 *PR* 536, 566. In 1820 C claimed that the *PR* from 1802 to 1816 "yielded" an average of about £2,500 a year, a figure hard to reconcile with C's financial condition at the end of the period. Statement of 1820 (Illinois).

80 The *Parliamentary History* and *State Trials* "were undertaken with the *certainty of sinking* money for some time . . . possibly for ever." 18 *PR* 19. In 1820 C claimed that these publications plus the *Parliamentary Debates* over their lifetime (presumably he meant up to the date he disposed of his interest, 1811) had cleared "not exceeding" £1,000. Statement of 1820 (Illinois).

81 A large number of the bills of exchange and notes for the period 1801–9 are in the Cornell library.

82 Much of the discounting was arranged by Swann, C's paper supplier. Swann to Wright, June 26, 1807, Add. MSS. 22906, fol. 296.

83 Money was borrowed from Richard Smith, George Crosby, Thomas Hughan, Richard Phillips, Lord Cochrane, Everard Tunno, Holt White, John Reeves, Timothy Brown, and probably others.

84 JPC, p. 22; letter to Wright, Nov. 29, 1807 (Illinois). The money laid out in improvements was not "spent." Letters to Wright, July 11 and Nov. 15, 1808, Add. MSS. 22907, fols. 24, 78.

85 The Pall Mall bookshop was taken over by E. Harding on January 1, 1803. In 1820 C claimed that when he began the *PR* he was about £5,000 in debt from losses from the *Porcupine* and from books published and books sent to America. Statement of 1820 (Illinois). In 1805 C put his loss from the *Porcupine* at £750. 8 *PR* 552.

86 8 *PR* 551. The "Mr. Penn" was John Penn, grandson of William Penn. C unsuccessfully urged Windham to retain John Penn's brother as undersecretary when Windham became minister in 1806. Letter to Windham, Mar. 2, 1806, Add. MSS. 37853, fol. 223; *Dropmore Papers* VIII:33.

87 Feb. 1, 1804, Dyckman papers, doc. 843 (New York Historical Society). C was also unable to pay his printers. Letter to Cadell & Davies, Feb. 18, 1804 (Yale).

88 Letters to Windham, July 15, 1804 and Oct. 27, 1804, Add. MSS. 37853, fols. 127–8, 144.

89 Petitions to State of Pennsylvania (Haverford, p. 4 and Historical Society of Penn-

sylvania, p. 5). The money paid out by C in 1804 had been set aside by him since 1800.

90 Letter to Wright [1804], Add. MSS. 22906, fol. 22.

91 Letter to de Daudon, July 18, 1806 (author's possession). Probable speculations: (1) Merino sheep imported from Spain: letter to Sir John Sinclair, June 20, 1809 (Bathurst papers); (2) rum: letters to Wright, Add. MSS. 22906, fols. 44, 116, 126, 287, 288; (3) tobacco: letter to North, June 25, 1806 (Boston Public Library); (4) Winchester turnpike: Anne, p. 32.

92 Letter to Wright, Nov. 27, 1807, Add. MSS. 22906, fol. 334.

93 Letter to Swann, May 9, 1809 (University of London). See also letter to Wright [Nov. 10, 1805], Add. MSS. 22906, fol. 102. C thought that land "will never depreciate." 19 PR 845.

94 Letter to Wright, Nov. 27, 1807, Add. MSS. 22906, fol. 334; Anne, p. 23.

95 Letter to Wright, Nov. 29, 1807 (Illinois): bond land "gives a man no weight in the county."

96 Visits: Mitford, Recollections, pp. 199f; letters to Wright, Add. MSS. 22906, fols. 70, 73, 164; Warren Derry, Dr Parr: A Portrait of the Whig Dr Johnson (Oxford 1966), p. 249. Coursing invitations: letters to Wright, Add. MSS. 22906, fol. 202, and Nov. 29, 1807 (Illinois).

97 Lord Dartmouth to Samuel Lysons (Dartmouth College). The letter has been misdated Jan. 9, 1796, but obviously was written in 1802 or 1803 before Lysons became keeper of Tower of London records in the latter year.

98 15 PR 817.

99 Letter to Wright, Oct. 10, 1807 (Illinois).

100 JPC, p. 92. 32 PR 917–18: "You, and all who have seen my family, know me to be the most kind and indulgent of parents, and, that my children fear neither my blows, nor my frowns, but fear only to give me pain." See also 56 PR 548–9.

11. Westminster elections

Motto: 10 PR 496. See also 30 PR 519 (1816): "The old appellations of Whig and Tory really have had no application in England for nearly half a century." Jonathan Swift, in his Letter to a Whig Lord (1712), had declared that the words were really obsolete.

1 The 100 members elected in Ireland resulted from the Act of Union effective January 1, 1801. Most of the figures referred to in the passages that follow relate to England alone. The electoral structure in Ireland and Scotland was, if anything, more reprehensible. Elie Halévy, A History of the English People in the Nineteenth Century (London 1924–47) II:116–22; Michael Brock, The Great Reform Act (London 1973), pp. 31–3.

2 The county members were increased to 82 in 1821 when Grampound was disenfranchised and its two members added to those already held by Yorkshire.

3 Blackstone I:172.

4 Namier, Structure of Politics, pp. 64–5.

5 Ibid. p. 80. The system remained practically unchanged from 1660 to 1832. Ibid. p. 75.

6 Edward Porritt, The Unreformed House of Commons: Parliamentary Representation before 1832 (New York 1963 repr.) I:4–5.

7 G. Lowes Dickinson, The Development of Parliament during the Nineteenth Century (London 1895), p. 6; Samuel Romilly, Memoirs of the Life of Sir Samuel Romilly, ed. his sons (3rd ed., London 1840) II:206.

8 Dickinson, p. 5.

9 ". . . probably not more than one in every twenty voters at county elections could

freely exercise his statutory rights." Namier, p. 73. This confirms C's claim that the freeholders in nineteen instances out of twenty had "nothing to do with the matter but to go to the polling place and utter certain words . . . their thoughts and wishes have no effect." 38 *PR* 714.

10 Namier, pp. 78–9. In 1754, when Wilkes was standing for Berwick, his opposition hired a boat to bring their supporters from London, but Wilkes bribed the captain to take them to Norway. C. B. Roylance Kent, *The English Radicals: An Historical Sketch* (London 1899), p. 32n.

11 Pares, *George III*, p. 9n.

12 Romilly, *Memoirs* II:206.

13 11 *PR* 578. See also 12 *PR* 47.

14 E. L. Woodward, *The Age of Reform 1815–1870* (Oxford 1939 repr.), p. 23.

15 Hansard XXX:795 (May 6, 1793). John Wilkes in 1776 asserted that 254 members were elected by 5,723 persons. George Rudé (ed.), *The Eighteenth Century* (London 1965), p. 179. Namier concluded that before the Act of Union, 235 borough seats were "under patronage" (*Structure of Politics*, p. 150). Cobbett in 1807 stated that parliament was "composed for one half of placemen and pensioners, and for nearly the other half, of dealers in the funds." 11 *PR* 802. According to Maddocks, "there were only 186 tolerably uninfluenced men" in parliament. Gray, *Perceval*, p. 207. John Wade's *Black Book* of 1820 claimed that 300 members of the lower house were returned by peers (p. 423); for another type of distribution see p. 445. John Wilson Croker in 1827 claimed that 276 seats were at the disposal of landed patrons. Woodward, *Age of Reform*, p. 24.

Approximately half of the House of Lords as it stood in 1811 had been promoted in or to the peerage by Perceval and "his predecessors of the same party and school" (i.e. since Pitt took office in 1783). 19 *PR* 22.

16 10 *PR* 679–80.

17 Henry Thomas Buckle, *History of Civilization in England* (new ed., Toronto 1878) I:500n.

18 Henry Stooks Smith, *The Parliaments of England from 1715 to 1847*, ed. F. W. S. Craig (2nd ed., Chichester 1973), pp. 207, 215.

19 10 *PR* 193.

20 According to the translation by H. J. Tozer (London 1902, p. 187), Rousseau's language reads: "The English nation thinks that it is free, but it is greatly mistaken, for it is so only during the election of members of Parliament; as soon as they are elected, it is enslaved and counts for nothing. The use which it makes of the brief moments of freedom renders the loss of liberty well-deserved." *The Social Contract*, bk. III, ch. xv.

21 10 *PR* 199.

22 10 *PR* 194.

23 Sheridan's great plays had been written when he was in his twenties. In his calmer moments, C was capable of a judicious appraisal of an opponent's merits. In 1824 he wrote: "Look at Sheridan: there was talent beyond that of all his contemporaries. There was eloquence; there was experience; there was extensive knowledge all on the subjects with which he had to meddle; and there was political philosophy, too, more profound than that of any other man of his day. Yet on this man, and chiefly because he was continually hunting after newspaper fame, nobody would rely, and he was at last shut disdainfully and justly out of the King's Cabinet by a man who had not a hundredth part of his talents." 53 *PR* 234–5.

24 Sheridan's election expenses for 1784 included 248 burgesses at five guineas each. Thomas Moore, *Memoirs of the Life of the Rt. Hon. Richard Brinsley Sheridan* (4th ed., London 1826) I:405.

25 10 *PR* 453.

26 10 *PR* 482. The Crown and Anchor on the Strand at Arundel Street was a favorite

public meeting place, since it had a room capable of seating upwards of 2,000 persons.

27 10 *PR* 483.

28 The facts seem to have been that on September 17, 1806, the day before he met his friends at the Crown and Anchor, Sheridan had "settled everything amicably" with Wilson, Lord Percy's man of business. Earl of Moira to Prince of Wales, Sept. 17, 1806. Arthur Aspinall (ed.), *The Correspondence of George, Prince of Wales 1770–1812* (London 1963–71), no. 2228. See also letter 2230, Duke of Northumberland to McMahon. Although C's initial hunch was, therefore, nearly correct, he later was given the false assurance that here had been no understanding between Percy and Sheridan. 10 *PR* 842. Francis Place (or his biographer) regarded Sheridan as "a sham candidate." Graham Wallas, *The Life of Francis Place* (rev. ed., London 1918), p. 41.

29 10 *PR* 513. Charles C. F. Greville, *The Greville Memoirs: A Journal of the Reigns of King George IV . . .* ed. Henry Reeve (new ed., London 1888) 1:233.

30 10 *PR* 545. See letter from Frederick Homan, 10 *PR* 554.

31 10 *PR* 552–3.

32 The dissolution occurred on October 24, 1806. The decision to dissolve had been taken at a cabinet meeting on October 13, and on October 14 Sheridan was advised that the government would accept "in a very handsome way" Sheridan's offer to stand for Westminster at the coming general election. Richard Brinsley Sheridan, *The Letters,* ed. Cecil Price (Oxford 1960) II:286n, 288.

33 41 *PR* 398, 403, 418.

34 9 *PR* 724. See 8 *PR* 14.

35 June 25 and July 7, 1806, Add. MSS. 22706, fols. 163, 168. See 41 *PR* 418: "His manners and habits were wholly contrary to my taste."

36 10 *PR* 675. Burdett supplied Paull with £1,000 for his campaign. C claimed that the election cost him nearly £500. 41 *PR* 415.

37 10 *PR* 709.

38 Samuel Foote's play *The Mayor of Garratt* portraying the tailor with goose and cabbages, first presented in 1763, was still popular with theatergoers in 1806.

39 R. Compton Rhodes, *Harlequin Sheridan: The Man and the Legend* (Oxford 1933), p. 215.

40 10 *PR* 755; Rhodes, p. 212. Lord Holland also managed to obtain "some reluctant assistance" for Sheridan from the ministry. On November 5 the accumulated vote was Hood, 1,281; Sheridan, 789; and Paull, 1,516. Sheridan, *Letters* II:293n, 295n. The conspiracy against Paull was described by C at 41 *PR* 398–411.

41 10 *PR* 812.

42 10 *PR* 1002.

43 According to Brougham, Windham was the most distinguished among the members of his party "agreeing ill" with Sheridan, and "treating him with little deference." *Historical Sketches* 1:269.

44 [George Gregory Smith], *The Dramatic Works of the Right Honorable Richard Brinsley Sheridan with a Memoir of His Life,* by G.G.S. (London, 1872), p. 174; Granville, *Correspondence* 1:427, 432; II:5n, 93, 307, 388; Brougham, *Historical Sketches* 1:267.

45 2 *PR* 837–8.

46 4 *PR* 426.

47 4 *PR* 481.

48 During 1803 C wrote a series of letters to Sheridan in the *PR* which, with an earlier unnumbered one (3 *PR* 385) and extracts from speeches of Sheridan, were published by him in 1804 as a book entitled *The Political Proteus: A View of the Public Character and Conduct of R. B. Sheridan, Esq.* Pearl, *Cobbett,* p. 75. Some of the other C attacks on Sheridan prior to the Westminster election of 1806 appear at 3 *PR*

76, 101, 127, 150, 444, 447, 605; 4 *PR* 96, 128, 159, 210, 324, 535, 567; 5 *PR* 27, 107, 287, 416, 443, 589, 614. Presumably out of consideration for Windham, C let up on Sheridan between May 1804 (when Pitt returned to power and the Grenville/Windham–Fox/Sheridan liaison became effective) and April 1806 (the month following C's breach with Windham).

49 10 *PR* 813, 842; 11 *PR* 492.

50 11 *PR* 15.

51 10 *PR* 836.

52 10 *PR* 992.

53 2 *PR* 90.

54 10 *PR* 915. See also 10 *PR* 811.

55 10 *PR* 812; 11 *PR* 197. See also 10 *PR* 812.

56 10 *PR* 839.

57 11 *PR* 193.

58 10 *PR* 812.

59 10 *PR* 865–6. See also 10 *PR* 811.

60 10 *PR* 837.

61 11 *PR* 198.

62 11 *PR* 369. See also 10 *PR* 814; letter to Wright, Feb. 9, 1807, Add. MSS. 31126, fol. 1, referring to Paull: "I will never take any statement from him again."

63 Hansard, 1st ser. IX:158 (Mar. 18, 1807).

64 William Drake, who had married a natural daughter of Sheridan, had gone to Paull with an elaborate story about Sheridan's conduct, after Drake and Sheridan had had a falling out. Hansard, 1st ser. VIII:1060f (Mar. 2, 1807).

65 Letters to Wright, Apr. 11? and 28, 1807, Add. MSS. 22906, fols. 278, 279.

66 Wallas, *Francis Place,* p. 44.

67 Letter to Wright, May 9, 1807, Add. MSS. 22906, fol. 280. C later claimed that the people of Westminster wanted Paull to be elected and that his failure was due to Burdett's perfidy. 41 *PR* 415–17.

68 11 *PR* 822.

69 Letter to Wright, Mar. 5, 1807, Add. MSS. 22906, fol 254.

70 Wallas, p. 45.

71 11 *PR* 838. This is inconsistent with C's later claim that the duel was due to Burdett's refusal to run as a candidate with Paull. 33 *PR* 73–4; 41 *PR* 416–17, 420.

72 11 *PR* 871.

73 11 *PR* 838–9.

74 Letter to Wright, May 17, 1807 (Illinois). Paull's "opposition" to Sir Francis's election seems to have been limited to the activities of a supporter of Paull, a Mr. Gibbons, former member of the committee that had nominated both men. *Times,* May 8, 1807.

75 Letters to Wright, Apr. 11? and May 14, 1807, Add. MSS. 22906, fols. 279, 283.

76 11 *PR* 957. The story of the 1806–7 elections was retold at 78 *PR* 517–24, where C stated that Cochrane's victory cost the sailor not less than £12,000.

77 11 *PR* 965; Sheridan, *Letters* III:9n. Wallas (*Francis Place,* p. 47) suggests that Cochrane, in order to soften the blow to Sheridan, took his inspectors away, allowing Sheridan to poll the same man "over and over again as many times as he pleased."

78 11 *PR* 972. An additional £500 was spent after close of the poll, mostly on the "chairing" of Sir Francis. 12 *PR* 283. Another £500 went for a share of the election expense of the sheriff and the cost of a nonsuited action brought by a pauper. 15 *PR* 820.

79 12 *PR* 1–3, 12–14.

80 Wallas, p. 1.

81 *Times,* May 8, 1807.

82 When, in 1814, Sheridan considered running again at Westminster, Byron wrote: "I fear for poor dear Sherry," but there was nothing to fear, as Sherry finally waived his pretensions. Aspinall, *Brougham and the Whig Party,* pp. 31, 34.

83 *ER* x (July 1807), 387. Burdett had been opposed by the papers of both parties, the *Morning Chronicle, Courier, Oracle, Morning Post, Times,* and *Sun.* 11 *PR* 922.

12. Reform and reformers

Motto: 11 *PR* 336.

1 Charles Grey served in the House of Commons from 1786 to November 1807, when he became a peer on the death of his father. In 1791 Grey and twenty-six other whigs had signed a declaration to the people of England favoring electoral reforms. 20 *PR* 464.

2 Hansard XXXIII:649–50 (May 26, 1797). Copyholder: one whose right was established through long occupancy as evidenced by copy of the manor roll.

3 Hansard XXVIII: 467 (Mar. 4, 1790). In 1806 C claimed that the "hurricane" was over. 9 *PR* 452. He later pointed out that the union with Ireland had been accomplished during the same war. 38 *PR* 156.

4 Quoted by G. S. Veitch, *The Genesis of Parliamentary Reform* (London 1965 repr.), p. 199.

5 Hansard XXXIII:645 (May 26, 1797).

6 F. D. Cartwright (ed.), *The Life and Correspondence of Major Cartwright* (London 1826) I:327–8.

7 9 *PR* 389.

8 Wallas, *Francis Place,* p. 63.

9 John Horne Tooke, supporter of Wilkes in the Middlesex elections of 1769, made a brief appearance out of the past to participate in the Westminster election of 1807 on the side of his disciple Burdett.

10 C apparently met Folkestone through Windham, and had been friendly with him since 1801. Ronald K. Huch, *The Radical Lord Radnor: The Public Life of Viscount Folkestone, Third Earl of Radnor* (Minneapolis 1977), p. 20; letter to Windham, Oct. 20, 1801, Add. MSS. 37853, fol. 16.

11 Hunt introduced himself to C sometime between May 1805 and January 1806. H. Hunt, *Memoirs* II:168. He appears in the *PR* of November 15, 1806 as the author of an address to Wiltshire freeholders, and in the *PR* of July 4 and August 8, 1807 as chairman of a meeting held in Bristol to endorse the action of the electors of Westminster. 10 *PR* 771; 12 *PR* 7, 210. He was an unsuccessful candidate for parliament at Bristol in 1812. 22 *PR* 110, 134, 193. A stirring speech delivered at a Westminster meeting in 1816 began his national prominence. Thereafter he was in great demand at reform meetings throughout England.

12 *Satirist,* Feb. 1809, p. 168. The issue of March 1809 refers to Folkestone as C's "pupil" (p. 250).

13 15 *PR* 977.

14 15 *PR* 962; 17 *PR* 601; Swann to Wright, May 29, 1809, Add. MSS. 22907, fol. 162.

15 15 *PR* 980.

16 9 *PR* 366.

17 1 *PR* 379; 2 *PR* 54.

18 3 *PR* 923–4; 4 *PR* 90, 792.

19 6 *PR* 245.

20 6 *PR* 82, 235, 247, 307, 881. The bread prices were for the standard "quartern loaf" weighing 4 lb 5 oz 8 drm.

21 7 *PR* 220, 222.

22   7 *PR* 300. The probable derivation of C's theory is discussed at a later point. See n. 52 below.

23   "... it appears impossible to account for the enormous increase in expenditure, on any other ground, than extravagance, corruption and intrigue." Paine, *Rights of Man*, p. 253.

24   15 *PR* 722. C coupled his exception of the principal servants with the remark "though I cannot see the *necessity* of it."

25   11 *PR* 1086. The law C proposed be restored was the 1701 Act of Settlement, which had been amended in 1707 to permit placemen to hold seats in the Commons if they were reelected after appointment to office.

26   11 *PR* 440.

27   1 *PR* 365. C denounced the close relationship between the government and the Bank. 4 *PR* 864.

28   11 *PR* 11.

29   2 *PR* 633; 9 *PR* 175.

30   9 *PR* 367.

31   10 *PR* 878.

32   8 *PR* 105; 9 *PR* 838; 10 *PR* 33, 65, 385; 12 *PR* 234.

33   15 *PR* 923; 12 *PR* 323.

34   Rosebery, *Pitt*, pp. 150–1. Arnold Toynbee, *The Industrial Revolution of the Eighteenth Century in England* (new ed., London 1908), p. 107: "During the war we had nominally borrowed £600,000,000 although owing to the way in which the loans were raised, the actual sum which came into the national exchequer was only £350,000,000."

35   As C's ideas developed, he claimed that the wars against France and the resulting expenditures were caused by the desire of the governing class to avoid reform in England. 32 *PR* 498–9.

36   Gladstone later demonstrated that the borrowing would have been unnecessary if Pitt had imposed the income tax in 1793 instead of in 1798. Rosebery, p. 153.

37   For example, see 3 *PR* 442.

38   At a later point C argued that the nation had no right to "burden its posterity." See e.g. 81 *PR* 779.

39   7 *PR* 224.

40   As early as 1803 C had said that he favored "annihilating" the national debt. 3 *PR* 923–4. But the form such annihilation was to take was not clear. In 1803 he supported a proposal to impose a 5 percent tax on the interest. In 1806 he said that he had never thought that the principal could be paid off (10 *PR* 392), and later: "is it not in the nature of things that the annihilation should come by degrees?" 10 *PR* 492. During the Westminster elections of 1806–7, his proposal was that a tax be levied on the funds, which were exempt from the income tax. 10 *PR* 166, 234. At one point he proposed that the funds be taxed at a higher rate than that imposed on other property. 7 *PR* 303. At another time he suggested that the interest paid on the debt be first lessened and then eliminated. 9 *PR* 100, 294. See also 10 *PR* 234. On several occasions he stated that his "annihilation" was based on the assumption that it would be done only if necessary for "the safety of the nation" and would be undertaken only after all other means had been resorted to. 9 *PR* 102, 301, 967; 10 *PR* 393. In 1835, after his breakdown, C claimed that he had "never called for a cancellation of the debt." 87 *PR* 7.

By 1820 C had come around to the view that the reduction in government debt should be accompanied by a comparable reduction in the obligations of private parties under leases, mortgages, and other commitments (36 *PR* 696), and this evolved into his principle of "equitable adjustment," which he vigorously promoted from 1823 on.

With the economic distress that followed the end of the Napoleonic wars, C became certain that the entire British financial structure was about to collapse, bringing down the political structure and forcing parliamentary reform. 30 *PR* 301, 307, 338, 369, 391; 31 *PR* 315, 354. He called attention to Paine's prediction of 1796 that the funding system was "on the last twenty years of its existence." 31 *PR* 217; Paine, *Political Works*, p. 487. Prophecies of imminent collapse became a regular feature of C's writings from 1816 to 1835. See, for example, 31 *PR* 595 (1816); 32 *PR* 48 (1817); 39 *PR* 409 (1821) etc. etc.

41 6 *PR* 243.

42 7 *PR* 304. See also 6 *PR* 868.

43 The 3 percent return on land used by C is confirmed by the examples cited in F. M. L. Thompson's *English Landed Society in the Nineteenth Century* (London 1971 repr.), pp. 37, 39, 40, 55. The latter observes, however, that "the costs of acquiring a given income from land or from Consols had remained roughly in step from 1790 to the 1840s," but then immediately adds an overwhelming exception: "apart from the period of the French wars and the special influence of the war finance in depressing the price of the Consols" (p. 122).

Later, C assumed that land produced a 3½ percent return. 19 *PR* 901.

44 "Our Government is to be found in each county . . . This is the Government of England." *Manchester Lectures*, p. 49.

45 6 *PR* 618. The moneymen had been rising for a long time. Swift complained of them in 1710. Leslie Stephen, *Swift* (London 1903 repr.), p. 91.

46 49 *PR* 602. "The whole race of *small country gentlemen* . . . has been swept away by the system of taxing and funding." 38 *PR* 166.

47 "In my native parish, Waverly Abbey, formerly the seat of Sir Robert Rich, is now the seat of a Mr. Thompson, a wine merchant; and Moor Park, rendered famous by being the seat of Sir William Temple, is now the seat of a Mr. Timson, a spirit merchant." 36 *PR* 771.

C claimed in 1823 that "a full third part of all the gentlemen in the county [have been] actually driven from their estates already." 48 *PR* 485. See also 49 *PR* 602. In 1829 he stated that "In every class of former English society, the second degree is destroyed except in that of the clergy." 68 *PR* 615.

48 38 *PR* 779; 78 *PR* 202.

49 39 *PR* 10; 64 *PR* 593. C regretted the loss of the practical education previously gained by young people "bred up under the eye and in the company" of the farmer and his wife. When C visited the north of England in 1832 he discovered that farm laborers there were generally still living, or at least boarding, with the farmer. 78 *PR* 5, 404, 458.

50 38 *PR* 750. He very shortly claimed that where there had been four farms there was now one. 39 *PR* 508. And a year later five or six farms had been made into one. 44 *PR* 471. In another six months he declared: "Nothing is more common" than a man occupying land that had once been "twenty farms." 46 *PR* 79.

The consolidation had been going on for some time, since C cited writings around 1801 testifying to the aggregation of as many as fifty small farms into one. 52 *PR* 147. See also 52 *PR* 352; Toynbee, *Industrial Revolution*, p. 68, citing contemporary reports.

Recent authority suggests that the decline of "small farmers" was not "very rapid or sweeping, or applied to all areas." G. E. Mingay, *Enclosure and the Small Farmer in the Age of the Industrial Revolution* (London 1976 repr.), p. 16. This analysis relies largely on an interpretation of the questionable estimates made by Gregory King in 1688, and assumes that anyone cultivating less than twenty acres was not a farmer. Yet, even adopting the latter assumption, a study based on firmer statistics shows that on the estates of one large landowner, not affected by enclosures, the tenanted area occupied by farms of from twenty to a hundred acres fell from 46.1 percent in 1714–20 to 14.9 percent in 1829–33, a drop of more than two-thirds.

J. R. Wordie, "Social Change on the Leveson-Gower Estates 1714–1832," *Economic History Review* XXVII (1974), 593.

51 40 *PR* 393–4. C's view of the decay of the small freeholders – the yeomanry and the squires – is confirmed by Toynbee (*Industrial Revolution*, pp. 34–44), who asserted that it constituted a "revolution, though so silent, of as great importance as the political revolution of 1831," but pointed out that the trend had started before the close of the eighteenth century. At times C had little good to say about the country gentlemen: a "set of greedy, proud, mean and servile wretches." 42 *PR* 202.

52 John Locke, *Civil Government*, bk. II, ch. v, para. 40. See also Adam Smith, *Wealth of Nations*, bk. I, ch. v: "What is bought with money or goods is purchased by labour." 6 *PR* 618; 16 *PR* 209; 47 *PR* 646 (*Rural Rides*, p. 225). In general, C was an admirer of the quakers. 36 *PR* 314–15. The Pennsylvania quakers were "the best people in the world." 12 *PR* 267. See Frank Whitson Fetter, *Development of British Monetary Orthodoxy* (Cambridge, Mass. 1965), pp. 128–9, on "Scots, Quakers and Jews."

53 10 *PR* 493; 13 *PR* 679.

54 10 *PR* 450.

55 "A small public debt is no harm to any country, nor, merely in a *pecuniary* point of view, is a large one . . . but not so in its political effects; there a great public debt is a tremendous evil." 3 *PR* 923.

   "The money is swallowing up the land" (4 *PR* 476); "thousands of small freeholds" had been swallowed by the moneymen (9 *PR* 361). See F. M. L. Thompson, *Landed Society*, pp. 38–9.

56 9 *PR* 368. What C meant by "the funding system" is not clear. Apparently he meant all the consequences of conducting government business on the basis of credit as contrasted with a system of pay-as-you-go using a metallic currency. He speaks of "the sinking fund . . . the consequent extension of the funding system together with the inevitable increase in paper money" (6 *PR* 243); "the present system of finance" (7 *PR* 303); "The taxing and funding, or, in other words, the *paper* system" (9 *PR* 361); "the funding and taxing and paper system . . . the money-system" (9 *PR* 367) – all, presumably, referring to the same thing.

57 Essay "Of Public Credit." Much of C's language follows that of Hume, as for example: "either that debt, or the independence of this nation, must be speedily destroyed." 3 *PR* 923.

   Bishop Watson's proposal to pay off the debt was attacked by Brougham on the ground, among others, that it would reduce the patronage of the crown, and thus constitute "a violent change in the balance of the Constitution." *ER*, Jan. 1804, p. 477.

58 The rates were 10 percent to 1802, 5 percent from 1803 to 1805, 6¼ percent in 1805–6, and 10 percent from 1806 to 1816, when the tax was repealed.

59 7 *PR* 300; Stephen Dowell, *A History of Taxation and Taxes in England from the Earliest Times to the Present Day* (3rd ed., London 1965) II:207, 257.

60 Paine, *Rights of Man*, p. 262; 31 *PR* 562; 42 *PR* 48.

   C at one time contended (although the figures used in the text do not appear to reflect his contention) that all taxes ultimately fall on labor. 7 *PR* 300, 381. See also 9 *PR* 485 and 10 *PR* 233. Apparently C's view was derived from Locke's theory of value referred to in n. 52 above.

61 In 1816 customs duties and excise taxes amounted to £44 million, or roughly £4 per capita, or £8 for husband and wife, taking no account of children. This was equal to 44 percent of the wages of a laborer paid seven shillings a week, and 31 percent of the wages of ten shillings.

   Toynbee (*Industrial Revolution*, p. 107) claimed that as late as 1834 half of a laborer's wages went for taxes.

62   12 *PR* 126. See also 9 *PR* 168; 10 *PR* 872–3; 12 *PR* 330.
      As might be expected, Karl Marx disagreed: "The great part that the public
      debt, and the fiscal system corresponding with it, has played in the capitalisation
      of wealth and the exploitation of the masses, has led many writers, like Cobbett
      . . . to seek in this, incorrectly, the fundamental cause of the misery of the modern
      peoples." Karl Marx and Frederick Engels, *Selected Works* (3 vols., Moscow 1969)
      II:138.

63   The Speenhamland system was practically legalized by the Poor Relief Act of 1796.
      In general, it fixed wages at the level necessary to sustain life in a single man, so
      that a married man had to apply to the parish for enough to support his family. A
      report of a special committee of the House of Commons in 1824 described the
      extent to which the Speenhamland system had been adopted in the several coun-
      ties. 51 *PR* 293.

64   30 *PR* 427. And see 38 *PR* 751. C also thought that "manufactories are one source
      of our pauperism" but did not expand on that statement. 12 *PR* 358. Considerably
      later, the "operation of the tithe system" was blamed for the deteriorating position
      of the farm laborer. *Manchester Lectures,* p. 55.

65   J. L. and B. Hammond, *The Village Labourer* (new ed., London 1920), p. 17; 6 *PR*
      245; 12 *PR* 842; 13 *PR* 367, 647, 719; 24 *PR* 139–40; 39 *PR* 329. Yet C in 1811
      suggested that a way be found to relieve enclosure bills "from the heavy expense
      that attends them." 20 *PR* 653. C claimed that he was the only one who publicly
      opposed enclosures. 39 *PR* 330. See John Stevenson, *Popular Disturbances in
      England 1700–1870* (London 1979), p. 41: "Population growth, rural unemploy-
      ment and the operation of the poor laws rather than enclosure were the major
      causes" of rural poverty and misery.

66   C frequently pointed out that wages lag behind prices. 6 *PR* 309, 882; 24 *PR* 641–
      2.

67   4 *PR* 794. But see 24 *PR* 482: "Depreciation of money has, and can have, no effect
      upon the man who lives by his labour." C was referring to "on an average of three
      or four years." 24 *PR* 641–2.

68   6 *PR* 235, 247, 307, 856, 883.

69   Blackstone IV:174.

70   7 *PR* 220. When a change was proposed in the law of settlement in 1819, C was
      ready with examples to show how burdensome the change would be on the various
      parishes affected, but was chiefly concerned about the rash of schemes "to get the
      greatest possible quantity of work performed from the giving the smallest possible
      quantity of food." 35 *PR* 105.

71   10 *PR* 873.

72   11 *PR* 336. C's contention that the poor were better off when he was born (1763)
      than in the early part of the nineteenth century is supported by Toynbee (*Indus-
      trial Revolution,* p. 46), who adds: "The middle of the eighteenth century was
      indeed about his best time, though a decline soon set in . . . By the end of the
      century men had begun to look back with regret upon this epoch in the history of
      the agricultural labourer as one of a vanished prosperity."
      What little evidence is available is to the same effect. Figures furnished by Tull
      show that the laborer in 1743 was paid three times as much in real wages as his
      counterpart seventy-five years later. 39 *PR* 322–6. For conditions in the fifteenth
      century C relied on the description of Sir John Fortescue. 32 *PR* 81–2; 51 *PR* 471;
      and see Charles Plummer (ed.), *The Governance of England . . .* by Sir John Fortes-
      cue (Oxford 1926), pp. 286–8. C also cited the statutes of the priory of Selbourne,
      which prescribed as *punishment* fasting on bread and beer. 51 *PR* 474. To this we
      can add that the real wages of a laborer in the fifteenth and sixteenth centuries
      paid 4d. a day, with wheat at six shillings a quarter (W. G. Hoskins, *The Age of
      Plunder: King Henry's England 1500–1547* (London 1976), pp. 112–13, 246), were

substantially higher than the 1s. 6d. a day paid Sussex farm laborers in 1788–90 or the 2s. 0½d. paid them in 1791–1819 (43 *PR* 519), when wheat was approximately fifty and eighty shillings respectively. A similar conclusion was reached by John Barton, *An Inquiry into the Causes of the Progressive Depreciation of Agricultural Labour* (London 1820), pp. 111–14. See also *Poor Man's Friend*, para. 55, and *Protestant "Reformation,"* paras. 464–6, for a comparison of wages provided in an act of 23 Edw. III with the prices in the *Preciosum* of Bishop Fleetwood. But cf. Norman Gash, *Aristocracy and People: Britain 1815–1865* (London 1979), pp. 34–5.

73   In these passages C used the word "poor" to refer to the bulk of the population, "who live wholly by the sweat of their brow." Elsewhere he used it in a different sense, to mean those who are paupers. Thus: "The man who, by his own and his family's labour, can provide a sufficiency of food and raiment, and a comfortable dwelling-place, is not a *poor man*." *Cottage Economy*, para. 6.

74   32 *PR* 79; 38 *PR* 515; 71 *PR* 643. See also 32 *PR* 1043; "It was a disgrace not to have window curtains, bed-curtains and feather beds."

75   14 *PR* 78.

76   14 *PR* 77.

77   31 *PR* 290. "The best savings-bank for the labourer . . . is a plot of land . . . a cow . . . a hog . . . and a barrel of beer, of his own brewing." 46 *PR* 241.

78   32 *PR* 639: "In vain did I say, that it would be better to give the poor bread, or, rather, to let them eat it when they had earned it, and leave them to enlighten themselves out of their own means." See also 16 *PR* 577–8; 46 *PR* 523; 47 *PR* 392.

79   37 *PR* 1061, 1242. See also 10 *PR* 811, 865.

80   "The *law of nature* bids a man *not starve* in a land of plenty, and forbids his being punished for taking food wherever he can find it." 34 *PR* 1026–7. See also *Poor Man's Friend*, paras. 1–53.

81   32 *PR* 25–32. See Appendix 2, "Cobbett and Malthusianism."

82   37 *PR* 651–2.

83   34 *PR* 924, 952. See also 36 *PR* 162.

84   C spoke of Brougham as one "engaged in the sublime and miraculous work of satisfying the cries of hunger by teaching the sufferers their A.B.C." 38 *PR* 139.

85   24 *PR* 747–8, 752, 781; 34 *PR* 925. C despised children's books that taught "the endless blessings of passive obedience, non-resistance, ragged backs, frozen joints, parching lips and hungry bellies." 34 *PR* 274.

86   Winch (ed.), *James Mill*, p. 90. See also G. M. Trevelyan, *History of England* (London 1926), p. 621: "Cobbett was the first who gave effective voice to their case."

87   See also "Address and Declaration" at a Select Meeting of the Friends of Universal Peace and Liberty, held at the Thatched House tavern, Aug. 20, 1791, J. Horne Tooke, chairman: "we hold that the moral obligation of providing for old age, helpless infancy and poverty, is far superior to that of supplying the invented wants of courtly extravagance, ambition and intrigue." Paine, *Political Works*, p. 592.

88   C's early respect for the monarchy and aristocracy weakened with the passage of time, but he never called for their elimination, as Paine did. At 34 *PR* 836–7 C warmly endorsed "a king with great prerogatives, and with advisers really responsible to his people, represented by a House of Commons really chosen by that people."

    The king was respected by C as a symbol: "The laws do not require us to believe that as a mortal man he is any better than any one of us." 86 *PR* 549. C became increasingly critical of the aristocracy "because so many of them have been such odious oppressors." They want "pulling down or, at least, putting down," C declared, describing them as "a prodigious band of spungers, living upon the labour of the industrious part of the community." 59 *PR* 649; 84 *PR* 74; *Life of Jackson*, p. 196.

89 3 *PR* 952; 5 *PR* 24; 7 *PR* 302. Paine favored the abolition of the law of primogeniture (*Rights of Man*, p. 272); C did not (52 *PR* 348).

90 45 *PR* 80; 65 *PR* 304, 464-5; 82 *PR* 715-18; 84 *PR* 519. "There has seldom been known in the world any very wicked and mischievous scheme, of which a *priest* of some description or other, was not at the bottom." 34 *PR* 478. Yet C said that he regretted that Paine had written his *Age of Reason*. 53 *PR* 257-8.

91 Letter to Wright, Mar. 30, 1807, Add. MSS. 22906, fol. 269; 6 *PR* 664, 1061; 11 *PR* 353, 587.

92 11 *PR* 588; 12 *PR* 741.

93 5 *PR* 933; 7 *PR* 219-22, 372, 446; 9 *PR* 844; 11 *PR* 80; 13 *PR* 860. His contempt for the slaveowner appears at 37 *PR* 1062. C was outraged by the administration of justice in the American slave states, where a white murderer of a black went unpunished. 43 *PR* 194-5. Yet he held to the view that the blacks were inferior and unable to distinguish between truth and falsehood. 40 *PR* 147, 150, 195; 76 *PR* 502.

94 69 *PR* 707-10, 813-14. By 1832 C was convinced that it would be better to abandon the British possessions in the West Indies than to uphold Negro slavery. He had made the discovery that the slaves were generally the property of the English boroughmongers, who used the profits derived from this source to enslave the white laborers of England. 77 *PR* 261.

95 10 *PR* 867, 972; 12 *PR* 199, 263, 801, 833, 846, 865, 897; 13 *PR* 106, 130, 213, 218, 241. According to William Spence, the principles urged by C and himself went back to Aristotle, Artaxerxes, etc. etc. 12 *PR* 923.

   But compare C's statement in 1814: "We are a commercial people; it is commerce that has elevated the country to the lofty station which she now occupies, and upon which, according to the system presently pursued, she must rely for future greatness." 25 *PR* 450.

96 James Mill expressed his disagreement with C in the pamphlet *Commerce Defended* published in 1808, although he stated that "Even on some pretty difficult questions of political economy (those, for example, respecting the corn-trade) he [Cobbett] has discovered a clearness and justness of thought, which but few of our scientific reasoners have reached." Winch (ed.), *James Mill*, p. 89. Mill's editor points out that C had agreed with Mill on the corn-trade issue.

97 11 *PR* 1082; Aspinall, *Brougham and the Whig Party*, p. 7. Barry Gordon, *Economic Doctrine and Tory Liberalism 1824-1830* (London 1979), p. 67: "James Mill . . . characterized the British Empire as 'a vast system of outdoor relief for the upper classes'."

98 Horace Twiss, *The Public and Private Life of Lord Chancellor Eldon* (London 1844) II:108.

13. Cobbett versus Perceval

Motto: Letter to Windham, Sept. 29, 1802, Add. MSS. 37853, fol. 54.

1 Gray, *Perceval*, pp. 1-27, 44, 47; Coupland, *Wilberforce*, pp. 325, 353, 362; Romilly, *Memoirs* I:91. In response to the comment that Perceval was a good father, Cartwright observed that "hyenas are remarkably fond of their young." 34 *PR* 209. Sydney Smith declared that "if public and private virtues must always be incompatible," he would prefer that Perceval "whipped his boys, and saved his country." *The Letters of Peter Plymley . . . by Sydney Smith* with an introduction by G. C. Heseltine (London 1929), p. 13.

2 Brougham, *Historical Sketches* I:301.

3 *George IV*, para. 77.

4 9 *PR* 560, 648. See also 12 *PR* 121; 13 *PR* 597.

5 Gray, *Perceval*, p. 23n.

6   11 *PR* 169.
7   11 *PR* 227.
8   Gray, pp. 3, 11; *Times,* July 1, 1809. In 1810, after there had been some rise in pay, C estimated that "the average wages of labourers, take all the kingdom through," was twelve shillings a week. 18 *PR* 333.
9   Letter to Wright, Apr. 11? [1807], Add, MSS. 22906, fol. 279.
10 Letter to Wright, May 10, 1807, ibid. fol. 282.
11 11 *PR* 857.
12 Letter to Wright, Apr. 10, 1807, Add. MSS. 22906, fol. 271.
13 Letter to Wright, Sept. 11, 1808, Add. MSS. 22907, fol. 44.
14 11 *PR* 241, 519; 12 *PR* 67. As a result of pressure from the opposition, the sinecure was altered from one for Perceval's life to one during the pleasure of the monarch.
15 12 *PR* 180. See also 12 *PR* 234.
16 12 *PR* 97.
17 12 *PR* 111.
18 11 *PR* 1017, 1091; 12 *PR* 65. See also 15 *PR* 651, 716.
19 12 *PR* 68, 70.
20 11 *PR* 836. See also 11 *PR* 825, 985.
21 11 *PR* 987. The *Courier* might have added that Perceval and the nine other ministers in the Commons had been returned by a total of 1,214 electors. Gray, *Perceval,* p. 139.
22 11 *PR* 988–9.
23 Michael Roberts, *The Whig Party 1807–1812* (2nd ed., London 1865), pp. 13–29.
24 11 *PR* 811.
25 11 *PR* 837.
26 12 *PR* 425; Arthur Bryant, *Years of Victory 1802–1812* (London 1944), p. 215, citing *Diaries and Letters of Sir George Jackson* II:208. See also 12 *PR* 280, 385; 13 *PR* 163, 204, 274, 323.
27 14 *PR* 385.
28 14 *PR* 513.
29 Letter to Wright, Sept. 17, 1808, Add. MSS. 22907, fol. 45. On hearing that there were *forty-seven* British generals in Portugal, C exclaimed: "What a deal of wine they will drink!" 14 *PR* 644.
30 Letter to Wright, Sept. 20, 1808, Add. MSS. 22907, fol. 46.
31 14 *PR* 515; 15 *PR* 521. C later turned against Waithman, finding that he did not have enough reforming zeal.
32 14 *PR* 653.
33 14 *PR* 656. See also 20 *PR* 463.
34 Letters to Wright, Oct. 28 and Nov. 1 and 2, 1808, Add. MSS. 22907, fols. 64, 67, 70.
35 Robert Sym ("Timothy Tickler") in *Blackwood's* XIV (Sept. 1813), 329.
36 Letter to Wright, Nov. 8, 1808, Add. MSS. 22907, fol. 72.
37 Letter to Wright, Nov. 25, 1808, ibid., fol. 81.
38 14 *PR* 711–27. On a show of hands, the vote appeared to be evenly divided between an address proposed by C and one proposed by Lord Northesk. When C refused the suggestion that a committee be appointed to combine the two proposals into a single one, the Northesk proposal was adopted. 14 *PR* 726–7.
39 Letter to Wright, Nov. 8, 1808, Add. MSS. 22907, fol. 72.
40 14 *PR* 963.
41 15 *PR* 2.
42 15 *PR* 7–8.
43 14 *PR* 715.
44 14 *PR* 202.

45 14 *PR* 230.
46 14 *PR* 257.
47 14 *PR* 353, 392.
48 14 *PR* 659.
49 *An Appeal to the Public* . . . pp. 36–7. It later appeared that C's friend Peter Finnerty was the publisher of the pamphlet, and possibly had a part in drafting it, George Manners, *Vindiciae Satiricae: or, A Vindication of the Principles of the "Satirist"* . . . (London 1809), pp. 15, 24n, 25.
50 13 *PR* 961; 14 *PR* 37, 38, 71. A few weeks later Perceval wrote to his brother: "How far this great struggle against French tyranny in Spain shall be effectually carried on without notions of independence and reform arising out of that very struggle itself, must at present be only a matter of conjecture." Perceval to Arden, July 20, 1808 (Perceval papers).
51 13 *PR* 914.
52 13 *PR* 1001.
53 Ibid.
54 13 *PR* 1003. The references cited in the text are far from inclusive of the taunts Cobbett directed at the junior members of the royal family. Not all of them were veiled. His attacks on the Duke of Clarence and his mistress Mrs. Jordan (10 *PR* 385; 11 *PR* 970; 15 *PR* 246) made her reluctant to visit the duke at St. James's Palace. Arthur Aspinall (ed.), *Mrs Jordan and Her Family* (London 1951), p. 64.
55 Although the principal charge related to the sale of army commissions, Mrs. Clarke's activities covered a far wider spectrum of corruption. See, for example, 15 *PR* 395–6 relating to the procuring of votes in parliament.
56 Letter to Wright, Jan. 29, 1809, Add. MSS. 22907, fol. 110.
57 Gray (*Perceval*, p. 204), relying on the *Sun*, a government-subsidized paper, asserts that Mrs. Clarke was "detected in twenty-eight falsehoods, but, under the rules of procedure, no witness could be examined under oath." The procedure was that recommended by the duke's friends. Hansard, 1st ser. XII:193 (Jan. 27, 1809). General Clavering, who volunteered evidence to prove that Mrs. Clarke was lying, was himself sent to Newgate for prevarication. Ibid. XIII:802 (Mar. 24, 1809). Since the duke lived with Mrs. Clarke for about five years, her shortcomings cast as much light on him as on her.
58 Looking only at the good of the nation, military appointments by the duke at the request of his mistress were undesirable whether or not he knew she was being paid, but this view does not appear to have been pressed.
59 15 *PR* 420. According to C, there was not a single pensioner or placeman among the 196 voting against the duke.
60 Gray, p. 201. It is not possible to determine the ultimate truth in the duke's case, and it is foolish, in attempting to do so, to rely on the demerits of Gwllym Wardle or Mrs. Clarke, who C thought was "a damned mercenary bitch." Letter to Wright, Apr. 11, 1809, Add. MSS. 22907, fol. 146. Sir Samuel Romilly, noted for his legal learning and integrity, voted against the duke. Leigh Hunt, after years of reflection, concluded: "there was some connivance on his part, but not of a systematic nature." Leigh Hunt, *The Autobiography of Leigh Hunt*, ed. J. E. Morpurgo (London 1959), p. 205. This conclusion has been accepted by Halévy, *History* 1:6. Compare, however, Gray, p. 204 and Roberts, *Whig Party*, p. 199.
61 Letters to Wright, Feb. 8 and 14, 1809, Add. MSS. 22907, fols. 121, 123.
62 Adam had acted as C's counsel in the "Juverna" case. While C was attacking Adam, he confessed his obligation to him. 15 *PR* 389.
63 15 *PR* 295–301, 321–3, 383–4. Gray (*Perceval*, p. 198) states that Miss Taylor "kept what she claimed was a boarding school for young ladies [there was no evidence to the contrary]; that she lied about her father's name [she said that her father's name

was Taylor; a witness testified that he sometimes went by another name]; and that she admitted being in debt [so was the Duke of York]."

64 15 *PR* 298.

65 15 *PR* 383–4.

66 15 *PR* 363–80.

67 Hansard, 1st ser. XII:729, 732 (Feb. 16, 1809).

68 Ibid. 732.

69 Ibid. 814–21 (Feb. 17, 1809); 15 *PR* 367–8. A few minutes before Perceval began his statement to the House on February 16 he learned that the note had not been destroyed.

70 15 *PR* 375. See also the shamefaced explanation of Adam. 15 *PR* 372–4. The accounts in Hansard, although well laundered, nevertheless reflect some of the embarrassment of the two gentlemen. 1st ser. XII:729–32.

71 15 *PR* 353, quoting Mic. 7:3.

72 15 *PR* 385.

73 15 *PR* 399. See also 15 *PR* 491.

74 15 *PR* 248.

75 15 *PR* 227.

76 15 *PR* 228. See also 15 *PR* 219, 385, 505.

77 15 *PR* 245.

78 Gronow, *Recollections*, p. 211; to the same effect: 32 *PR* 1146. Several officers, including Arthur Wellesley, testified to the general state of the army under the duke's command. C commented: "If a shepherd be tried for sheep-stealing, is evidence ever brought respecting the healthy and excellent state of the flock?" 15 *PR* 331.

79 15 *PR* 360.

80 Letter to Wright, Feb. 2, 1809, Add. MSS. 22907, fol. 115.

81 Wright, however, continued to be alarmed. Letter to Wright, Mar. 1, 1809, ibid. fol. 129.

14. Perceval versus Cobbett

Motto: 12 *PR* 202.

1 15 *PR* 513.

2 15 *PR* 580, 673, 677, 684, 813, 1002.

3 15 *PR* 577f.

4 Roberts, *Whig Party*, pp. 201–2.

5 15 *PR* 677. The terror created by C among his opposition is reflected in Wilbraham Bootle's letter to Perceval of April 23, 1809, declining to take part in the debate on Lord Hamilton's motion. (Perceval papers.)

6 15 *PR* 678–9.

7 15 *PR* 684.

8 Lord Colchester (ed.), *The Diary and Correspondence of Charles Abbot, Lord Colchester* (London 1861) II:183.

9 15 *PR* 709, 737; Gray, *Perceval*, p. 207.

10 15 *PR* 767–8.

11 15 *PR* 758, 769–70.

12 15 *PR* 770–1. See also 15 *PR* 753.

13 15 *PR* 754.

14 15 *PR* 874. See 30 *PR* 522: "Since the 12th of May, 1809 there has not been to be found one unbought pen or tongue to pretend that one of the parties is a straw better or worse than the other."

15 15 *PR* 545.

16 15 *PR* 685. "The public meetings begin to assume a new shape and character, requiring vigilance and consideration." *Courier,* May 3, 1809.
17 *Times,* May 16, 1809.
18 Roberts, *Whig Party,* p. 212; 15 *PR* 835, 865, 961.
19 15 *PR* 865; *Satirist,* July 1809, p. 50; letter to Wright, Mar. 26, 1810, Add. MSS. 22907, fol. 257.
20 Curwen and Coke both asserted in 1822 that seats were still being sold. *Collective Commentaries,* p. 177.
21 15 *PR* 882.
22 David B. Smith (ed.), *Letters of Admiral of the Fleet the Earl of St. Vincent* (London 1927) II:231.
23 Lord Holland, *Further Memoirs of the Whig Party, 1807–1821* ... ed. Lord Stavordale (London 1905), p. 387; *ER* x (July 1807), 386–421. Francis Horner opposed the attack on Cobbett.
24 *ER* XIII (October 1808), 185–205, 215–34, reviews with the short titles "Don Pedro Cevallos on the French Usurpation of Spain" and "Leckie on Foreign Policy of Great Britain." See 14 *PR* 907–10; 15 *PR* 179–80; John Clive, *Scottish Reviewers: The "Edinburgh Review" 1802–1815* (London 1957), pp. 110ff. Jeffrey's article gave rise to an error that has persisted for 150 years. William Hazlitt, otherwise an admirer of Cobbett, accused him of cowardice in an article published in 1825: "Whenever he has been set upon, he has slunk out of the controversy. The Edinburgh Review made (what is called) a dead set at him many years ago, to which he only retorted by an eulogy on the superior neatness of an English kitchen-garden to a Scotch one." *The Spirit of the Age,* p. 350. Hazlitt was referring to Jeffrey's essay of July 1807, and to an article that appeared in the *Political Register* of August 29, 1807 in which Cobbett spoke of the English laborers who "spend the twilight in works of neatness round their cottages" as compared with the "garden-less ... cabbins of Scotland." 12 *PR* 337. But that was not Cobbett's retort to Jeffrey, which appeared in the issue of October 17, 1807 (presumably never read by Hazlitt), in which Cobbett, in a return compliment, showed the inconsistency of the *Edinburgh Review,* and neatly demolished Jeffrey's main argument. 12 *PR* 577. See also 12 *PR* 600, 722, 824, 982.
25 C stated in 1815 that "more than twenty publications" were "set up for the express purpose of writing down the Register." 29 *PR* 355. Papers clearly of this description include, in addition to the *Satirist, Mr. Redhead Yorke's Weekly Political Review* (1805–11), the *National Register* (1808–12?), *Blagdon's Weekly Political Register* (1809–11), the *Weekly Register and Political Magazine* (1809–11), the *National Adviser* (1811–12), the *British Commoner* (1812–13), and the *Anti-Gallican Monitor* (1811–18). See Aspinall, *Politics and the Press,* pp. 85–93.
    C probably also had in mind the *Quarterly Review,* the tory response to the *ER.* The *Quarterly Review's* editor, William Gifford, and principal contributors, Southey and Walter Scott, were frequent C targets. See e.g. 32 *PR* 253.
26 The *DNB* entry gives no information on parentage, birthplace, or education. In his *Vindiciae Satiricae: or, A Vindication of the Principles of the "Satirist", and the Conduct of its Proprietors* (London 1809), an attack on C and his friend Peter Finnerty, Manners stated that he was six feet four inches, one of twenty children, several of whom were army officers, went to Westminster school (which has no record of his attendance), married, and lived in Wales for six years (pp. 6, 30n, 38). In 1811 he was imprisoned for three months for a libel on William Hallett, one of C's supporters. In 1812 he sold the *Satirist,* which thereafter followed a less vitriolic course. In 1817 Manners was appointed British consul for Massachusetts. C stated that Manners used to boast that he was related to the Duke of Rutland's family, "although his mother was never *married* to any of them." 32 *PR* 928.

27 *Satirist*, June 1809, p. 606n. For Brougham's adverse comments on Manners see Hansard, 1st ser. XLI:1563 (Dec. 23, 1819).
28 *Satirist*, Nov. 1808, pp. 340–2.
29 *Satirist*, Dec. 1808, p. 516.
30 C himself had drawn attention to the story in 1805 when he said that he had left the army because of "shocking abuses as to money matters," and that the records of the war office would show how he had endeavored but failed to obtain redress. 8 *PR* 521–2.
31 15 *PR* 46; *Satirist*, Feb. 1809, p. 126.
32 At the Hampshire county meeting held on November 2, 1810 Baker had seconded C's resolution condemning the Cintra convention. 14 *PR* 720, 723. C may have taken offense at the appearance in the *Satirist* for November 1808 (p. 345n) of a remark allegedly made by him "at the Rev. Mr. B—'s table."
33 *Satirist*, Apr. 1809, p. 375. The January 1809 issue (pp. 44–5) had carried an account of a notice posted in the kitchen of the Dolphin in Botley in which C threatened to prosecute anyone detected in cutting his trees or found trespassing on his property.
34 15 *PR* 816–17.
35 The *Courier*, June 15, 1809, suggests that the pamphlet had been issued not later than the last week in May.
36 *Satirist*, June 1809, p. 573.
37 15 *PR* 851.
38 *Courier*, June 9, 1809.
39 *Courier*, June 15, 1809.
40 Gray, *Perceval*, p. 132, citing Add. MSS. 38737, fol. 413. See also Aspinall, *Politics and the Press*, p. 88.
41 15 *PR* 897–9, 907.
42 I have been unable to identify more than eight or nine letters written by C to the government which were not in the pamphlet, including the letter C allegedly wrote from Fratton about the discharge of Bestland, which has not been found. See ch. 2, n. 36.
43 *Courier*, June 22, July 8 and 20. Brougham wrote to Earl Grey on June 19, 1809: "Cobbett is seriously damaged. His court martial business is much against him, and would probably have been much more if Sir George Yonge had behaved with tolerable fairness and prudence." Henry Brougham, *The Life and Times of Henry Lord Brougham Written by Himself* (2nd ed., London 1871) 1:437.
44 Letters to Wright, June 20, 23, and 26, 1809, Add. MSS. 22907, fols. 172, 175; 31126, fol. 65. The *Morning Post* had claimed that Cobbett's letter to Pitt had been a "fabrication," and Cobbett asserted that it would make the same claim about whatever he might publish.
45 16 *PR* 98. See also 65 *PR* 496.
46 16 *PR* 111.
47 16 *PR* 97.
48 Letter to Wright, July 22, 1809, Add. MSS. 22907, fol. 177.
49 16 *PR* 97–120. The version given in the pamphlet *Cobbett's Oppression!!*, allegedly based on a shorthand account of the trial, portrays C as short-tempered and addicted to the use of abusive and threatening language.
50 Blackstone 1:425.
51 Anne, p. 26.
52 16 *PR* 117.
53 Letter to Wright, July 22, 1809, Add. MSS. 22907, fol. 179; 16 *PR* 124.
54 15 *PR* 996–1002.
55 15 *PR* 993; *Courier*, June 24, 1809. C later explained the phrase "stoppage of their knapsacks" as follows: "the law had awarded a sum of money called the 'marching

guinea'; but knapsacks had been given, or tendered to them instead of the money." *Corn*, para. 187.

56 See, for example, the references to foreign troops in one six-month period: 11 *PR* 46, 106, 164, 167, 206, 230, 330, 354, 417, 426, 436, 439, 487, 498, 810, 1088, 1118. Paine, like C, objected to the cost of maintaining foreign troops. "Prospects on the Rubicon," in *Political Works*, p. 271.

57 15 *PR* 993.

58 Letter to Wright, July 27, 1809, Add. MSS. 22907, fol. 179; 16 *PR* 124.

59 Letter to Wright, Aug. 18, 1809, Add. MSS. 22907, fol. 189.

60 Letters to Wright, Nov. 9 and 22, 1809, ibid. fol. 218.

61 16 *PR* 193, 257, 289, 321, 353, 385, 491, 520, 627.

62 16 *PR* 173, 373, 397, 909. "Can it possibly be intended to succumb under these most scandalous & outrageous libels which are now daily & hourly circulating with so much malignant assiduity against . . . Lord Chatham?" Charles Yorke to Perceval, Sept. 12, 1809 (Perceval papers).

63 16 *PR* 417, 424, 481, 487, 515, 609, 750, 784, 833.

64 16 *PR* 897.

65 Letter to Wright, Jan. 30, 1810, Add. MSS. 22907, fol. 244.

66 Letter to Wright, Mar. 25, 1810, ibid. fol. 253. Perry was prosecuted for inserting in the *Morning Chronicle* of October 2, 1809 a paragraph from the *Examiner* stating that the successor of George III would have "the finest opportunity of becoming nobly popular." An action against the editor of the *Examiner* was dropped after Perry's success.

67 Swann to Wright, Feb. 15 and May 21, 1810, Add. MSS. 22907, fols. 248, 271. At C's trial, the attorney general claimed that the delay was due entirely to C, who had "industriously circulated" the information that the attorney general had given up the trial, "when he had no such intention." *Times*, June 16, 1810. C's denial of responsibility for the delay is supported by his letter to Mitford of Jan. 7, 1810 (Bodleian), from which it is clear that he expected the trial to occur in that month.

68 The editor of this new publication was Francis Blagdon, whose rascally activities are described in Aspinall, *Politics and the Press*, pp. 86–8, 168, 407–8; and Gray, *Perceval*, pp. 87–8.

69 17 *PR* 193.

70 Gray, p. 289.

71 17 *PR* 421.

72 Colchester, *Diary* II:240.

73 Letter to Wright, Mar. 28, 1810, Add. MSS. 22907, fol. 257. See also fol. 256.

74 Letters to Wright, May 16, 21, 22, and 30, 1810, ibid. fols. 270, 272, 274, 277.

75 Swann to Wright, May 21, 1810, ibid. fol. 271.

76 Gray, *Perceval*, pp. 290–8; Cobbett's eyewitness account of some of the scenes is reported in 17 *PR* 545f.

77 Wallas, *Francis Place*, p. 55. Gale Jones had previously been released as a result of a motion carried against the government on April 17 in the House. Hansard, 1st ser. XVI:726 (Apr. 17, 1810); Gray, *Perceval*, p. 298.

78 *Times*, June 22, 1810.

79 Burdett's explanation of his failure to participate in the procession was that it might have led to bloodshed. Place, who had helped arrange the procession, called Burdett "a d—d coward and paltroon," and until 1817 they did not speak to each other. Patterson, *Burdett* II:289; H. Hunt, *Memoirs* II:423. Cf. Wallas, p. 56. See also 33 *PR* 13–14.

80 34 *PR* 741; Anne, p. 13. C wrote the taunting introductory address; the body of the paper, an analysis of legal precedents and the pertinent facts, was the joint work of Burdett, Wright, and Thomas Howell with only a few sentences by C. C was also the author of the "flaming address" from the people of Westminster

"highly approving of every part" of Burdett's conduct. 33 *PR* 12; 34 *PR* 334. C claimed that in 1812 he wrote a Burdett address to the House of Commons, later published as a pamphlet under Burdett's name. 65 *PR* 631.

15. Into Newgate

Motto: Letter to Wright, Nov. 25, 1807 (Illinois).

1 Gray, *Perceval,* p. 136. The ex-officio information was intended to apply only to "such enormous misdemeanours as peculiarly tend to disturb or endanger" the king's government or to "molest or affront him in the regular discharge of his royal functions" where the usual grand jury proceeding could not be followed because "a moment's delay would be fatal." Blackstone IV:308–9. The evil effects of the ex-officio information were described by C in 19 *PR* 428, 833 and 22 *PR* 66. In 1811 Lord Holland's motion for a list of ex-officio informations filed in the past ten years was opposed by Lord Ellenborough and lost in the House of Lords by a vote of 24 to 12. 19 *PR* 621. A similar motion by Lord Folkestone, opposed by the attorney general, failed in the House of Commons 121 to 38. 19 *PR* 832.

The original protection intended to be afforded by the grand jury was whittled away by practices such as prevailed in Lancashire, where, over a twelve-year period, only thirty-eight persons were called to serve on the grand jury. 46 *PR* 809.

2 *The Trial of Messrs Lambert & Perry to Which Is Added the Trial of William Cobbett, for Libelling his Present Majesty, George III, King of England and His Government* (New York 1810), p. 44.

3 *Times,* June 16, 1810. The succeeding quotations are from the same source.

4 *Courier,* June 16, 1810. The succeeding quotations are from the same source.

5 When later describing his argument, C claimed that he had stressed the cruelty and injustice to a greater extent than appears in any of the unofficial accounts of the trial. 22 *PR* 71. No official account seems to have been published.

6 *Times,* June 22, 1809. C later referred to the incident as involving "Some local militia men; young fellows who had been *compelled* to become soldiers, and who had no knowledge of military discipline; who had, by the act of parliament, been promised a guinea each before they marched; who had refused to march because the guinea had not been wholly paid them . . ." *Year's Residence,* pp. 591–2. See also 77 *PR* 178.

7 The practice of the day was to use a whip with nine lashes fifteen or sixteen inches long, each of the lashes with nine knots. 76 *PR* 715. Burdett's efforts in 1808 and 1811 to minimize the evils of flogging in the army met with no success. Hansard, 1st ser. XI:1117 (June 30, 1808); XX:698 (June 18, 1811).

C's proposal to defend himself goes back at least to 1807 (Add. MSS. 22906, fol. 271). Perhaps as an attempt to justify his conduct, C later claimed that barristers were so dependent on the government that "any man is a fool, in the present state of things, to employ a barrister, in a case where the government is the prosecutor." 31 *PR* 280. At a council of war in 1809 with Francis Place, Cochrane Johnstone, John Wright, Lord Cochrane, and Henry Clifford it was decided (the barrister Clifford dissenting) that C should defend himself, as "there was not a man at the bar who would defend Cobbett as he ought to be defended. It was equally well-known . . . that the judge would be against him, and that no man at the bar would offend Lord Ellenborough." Place papers, Add. MSS. 35145, fol. 9.

8 Place papers, Add. MSS. 35145, fols. 10, 13. Francis Place, with whom C had rehearsed the use of the letters, was astounded to hear C conclude without using them. Place refers also to letters from "Mr. Perceval himself and two from the Speaker," who sent C speeches to be inserted in the *PR.* But the Perceval letters were probably from an early period when C was still supporting him.

9 Within eight months of C's trial, Henry Brougham, a talented barrister, secured a not-guilty verdict in a libel action brought by the attorney general against Leigh and John Hunt, proprietors of the *Examiner,* for reprinting an article that criticized military flogging, despite Lord Ellenborough's declaration that the publication was a seditious libel. In the Hunt case there were only two special jurors out of twelve. 19 *PR* 495.

According to C, the "defendants had to thank the jury themselves much more than their advocate." 19 *PR* 546. Although this may have been true, it is also true that Brougham made out a better case. For example, he showed that two distinguished British army officers had written pamphlets criticizing flogging. Yet Brougham was unsuccessful a month later in defending Drakard, the original publisher of the same article, in a proceeding held in Lincoln before Judge Wood and a jury with six special jurors out of twelve. 19 *PR* 684. Drakard was sentenced to eighteen months in prison and fined £200. 10 *PR* 1319.

10 16 *PR* 582–5, 636, 745. C's loyalty to the king was as *king,* not as a man; according to his theory, the title and office were "the repository of all that is necessary to the preservation of the national character." 6 *PR* 616; 18 *PR* 865; 86 *PR* 549.

11 10 *PR* 33, 65, 385.

12 9 *PR* 809; 10 *PR* 42; 11 *PR* 263.

13 14 *PR* 417, reprinted in 19 *PR* 559. C had also attacked Ellenborough's appointment to the cabinet in 1807 as inconsistent with his position as chief judge.

14 Place papers, Add. MSS. 35145, fol. 13; Wallas, *Francis Place,* p. 117n. The barrister John Campbell, future lord chancellor, who attended the trial, thought C's speech "the poorest trash I ever heard." Mrs. Hardcastle (ed.), *Life of John, Lord Campbell, Lord High Chancellor of Great Britain* (London 1881) 1:259.

15 Swann to Wright, June 18, 1810, Add. MSS. 22907, fol. 278.

16 18 *PR* 2.

17 18 *PR* 16. His two brothers, George and Thomas, had at least fourteen children between them.

18 Letter to Wright, June 25, 1810, Add. MSS. 22907, fol. 279. Dr. Mitford, who claimed relationship to Lord Redesdale, Perceval's brother-in-law, may have been the source of the proposal. See undated letter to Wright, which seems to have been lost. Edward Smith, *Cobbett* II:119; Lewis Melville, *The Life and Letters of William Cobbett in England and America Based upon Hitherto Unpublished Family Papers* (London 1913) II:44; letters to Wright, Jan. 3, 1810 (Illinois) and to Mitford, Jan. 7, 1810 (Bodleian). In 1819 Wright testified that he first heard of the proposal from Mitford in 1810 (*Courier,* Dec. 31, 1819), although C's letter to Wright of Aug. 18, 1809 (Add. MSS. 22708, fol. 189) suggests that Wright himself had "half-solicited" conversations on this subject with Reeves in 1809.

19 Report of action *Wright* v. *Clement* (London 1819), pp. xiv–xviii. A copy of the farewell article appears at Melville II:45 and in the *Courier,* Dec. 31, 1819.

20 *Wright* v. *Clement,* p. x. The avenue selected was curious, for only a short time before, C had attacked Yorke as the "constant supporter of every measure hostile to the public purse, and to public freedom" (17 *PR* 385), and had bitterly opposed Yorke in various matters in which he had been involved in 1810. See, for example, 17 *PR* 174, 225, 321, 353, 374, 499, 512, 692. Yorke had, however, been the channel through which C had transmitted his "Important Considerations" to the government in 1803. 69 *PR* 457.

21 Letter to Wright, June 28, 1810, Add. MSS. 22907, fol. 283.

22 Letter to Wright, June 29, 1810, ibid. fol. 285. When C described the transaction in 1817, he stated that his solicitor, Holt White, had been the person to whom he had communicated his proposal to cease publication of the *PR,* and that White had been prevented, as a result of the message carried by Finnerty, from acting on the proposal. 32 *PR* 13. Either C had forgotten about Reeves, which seems

unlikely (although C's correspondence relating to the matter that is now available to us was then in Wright's hands) or both White and Reeves were acting as intermediaries.

23 Wright, after falling out with C, claimed that Perceval "addressed a letter to Mr. Reeves, in which Mr. Cobbett's offer was treated by him with the scorn it deserved." *Courier*, Dec. 31, 1819. There is, however, no evidence that C knew of the decision before he withdrew the proposal. Although these maneuvers were supposedly made behind the scenes, C was shortly called on to deny that he had sought "to evade punishment by a compromise with Mr. Perceval and his Gang!" *Independent Whig*, Aug. 5, 1810. So far as can be determined, C made no reply to the challenge, but subsequent challenges (see ch. 16) were met with evasive answers.

24 Letter to Wright, June 29, 1810, Add. MSS. 22907, fol. 285.

25 Letter to Wright, July 1, 1810, ibid. fol. 286.

26 18 *PR* 8. C later claimed that Gibbs had urged the court to make C a "blighted example of the vengeance of the law" (33 *PR* 481), but these words have not been found in any of the accounts of the hearing.

27 During the four days in King's Bench prison, C occupied accommodations generously relinquished by Henry Hunt. Hunt, *Memoirs* II:413–14.

28 18 *PR* 2; *Times*, July 10, 1810.

29 *Times*, July 10, 1810.

30 *Courier*, July 6, 1810; *Times*, July 6 and 10, 1810. The *PR* stated that it was "published" by Bagshaw, "sold also" by Budd.

31 Anne, p. 25.

32 32 *PR* 898. Peter Walker was the friend. Anne's recollection was that Mr. Crosby had put up the bedstead. Anne, p. 25.

33 44 *PR* 145–6, except sentence beginning "the youngest," which was taken from *Advice*, para. 301.

34 30 *PR* 621. 34 *PR* 10: "Chucklehead but crafty Curtis met Tierney in the Hall. 'Ah, a, ah! We have got him at last' said Curtis. 'Poor Cobbett! Let him be *bold now!*' The old place-hunter answered: 'Damn him! I hope they'll *squeeze* him!' " 30 *PR* 621.

35 Anne, pp. 25–7. According to her account, Alderman Goodbehere accompanied Wood.

36 C occupied several different rooms in the keeper's house at first, not taking over Davison's quarters until late in 1810. Anne, p. 27. C claimed that he had "ransomed" himself from the society of felons at a cost of £2,000. 41 *PR* 294; 69 *PR* 460–1; *Legacy to Labourers*, p. 32.

37 Anne, p. 28.

38 *Advice*, paras. 302, 304.

39 *Advice*, para. 169.

40 *Advice*, para 303.

41 Melville, *Cobbett* II:69. Present whereabouts of letter unknown.

42 Henry Crabb Robinson, who saw William junior in 1817, "thought he looked chuckle-headed. They say he is *dignus filius dignioris patris.*" Edith J. Morley (ed.), *Henry Crabb Robinson on Books and Their Writers* (London 1938) I:203–4.

43 *Advice*, para. 302.

44 Manchester Cobbett papers, no. 26 (Nuffield).

45 Ibid. no. 27 (Nuffield).

46 Anne, p. 29.

47 Manchester Cobbett papers, no. 28 (Nuffield).

48 Anne, pp. 27–8. Prisoners in Newgate were given about a pound of bread each day. 18 *PR* 139, 1344.

49 *The Creevey Papers* . . . ed. Sir Herbert Maxwell (London 1923), p. 134.

50 18 *PR* 1.

51 18 *PR* 13–14.

52 18 *PR* 14–17.

53 Swann to Wright, July 20, 1810, Add. MSS. 22907, fol. 290.

54 69 *PR* 461.

55 18 *PR* 182–4. In 1832 a newspaper account of an after-dinner speech by C had him saying that Bosville had declared that "if Burdett would give £1,000 he would also give £1,000 to relieve him." 78 *PR* 359. In 1833 C said that this was to reimburse C for Paull's election expenses incurred at Bosville's request. 82 *PR* 14.

56 Before the partnership arrangement was agreed to, C paid Wright a straight salary of £2 a week for his work as editor. Add. MSS. 31126, fol. 127. Wright's actual drawings, plus the remaining balance in his cash account, averaged more than £8 a week for the period 1804–10. Ibid. fols. 145, 157. In 1819 C evasively denied that Wright had ever been his "partner." 34 *PR* 739–41.

57 "He had been lodged, fed, nursed, in my house, weeks and months, without the cost of a farthing!" Add. MSS. 31126, fol. 111.

58 C later alleged that he had transferred more volumes to Budd than he had intended, through Wright's understatement of the total stock on hand. Ibid. fol. 80.

59 Ibid. fols. 3–8.

60 Letter to Wright, Oct. 28, 1808, Add. MSS. 22907, fol. 64.

61 Add. MSS. 31126, fols. 97–9.

62 An earlier "reference" and arbitration had broken down for reasons that do not appear. Letter to Swann, June 27, 1811 (Bodleian). Thomas Denman, later lord chief justice, acted as arbitrator for Wright. 41 *PR* 510.

63 Add. MSS. 31126, fol. 81; letter to Hansard, Mar. 11, 1812 (Nuffield).

64 Add. MSS. 31126, fols. 81–2. In 1819 C claimed that Wright had obtained £300 from Burdett on the allegation that he needed that amount to pay a bill for C, but that Wright had given C no credit for it in his accounting. At the arbitration, Wright contended that he had borrowed the money for himself and hence owed it to Burdett. C, however, voluntarily assumed the debt to Burdett. 34 *PR* 745–6; 69 *PR* 468.

65 Add. MSS. 31126, fol. 89. The number of unsold volumes is a rough computation based on an estimate of the numbers printed less those sold. Ibid. fols. 115–16, 124, 129. C estimated the value of the volumes held by Hansard, before he bought the Budd stock, at about £9,000. Ibid. fol. 133. Budd died shortly after December 1811, so Hansard dealt with his heirs.

66 According to C, Howell killed himself in a hackney coach in 1815 after an attempt to enlist C's help "in saving himself from the schemes" of Wright. 34 *PR* 742. This claim was denounced as completely untrue by Wright's counsel in the action for libel Wright brought against C in 1820. *The Book of Wonders: Part the Second* (London 1821), p. 23.

67 By letter to Hansard dated Mar. 11, 1811 (Nuffield), C had demanded that Hansard deliver to him the stock of books held by Hansard and mortgaged to C.

68 Another claim made by Wright was that he received no remuneration for the services he rendered to C. This is true only on the doubtful assumption that Wright had reimbursed C for the advances he had received amounting to more than £3,000 and for the value of the room and board provided Wright while living with C and his family.

69 C made other serious charges against Wright: that Wright had charged C with the cost of discounting a note of one of Wright's friends (Add. MSS. 31126, fol. 106); that Wright had pocketed the money derived from the sale of a pony C had lent him (ibid. fol. 113); that Wright had charged C twice for the same expenditure (ibid. fols. 134, 136); that Wright had fabricated entries in the "New Account

Book" which were revealed when the "Old Account Book," believed lost, was found (ibid. fols. 146, 152–3). See also letter to Swann, Dec. 7, 1819 (Bodleian).

In 1819 C alleged that Wright had been "discarded" by Canning, Frere, and George Ellis for publishing a pamphlet written by William Gifford which insinuated that John Wolcot ("Peter Pindar") was guilty of "unnatural propensities." 34 *PR* 748, 982; 43 *PR* 581. See ch. 7, n. 5.

Sources

~~~~~~

Principal published writings of Cobbett

The pamphlets Cobbett wrote in America between 1794 and 1800 were nearly all reprinted (sometimes with considerable modification) in *Porcupine's Works*, consisting of twelve volumes published in 1801. Many of Cobbett's later books and pamphlets first appeared in his weekly *Political Register*. In the following list of Cobbett's writings, those reprinted in *Porcupine's Works* are marked with an asterisk (*), and those that first appeared in the *Political Register* are marked with a dagger (†). The compilation is arranged alphabetically by the short titles that are used in the text and notes.

A Little Plain English: *A Little Plain English, Addressed to the People of the United States . . . by Peter Porcupine. Philadelphia 1795.

Advice: Advice to Young Men and (Incidentally) to Young Women in the Middle and Higher Ranks of Life . . . London 1830. First issued in 14 monthly parts. June 1829–Sept. 1830.

American Gardener: The American Gardener; or, A Treatise on the Situation, Soil, Fencing and Laying-Out of Gardens . . . London 1821.

American PR (American Political Register): Cobbett's American Political Register. Jan.–June 1816; May 1817–Jan. 1818. New York. Published by Henry Cobbett, Cobbett's nephew.

Big O and Sir Glory: †*Big O and Sir Glory: or, "Leisure to Laugh." A Comedy. In Three Acts.* London 1825.

Bloody Buoy: *The Bloody Buoy, Thrown Out as a Warning to the Political Pilots of America; or A Faithful Relation of a Multitude of Acts of Horrid Barbarity* . . . By Peter Porcupine. Philadelphia 1796.

Bone to Gnaw: *A Bone to Gnaw, for the Democrats* . . . By Peter Porcupine. Philadelphia 1795.

Cannibals' Progress: *The Cannibals' Progress; or The Dreadful Horrors of French Invasion* . . . Translated from the German by Anthony Aufrer . . . republished at Philadelphia by William Cobbett. [1798.]

Collective Commentaries: Cobbett's Collective Commentaries . . . London 1822. Mostly articles Cobbett published in the *Statesman* during 1822.

Corn: A Treatise on Cobbett's Corn . . . London 1828.

Cottage Economy: Cottage Economy: Containing Information Relating to the Brewing of Beer, Making of Bread, Keeping of Cows, Pigs, Bees, Ewes, Goats, Poultry and Rabbits, and Relative to Other Matters Deemed Useful in the Conducting of the Affairs of a Labourer's Family. London 1822. First issued in 7 monthly parts. 1821–2.

Country Porcupine: Country Porcupine. Triweekly newspaper, March 5, 1798–Aug. 26, 1799. Philadelphia.

Democratic Judge: *The Democratic Judge: or The Equal Liberty of the Press, as Exhibited, Explained and Exposed, in the Prosecution of William Cobbett, for a Pretended Libel against the King of Spain and His Ambassador, before Thomas M'Kean, Chief Justice of the State of Pennsylvania.* Philadelphia 1798.

307

Detection of Conspiracy: *Detection of a Conspiracy, Formed by the United Irishmen, with the Evident Intention of Aiding the Tyrants of France in Subverting the Government of the United States of America. By Peter Porcupine. Philadelphia 1798.

Emigrant's Guide: The Emigrant's Guide; in Ten Letters, Addressed to the Taxpayers of England; Containing Information of Every Kind, Necessary to Persons Who Are About to Emigrate . . . London 1829.

English Gardener: The English Gardener; or, A Treatise on the Situation, Soil, Enclosing and Laying-Out, of Kitchen Gardens . . . London 1828.

English Grammar: A Grammar of the English Language, in a Series of Letters. Intended for the Use of Schools and of Young Persons in General; but, More Especially for the Use of Soldiers, Sailors, Apprentices, and Plough-Boys. New York 1818.

Evening Post: Cobbett's Evening Post. Daily newspaper, Jan. 29–Apr. 1, 1820. London.

French Arrogance: French Arrogance; or, "The Cat Let Out of the Bag"; A Poetical Dialogue between the Envoys of America and X.Y.Z. and the Lady. By Peter Porcupine. Philadelphia 1798.

French Dictionary: A New French and English Dictionary. In Two Parts . . . London 1833.

French Grammar: A French Grammar, or, Plain Instructions for the Learning of French. In a Series of Letters. London 1824.

French Lectures: Eleven Lectures on the French and Belgian Revolutions, and English Borough-mongering: Delivered in the Theatre of the Rotunda, Blackfriars Bridge. London 1830. First issued in 11 parts, Sept.–Oct. 1830.

Geographical Dictionary: A Geographical Dictionary of England and Wales . . . London 1832.

George IV: History of the Regency and Reign of King George the Fourth. 2 vols. London 1830–4. First issued in parts, 1830–4.

Good Friday: Good Friday; or, The Murder of Jesus Christ by the Jews. London 1830.

Gros Mousqueton: *The Gros Mousqueton Diplomatique; or Diplomatic Blunderbuss, Containing, Citizen Adet's Notes to the Secretary of State . . . By Peter Porcupine. Philadelphia 1796.

Impeachment: Impeachment of Mr. Lafayette . . . Translated from the French by William Cobbett. Philadelphia 1793.

Important Considerations: Important Considerations for the People of This Kingdom. Anonymous. London 1803.

Kick for a Bite: *A Kick for a Bite; or, Review upon Review; With a Critical Essay, on the Works of Mrs S. Rowson . . . by Peter Porcupine. Philadelphia 1795.

Legacy to Labourers: Cobbett's Legacy to Labourers; or, What Is the Right Which Lords, Baronets, and Squires Have to the Lands of England? . . . London 1834 [1835].

Legacy to Parsons: Cobbett's Legacy to Parsons; or, Have the Clergy of the Established Church an Equitable Right to the Tithes, or to Any Other Thing Called Church Property, Greater Than the Dissenters Have to the Same? . . . London 1835.

Letters to Hawkesbury: Letters to the Right Honourable Lord Hawkesbury, and to the Right Honourable Henry Addington, on the Peace with Buonaparte . . . London 1802.

Letters to Thornton: Letters from William Cobbett to Edward Thornton Written in the Years 1797 to 1800, ed. G. D. H. Cole. London 1937.

Life and Adventures: *The Life and Adventures of Peter Porcupine, with a Full and Fair Account of All His Authoring Transactions; Being a Sure and Infallible Guide for All Enterprising Young Men Who Wish to Make a Fortune by Writing Pamphlets. By Peter Porcupine Himself. Philadelphia 1796.

Life of Jackson: Life of Andrew Jackson, President of the United States of America. Abridged and compiled by William Cobbett, M.P. for Oldham . . . London 1834.

Manchester Lectures: Cobbett's Manchester Lectures, in Support of His Fourteen Reform Propositions; Which Lectures Were Delivered in the Minor Theatre in That Town, on the Last Six Days of the Year 1831 . . . London 1832.

Martens's *Law of Nations:* Summary of Law of Nations . . . By Mr Martens . . . Translated from the French by William Cobbett. Philadelphia 1795.

Mercure Anglois: Le Mercure Anglois. Feb.–Apr. 1803. London. A French version of parts of the *Political Register.*

New-Year's Gift: **A New-Year's Gift to the Democrats; or, Observations on a Pamphlet Entitled 'A Vindication of Mr Randolph's Resignation.'* By Peter Porcupine. Philadelphia 1796.

Observations on Priestley: **Observations on the Emigration of Dr. Joseph Priestley, and on the Several Addresses Delivered to Him on His Arrival at New York.* Anonymous. Philadelphia [1794].

Paper against Gold: †*Paper against Gold and Glory against Prosperity. Or, An Account of the Rise, Progress, Extent and Present State of the Funds, and of the Paper-Money of Great Britain . . . Brought Down to the End of the Year 1814.* London 1815.

Parliamentary Debates: Cobbett's Parliamentary Debates. Published by Cobbett 1804–12; thereafter by T. C. Hansard, from whom it took the name "Hansard."

Parliamentary History: Cobbett's Parliamentary History of England . . . Published by Cobbett 1804–12; thereafter by T. C. Hansard.

Political Censor: **The Political Censor, or Monthly Review of the Most Interesting Political Occurrences, Relative to the United States of America.* By Peter Porcupine. Nine issues, Mar. 1796–Mar. 1797. Philadelphia.

Poor Man's Friend: Cobbett's Poor Man's Friend: or, Useful Information and Advice for the Working Classes; in a Series of Letters, Addressed to the Working Classes of Preston. London. First published in parts 1826–7; shortened and revised edition 1833.

Porcupine: The Porcupine. Daily paper, Oct. 30, 1800–Oct. 12, 1801. London. Continued as *The Porcupine, and Antigallican Monitor* Oct. 13–Dec. 31, 1801.

Porcupine's Gazette: Porcupine's Gazette. Daily, Mar. 4, 1797–Aug. 28, 1799. Philadelphia. Six weekly numbers, Sept. 6–Oct. 11, 1799 and two further pamphlet issues, Oct. 19 and 26, 1799. Bustleton. Final number, Jan. 1800. New York. Selections were reprinted in *Works.*

PR (Political Register): Cobbett's Weekly Political Register, Jan. 1802–June 1835, in 88 vols., with various name changes. Vol. 89, July–Sept. 1835, published by William Cobbett junior.

Prospect from the Congress-Gallery: **A Prospect from the Congress-Gallery, during the Session, Begun December 7, 1795 . . .* By Peter Porcupine. Philadelphia 1796.

Protestant "Reformation": A History of the Protestant "Reformation," in England and Ireland: Showing How That Event Has Impoverished and Degraded the Main Body of the People in Those Countries . . . First published in parts, London 1824–6. A second part, listing abbeys etc. confiscated, published 1827.

Republican Judge: **The Republican Judge: or The American Liberty of the Press . . .* By Peter Porcupine. London 1798. Revision of *Democratic Judge* for English consumption.

Roman History: Elements of the Roman History, in English and French, from the Foundation of Rome to the Battle of Actium . . . The English by William Cobbett; the French by J. H. Sievrac. London 1828. *An Abridged History of the Emperors, in French and English.* By the same. London 1829.

Rural Rides: †*Rural Rides in the Counties of Surrey, Kent, Sussex, Hampshire, Wiltshire, Gloucestershire, Herefordshire, Worcestershire, Somersetshire, Oxfordshire, Berkshire, Essex, Suffolk, Norfolk and Hertfordshire: With Economical and Political Observations Relating to Matters Applicable to, and Illustrated by the State of Those Counties Respectively.* London 1830. Quotations are from the Penguin edition of 1967.

Rush-Light: **The Rush-Light.* Five numbers published in New York in 1800; a sixth, after Cobbett's return to London.

Scare-Crow: **The Scare-Crow; Being an Infamous Letter, Sent to Mr. John Oldden, Threatening Destruction to His House, and Violence to the Person of His Tenant, William Cobbett, with Remarks on the same by Peter Porcupine.* Philadelphia 1796.

Selections: Selections from Cobbett's Political Works: Being a Complete Abridgment of the 100 Volumes Which Comprise the Writings of "Porcupine" and the "Weekly Political Register."

With Notes, Historical and Explanatory. By John M. Cobbett and James P. Cobbett. 6 vols. London: Anne Cobbett [1835–7].

Sermons: Cobbett's Sermons . . . First issued in 12 monthly parts. London 1821–2.

Soldier's Friend: The Soldier's Friend: or, Considerations on the Late Pretended Augmentation of the Subsistence of the Private Soldiers. Anonymous. London 1792.

Spelling Book: A Spelling Book, with Appropriate Lessons in Reading, and with a Stepping-Stone to English Grammar. London 1831.

Spirit of Public Journals: Cobbett's Spirit of the Public Journals. Vol. 1 for 1804. London. Not continued.

State Trials: Cobbett's Complete Collection of State Trials . . . Published by Cobbett 1809–12; thereafter by T. B. Howell, from whom it derived the name *Howell's State Trials.*

Surplus Population: †*Surplus Population: And Poor-Law Bill. A Comedy, in Three Acts.* London [1835].

Tour in Scotland: †*Cobbett's Tour in Scotland: And in the Four Northern Counties of England: In the Autumn of the Year 1832.* London 1833.

Two-Penny Trash: Cobbett's Two-Penny Trash; or, Politics for the Poor. 2 vols. London 1831–2. First appeared in monthly parts July 1830–July 1832.

Woodlands: The Woodlands: or, A Treatise on the Preparation of the Ground for Planting; on the Planting; on the Cultivating; on the Pruning; and on the Cutting Down of Forest Trees and Underwoods . . . London. First published in 7 numbers Dec. 1825–Mar. 1828.

Works: Porcupine's Works; Containing Various Writings and Selections, Exhibiting a Faithful Picture of the United States of America . . . from the End of the War, in 1793, to the Election of the President, in March 1801. 12 vols. London 1801.

Year's Residence: A Year's Residence in the United States of America. Treating of the Face of the Country, the Climate, the Soil . . . In three parts. New York 1818–19.

Index of names